MW01196072

BOWSTRING

OTHER WORKS BY VIKTOR SHKLOVSKY IN ENGLISH TRANSLATION

Theory of Prose

A Sentimental Journey: Memoirs, 1917–1922

Literature and Cinematography

Zoo, or Letters Not About Love

Knight's Move

Third Factory

Mayakovsky and His Circle

Lev Tolstoy

Energy of Delusion: A Book on Plot

BOWSTRING: ON THE DISSIMILARITY OF THE SIMILAR

VIKTOR SHKLOVSKY

TRANSLATED BY SHUSHAN AVAGYAN

DALKEY ARCHIVE PRESS
CHAMPAIGN • DUBLIN • LONDON

Originally published in Russian as *Tetiva: o neskhodstve skhodnogo*, Sovetskii pisateľ, 1970
Viktor Shklovsky's Russian text copyright © 1985 by Varvara Shklovskaya-Kordi
Translation rights into the English language are granted by FTM Agency, Ltd., Russia, 1994
English translation copyright © 2011 by Shushan Avagyan
First edition, 2011
All rights reserved

Library of Congress Cataloging-in-Publication Data

Shklovskii, Viktor, 1893-1984.
 [Tetiva. English]
 Bowstring : on the dissimilarity of the similar / by Viktor Shklovsky ; translated by Shushan
Avagyan. -- 1st ed.
    p. cm.
 Includes bibliographical references.
 ISBN 978-1-56478-425-4 (pbk. : alk. paper)
 1. Literature--History and criticism--Theory, etc. I. Title.
 PN441.S4813 2011
 801--dc22

                              2011012936

Partially funded by a grant from the Illinois Arts Council, a state agency, and by the University
of Illinois at Urbana-Champaign

www.dalkeyarchive.com

Cover: design and composition by Danielle Dutton, photo by Yuriy Palmin
Printed on permanent/durable acid-free paper and bound in the United States of America

For Serafima Shklovskaya

For your support, patience, doubts;
for your inferences, revisions,
for days and months of work,
thank you, dear.
The day is always short,
we move on.

TRANSLATOR'S PREFACE

Giving up giving, in other words, because in the first place the thing does not belong to you, and in the second it will not in any case have been handed over intact.[1]

In a conversation with Viktor Shklovsky in 1981, his former student Marietta Chudakova asked him about living and working under the regime of Stalin. "Just before 1937," he recalled, "an acquaintance of mine who worked in the Cheka (Soviet Secret Police) brought me a file he wanted to show me, with documents against me. I saw that they were doing a poor job, that there was a lot they didn't know about me. But they knew enough to make me a center (of a conspiracy)."[2]

Shklovsky, of course, foresaw the age of terror as early as the 1920s, when he had to flee to Finland, then to Berlin, to escape arrest for the charges of his anti-Bolshevik activities—as described in *A Sentimental Journey: Memoirs, 1917–1922* (1923). Many Russian intellectuals from the pre-revolutionary period emigrated during

---

1   Eric Prenowitz, Translator's Note. *Archive Fever* by Jacques Derrida. U of Chicago P, 1996. 105.

2   Chudakova was a graduate student at Moscow State University in 1960–63 and met Shklovsky in spring 1962. "Conversation with Viktor Borisovich Shklovsky, January 9, 1981." Translated by Karen Evans-Romaine. *Poetics Today* 27:1 (Spring 2006). 237–244.

those years, most of them settling in Europe and North America—in 1919, the Nabokovs escaped to London, then to Berlin; Ivan Puni and his wife went to Finland, eventually arriving in Berlin in 1921. Marc Chagall left Russia for good in 1922, and the same year Marina Tsvetaeva emigrated with her family to Berlin, later to Prague, and then to Paris. In 1920, Roman Jakobson moved from Moscow to Prague to continue his doctoral studies and eventually ended up in New York. Some expatriates, however, like Shklovsky and Tsvetaeva, found exile intolerable and were compelled to return home.

Shklovsky went back to Russia in the fall of 1923, when his petition to the Central Committee of the Communist Party received a favorable response, the details of which are recounted in his epistolary novel *Zoo, or Letters Not About Love* (1923). But the homecoming was excruciatingly difficult; for one thing, it meant being a witness to the degradation and death of many of his friends—including Mayakovsky, who committed suicide on April 14, 1930. It was the beginning of the Great Purge, which was characterized by widespread government surveillance, constant suspicion of possible "saboteurs," public trials, and executions. The madness and confusion of this period lurks in the background of Shklovsky's part-fictional, part-autobiographical book *Poiski optimizma* (Hunt for Optimism, 1931), which he ends with the following sinister remark: "Life is difficult. It's big. One should live as long as possible. Let's take care of one another in the name of this great epoch. We have to be calm, like being at war or inside an incubator."

Compared to the epoch of revolutions, the period between the 1930s and 1950s was relatively quiet, but dramatic in other ways. It became excessively difficult and dangerous for Shklovsky to publish anything after the heavy criticism of his book on Mayakovsky

(*Mayakovsky and His Circle*, 1940) for its emphasis on the influence of Futurism and its attempt to rehabilitate discredited Formalist theories. Shklovsky was evacuated to Alma-Ata during World War II, and later he was greatly affected by the death of his son, Nikita, who was killed on February 8, 1945, a few months before the end of the war. The final blow came with the campaign against the so-called "Cosmopolites" in 1949, when Konstantin Simonov attacked Shklovsky's *Gamburgsky Schyot* (Hamburg Account, 1928) for being an "utterly bourgeois book" that was "against Soviet art." With the exception of documentary screenplays and several translations of works from other Soviet nations and languages, almost nothing written by Shklovsky appeared in print between 1949 and 1953. To get a sense of how Glavlit (the State Committee on Censorship) worked to silence writers, we only need to look into the case of Yefim Etkind, who in 1968 dared to make the following statement in his introduction to the two-volume collection *Mastera russkogo stikhotvornogo perevoda* (Masters of Russian Verse Translation):

> During a certain period, particularly between the 19th and 20th [Party] Congresses, Russian poets were deprived of the possibility of expressing themselves to the full in original writing and spoke to the reader in the language of Goethe, Orbeliani, Shakespeare, and Hugo. Whatever the reason, the 1930s, the 1940s, and the 1950s were fabulously productive for the development of verse translation in the USSR.[3]

---

3   Quoted in Lauren G. Leighton's *Two Worlds, One Art: Literary Translation in Russia and America*. Northern Illinois UP, 1991. 37.

The above might seem a casual—if somewhat ironic—aside, but because of those two short sentences, an entire printing of twenty-five thousand copies of two volumes was rebound; three members of the editorial staff of Poet's Library, which publishes a prestigious series of scholarly editions of Russian poets, were immediately fired; the Editor-in-Chief was soon forced to retire; those held responsible were asked to publicly recant; Etkind was called to a *pro-rabotka*, a public criticism and rebuke, by his colleagues at the Herzen Institute in Leningrad, and was subjected to a series of public humiliations, including dismissal from his university post, until he emigrated in 1974.[4] Despite the modest freedoms that were allowed in the arts during the Khrushchev years, Stalin's system still persisted even after his death—and it was in this climate that Shklovsky was writing *Bowstring*.

"Myths do not flow through the pipes of history," writes Shklovsky, "they change and splinter, they contrast and refute one another. The similar turns out to be dissimilar." Published in Moscow in 1970 and appearing in English translation for the first time, *Bowstring* is a seminal work, in which Shklovsky redefines estrangement (*ostranenie*) as a device of the literary comparatist—the "person out of place," who has turned up in a period where he does not belong and who must search for meaning with a strained sensibility. The book's title comes from Heraclitus: "They do not understand how that which differs from itself is in agreement: harmony consists of opposing tension, like that of the bow and the lyre." Comparison, in this sense, does not involve the assimilation

---

4   Yefim Etkind, *Notes of a Non-Conspirator*. Translated by Peter France. Oxford UP, 1978. 112, 129–30, 145–46.

of someone else's "otherness"—rather, it catalyzes one's own "otherness" and the otherness of one's own language. As Shklovsky experiments with different genres, employing a technique of textual montage, he mixes autobiography, biography, memoir, history, and literary criticism in a book that boldly refutes mechanical repetition, mediocrity, and cultural parochialism in the name of art that dares to be different and innovative. *Bowstring* is a brilliant and provocative book that spares no one in its unapologetic project to free art from conventionality.

ACKNOWLEDGMENTS

I have used existing translations, when possible, for quotations from texts originally in other languages, while I have compared texts originally in Russian with existing translations and revised some of them (all revisions are indicated in the footnotes). Texts that began life in English have been restored to their original form.

For the opportunity to share this work with various English-speaking audiences in the United States and abroad, and for helping me with information, interpretation and nuance, I thank Marina Balina, Oren Whightsel, and Jonathan Druker. I also wish to thank the staff of Milner Library at Illinois State University. I was intellectually sustained throughout the research and translation process by my many meetings and conversations with Rebecca Saunders and Kristin Dykstra, to whom I am enormously indebted. Finally, I thank my parents for their guidance and support.

S. AVAGYAN

Bloomington, Illinois
October 2010

BOWSTRING

PROLOGUE

Everyone has his own habits. I have grown accustomed to starting a book with a landscape.

Yalta.

It's the end of April.

The coiling snow patches in the mountains look like streams of wax on a wide candlestick.

A few corpulent crows swing on the treetops, balancing themselves with their spread tails and drooped wings.

They are large gray birds with black wings.

The cypresses bloom timidly. Sparrows raise clouds of yellow dust as they perch on their steep branches.

Unfortunately, the blossoms on the almond tree are almost gone, though they lasted a long time. The white petals are scattered on the ground, and occasionally the wind makes light "blizzards" out of them.

The air is permeated with the dense, docile scent of the small-leaf plum tree.

Another page of spring—the seventy-sixth.

Youth and friends are gone. There is almost no one I can write letters or show manuscripts to. The leaves have been falling, and not just this past autumn.

Leaves fall surreptitiously here, almost unnoticed, like words change in a language; the tree, too, grows new pointy leaves with thorns and seemingly tougher skin.

People go in strange ways. Tynjanov, Polivanov, Jakubinksy, Eichenbaum—they are all gone.

The pages keep turning. I'll try to turn back the pages and read them again.

When one is old, one likes to reread.

Old age will soon come to an end.

But I am not going to sit by the sea and scoop out water with my embossed plastic hat. A grateful crawfish or a frightened devil won't bring back the golden rings, tossed into the water by the imprudence of youth.

Youth boldly projects its piers far into the future, then finds them elsewhere, not in the same place—but it does find them.

That's how a bird finds a perching spot on a branch.

I reflect, write, piece things together, then keep rearranging them; I do only what I know I can do.

These are old pathways. I hope to intersect them.

It was evening when I started writing this.

Almost dropped on its back, the new crescent moon was floating in the sky and right above it was the familiar gray shadow, completing the circular form illuminated by earth-shine.

Nightingales sang below my window, or maybe they weren't nightingales at all.

They don't care that they have been exhausted in poetry; they don't know that they've been refuted.

Then spring comes. Trees bloom one after the other, nightingales sing, and crows caw.

Someone even heard the blackbirds. They imitate other birds.

The nightingales are still on their way.

FOREWORD

I lived once by the river near Chudovo when I was a boy. It was springtime. The bird-cherry trees had finished blooming. At dusk, when the slanting rays of sunlight lit up the forest, the nightingales would start singing.

They would start their song in the crimson light, and continue singing through the short night.

At daybreak, when the sun rose above the bluish lumps of plowed soil, the chaffinch continued the song of nightingales in that quarter hour when shadows are long. He would pick up their tune. If his song was clear and coherent, people said the weather was going to be nice.

Am I to sing the song of the chaffinch? And what is he singing now?

I began writing when I was a young man, a university student who didn't have time to graduate. I was born in 1893, before the Revolution of 1905, but was awoken by the first revolution and anticipation of the new. We knew that the revolution was around the corner, that it would happen soon. In our poems, we tried to guess the date of its arrival. We were waiting for a revolution in the radical changes of which we would partake. We didn't want to replicate or receive the world as it was, we wanted to understand and change it. But how—we didn't yet know.

The poetry of Mayakovsky, Khlebnikov—and the new movement in painting—wanted to perceive the world anew and thus changed the sound of the poem itself.

But we saw that we weren't alone in our arguments. Poets and writers from the past have also tried to speak in new ways because they, too, envisioned things in their own way.

The theory of *ostranenie* appeared in 1916.[1] I tried to sum up in it the method of renewing perception and representation of phenomena. Everything was connected with the time period, with pain and inspiration—the world that kept surprising us. At the same time, I wrote in *Theory of Prose* (1925):

> A literary work is pure form; it is neither a thing nor material but a relationship of materials. And, like any relationship, this one, too, is zero-dimensional. Which is why the ratio of a composition is irrelevant, the mathematical value of its numerator or denominator doesn't matter; what matters is their relationship. Comic or tragic works, well-known or small-scale works—the juxtaposition of a world

---

1   Shklovsky first used the term *ostranenie* (estrangement) in his essay "Art as Device" (1917), where he conceptualized it, based on the Aristotlean notion of poetic language, as the defining feature of language in its artistic usage in both verse and prose. As Shklovsky posited, after encountering objects or phenomena several times, the process of recognition switches to an automated mode in our minds and in order to renew perception of the familiar, poetic language must shift the familiar into an unfamiliar semantic axis. The function of estrangement then is to render the familiar in unfamiliar terms in order to return the palpability of the experience on the page by slowing down automated perception and increasing the difficulty of perception by impeding and retarding the process of recognition.

to another world is equal to the juxtaposition of a cat to a stone.[2]

There are small fruit flies called *Drosophila*.

They are remarkable because they have a very short lifespan.

It is possible to follow the crossbreeding between these minute species in an extremely precise and short period of time.

There was a time when we were told: "You study the crossbreeding of Drosophila flies, but they are good for nothing, they don't produce milk or meat."

But behind the experiment lie attempts to study the laws of genetics. Here, as Vladimir Mayakovsky once said, "life arises in a completely different context, and you begin to understand the most important things through nonsense."

If in art we are comparing a cat with another cat, or a flower with another flower, the artistic form as such is not constructed solely in the moment of such crossbreeding; those are merely detonators for triggering much larger explosions, entryways into knowledge, explorations of the new.

By refuting emotion or ideology in art, we are also refuting the knowledge of form, the purpose of knowledge, and the path of experience that leads to the perception of the world.

Form and content then are separated from each other. The brilliant formula is actually a formula of capitulation; it divides the realm of art—destroys the wholeness of perception.

---

2   Viktor Shklovsky, *Theory of Prose*. From Chapter 9, "Literature without a Plot: Rozanov." Translated by Benjamin Sher. Dalkey Archive, 1990. Revised by Shushan Avagyan. All subsequent quotations from *Theory of Prose* are taken from this standard version.

The Drosophila flies are not sent into space for a vacation. They enable the study of how the cosmos affects living organisms.

You can send the cat and flies into the cosmos, but there ought to be a purpose to these expeditions.

Art cognizes by implementing old models in new ways and by creating new ones. Art moves, transforming. It changes its methods, but the past does not cease to exist. Art moves using its old vocabulary and reinterpreting old structures and, at the same time, it seems to be static. It changes fast, changes not for the sake of changing, but to impart the sensation of things in their difference through rearrangement.

BORIS EICHENBAUM

The Beginning

There are names of people in my old phone book that I can't call anymore. But names don't get erased from memory. I lived with my friends and thought along with them. My mistakes form a major part of their mistakes. Generally speaking, I haven't been able to make them happier in life. Still, my suppositions and conversations have played a part in their discoveries.

 I got acquainted with Boris Mikhailovich Eichenbaum in 1916. He was a successful and promising young scientist who wrote good articles. He was poor, but he wasn't burdened by poverty. A violinist who had stopped playing, but who hadn't lost his love for music. A poet who had stopped writing poetry, but continued to translate poems—Aleksandr Blok liked his translations very much.

Eichenbaum was an accomplished academician and, even though he was young, he had a great deal of experience.

He took violin lessons as a child. Later he attended the Lesgaft Academy.

He was passionate about music and kept his violin, despite passionately hating it.

He had unusually beautiful hands, his body was light and strong.

We met on Sapyorny Lane, by a house, the balcony of which was upheld by four titans made of plaster and painted gray to simulate the color of granite.

It was during the war. The titans looked worn out, you could see their wounds—the white plaster underneath.

We got acquainted and became friends.

By then, having gone through various paths, Boris Mikhailovich was already a proficient philologist.

He was headed toward a bright future.

I ruined his life by engaging him in an argument.

This polite, calm, eloquent man knew how to argue until the end. He was polite but he would never concede.

He was a man of politely extreme convictions.

We were surrounded by streets and lanes such as Znamenskaya, Baseinaya, Manezhnaya, and Batareinaya.

Between the Neva and us were Kirochnaya, Zakharinskaya and Shpalernaya streets. The long barracks stretched across, guarded by sentries at the gates—bleak vicinities.

The war dragged on. There appeared wounded people wearing robes in the streets and lines snaking in front of shops selling frozen Siberian meat.

The empire was coming to an end.

In the streets, noncommissioned officers were teaching the new recruits how to form a unit.

They had to click smartly with their heels when turning around, but the worn, third-hand boots only made a shuffling sound.

I remember my grandmother standing on the sidewalk and objecting in a low voice: "How is he supposed to be a good soldier if they won't give him any decent clothing?"

I served as an instructor in the armored division. I enrolled as a volunteer out of confusion.

I used leave passes to sleep at home.

Met with my philologist friends.

I wasn't sure who I was.

A private who supervised a drivers' school. Not quite a soldier, not quite a Futurist.

With the help of Osip Brik and my friends I managed to publish two thin volumes titled *Studies on the Theory of Poetic Language*.

We were claiming that the poetic function of language has its own laws.

Everything around us was old and everything was changing.

Amid the one-story barracks on the Shpalernaya Street rose the thickset Tauride Palace, separating itself with difficulty from the low embankment.

Here, once, Prince Potyomkin-Tavrichesky shined in his prime: he would enter the ballroom dressed in such elegant clothes that his adjutant had to carry in his hat separately behind him—it was adorned, like a crown, with emeralds and diamonds.

Back then the Tauride Palace served as a ballroom with large halls, parquet floors, and swampy, labyrinthine gardens.

During the war, the palace was transformed into the seat of the Imperial State Duma—a moldering displeasure was quietly brewing inside.

The insurgent troops came very close to the State Duma during the revolution, they were practically in the neighborhood.

I slept between the white columns, wrapped in my driver's fur coat. Later I saw the steep amphitheater of the Duma transform into the Petrograd Soviet.

Fifty years ago I got to see Lenin in that same hall—with his broad shoulders and high chest—talking from a small, raised tribune. He moved spontaneously and effortlessly on the tribune, addressing different parts of the audience.

I witnessed everything from the very beginning, I began to understand things much later.

I recall him now as the flame that burns on the Field of Mars.

The revolution came and ascended the stairs.

Uplifted by the wave of the revolution, without really comprehending it, we were immersed in it, and we were in love with it as young people can be in love.

We lived a difficult life.

It was very cold in Petrograd during the revolution years. We had very little food; the bread was variegated, kind of tousled, mixed with straw—you could only eat it if you were distracted by something else, when you had no time to look. Fortunately we were very busy.

Boris Mikhailovich had two children, a son—Viktor, and a daughter—Olga. The family lived on Znamenskaya Street. Today it's called Vosstaniya Street.[3]

They had two rooms. He lived in the smaller one to keep warm, and sat on the floor on a pile of books in front of the iron woodstove. He would read a book, tear some pages out of it and then throw the rest into the stove. He was very knowledgeable, knew everything about Russian poetry and Russian journalism. During those years he passed his library through fire.

---

3   Vosstaniya Street (literally meaning "insurrection"), known as Znamenskaya Street (named after the Church of the Sign), was renamed after the February Revolution.

Books burn very badly—they create a lot of ashes, preserving the printed words that turn white for a long time.

Eichenbaum's children got sick. His son died.

One day it was unusually warm in the hunger-stricken and frozen Petrograd. The snow that never got plowed started to melt, the walls got damp and you could tell from the black patches which apartments were still being heated.

Snow was melting everywhere. Human footprints in the snow emerged in their blackness.

Then I saw sleds on the street. Boris Mikhailovich, wrapped in layers of clothing, was pulling his daughter Olga on a sled. She wore a fur coat and over it she was bundled in an old knitted shawl that was crossed across her chest and tied behind her back.

The sleds moved with difficulty on the melted snow.

"Boris, it's warm," I told him.

"I didn't even notice . . . yes, it's warm."

Later we were eating apple porridge. There were many apples in those days. We had been standing in lines for them in the summer.

I remember how I stood next to Blok. He had a suitcase in his hand, and asked me if ten pounds of apples would fit inside.

We ate apples all winter long.

Those were difficult times.

I am not writing about this in a book to criticize the past, or brag about my health. I want to recall how happy we were despite those difficulties.

We read reports in abandoned apartments, at Brik's or Sergei Bernstein's: there, too, we burned books and cornices to heat up the rooms, taking turns sticking our feet in the stove in order to warm them up.

That's how some issues of *Starye gody* (Bygone Years) got burned in the Briks' apartment.

Boris was editing an anthology of classics, he was working on it with Kholobaev; the texts were carefully proofed and corrected.

We read papers. With a tortured face, the young Sergei Bondi would enter the room with a heavy load on his shoulders.

We talked about rhythmic-syntactic figures, the laws of art, and the laws of prose.

Boris Mikhailovich was writing a book about the young Tolstoy.

It was the beginning of the NEP.[4] There were newly opened markets and stores.

I lived in the House of Arts, next to Mikhail Slonimsky, Akim Volynsky, Vladislav Khodasevich, Olga Forsh, Vladimir Piast, Aleksandr Grin, and Marietta Shaginian.

My apartment was old. It was a large apartment with several floors where the fruit merchant Yeliseev once lived, with a small concert hall, libraries, two bathrooms, and a separate bath. My room was behind the lavatory that had four windows, a fountain, and a bicycle with no wheels—for exercising.

I didn't need the bicycle but people envied me for living so extravagantly.

---

4   The New Economic Policy (1921–28) formulated by Lenin, with the aim of reviving production, especially in the field of agriculture. The main goal was to secure the food supply necessary to feed Russia's population.

New Petrograd and *The Overcoat*

In 1919, in revolutionary Petrograd, the Futurists under the editorship of Mayakovsky published *Poetics* through IMO (*Iskusstvo molodykh*—Art of the Young).

I showed the essays to the soft-spoken yet domineering art critic Isaac Babel. We became acquainted through Gorky's periodical *Letopis* (The Chronicle).

He was short, round-shouldered, with a high chest—he reminded me of an egg. But I want to talk about Eichenbaum's essay in *Poetics*. It was called "How Gogol's *Overcoat* Is Made."

Boris Mikhailovich examined the structure of the novella as thoroughly as Goethe once studied the morphology of the flower and skull, comparing the relation of floral and foliar parts with the vertebral structure of the skull.

The essay analyzed the novella as though it was a musical piece: first came an analysis of the name—Akaki Akakievich—as a stutter.

The story is narrated in the hero's language. Gogol transmitted muteness not only through the stuttering of his hero, but also by replicating the morphology of muteness in the narrator's discourse.

The hero's hemorrhoidal, astigmatic appearance was fused with his impededly insignificant vocabulary; the image of the character was born out of his own mutterings. He was unable to articulate himself, he couldn't find the words. The only source of happiness for Akaki Akakievich, his sole aim in life, was the overcoat, which was made with incredible difficulties because Akaki

Akakievich's life was a muttering, a convulsion from unuttered words and poverty.

Only the overcoat, like a heroic deed, fluttered above the distinct calligraphic lines of the copyist and mutterings of a "private life."

There used to be an old Russian saying: "to build boots."

It is much more difficult to build an overcoat. It consisted of various fabrics: the coarse textile, lining cloth, and the collar. For Akaki Akakievich, the making of the overcoat was as difficult as building a cathedral.

Eugene threatened the bronze idol:

> "Well, builder-maker of the marvels,"
> He whispered, trembling in a fit,
> "You only wait! . . ."[5]

"Wait" is a reference to the future.

These incomprehensible, prosaic words arranged in free verse appear in the ominous, architecturally poetic landscape of *The Bronze Horseman*.

The incomprehensibility introduces a difference between the narrative voice and the intentionally lowered, demoted voice of the hero.

In *The Overcoat*, the incoherence is exposed through the voice of the hero.

---

5   Aleksandr Pushkin, *The Bronze Horseman*. Translated by Yevgeny Bonver.

Eichenbaum wrote his essay at a time when everyone was enamored with *skaz*.[6] It was the age of Mikhail Zoshchenko, Vsevolod Ivanov, and Isaac Babel.

There are a few extraordinary things happening in *The Overcoat*: one of them is how unified it is in terms of voice, particularly how the narrative voice isn't clear. But there are instances where the narration becomes more distinct, as, for example, in the part about the young clerk who perceives the human voice in the incoherent mutterings of Akaki Akakievich, given directly, not yet as a sign of threat, but rather as pity toward the hero. The threat, as Herzen noted, is concentrated at the end of the story.

Let's look at plot construction—the conflict of semantic values—in *The Overcoat*. Akaki Akakievich curses from his deathbed, and then rebels as a ghost; the story has a fairy-tale-like, folkloro-prophetic resolution that constantly hovers over the reader.

In "How Gogol's *Overcoat* Is Made," everything evolves on the level of direct discourse and narration, which, while masking the internal conflicts, is at the same time accentuating them. The tragic nature of the trivialities exaggerates the tragedy because it makes the tragedy universal.

---

6   The term *skaz* comes from the Russian verb *skazat* (to tell) or such words as *rasskaz* (short story) and *skazka* (fairy tale). It was designated to classify oral "folk" narratives and essentially anything that had to do with "storytelling." Boris Eichenbaum further developed the concept of *skaz* as a form of narrative technique in literary works that comes in a register of language marked as being in some way distinct from the author's own. This may involve idiosyncrasies of style, as well as more obvious instances of substandard speech, slang, or regional dialect. According to Eichenbaum, the narrator's lexicon, grammar, and intonation are significant in themselves, sometimes outweighing the composition or the interplay of narrative motifs.

It is very difficult to distinguish between the narrative voice and the style of the composition—they are integrated, interconnected, and yet they are dissimilar.

"How Gogol's *Overcoat* Is Made" is an excellent essay. It has already been reprinted. In order to resolve it, one should reread it again.

It facilitated the development of many things.

The overcoat—not the overcoat of Akaki Akakievich, but Gogol's *Overcoat*—is built as a Gothic structure: the composition of the novella pulls the strain of events into electric power lines. The walls between the arches can be taken out. The composition surpasses its material by materializing it.

The dejected, grotesque Russia of Nicholas I stretches outside its windows. The wind of the empire bursts into the novella's structure.

The story is at once microscopic and colossal in its construction. It transmits Petersburg and its suburbs through the thin power lines carrying the mumblings of an impoverished clerk who has been crushed by the weight of the empire.

This is done with the help of words. They build a model of the world.

Akaki Akakievich's words are incoherent. So are his threats to the chief of staff, uttered in delirium.

The work of Boris Mikhailovich is straightforwardly brilliant; it still raises questions half a century later. It has charted new grounds for the future study of prose. One can clearly see the connection between Viktor Vinogradov's method in his analysis of *Poor Folk* and the work of the young Eichenbaum.

The world of Akaki Akakievich is narrowed not through his bizarrely unfinished thought; his language is almost like mimicry. It is as though human speech either hasn't originated yet, or it is dying on the worn stairs of Petersburg.

Akaki Akakievich's speech isn't the only incoherent discourse in the story; the shrieks of the chief of staff to whom the poor clerk appeals with a complaint are full of bureaucratic incoherence.

The incomprehensible mutterings of the dying Bashmachkin are terrible.

Incomprehensibility can be a terrible thing.

The fate of Gogol's *Overcoat* is quite interesting. The Factory of the Eccentric Actor (FEKS) led by Grigori Kozintsev and Leonid Trauberg produced a film "based" (as we erroneously like to say) on the story of *The Overcoat*. The script was written by Yuri Tynjanov, who consulted with Eichenbaum. It was a silent film, but it was produced by people who knew the meaning of the word, what it expresses. The poor, petty clerk, who practically couldn't speak, his sole petty joy consisting of his attempts to survive the cold, became a reproach not only to our past history, but a reproach to the contemporary world. We saw the fate of the hero in silent film made by people who could speak. Akaki Akakievich was now on a circus stage.

Recently in Paris there were two simultaneous productions of *The Overcoat*. In the first version, Akaki Akakievich was born in Petersburg and he was being scolded by a high-ranking Russian clerk. In the second one, Akaki Akakievich was a French clerk. He lived in de Gaulle's Paris, but his fate was still the same: he built his overcoat with the same difficulty and lost it in the same wretched way.

The essay "How Gogol's *Overcoat* Is Made" is in some way connected to my "How *Don Quixote* Is Made." The connection is laid bare in the word "made." The word is confusing, I suppose, because a literary work can't be stitched together as an overcoat.

Compositions are made, they are developed; the author creates in them semantic knots that are correlated, intensifying the perceptibility of the composition. New structures emerge.

It is a complicated process. The investigation of the new material of being and the comparison of that new material with old structures generate new knowledge, new perception, new experience of the work.

The language system in *The Overcoat* is based on the decomposition, impoverishment of, ordinary speech; it reveals the disparagement of language. However, the new linguistic structure simultaneously changes all preexisting compositional constructions; the artist-investigator moves the spotlight onto something else that was in the dark before.

A shift in the realm of cognition changes art. I once said that art is completely devoid of emotion. But you can find both pain and sympathy in Herzen's *My Past and Thoughts*, Lermontov's *A Hero of Our Time*, Dostoevsky's *Crime and Punishment*, the poems of Mayakovsky and Pasternak, except they become modes of understanding sympathy and indignation. A projector is not an instrument in and of itself, it merely illuminates the object of interest, it changes the landscape.

It is possible to live without the life-sensation of one's existence, or to analyze without fully perceiving. The use of such methods of intelligibility is on the rise.

Already there are machines that know our life by comparing its phenomena. The human brain has deep interstitial paths that help a person to orient in life, quicken his decisions, and also stifle his original sensation for the sake of a quick reaction.

Analyzing machines are boring, and they can't belong to the realm of art because they use shortcuts.

Now I think about how art is made, I think about Cervantes, who invented the logic of the novel by signifying the interrelation of parts. In the end, after a number of disappointments, with the help of humor and tragedy he taught people how to see life anew, how to have compassion for others, how to strive for independence, how to joke, and how to fight.

I think about how literary criticism, the life of Boris Eichenbaum, the life of Yuri Tynjanov have also been spent on the analysis of the phenomena of existence, on removing the shroud of time from the art of the past, and restoring our perception of the classics.

According to the ancient Greeks, the cicadas used to be human poets and musicians who got so carried away with music they couldn't engage in practical things in life anymore; they were among those whom Pushkin's Mozart called "the priests of beauty."

We were in love, we experienced death, we saw our children die, and we saw our own history unfold.

The sound of the cicadas is not art (yet), but it has potential.

Barefooted, Socrates rested under the plane tree, listening to the cicadas, and retelling life, turning its pages anew.

The Young Tolstoy

The Young Tolstoy is a thin book—it's almost a brochure. To write it, Boris Mikhailovich went through many archives.

It's easy now to see through reference books how Lev Nikolaevich mentioned Sterne at least sixty times and translated some of his works. But back then Tolstoy's relationship with world literature wasn't understood properly—influence was taken for similarity.

Eichenbaum helped broaden the area of study in intertextuality.

There was a lot of talk on influences, but what "influence" means is still unclear even today.

Is it perhaps something like filling an empty vessel, or is it the rotation of a dynamo rotor in an electric field that, as a result, creates a new kind of electricity?

It seems they hadn't even noticed that when Karamzin introduced the word "influence," he meant an influence "in."

Then they started talking about an influence "on."

Eichenbaum tried to understand the relationship between the writer's perception of his own writing and the literary experience from the past. The writer analyzes the world twice, based on his own personal impressions and also past knowledge—seeing the world as of today, but also knowing its previous constructions. We often examine the diary as a record of one's internal spiritual world, as an original document written for oneself, but diaries are often read by others, and usually the memoirist censors his writing from the beginning.

As Pushkin wrote: "The pen will sometimes stop, as if before a leap over an abyss—it will stop at something that a stranger would have read with indifference."

It is conceivably easier to write about yourself in a purely fictional work with invented characters because you are not really writing about yourself. In order to see something, you must know what you were hoping to see.

The diary is a particular kind of literary fact.[7] The writer's diary is a particular kind of diary—it has a specific purpose.

The diaries of the young Tolstoy aren't just the traces of his internal life, but also experiments of literary mastery. They are tests for learning different methods of description, for selecting traits to identify characteristics. Eichenbaum wrote:

> This is why a purely psychological analysis of such documents as letters and diaries requires special methods for cutting *through* self observation in order to observe psychic phenomena as such—independent of form and of the ever-conventional stylistic shell.
>
> Entirely different methods must be employed in literary analysis. In this case the form and devices of one's self-observation and psychic formulation are immediately significant material from which we ought not to digress. Here, precisely in the stylistic shell, in the conventional forms, it is possible to detect the embryos of artistic devices, to trace a specific literary tradition.[8]

---

7   A reference to Yuri Tynjanov's seminal essay "The Literary Fact" (1924), in which Tynjanov explored the historical dimension of literature and the phenomenon of literary change, showing that what is defined as literary— "the literary fact" as distinct from a fact of everyday life—constantly shifts, as genres evolve, compete with one another, and change their positions in the hierarchy of genres.

8   Boris Eichenbaum, *The Young Tolstoy*. Translated by Gary Kern. Ann Arbor: Ardis, 1972.

Lev Nikolaevich was interested not so much in self-analysis, as in the analysis of the world. He took notes on the most indiscernible things from his daily readings and reformulated them in his own words.

He learned literary construction from the historian, the geographer, and Sterne—by unraveling his digressions.

The young Tolstoy loved Rousseau and carried his portrait on a chain around his neck.

Tolstoy imitated many of Rousseau's stylistic devices in his sentimental-romantic correspondence with his aunt Aleksandra Andreevna. He lived on the shores of Lake Geneva, the birthplace of Rousseau's creativity. Later he crossed the Alps, carrying with him Rousseau's books to compare the fictional landscapes with the natural terrain.

In the Caucasus he began a series of sketches and portraits, describing people, searching for the universal through the particular.

In his diaries, next to an analysis of romantic feelings you find writings about lust and also plans for restructuring the government. Tolstoy related to the Cossack village as a model of a different social order. Going over Tolstoy's diaries, you get a sense of looking at the blueprints of an experimental shop in a huge factory.

Tolstoy's later diaries become more personal and monotonous; registering the already invented structure, they repeat and suddenly break at certain points with some unexpected remark, a painful observation that is contradictory, yet precise.

While writing *Childhood*, Tolstoy served as a volunteer in a regiment stationed in a Cossack village on the Terek: he went wild-boar hunting, drank wine, fell in love with a Cossack woman, was ready to leave everything behind and settle there, amid river thickets and deserted lands.

The fact that there is not a single account of those years in *Childhood* is simply astonishing. Instead, it is an altered autobiography with stylistic details assimilated from Sterne, but without the Sternean digressions. *Childhood* depicts an unexciting existence, filmed as though in slow motion and examined through the magnifying glass of time.

Eichenbaum's analysis is remarkable, but it is not complete. Tolstoy took from Sterne whatever he needed at the time. The Sternean digressions are knotted for the purpose of parody; they take the reader farther and farther from the hero of the book—Tristram Shandy. The *evental* pace of life,[9] the chronological continuity is deliberately disrupted. The story narrates the conception of the hero, what had happened before the marriage of his parents, then it gives a characterization of the hero's father, uncle, uncle's servant, and the doctor, after which we read a detailed account of the hero's birth. Life evolves in a thread of knots that get more and more tangled. The narrative segments are intentionally dislocated and rearranged, so the knots become the characters, as it were.

---

9   At the root of the term *sobytiinyi* (evental) lies the Russian word *bytie* (existence or being), and *so-bytie*, which can be read both in its ordinary meaning of "event," and in a more literal rendering as co-existing or co-being. The *evental* describes the qualities of events that happen in real time and in real space—a material specificity, a moment that constrains abstract transcription. The term *evental* in Shklovsky is used specifically in relation to the concept of *fabula* (story), the linear, chronological narration of real or fictionalized events taking place in a narrative.

Tolstoy's temporal magnifying glass examines events in strictly chronological order. The Sternean parody is completely removed. The tensions that Sterne creates through his eroticized descriptions are concealed, but you can see their traces in the drafts of the manuscript.

The style of the young Tolstoy can be compared with Sterne's style as an example of noncoincidence of two analogous things—a dissimilarity of the similar—whereas dissimilarity was part of Tolstoy's intention.

Tolstoy wrote in a linear chain, giving long but intermittent descriptions. He described people's movements, examined their lives with particular sentimentalism, but he invented something that Sterne hadn't discovered yet by separating the hero's psychology from his actions. The boy who loves his mother stands unflinchingly by her coffin, not grieving. He is in a state of shock and, at the same time, he impersonates grief, as it were, acting as a child who has lost his mother. And only the horror (scream) expressed by the little peasant girl makes him realize the reality of death, which is given through the most dreadful detail—a fly on the dead face.

Tolstoy's suspicion toward quotidian descriptions about people's lives is already present in this early work.

One can easily trace Sterne's, as well as Rousseau's experiments in *Childhood*.

He writes in a way that's similar to Sterne, but is also different.

Eichenbaum's life during the years of writing *The Young Tolstoy* didn't reflect on his own work.

The work is larger than life. The writer is like a bee, but he is also the honeycomb. His work contains the work of many other bees, both from the past and also from the future. The whole world was moving. The Soviet Union was pulling the world and it was changing slowly—from our perspective, and quickly—from the historical point of view.

Eichenbaum's First Book on Lermontov

Eichenbaum's study of Lermontov was published in 1924. Later the author grew tired of his book and disowned it, yet the book is interesting to say the least—interesting for the inevitability of its errors. They were inevitable for a group of people who were then called the Formalists, and inevitable for those years, however brief they were.

The *Complete Works of Mikhail Lermontov* was compiled only by 1891, for the fiftieth anniversary of his death. "For the readers of the '30s and '40s," wrote Eichenbaum in his first chapter, "Lermontov was the author of *A Hero of Our Time* and some seventy or eighty poems (of which only forty-two poems were published during his lifetime)."[10]

To clarify, Eichenbaum wrote that, "besides *A Hero of Our Time*, Lermontov succeeded in publishing only one collection (1840) of twenty-eight poems."

Analyzing Lermontov's early verses which get published today alongside his more mature work, Eichenbaum established that the poet was what Shevyrev called (during the poet's lifetime) "protean," i.e., capable of assuming various forms.

Going over Lermontov's early poems, Eichenbaum arranged them in columns—next to poems by Dmitriev, Batyushkov, and even Lomonosov, who may have influenced the young poet.

---

10   Boris Eichenbaum, *Lermontov*. Translated by Ray Parrott and Harry Weber. Ann Arbor: Ardis, 1981.

Back then Eichenbaum believed that it was the juxtaposition of Russian poetry with foreign poetry that determined Lermontov's path.

The book was subtitled *A Study in Literary-Historical Evaluation*.

And even though Eichenbaum was later disappointed with his own book, it is an interesting phase in his literary career. The first chapter is entitled "Youthful Verse." Lermontov died very young, but the chapter on his youthful verse takes up only forty pages in the entire book that altogether (including preface and notes) consists of a hundred and sixty-six pages.

Lermontov himself never published these poems, for they were his preliminary work. They weren't even drafts of poems, but rather outlines or notes on how to approach art.

Mayakovsky was glad that his youthful poems had been lost in prison. Youthful poems can be examined only in a particular context.

"Thus," Boris Mikhailovich wrote, "Lermonotov's creative work naturally divides into two periods, the school period (1828–1832) and the mature period (1835–1841)."

The poems of the first period were unknown to Lermontov's contemporaries. Boris Mikhailovich wrote that had these youthful poems not been preserved, then "of course, the study of Lermontov's artistic development would have been greatly hampered, but his literary-historical portrait would have probably acquired more distinct outlines because it wouldn't have been complicated by the enormous material of the school years, which researchers have not known how to analyze until now."

Not to mention Senkovsky's strong protest and indignation against the publishers who, against Lermontov's wishes, included his first poetic attempts in the 1842 collection, or Belinsky's comment against the complete collection in his *Notes of the Fatherland* in 1844.

Belinsky proposed having two condensed books: one containing *A Hero of Our Time*, and the other—a collection of best poems, at the end of which would be included additional pieces of the lowest merit. Eventually Eichenbaum came to the same conclusion.

During his first, "school" period—a term used by Eichenbaum—Lermontov wrote over three hundred poems, and only about a hundred during his second period. Some of the poems from his "school" period appear to be what they called centos in poetics; they are composed of fragments taken from other famous works. Almost every writer goes through a similar phase. Pushkin as a boy wrote a play which he "stole from Molière."

It is typical for young writers to write centos. They often submit this type of work for publication, sometimes even in disguised form.

But Boris Mikhailovich wrote in particular about Lermontov that "these youthful poems are a unique exercise in the pasting together of ready-made bits and pieces."

Then he discussed foreign literary influences. Eichenbaum's interest in the comparative columns is connected to the kind of work we did back then. I used to say at the time that we were not *dethroning* literature, only *unscrewing* it.[11]

---

11 The pun with the homophones *razvenchivat* (to dethrone, debunk, remove from a powerful position) and *razvinchivat* (to unscrew, take apart, upset the balance or stability) illustrates Shklovsky's method of literary analysis, in which literary phenomena are not repudiated or refuted but rather disjointed and understood through a rearrangement or displacement of the parts in newly formed relationships.

It is rather easy to "unscrew" one's youthful work, but here Boris Mikhailovich fell victim to the method. He underestimated the fact that he was looking at the manuscripts of a young adolescent.

A writer finds his own pathway through the literary works of other famous writers; he goes through a stage of contamination, so to speak.

Boris Mikhailovich applied this principle to other poems, too; he thought that in "The Dying Gladiator," for example, "the images and set phrases in themselves do not represent anything especially original or new; for the most part they are completely traditional and go back to Zhukovsky's epistle."

This is somewhat true, but not completely.

Zhukovsky was not a bad writer, but Lermontov wrote differently. The similar is what they call "structure" today—it has nothing to do with common parts; rather, it is a selection of separate knots in a composition, the juxtaposition of which creates a new construction.

Pushkin said that the dictionary contains all the words, but even so the writer creates something new.

This rather broad concept of "influence" and "borrowing" became very advantageous for Eichenbaum. In an unusually evocative way he showed the literary epoch in which the artist functioned. Analyzing Tolstoy in the first volume, written in 1928, Boris Mikhailovich pointed at the resemblance of Panteleymon Kulish's story about his childhood to Tolstoy's *Childhood*. On September 29, 1852, Tolstoy recorded in his diary: "I was reading the new issue of *Sovremennik* (The Contemporary). There is one good story similar to my *Childhood*, but it's insubstantial." In terms of genre, Eichenbaum thought that both of these works resembled the work of Dickens. When examining Tolstoy's Caucasian sketches, he wrote about military sketches and Kostenetsky's *Notes about the Avarian Expedition*, pointing at the similarity of Tolstoy's

"Two Hussars" to Thackeray's works; when discussing Napoleon, he brought up Proudhon, and aphorisms by Pogodin; talked about Urusov's and de Maistre's influences, and wrote extensively on the cheap popular *lubok* literature, drawing on important and generally true examples. But the precision of the composition's framework, Tolstoy's "distinctiveness," how he consciously separated, and distinguished him from the world of literature, which in fact brought objections from his contemporaries—these aspects Eichenbaum hardly ever mentioned.

The omission, of course, is not accidental.

In *War and Peace* Tolstoy used the forms of both the old "domestic" novel and what he calls the "military" novel. But the domestic novel conventionally ended with a wedding, after a set of lucky incidents, delayed by traditional impediments such as, for example, suspecting the bridegroom of unfaithfulness.

Tolstoy intentionally destroyed the conventional structures and started his novels such as *Family Happiness* or *Anna Karenina* from a point where the wedding had already taken place.

This was, in fact, a purposeful invention of a unique structure.

Tolstoy wrote in his foreword to *War and Peace*: "I couldn't help thinking that the death of one character only aroused interest in other characters, and a marriage seemed more like a source of complication than a denouement of the reader's interest."

The beginnings and endings in Tolstoy are different, though people do get married and they die, but these are "storied" facts.[12] The difference is in the compositional meaning.

---

12   Shklovsky differentiates between *syuzhet* (plot), the compositional structure or architecture of a literary work, and *fabula* (story), which is defined as the chronological sequence of events that are used as material for the construction of the plot.

"The Death of Ivan Ilych" begins from a point where Ivan Ilych is already dead; he is a corpse.

His wife quibbles over his pension, but the idea behind the work, the direction of interest, is not whether or not Ivan Ilych will die, or what pension his wife will receive, but rather in the question of why Ivan Ilych's life had been "most simple and most ordinary and therefore most terrible."[13]

Pierre Bezukhov's life after the wedding, Princess Maria's life after she becomes Nikolai Rostov's wife—this is a new kind of beginning, a new collision and disillusionment. Yet in the original conception of the novel that was provisionally titled "The Decembrists," Tolstoy showed Pierre and Natasha as an old couple; they had already been predestined for new disillusionments, for witnessing a new epoch—Russia's reality after the Crimean defeat.

It is true, the old exists in Tolstoy, the literature of all past epochs is present in his work, and it is important to analyze that. But in order to understand a literary work it is important to ask the following: What did the author create? What did he change in the field of art? How was he innovative?

Boris Mikhailovich showed the most unexpected sources that had influenced Tolstoy's fiction. He analyzed the lower genres and showed how the very concept of the literary fact changed, how the material itself evolved in a literary work. He introduced and developed topics such as "Tolstoy and Paul de Kock"—the essay was published in *Zapadny sbornik* (Western Anthology) in 1937. It's an interesting essay. Every single suggestion, the precise

---

13   Lev Tolstoy, "The Death of Ivan Ilych." Translated by Louise and Aylmer Maude. Borders Classics, 2007.

correlations of *Anna Karenina* to the novels of Dumas, *fils* are all very interesting, but they don't explicate, while pointing to similarities, the change in their functions. Eichenbaum arrived at this only in his third volume, which he was writing in the besieged Leningrad.

I have seen the work. It was finished during that dreadful winter.

Boris Mikhailovich kept the manuscript in a briefcase, and during evacuation hung the briefcase around his neck. The truck carrying people out of Leningrad broke down.

Eichenbaum stood on the ice for a long time and somehow lost the manuscript. He wasn't able to recover it in full. The archive had been burned. Some parts, like the most significant chapter on *Anna Karenina*, were recovered by memory.

Scientific discoveries cannot be inherited by anyone; you must get there on your own, through a great and difficult path.

I am deeply grieved by those scholars who present Boris Mikhailovich Eichenbaum as a scientist whose career ended in 1934. His works from 1957 are exceptional.

I said once that in order to bring a change of form in literature one must make use of minor genres. Before becoming a published poet, Derzhavin wrote odes and even epistles to his garrison friends, the Guards, or the so-called "aristocratic imbeciles." The mixture of elated tone with the intimate, the intrusion of mundane reality into the high forms of art, became Derzhavin's poetic invention. He wrote in the "amusing Russian style."

But one must add that this style became a literary fact, it grew stronger with the victory of Derzhavin's friends. The officers of the Leib Guard, the aristocrats who proclaimed Catherine as

Empress, and before her—Elizabeth, were as if promoting their own genre—the genre of their own songs and garrison jokes. Let's not forget that Elizabeth Petrovna herself wrote songs that were not without the influence of popular culture or, at any rate, of colloquialisms.

The comparisons that Eichenbaum constructs in his first book on Lermontov are very realistic and accurate. But they don't explicate the subject fully.

When Lermontov wrote:

> No, I'm not Byron—I am yet
> Another choice for the sacred dole,
> Like him—a persecuted soul,
> But only of the Russian set.[14]

—the very fact of disassociation, the mentioning of his soul, I think, is more important than when he mentions Byron's name.

The poet always has predecessors, and what unifies them is not so much tradition as negation.

Human speech is made of words that have been created a long time ago; those words are preserved in dictionaries, but poets and writers change.

At first Eichenbaum compared, just as I did, similar parts in different structures. The similar then became identical.

This conversation has been going on in literature for a very long time; Shakespeare too has old elements in his works and, in fact,

---

14   Mikhail Lermontov, "No, I'm Not Byron" (1832). Translated by Yevgeny Bonver.

his plots are not original. But his compositions are his own, and the hardest thing of all to understand is why they are so dissimilar from what appear to be the sources of those works.

The book on Lermontov showed the need not for just broad parallel comparisons but also for the importance of analyzing the dissimilarity of the similar. It was a difficult task: one should have been another Nekrasov to have found and extolled someone like Tyutchev in the course of poetry from Pushkin's age. Nekrasov's essay "On Minor Russian Poets" is a remarkable piece about the new within the old.

Eichenbaum's task was difficult—he worked hard and was rewarded. After a long search he finally found the new Lermontov who turned out to be the true Lermontov.

About How Lermontov Was Rediscovered in the Soviet Age

Time went by. The Eichenbaums had another son, Dmitri. Boris was immersed in his work.

He wrote several books and monographs on Lermontov. There had been previous publications and studies on Lermontov before Eichenbaum, of course. But let's see how others understood Lermontov and how difficult he was for even the most renowned critics and, perhaps, everyone else, except for Herzen and Belinsky.

The road to Lermontov was difficult.

In 1861 Dostoevsky wrote about Lermontov, drawing parallels between the fates of Lermontov and Gogol:

We had Demons too, real Demons. There were two of them, how we loved them! And we still love and regard them to this day! One of them laughed all the time; he laughed all his life, mocking himself and us, and we kept laughing with him. We laughed so hard that we cried from laughing. He got promoted to the rank of Lieutenant Pirogov and made such an awful scene over a clerk's lost overcoat. He told us everything about the Ryazan Lieutenant in three lines, everything to the last dash ... O, he was a colossal Demon and you in Europe never had anyone like him and probably wouldn't have endured someone like him anyway.

The other Demon—perhaps we loved him even more...[15]

For Dostoevsky, Lermontov was Gogol's equal: "We followed him for a long time, but he finally died somewhere in a manner that was aimless, erratic, and even ridiculous. But we didn't laugh."

In these excerpts, which I am not quoting fully, Gogol and Lermontov take up the same amount of lines, whereas Gogol, for Dostoevky, was a teacher.

So, there were at least two Lermontovs: the true Lermontov—who is revealed in his poems about Pushkin and other poems, which he himself included in his collection of works, the genius who authored *A Hero of Our Time*, which was a pinnacle for Chekhov, and the other—the "aimless," "erratic" Lermontov.

Why did Dostoevsky think that Lermontov's death was "even ridiculous," why did he call Lermontov a "mystificator"?

---

15   Fyodor Dostoevsky, *Ryad statei o russkoi literature* [Articles on Russian Literature], 1861.

These words epitomize the tragedy of social taste and illustrate what literary criticism should have been.

Readers sometimes mistook Grushnitsky for Lermontov, but Lermontov turned out to be a demon and continued to tempt Dostoevsky.

Dostoevsky argued with Lermontov because the latter antagonized the idea of humility and obedience.

According to Varvara Timofeeva, who worked with Dostoevsky between 1873–74 when he was the editor of the weekly *Grazhdanin* (The Citizen), he came to the office one day in a grave mood: "... Only during those gloomy, silent days he turned to me once—he raised his eyes from the galley proofs for a moment and muttered in a cold, broken voice: 'And how much better it is in Lermontov's translation':

> Уста молчат, засох мой взор, / These lips are mute, these eyes are dry;
> Но подавили грудь и ум / But in my breast and in my brain,
> Непроходимый мук собор / Awake the pangs that pass not by,
> С толпой неусыпимых дум . . . / The thought that ne'er shall sleep again.[16]

" 'This is Byron writing to his wife. But this is not like any of those translations by Gerbel and others—this is Byron in his true form. The proud, impenetrable genius . . . Lermontov's ver-

---

16 George Byron, "Farewell! If Ever Fondest Prayer" (1808).

sion, Непроходимый мук собор, goes so much deeper![17] Byron doesn't have this. What force and grandeur! A whole tragedy in just one line. The word собор (cathedral) alone is worth everything! A pure Russian word, and so visual. This is a remarkable poem, much greater than Byron's!' "[18]

Dostoevsky was right. The line that fascinated him wasn't Byron's.

It belonged to Lermontov.

Dostoevsky's favorite poem was Pushkin's "The Prophet"; he thought it was an "above worldly" poem. He read it with great passion at the Pushkin Jubilee. It was as though Dostoevsky was taking an oath on that poem. He also read Lermontov's "The Prophet."

He said, "*They* are here!" in the poem. By "they" he meant the nihilists. After stressing the word "they," according to Timofeeva, Dostoevsky "read in a wrathful and venomous voice:

> I spoke of love to all the world,
> And truth, the Master's teaching clear;
> And those I loved the most, they hurled
> Mad stones at me in hate and fear.

"And when he reached the following lines—

---

17   In Lermontov's translation, "pangs" (*muk*) in the line "Awake the pangs that pass not by," becomes "the cathedral of pangs" (*muk sobor*).
18   *F. M. Dostoevsky v vospominaniakh sovremennikov* [F. M. Dostoevsky in the Memories of his Contemporaries], Moscow, 1964.

A fool, who'd have us all believe
That God speaks through *his* lips alone![19]

"—Fyodor Mikhailovich looked at me as if trying to catch—again!—my 'wicked,' skeptical smile."

For Dostoevsky, Lermontov was a forerunner of the nihilist movement and also his predecessor.

The line with "the cathedral of pangs" that Dostoevsky discovered in Lermontov was also Dostoevsky's own exulted line that could have been an epigraph to "The Grand Inquisitor."

Dostoevsky understood Lermontov deeper than anyone else, but he tried to fence himself off.

He did this by believing the well-constructed and equally well-established lies and slander about Lermontov.

The second—false—Lermontov belongs to the tasteless, indulgent liberal tradition. The liberal criticism continued its conspiracy against the poet. Not only did they kill him in Pyatigorsk, but they also misconstrued his story, discredited him politically, and even cleared the name of his murderer.

Let's take the famous Brockhaus and Efron Encyclopedia and look up Martynov: "Nikolai Solomonovich Martynov (1816–1876), an officer who had the misfortune of killing Lermontov in a duel."

The entry is short. Its tone is very sympathetic toward Martynov, though it was obvious even then that it wasn't Martynov's

---

19   Mikhail Lermontov, "The Prophet" (1841). Translated by C. E. L'Ami and Alexander Welikotny. All subsequent quotations from "The Prophet" are taken from this standard version.

"misfortune"—he lived a long life—but Lermontov's, because he got killed.

They wrote that Lermontov had supposedly insulted Martynov's sisters by opening a letter addressed to them. These slanders were finally refuted recently by Irakli Andronikov.

And so, there were two Lermontovs: the true Lermontov and the other. This is plainly evident from Chekhov's letters. In 1901 he wrote to Tikhomirov from Nice—I'm quoting from the end (this is probably a response to the actor's question in regards to *Three Sisters*):

> Indeed, Solyony thinks that he resembles Lermontov; but, of course Solyony's nothing like him—it's ridiculous to even think that . . . He should be dressed and made up to look like Lermontov. They are similar, almost identical, but only in Solyony's mind.

Solyony was supposed to personify the second Lermontov, the one whom Martynov "had the misfortune of killing," the Lermontov who was portrayed by slanderers and liberals.

In 1891, the literary historian Nestor Kotliarevsky wrote a book titled *Lermontov: The Poet's Character and His Work*, which was reprinted in 1905. Blok reviewed it during the years of the first Russian Revolution—he wrote with indignation and rightly so:

> Lermontov is a writer who had neither luck in the quantity of monographs written about him, nor any kind of genuine appreciation from his successors: scholars usually find

a way to circumvent Lermontov because he is beyond their capacity. For the "larger audience," Lermontov was for a long time (and still is) the officer-troubadour with twirled moustache who wrote romantic ballads. "Lead in breast and vengeful fire"[20] were taken as motto for bad companionship and debauched fraternal military camaraderie. This representation has many profound reasons, and one of them is that Lermontov, analyzed through the infamous lens, can be *almost completely* understood only in *those terms* and no other.[21]

Blok argued that critics should evaluate Lermontov anew, and that there is almost nothing written about him—"silence and more silence."

Though a man of calm termperament, Blok's review is scathing. He uses phrases like "gibberish," and talks about professor Kotliarevsky's "playful wit," whose book is simply astounding in its flatness of liberal mentality. Blok wrote:

> There is no groundwork for scholarship on Lermontov—
> his biography is scant. What's left but to "speculate" about
> him? But his face is still dark, distant and terrible. One might
> look for *impartiality*, for clever and pithy yet futile guesses
> in order not to "disturb the beloved ashes." But in order
> to find treasures, one needs to figure out the meaning of

20   Mikhail Lermontov, "Death of the Poet" (1837). Translated by Yevgeny Bonver.
21   Aleksandr Blok, *Sochinenia* [Selected Works], 1955.

the *code* first that will direct to the hidden place, one must "measure seven times"—and only then, once and for all, unmistakably "cut" the piece of land where the treasure is buried. The treasures of Lermontov require persistent efforts.

After writing his first work on Lermontov, Eichenbaum dedicated his life to finding the "treasures of Lermontov." He refined Herzen's analysis of Lermontov and pointed at the importance of Lermontov's Circle of the Sixteen, the members of which were followers of the Decembrist movement. He connected Lermontov to the ideas of the time and showed in him the "exaltation" of civic society. He "figured out the meaning of Lermontov's code."

He saw in Lermontov the man whom Dostoevsky called "they."

There are many detective stories in the world. The characters in those stories search for treasures that never existed. But had they been found, we still wouldn't get anything. Soviet treasure-hunters search for literary treasures from which we're sure to get a fraction. They chart the map of literature, show the true meaning of poetry and prose, clarify the paths passed by men, and give the exact meaning of words. People's lives are spent on this.

Eichenbaum had students and, first, I would like to mention among them Irakli Andronikov, who verified all the facts of Lermontov's biography. We can't forget Emma Gerstein, who did quite the impossible, sorting through the piles of *Hofmarschall* journals that were kept in the royal court in a strange mix of languages.

From insinuations and hints we learned that people were afraid of Lermontov, they considered him a potential leader of some resistance movement. We also found out that d'Anthès wasn't incidental, and Lermontov knew what he was doing when he revealed the crowd that killed Pushkin.

The most remarkable thing about Eichenbaum's students was that they were all different and they kept their individuality. They learned a lot from Eichenbaum.

He taught them how to see Lermontov not as an accidental person or an embittered poet, but a fighter, whose pathos was crucial for everyone.

Boris Mikhailovich Eichenbaum was a professor from Leningrad—herein lies his fame: he was not alone and he could never have been alone.

Old age wasn't an obstacle for him; he kept finding new material that finally convinced him. He was the first to understand the kind of people that surrounded Lermontov, showed his role as the forerunner of the Decembrists, constructed the true image of Pechorin, and overcame all prejudices against the man of "bad character" that got in the way of understanding the man of "wide worldviews."

The City without Smoke

The Writers' House in Leningrad was on Griboedov Canal.

There are other houses in the city today.

But the original Writers' House was an expanded building that once used to be the quarters of imperial choristers.

It had long corridors and a stairwell on sloping arches.

The windows in Eichenbaum's apartment looked into a small courtyard. The doors opened into a corridor filled with books. In his office he had more books, a record player, and numerous gramophone records catalogued in a strict order.

Boris lived through the great Leningrad blockade in this apartment.

The city was tightly constricted. Its suburbs had disappeared.

There was no smoke above the city. Plants and factories had stopped working.

The city was holding up with its artillery.

Battleships sat motionless in the ice. There had been the Kronstadt uprising.

Frozen to the white aorta of the Neva, Leningrad was dying in a crown of explosions.

But it survived.

Boris lived with his wife, daughter, and granddaughter. His daughter's husband died in the blockade. His son was in the infantry in Stalingrad, he never returned.

They waited for him, and believed that letters got lost in the way.

Boris was writing his book about Tolstoy.

In the first two volumes Eichenbaum exhaustively and convincingly analyzed the literary milieu of Tolstoy and his contemporaries.

He was working out the methods of selection from Tolstoy's texts and depth of impression from his works.

Everything was new and consistent.

I already said a few things about metamorphosis, about how something similar becomes dissimilar, individualized, or unique.

When a sparrow feels the freezing cold air, he puffs up his feathers and gathers his feet under his body; he bears the surrounding cold by countering it with his inner warmth. The writer, who is also warm-blooded, fights even harder.

Separateness, distinction, and singularity characterize every living thing, though all living things are interconnected as a whole.

The great writer is consanguineous with the nation, but his blood is his own and not received by infusion or influence.

Eichenbaum was selflessly conscientious. A single line sometimes took him a month's work, though he always considered it unfinished.

The walls of his apartment became covered with hoarfrost. The old wood stoves came to life once again, they started devouring more books.

Eichenbaum lived the life of the besieged Leningrad. He wrote his book. Dined at the Mayakovsky House cafeteria by the Neva. Ate yeast soup. Exchanged things for barley. Waited for letters from the front. Listened to the radio.

It took him years to finish the book. The index cards kept piling up, comparisons were being made and then disproved.

Eichenbaum had a great ability to see anew each time he read something. He spent endless hours reading without rushing through, and after being persuaded by his discovery, he labored on it as though his work had just begun.

His index cards never got stale.

And now Eichenbaum was working at a faster pace; he hurried, perhaps for the first time in his life.

Death lurked everywhere—in the apartment, in the academy library, in the Mayakovsky House cafeteria.

There were messages painted on the walls in Leningrad warning which parts of the streets were dangerous or under fire.

The cupola of St. Isaac's Cathedral and the spire of the Admiralty had been covered up. The enemy was using detailed maps to bombard the city.

The tram car stations and bridges were all under fire. The sound from the shrapnel echoed in the streets that were overgrown with grass or covered in snow.

The winter dragged on. The water-supply system had stopped working. There were no newspapers. The news was transmitted only by radio. Between news reports you could hear the continuous beat of the metronome—an air-raid warning!

This was the pulse of the city—it was still alive.

In the winter, the Germans declared that they would occupy Leningrad on such and such date.

The city was covered in snow. There were narrow paths along the wide, seemingly abandoned streets—they looked like trails in a forest.

Olga Berggolts told me from her recollections: "The Radio House was on Rakova Street, not too far away from Nevsky Prospect, close by the Public Library and across from the Manezh, where Lenin spoke in April 1917.

"One morning Boris Mikhailovich Eichenbaum came to the Radio House. It must have been a very difficult walk; he had to cross Griboedov Canal, pass through several quarters of the city. Eichenbaum asked to speak on the radio—he wanted to talk to the Germans. This is what he said":

I am an old professor. My son Dmitri is at the front. My son-in-law was killed. I live with my wife, daughter, and granddaughter in a single room and write a book about Tolstoy. You know him—he is the author of *War and Peace*. I know you are afraid of Tolstoy—you have read his book about victory after defeat.

I left my desk with frozen ink to come here and tell you that I despise you. You can refute culture only with culture. We have cannons too—you can't prove anything with cannons. You can't destroy our culture, you can't break into our city.

The speech wasn't recorded. People recall it from memory.

Boris Mikhailovich walked back home. He went past houses with windows blocked up with bricks and machine-gun emplacements made of earth and timber at their corners.

The city was both dead and alive.

Boris Mikhailovich returned along the old Italianskaya Street,[22] passing the Philharmonic, crossing the bridge on Griboedov Canal, entering the house, and walking up the cold stairwell with endless steps covered in ice (water spilled from buckets that people carried home).

He walked over the squeaky floors of the narrow corridors, opened the half-frozen door of his apartment and entered his cold lodging.

He survived somehow. He was transported with his wife, daughter, and granddaughter on a truck across the frozen Lake Ladoga. From his neck Eichenbaum hung the briefcase with the third vol-

22 Italianskaya Street, running from Griboedov Canal to the Fontanka River, was renamed Rakova Street after the revolution.

ume of the manuscript on Tolstoy. It was a long journey through snowstorms and German planes hanging over the head.

When Boris Mikhailovich and his family reached the first train station, it turned out that the manuscript had been lost: the rope on which the briefcase was hanging had torn.

Later Eichenbaum lectured in Saratov where the University of Leningrad had been evacuated.

The drafts left in Leningrad were lost too.

The Professor Departs

It was Eichenbaum's fortieth year at the university.

They were publishing the jubilee edition of Tolstoy's works and Eichenbaum was involved in the publication. At the time, he was immersed in dramaturgy, writing an article on *Hamlet*, and trying to restore the lost part of his book on Tolstoy, while simultaneously revising many things in it.

Eichenbaum was reorganizing his archive. Most of it had been burnt in Leningrad during the blockade and his absence.

He had to begin working on the second half of the book anew.

His wife had passed away. His granddaughter was growing up.

The professor kept working on his book that didn't yet have a publisher. He was starting from scratch.

A scientific work usually requires the establishment of a specific terminology.

Eichenbaum had long been working on Lenin's stylistic tendencies and his essays on literature. In 1924, he had published an essay called "Basic Stylistic Patterns in Lenin's Speech" in the first issue of *LEF*.

Working on Tolstoy after the war, Eichenbaum once again turned his attention to Lenin's essays.

He was trying to determine what Lenin meant by his remark that, "it is necessary to aspire to *elevate* spontaneity to consciousness."[23]

In the essay "Lev Tolstoy and His Epoch" (1911), Lenin saw Tolstoy's teachings as a phenomenon brought on by the period of 1862–1904, a period of upheaval in Russia, "that could give rise to Tolstoy's teachings and in which they were inevitable, not as something individual, not as a caprice or a fad, but as the ideology of the conditions of life under which millions and millions actually found themselves for a certain period of time."

The professor explicated what Lenin meant when he wrote that "Tolstoy's doctrine is certainly utopian and in content is reactionary in the most precise and most profound sense of the word."

He found the same expressions in another text by Lenin, *A Characterization of Economic Romanticism*, "where the discussion is about the 'utopian' and 'reactionary' nature (in this exact combination) of Sismondi's and Proudhon's theories."

Lenin wrote the following footnote to the word *reactionary*: "This term is employed in its *historico-philosophical* sense, describing only the *error* of the theorists who take models for their theories from *obsolete* forms of society. It does not apply at all to the personal qualities of these theorists, or to their programs. Everybody knows that neither Sismondi nor Proudhon were reactionaries in

23   From Vladimir Lenin's article "A Talk with Defenders of Economism" (1901).

the ordinary sense of the term. We are explaining these elementary truths because, as we shall see below, the Narodnik gentlemen have not grasped them to this day."

We don't simply live *in* our country—we live *with* it. Our generation isn't a generation of people who were sent in the wrong direction by a casual passerby because they were lost. That method of correcting mistakes belongs to Salieri. He changed his direction because they advised him to do so, but he poisoned a genius, envying his destiny.

The period of Tynjanov, Eichenbaum, Polivanov, Jakubinsky, and others was a movement of explorers, not followers. We conducted extensive experiments. We have always refuted the old but that doesn't mean we renounce it. There is a big difference there.

Eichenbaum's oeuvre is an inseparable whole.

He was very ill. His heart began to fail. But Boris still looked very young. He attended concerts, and conducted music at home, while standing above his record collection. Boris liked classical music very much and knew it well. He lived in music, wanted to write the history of the orchestra and the history of change in musical instruments.

He wrote about new instruments and how they come into use: how they first get evaluated and analyzed according to their timbre.

This is how Plato treated the flute, and how they appraised the violin. That's how they debated about the saxophone. The instruments are thus introduced into the orchestra anew, generating a complementary nuance.

In the evolution of art, an instrument finds its new and contested place differently each time, or it doesn't find a place at all.

One ought to be purposefully prudent.

Eichenbaum had a friend—a rather capable poet—who finally exhausted himself and turned to sketch comedy.

Eichenbaum was pretty old then. They had organized an evening dedicated to the poet at the Mayakovsky House. The opening speech was to be made by a popular variety actor. It turned out that the actor wasn't going to make it to the event. The poet then called Eichenbaum and asked his old friend to come to his rescue:

—I'll be mortified if the evening is canceled.

The old professor wasn't too fond of sketches but he was a loyal friend.

Boris had talked at the Mayakovsky House, let's say, hundreds of times. He was certain that he could handle someone else's audience. He quickly went to work, found some examples on the meaning and purpose of the genre.

He carefully read and reinterpreted the poor sketches, wrote a short introduction about the meaning of moral, the significance of the repetition of simple didactic rules, and how that too can become a phenomenon of art.

When Eichenbaum appeared on the stage instead of the actor, there was a sigh of disappointment in the audience. He often gave speeches to young sailors, students, and Red Army soldiers; he was very proficient at improvising at such lectures. In fact, he took great pleasure in conducting the audience and delivering an idea to a point of clarity.

But this was someone else's audience.

As he spoke the audience grew bored. He finished—there was a grave silence.

The professor came down, joining the mute, offended audience, and sat in the front row.

The curtains went up and the performance of the sketch began.

Boris Mikhailovich turned to his daughter and said:

—What a stupid flop!

The actors were already on the stage, mumbling idiocies.

Suddenly, the actress stopped and jumped off the stage. The professor was stiff in his chair—dead.

There are no accidental works for the artist's heart.

The heart was prepared to lift a heavy weight.

But the barbell turned out to be empty.

An unnecessary sacrifice.

His heart was seventy years old. It had withstood many blows but it was worn out by three infractions.

They spoke of his contributions at the funeral.

He was buried in the new cemetery at Vyborgskaya Side.

Crows sat perched on bare November birches.

The varnish of the yellow coffin glistened by his gray tombstone.

How sadly Pushkin wrote: only a few of us are left, and alas the best ones are gone.[24]

People walked together, then they dispersed.

There had been arguments and fights as in a marriage.

There had been works as battles, as feasts.

But the blood-wine wasn't enough for all.

---

24   A paraphrase from *Eugene Onegin*'s final stanza:

"Some are no more, others are distant,"
as erstwhiles Sadi said. (Translated by V. Nabokov)

Death doesn't offer apologies.

Even old age has passed. Crows cover the battlefield with their wings.

Death replaces the rows of people; it is preparing a new edition, restoring life.

Let's preserve the memory of the work.

ON UNITY

The Strained Bowstring

The Greek philosopher Heraclitus was commonly referred to as "the Obscure" in the antiquity. He received this epithet because he spoke about contradiction, and also because his philosophical writings were preserved only in fragments and inaccurate paraphrases.

In Plato's *Symposium*, one of the interlocutors speaks about contradictions—about "opposite" or "hostile" beginnings:

> Anyone who pays the least attention to the subject will also perceive that in music there is the same reconciliation of opposites; and I suppose that this must have been the meaning of Heraclitus, although his words are not accurate, for he says that the One is united by disunion, like the harmony of the bow and the lyre . . . What he probably meant was, that harmony is attained through the art of music by the reconciliation of differing notes of higher or lower pitch which once disagreed.[25]

---

25   Plato, *Symposium*. In *The Dialogues of Plato*. Vol. I. Translated by Benjamin Jowett. Oxford UP, 1964.

In the translator's note, V. Asmus writes that Plato was referencing the following fragment preserved from Heraclitus: "They do not understand how that which differs from itself is in agreement: harmony consists of opposing tension, like that of the bow and the lyre."

These ideas repeat variously in his other fragments.

Heraclitus's undeniably "obscure" proposition had different interpreters. Those who tried to interpret what he meant are individuals whom we can trust.

They paid particular attention to it.

If we look at the proposition ourselves, we will clearly see that opposites, moving in different directions, seem to harmonize one another.

The remaining energy, born from opposition, exists in every work of art and its fragments; if it maintains its artistic composition, it creates a new unity.

The wooden stick is a single unity. The string made of sinew is another unity. The arched stick, bent by the string, becomes a bow.

This is a new unity and it represents the first model of an artistic composition.

This idea can be clarified with the help of another quote from Plato's *Phaedo*: ". . . but first the lyre, and the strings, and the sounds exist in a state of discord, and then harmony is made last of all, and perishes first."[26]

The bow's harmony arises from the strained stick forced by the bowstring. Subsequently, harmony resides in unity and contradiction.

It is kinetic energy that's about to become dynamic energy.

---

26   Plato, *Phaedo*. In *The Dialogues of Plato*. Vol. I. Translated by Benjamin Jowett. Oxford UP, 1964.

Lenin wrote about this in his *Philosophical Notebooks*.

In his conspectus of Hegel's *Lectures on the History of Philosophy*, Lenin quotes Hegel and comments:

> Aristotle (*De mundo*, Chapter 5) quotes this from Heraclitus: "Join together the complete whole and the incomplete" (the whole makes itself the part, and the meaning of the part is to become the whole), "what coincides and what conflicts, what is harmonious and what discordant; and from out of them all (the opposite) comes one, and from one, all."

Plato, in his *Symposium*, puts forward Heraclitus's views (applicable to music: harmony consists of opposites) and the statement that "the art of music unites the discordant."

Lenin quotes Hegel's analysis of harmony and writes in the margin:

> . . . difference is clearly necessary to harmony, or a definite antithesis; for it is the absolute becoming and not mere change. The real fact is that each particular tone is different from another—not abstractly so from any other, but from *its* other—and thus it also can be one. Each particular only is, in

Quite true and important: the "other" as *its own* other; development into *its* opposite.

so far as its opposite is implici-
tly contained in its Notion.[27]

I will try to summarize what I just said without formulating anything concrete just yet.

Something new is registered in the similar (predictable) as "its
own—foreign." The sign or feature delineating the removal of a previous whole becomes the main content of the new message.

As a result something new is formed—it is different, separate
from "its own other," which is also contained in it.

The dissimilarity requires a similarity in order to transmit "its
own," to create its own distinct system.

Fixed forms in art exist through changes.

I will call laws determining the meanings of parts in given con-
texts "conventions," i.e., conditions accepted both by the author of the
given system of signs and those who perceive them. A changed feature in the similar can change the entire system by its dissimilarity.

Therefore, the dissimilarity of the similar is economical in its own
way, because it uses the system as part of its new message without
destroying the entire system.

Tropes—uncommon applications of the word—don't destroy the
quotidian, conventional meaning of the word-sign, but represent a new
(found in the ordinary) consciousness of the dissimilarity of the similar.

The image-trope is a specific example of how a new model is constructed through an analysis of the dissimilarity of the similar.

---

27   G. W. F. Hegel, *Lectures on the History of Philosophy*. Translated by E. S.
Haldane. U of Nebraska P, 1995.

The Whole and the Part

We experience both "finished" works and fragments as a whole, whether they are fragments from an ancient poet, Venus de Milo without her arms, Sterne's novel stopped in the middle of a phrase, the abruptly ended *Eugene Onegin* in its moment of high tension, *Dead Souls*, or Tolstoy's trilogy *Childhood, Boyhood,* and *Youth*—though *Youth* is finished, there is a promise of continuation: "How long that moral impulse lasted, what it consisted of, and what new principles I devised for my moral growth I will relate when speaking of the ensuing and happier portion of my early manhood."[28] There are records about the work's continuation, but it is not finished.

The Cossacks wasn't finished either, nor was *Resurrection*. Despite the promise of a continuation, Dostoevsky didn't "finish" *Crime and Punishment*. There are many such examples of unfinished but fully exposed works in literature.

There are books that have been finished but are hardly ever read to the end such as, for example, *The Divine Comedy*.

We expect more decisive closures in drama. The canonical endings—wedding or death—were mostly developed in plays.

The laws of drama seemed rigidly strict. The beginning of the play already separated the work with a stage, Chorus, and expectation of the audience.

The ancient Greeks had a different perception of the whole. Let me repeat.

---

28 Lev Tolstoy, *Childhood, Boyhood, and Youth*. Translated by C. J. Hogarth. New York: Alfred A. Knopf, 1991.

For Aristotle, "parts" made up a whole: "Now a whole is that which has a beginning, a middle, and an end. A beginning is that which does not itself follow anything by causal necessity, but after which something naturally is or comes to be. An end, on the contrary, is that which itself naturally follows some other thing, either by necessity, or as a rule, but has nothing following it. A middle is that which follows something as some other thing follows it."[29]

In Aristotle's definition the whole here is, first of all, a myth or *fabula*—a story. But the *fabula* that unfolds, for example, in a tragedy or an epic, naturally being a whole, is not the only whole and in itself is divided into its own integral parts, which can be not only arranged in a new whole but also isolated and evaluated on their own. The catalogue of ships in *The Iliad*, for instance, can be seen as a whole. And Mandelstam imagined or, more precisely, grasped the catalogue of ships through his poem:

> Insomnia. Homer. Taut sails.
> I've read to the middle of the list of ships.[30]

But in this catalogue too there are parts that, if separated, represent a certain whole and can be evaluated and compared.

Osip Mandelstam read the catalogue of ships not only to fall asleep. For him this description was a whole. Perhaps it was so for the Greek Chorus. The catalogue of ships represented Greece, the

---

29   Aristotle, *Poetics*. Translated by S. H. Butcher. New York: Hill and Wang, 1961. All subsequent quotations from *Poetics* are taken from this standard version.
30   Osip Mandelstam, "78" (1915). Translated by Joan Aleshire.

forces that were gathering around Troy, and the interrelation of those forces. The number of ships represented separate kings and the degree of their involvement in the war.

But this description is simultaneously an independent composition, and its part can also be perceived as independent. This could be done through a stylistic strain.

Among others, there were three ships that came from Syme.

Here is what Cicero said about them:

> Ordinary things are ignoble and hence, do not provoke a surprise. By extolling Nireus, a nonentity, and his measly military means—only three ships and a few men, Homer presents something trivial as something grand when he employs a double-hybrid figure that combines anaphora and division:
>
> > Nireus led his three ships from Syme,
> > Nireus the son of Aglaea and King Charopus,
> > Nireus the handsomest man who ever came to Troy,
> > of all the Achaeans after Peleus's fearless son. (Book 2, 767–770)[31]
>
> The anaphora pulls Nireus forward, the division gives the impression of a multitude of means, although they consist of two or three objects. And though he mentions Nireus only once in his epic poem, we remember him as vividly as Achilles or Odysseus who appear in almost every stro-

31   Homer, *The Iliad*. Translated by Robert Fagles. New York: Viking, 1990. All subsequent quotations from *The Iliad* are taken from this standard version.

phe. This is due to the power of the rhetorical figure. Had he said "Nireus, the son of Aglaea from Syme, came with three ships," it would have been the same as never having mentioned Nireus.[32]

The anaphora here is used as a method of selection.

In rhetoric, the anaphora is a repetition of opening phrases. In all three lines, Nireus's name is positioned in the same identical place. Hence it is stressed and singled out. If the excerpt, which is only four lines long, doesn't give us an image then it certainly gives us a sign that we will remember. The sign is repeated, intensified. Never being mentioned in the battle again, the hero's name nonetheless remains in our memory. The name with triple emphasis gives us the impression that there were many people on Nireus's ship and that they were all different—it gives us the depth of the stage, though the name itself seems irrelevant.

The anaphora turns a part into a whole.

The autonomy of this verse is based on something that was called word-arrangement in antiquity, it is created by the poem's movement—the poetic strain.

We can say here that this strain introduces the element of surprise, which in turn fixes a certain phenomenon. We experience it as if it were loaded. We hear the sound of the strained bowstring.

In literature, "the parts" are usually perceived as "the whole," and if a part is separated it becomes strained.

---

32   *Antichnye teorii yazyka i stilya* [Theories of Language and Style in Antiquity], edited by Olga Freidenberg, 1936.

What Are the Distinguishing Features of Art and What Is Unity?

Every so often an artistic composition will be measured by its imagistic qualities. But what does that mean? The term *image* has been perceived as a means of depiction, a measure of artistic quality in description, and at the same time people talk about "the image of Tatyana" or "the image of Onegin." By this they mean a character, a representation. The word *image* also means an image.

This is not an exact definition—it isn't a term.

If we take a scientific dictionary from Pushkin's period, we'll find various contradictory definitions of the word *image*.

According to the Dictionary of the Russian Academy, published in 1822:

> **Image** *n.* 1) aspect, external appearance; 2) reproduction, portrayal or likeness of a person; 3) model; 4) method, mode, way; 5) order, way of thinking.

For instance, we describe something "as an image of" something else. The word *image* in this case refers to "content" or "essence."

There is only one method in art and it doesn't change during the process of a work's creation.

Let's take one of the meanings of the word *image*. The phenomena of art move from one realm to another.

So what is the "order" of art?

There are various disciplines in art, though obviously they are somehow connected to one another.

When referring to "reproduction" or "portrayal," the word *image* generally fits best in the context of painting or sculpture, but it is completely unsuitable when used in architecture or music. We hardly ever apply it in the context of the performing arts; however, occasionally we may use it to refer to a "way of dancing."

But the ancient philosophers argued that the concept of *image* had little to do with lyric poetry because it doesn't depict anything, rather it transmits emotion, which may not necessarily contain any concrete image in itself.

To complicate the question, or better yet, to pinpoint the difficulty of the question, we will see that figurativeness isn't clear even in the discipline of physics, though it has its "methods—means." The physicist thinks, somehow imagining and fixing his ideas.

But we have no way of knowing exactly how he imagines those things.

We often believe that we think in words, but mathematical thought, in its quest for veracity, is usually expressed in mathematical formulas and cannot be transmitted in any other form, including the verbal system. It can be reformulated in words with great difficulty, but this reformulation doesn't get any more visual, voluminous or representational.

Albert Einstein wrote in his *Autobiographical Notes*:

> I have no doubt but that our thinking goes on for the most part without use of signs (words) and beyond that to a considerable degree unconsciously. For how, otherwise, should it happen that sometimes we "wonder" quite spontaneously about some experience? This "wondering" appears to occur when an experience comes into conflict with a world of concepts already sufficiently fixed within us. Whenever such a conflict is experienced

sharply and intensively it reacts back upon our world of thought in a decisive way. The development of this world of thought is in a certain sense a continuous flight from "wonder."[33]

So the ordinary, real, existing world that gives birth to all our experiences and knowledge simultaneously, in the process of cognition, creates something else—the fact of surprise, the fact of some superiority of essence over our knowledge.

The primary motive or one of the primary motives for scientific thought, according to Einstein, is this sensation of surprise.

In his essay "Principles of Research" (1918), Einstein uses artistic terms:

> Man tries to make for himself, in the fashion that suits him best, a simplified and intelligible picture of the world; he then tries to some extent to substitute this cosmos of his for the world of experience, and thus to overcome it. This is what the painter, the poet, the speculative philosopher, and the natural scientist do, each in his own fashion. Each makes this cosmos and its construction the pivot of his emotional life, in order to find in this way the peace and security which he cannot find in the narrow whirlpool of personal experience.

---

33 Albert Einstein, *Autobiographical Notes*. Translated by Paul Arthur Schilpp. La Salle: Open Court, 1979.

We come across the concept of simulacrum, the idea of a model, the construction of another world, and these representations are created for the purpose of understanding what we call reality, for the speculation and discovery of possibilities.

What goes into the creative work is selected by the artist from his surroundings for the construction of his model of reality— it is not a simple replica. It is unique. It's a reflection in which the features of the perceived thing are juxtaposed in their dissimilarity.

In his conspectus of Hegel's *Lectures on the History of Philosophy*, Lenin copies the following sentence: "The strife is not due to the opposition between observation and the absolute Notion, but between the one Notion and the other,"—and writes in the margin: "Correct!"

The book which you are reading attempts to show that literature is not a subdiscipline of linguistics, and that linguistics is not a science of all-encompassing universal thought.

Aristotle, discussing tragedy in *Poetics*, wrote: "Now, according to our definition Tragedy is an imitation of an action that is complete, and whole, and of a certain magnitude; for there may be a whole that is wanting in magnitude. A *whole* is that which has a beginning, a middle, and an end."

This is apparent in and specific to Greek tragedy. *The Iliad*, too, has a beginning—the rage of Achilles against Agamemnon, a middle—the repercussions from that rage, and Patroclus's death. But, in essence, there is no ending—Achilles's fate is foretold by his horse, Xanthus: "But the day of death already hovers near," and then by Hector.

There is a beginning, a middle, and an end in *The Odyssey*. Fairy tales, too, have beginnings and endings.

They typically begin with: "Once upon a time . . ."—or: "In a land far, far away . . ."

This customary lead signals to the listener that he is about to enter a particular structure with its own laws.

The ending of the fairy tale is traditional: "And they lived happily ever after."

But works of art are often discontinuous, they may not have a proper beginning, or they may have a distinctive "unendedness" or "infinality." They create a stimulus for attention.

Pushkin begins *Eugene Onegin* with the following:

> "My uncle has most honest principles:
> when he was taken gravely ill,
> he forced one to respect him
> and nothing better could invent."[34]

We don't know yet who is saying this and why.

The hero is identified and described later on—the explanation of Onegin's arrival in the countryside is deferred.

This kind of a beginning is crucial here. It forces us to study the stranger's face. It prompts what Onegin is engaged in. The beginning serves as an exposition to Onegin's appearance in the estate where he meets Lensky and Tatyana.

---

34 Aleksandr Pushkin, *Eugene Onegin*. Vol. I. Translated by Vladimir Nabokov. New York: Pantheon Books, 1964. All subsequent quotations from *Eugene Onegin* are taken from this standard version.

Onegin's "character" is a riddle to Tatyana.

Onegin's love is a riddle even to himself.

We must understand the heroes by studying the digressions—the social milieu that surrounds them.

The "encyclopedia of life" in *Eugene Onegin* is unified through various elements: the landscapes of changing seasons, the author's fleeting remarks about himself and others.

The serpentine bends of the strophes give breadth and multi-angle perspectives to the narrative.

Eugene Onegin is a river, the shores of which have been described, but which hasn't been fully explored yet.

The hero and his place in the world are still not understood.

His love passed by unrecognized, the recognition of which is tragic. The happy ending—a conventional resolution that creates an illusion of closure and completion—is expunged.

This is not a coincidence. It's how conformity is determined.

The concept of the whole is historical and it changes.

Beginning from familiar places, from ordinary fairy-tale situations, as we would say, the storyteller changes them, weaving a new tale and is surprised by it, as it were. He is building his own *skaz*.

Pushkin didn't follow in the footsteps of Byron or Sterne.

Giving a direction to his search, he pushed away from the traditional ending that doesn't contain any information.

He replied to his friend:

> You give me the advice, my dear Pletnyov,
> To go on writing <our> abandoned novel

<and> to amuse <this austere> age, this iron
age of accounts, with empty narratives.[35]

There won't be such an ending, there won't be an epilogue.

Pushkin evaded the answer. The ruthless epoch reproached him for that.

No more old prologues.

The traditional ending is pushed away—rejected.

Chekhov in his letters to his brother wrote: "Start writing from the second page."

He was more blunt in conversations: "Tear out the first half of your story; you'll only have to change a few things in the beginning of the second half and the story will be perfectly clear."

The unity of a composition is not based on whether it has a beginning, a middle and an end, but whether it creates a unique interrelation between its parts.

The concept of unity (the whole) is historically changing.

Unity and the Hero

Anyone can think of literary works titled after their eponymous heroes such as *The Odyssey, Candide, Eugene Onegin, Anna Karenina* Turgenev's *Rudin*, Gorky's *The Life of Klim Samgin*, Tvardovsky's *Vasili Tyorkin*. As a result of this, there is a general assumption that

---

35 Aleksandr Pushkin, *Eugene Onegin*. Vol. III. Translated by Vladimir Nabokov. New York: Pantheon Books, 1964. In 1835 Pushkin wrote this verse epistle to Pyotr Pletnyov, who had urged him to continue *Eugene Onegin*. He began the epistle in iambic pentameter but then switched to his old *Eugene Onegin* stanza.

a work's unity is based on the unity of the story about a single or several heroes.

But this assumption has been refuted a long time ago.

Aristotle wrote in *Poetics* (Chapter 8):

> Unity of plot does not, as some people think, consist in the unity of the hero. For infinitely various are the incidents in one man's life which cannot be reduced to unity; and so, too, there are many actions of one man out of which we cannot make one action.

The incidents are always selected—we would have drowned in the number of incidents even if we had only one character. Attempting to write "A History of Yesterday," the young Tolstoy noted that there wouldn't be enough ink or paper in the world had he recorded everything a person goes through in a single day. About a century later, Joyce attempted the same on a much larger scale. The whole for him was a link of associations—a path through their contradictoriness. Perhaps this is why he titled his book *Ulysses*— naming it after the traveler who passed through the lands and the myths of classical antiquity.

The unity of *Ulysses* is in the juxtaposition of conscious and subconscious constructions—the search for the purpose of juxtaposition.

The book's peculiarity is in its emphasis on the noncoincidence of the juxtaposed.

The unity of a literary work is based on its structure.

We are approaching the concept of unity between action and situation not only in terms of evental linearity or continuity, but also in terms of artistic construction—the unity of intention.

In his "Introduction to the Works of Guy de Maupassant," Tolstoy interrupted the description of separate constructions with the following words:

> People of little artistic sensibility often think that a work of art possesses unity when the same people act in it throughout, or when it is all constructed on one plot, or describes the life of one man. That is a mistake. It only appears so to a superficial observer. The cement, which binds any artistic production into one whole and, therefore, produces the illusion of being a reflection of life is not the unity of persons or situations, but the unity of the author's original moral relation to his subject.[36]

I should note here that the "original moral relation" shouldn't be understood solely in relation to Tolstoyan morality. The word "original" should orient us to the notion that this is an author's attitude toward his own epoch.

Tolstoy himself hesitated in this question. In *What Is Art?* he thought that a work had aesthetic value if it was based on morality, that is—in Tolstoy's understanding—on peasant morality. Tolstoy further argued that this kind of morality was inherent in any genuine art. To prove his point, he used the analysis of ancient theories of literature that discuss the concept of *kalokagathia*.

This is an idiomatic phrase made up of two adjectives—*kalos* (beautiful) and *agathos* (good, prudent). So, in a way, the ethical

---

36   The article served as preface to a Russian edition of a selection of Maupassant's stories published for the first time in 1894 by Posrednik Press.

and aesthetical features are united in the word *kalokagathia* as a single characterization.

This concept isn't descriptive of all aesthetical values of antiquity. It belongs to a different system in connection to an assertion of well-being and health. Aristotle wrote in *Politics*:

> For the noble are citizens in a truer sense than the ignoble, and good birth is always valued in a man's own home and country. Another reason is that those who are sprung from better ancestors are likely to be better men, for nobility is excellence of race. Virtue, too, may be truly said to have a claim, for justice has been acknowledged by us to be a social virtue, and it implies all others.[37]

In *Oeconomicus*, Xenophon constructs a dialogue between Socrates and Critobulus about the ideal master. We are introduced to a certain Ischomachus who possesses the qualities of *kalokagathia*. Socrates leads the conversation about good carpenters, blacksmiths, painters, sculptors, and then he adds that one cannot link the word "beautiful" to the word "good" always, but only when one possesses a good soul. But then Socrates says how beauty can be found in the way that shoes are lined up or coats are sorted. Brass earthenware, tablecloths, and even flower pots arranged in good order can be beautiful as they represent something well-proportioned and harmonious.

Kalokagathia is a good man's household, something that Levin was trying to attain in *Anna Karenina* but was unable to because

---

37 Aristotle, *Politics*. Translated by Benjamin Jowett. New York: Random House, 1943.

the social structure was changing in Russia and nothing would fit in properly. *Kalokagathia* was an impossibility.

So the idea of *kalokagathia*, which Tolstoy used to base his claim of genuine art, was a historical concept. Tolstoy—to whom the contemporary everyman was a good master, a self-sufficient peasant working with his own hands—couldn't possibly measure art with such a yardstick. This is why he went through endless divergences of opinion. He said, for example, that art was good when it flowed from a religious consciousness: "Art was perceived in that way by the ancient philosophers—Socrates, Plato, Aristotle. That is how the Jewish prophets and old Christians viewed art, so did the Mohammedans, and that is how the religious people of my time continue to perceive it."

This was the opinion of Tolstoy the theoretician.

Beauty meant moral decency.

What would happen if we approached art with this kind of a measure? It would mean that Pushkin who wasn't "a divine man and teacher of kindness," but "a man of immoral behavior," didn't produce any kind of genuine art.

Tolstoy went back and forth; he kept acknowledging Pushkin and then refuting him, while maintaining his theory.

The Contradictoriness of the Definition
that Doesn't Encompass History

Tolstoy anticipated objections—and much of that remained in his drafts, where he argued that "the epics of Virgil, Dante, Tasso, Milton, a great many plays of Shakespeare, a great part of Goethe, the last compositions of Beethoven, some compositions of Bach" are tasteless, vile, repulsive, and boring to a majority of people.

In other drafts Tolstoy wrote that, "first of all, it is necessary to eliminate the so-called works of art that don't infect but are now considered art because they are *interesting*," and proceeded to give a list of rejected works. "And in the next column, as an exception, are the works that call for praise and should be considered as high art, beginning from the antiquity with Pheidias and *Venus de Milo*, and most importantly, the wild tragedians Sophocles, Euripides, Aeschylus, Aristophanes. . . ." Then he listed Corneille, Racine, Raphael, Michelangelo. And the list went on—Ibsen, Maeterlinck, Verlaine, Mallarmé, from composers—Brahms and Strauss.

One can certainly talk about morality and *kalokagathia* in art. But to do so without dismissing all of art, it's important to understand that morals change, they are historical. Tolstoy took the morality of one particular period and turned it into a universal measure. Consequently, whatever didn't fit within those limitations was immoral to him. Yet he considered the biblical story of Joseph to be a moral one. He even taught it to the peasant children in his school, included it in the *Primer*, and discussed it in the context of both history and analysis of art. Joseph is mentioned a dozen times in his essays about art. Let's look at what he did.

After Joseph interpreted Pharaoh's dream about the seven fat and seven thin cows as the seven years of prosperity, followed by seven years of famine, Pharaoh ordered that they store away all the food: "So Joseph stored up grain in such abundance—like sand of the sea—that he stopped measuring it; it was beyond measure"

(Genesis 41:49).[38] When the famine arrived, Pharaoh first sold the grain through Joseph to the Egyptians, and Joseph brought all the money back to Pharaoh's treasury. He then exchanged food for their livestock and land, and finally Joseph bought "all the land of Egypt for Pharaoh" and "as for the people, he made slaves of them from one end of Egypt to the other" (47:20–21). And then: "Only the land of the priests he did not buy; for the priests had a fixed allowance from Pharaoh, and lived on the allowance that Pharaoh gave them; therefore they did not sell their land" (47:22).

This whole story is an interpretation of how the land of Egypt became the property of Pharaoh. But Joseph's actions, the actions of Pharaoh's right-hand man—in the way in which they were transcribed in the Bible—couldn't have been perceived as *kalokagathia* from the peasants' perspective of Tolstoy's time. It was more like pawning or exploitation. But in the context of the Bible, in the system of that worldview, Joseph's actions were believed to be good. Likewise, Engels explains how in old tales a man could marry his own sister and how it was morally accepted. It was another system of morality. But when reading a literary work, we often accept against our own will the system of moral codes that operated during the writing process.

The originality of moral relations in this biblical story stems from the fact that the author portrayed Joseph as a steady, wise, but not vengeful man.

---

38 The New Oxford Annotated Bible (New Revised Standard Version). Ed. Bruce M. Metzger and Roland E. Murphy. Oxford UP, 1991. All subsequent quotations from the Bible are taken from this standard version.

The pupils at Yasnaya Polyana accepted Joseph's system of moral codes. Even Thomas Mann agreed that Joseph's land politics were right. Or, let's just say, that it corresponded well with that epoch.

The Unity of Structures

Now let us return to the unity of artistic compositions. This unity is doubtlessly the unity of artistic construction created through the author's sensibility. It strives to create models of universal phenomena.

The artistic composition is monolithic: it brings us into the possibilities of proposed human relationships and doesn't disconnect us from the past because we see the appropriateness (or inappropriateness) of not just a single action but of the whole system. For example, we ignore (though we read about it) that Penelope provokes her suitors to bring her gifts and even accepts those gifts knowing that Odysseus has already returned and is about to take revenge on the suitors.

So how can we explain the continuity of our perception of art when art in itself is discontinuous? Aeschylus was refuted by Sophocles, and Shakespeare was refuted by Tolstoy. According to Lenin, who spoke at the anniversary of Tolstoy's death, Tolstoy was not understood by the majority of Russians. Yet today he is recognized. Everyone reads *Anna Karenina*. What people have abandoned and won't read now are Tolstoy's folktales.

Eichenbaum told me once about Tolstoy's copy of *Romeo and Juliet*, on the margins of which Tolstoy had made ironic remarks to

Shakespeare. In the part where Romeo utters: "Hang up philosophy! / Unless philosophy can make a Juliet," Tolstoy wrote something in the margins which he crossed out, then wrote another comment that he crossed out again. Finally he wrote in large and irritated letters: "Evidently a lucky accident."

He was unable to disprove the truth of these words. But he formed his own aesthetic system founded on a specific worldview and tried to apply it to all cultures of mankind, and consequently crossed out the larger part of art.

I am writing this book to refute the very convincing and ingeniously articulated idea of art censorship carried out by Tolstoy, and to refute his relationship and methods of crossing things out. I should mention that those methods always changed and Tolstoy frequently recorded his admiration of Chopin and Beethoven. Russian composer Aleksandr Goldenweiser recorded one of Tolstoy's remarks about how Chopin was not understood when Tolstoy was younger.

A person uses words that were invented for him. They contain echoes of the past, traces of old traditions.

Words, as Horace observed, are like leaves. They sprout and then they wither away. He wrote this by the Mediterranean Sea where the trees are evergreen. Leaves fall very quickly in our climate, in our life, and different ones appear the following year. But forests change, too. According to Russian folklore, the birches were advancing and appeared behind the Volga with the Russians. Nature changes. But most importantly, life changes, while preserving its nominative forms, and we live without destroying the past.

We think through negation in art. The Bible, Homer, and Tolstoy all co-exist in Russian literature. We still use religious terms to say something antireligious. You can see this in Yesenin and Mayakovsky. The rhetoric of the Russian Revolution incorporated biblical phrases in their antithetical forms. Everything was refuted—the old style, definition of terms, rhythms—yet it was refuted not through parts but as a reinterpretation of the whole system. So in order to understand Mayakovsky's poetry one must know the poetry of Pushkin who exists through Mayakovsky and is illuminated by him.

Aleksandr Blok wrote how the Futurists unintentionally renewed the perception of Pushkin: "What if I said that we were taught to *love* Pushkin again in a *new way* not by Bryusov, Shchyogolev, or Morozov, but . . . by the *Futurists*. They scold him in new ways, and he becomes closer to us anew. I felt this with *Eugene Onegin*."[39]

The poet continued: "Scolding in the name of the new is not the same as scolding in the name of the old, even if the new is unrecognized (isn't it always?), and the old—great and renowned. This is true because scolding in the name of the new is *much more difficult and requires great responsibility.*"

Contradictions within the Concept of Image

Let's see how the meaning of description or characterization of the referent changes. Let's look at a few examples from Chinese and Japanese art.

---

39   Aleksandr Blok, *Zapisnye knizhki 1901–1920* [Notebooks: 1901–1920], 1965.

"A lonesome tree" is an easily discernible semantic sign. Everyone recognizes the figure of "a lonesome oak": it appears in Russian folksongs, in Pushkin's verses and in Tolstoy's *War and Peace*.

But there are various degrees of lonesomeness.

Seventeenth-century poet Matsuo Basho juxtaposes an oak to a cherry tree:

> The lonesome oak
> stands dignified, not noticing
> the cherry blossoms.

And there are countless haiku poems of this sort. But this isn't due to poverty of imagination—it's the selection that poetry made in a given epoch. It stems from the structure of the short poem that doesn't have room for long explanations.

In Chinese poetry, the monkey's cry in the forest is usually a sign of solitude.

Eighth-century Chinese poet Li Po writes about a clear river:

> The reflection of birds
> is like a vibrant painting on the screen.
> And in the evenings, amid the silence,
> the cries of monkeys alone
> torment the travelers
> wandering under the clear moon.

The cries of monkeys, wilderness, absence of people—these familiar signs of the woods are contrasted with the habitable room:

the reflection of birds seen as a painting on the screen. But the "monkey's cry" turns into a platitude. Disconnected from the real experience, it's like the screen with painted birds.

Basho writes:

> For those touched by the monkey's cry
> How is it when they hear the crying child
> Abandoned in the autumn wind?

Here the conventional image is contrasted with a real image; each line intensifies the next one, and they simultaneously move poetry away from ordinary poetic embellishments. Monkeys are a common sight in the markets and squares in China and Japan. The monkey is thought to have a caricature-like face, but on special holidays it is paraded in a monkey's mask: its features are amplified through repetition and the face becomes a mask.

Another Japanese poet, describing autumn rain in a haiku, writes how in such weather the monkey longs for a raincoat.

A raincoat made of straw is a poor man's clothing. The poet's words convey an ironic pity toward himself. The juxtaposition was so powerful that the collection of poems, including that particular poem, was titled "The Monkey's Straw Raincoat."

Images are juxtaposed, creating a poetic phrase, forming though the foundation of a new plot—a new strain.

IMAGE AND RIDDLES

About Riddles and the Baring of Conflict in the Habitual

Hegel wrote in his *Lectures on Fine Art* that "the riddle belongs to conscious symbolism."[40] What is the riddle's answer? It is derivation of meaning. According to Hegel, the riddle consists of "individual traits of character and properties drawn from the otherwise known external world and, as in nature and in externality generally, lying there scattered outside one another, they are associated together in a disparate and therefore striking way. As a result they lack a subject embracing them together [as predicates] into a unity . . ." This disparity of signs hinders the immediate solution as to which whole they all belong to.

In veiling the whole, the riddle forces us to rearrange the signs of a given object, thus showing the possibility of diversity, the possibility to combine the previously irreconcilable in new semantic arrangements.

The great realist Sancho Panza said that he would rather be given the answer first and the riddle afterwards.[41]

But Sancho Panza amused himself by constructing his own riddles and then solving them himself.

---

40   G. W. F. Hegel, *Aesthetics: Lectures on Fine Art*. Vol. I. Translated by T. M. Knox. Oxford UP, 1998. All subsequent quotations from *Lectures on Fine Art* are taken from this standard version.
41   Sancho Panza's remark, which Shklovsky is paraphrasing from Hegel, seems to be in character, but cannot be found in *Don Quixote*.

His short term of governorship itself appears to be a program of solving riddles. The riddles and their solutions are folkloric.

The trials of Tom Canty, whom Mark Twain turned from pauper to prince, also represent a collection of folkloric riddles and solutions of a free simpleton. Tom learns the great art of solving riddles in Offal Court, one of the poorest districts of London.

Folkloric riddle solvers—the paupers and the peasants, sometimes turn out to be great decipherers and mystery solvers when they appear on the hill where the great decipherer Solomon's throne was buried.

We are great or insignificant not in and of ourselves, but because sometimes we stand on the foundations of the past.

The task of the solution is to renew meaning through a rearrangement of signs. As we solve the riddle, we reposition the signs and get excited over the fact that before we didn't know the meaning of disunity. The assembled object is something that we recognize. So the riddle is a pretext of the excitement of recognition. But the riddle usually has two answers. The first one is a literal solution, but it is wrong. The second one is the true answer.

The riddle that the Sphinx posed to Oedipus was the following: What goes on four legs in the morning, on two legs at noon, and on three legs in the evening?

The difficulty of putting the proposed clues together and solving the riddle is that there are creatures with two legs (humans and birds) and four legs (mammals and some reptiles) but there are no creatures with three legs—it's a confusing question. This is precisely how a lock is made with winding pins; it is quite impossible to open it with a lock pick.

The answer to the riddle is a man, who crawls on all fours as a baby, walks on two legs as an adult, and walks with a cane in old age.

The answer is slightly deceitful because the cane is equated to a limb.

The riddle often has two answers—both are correct but one is illicit, as it were. Russian ethnographer Dmitri Sadovnikov in his famous collection of riddles wrote that almost all the "lock-and-key" riddles had a double meaning, and that some of them were quite impossible to include in the collection. Since the percentage of such riddles was large, he safely concluded that they were rather widespread.[42]

Many riddles unfold into whole fairy tales. The Belarusian collection by Yevdokim Romanov includes many such fairy tales. We can also find them in Russian *bylinas* (legendary epic tales). A woman, unrecognized by her husband, asks him a question.[43] She is dressed as a foreign consul; she is in a man's suit. She offers to her husband a number of metaphorically erotic riddles. He is unable to solve them. Two meanings are offered simultaneously—they exist side by side—as though competing with one another, one complementing the other.

Occasionally riddles will have only one unique answer. For example, Samson, after slaying the lion notices that a swarm of bees have nested in the carcass of the lion and made honey. He gives some to his parents and then proposes a riddle to the Philistines: "Out of the eater came something to eat. Out of the strong came something sweet" (Judges 14:14).

---

42   *Zagadki russkogo naroda*, a collection of over 2,500 Russian riddles, first published in 1876. *Riddles of the Russian People: A Collection of Riddles, Parables and Puzzles.* Compiled by Dmitri Sadovnikov. Translated by Ann C. Bigelow. Ann Arbor: Ardis, 1986.
43   One of the oldest epic tales *Stavr Godinovich: A Russian Bylina* (circa 1500s).

The eater and the strong is the lion and the something sweet is the honey. The passage uses the classic form of a riddle but it has no solution, or more precisely—it has only one literal solution.

Then there are the so-called detective stories, which are in essence multi-level and complex riddles. We are given various clues that can be connected in numerous ways; the correct combination of clues and traces lead us to the criminal. First, the investigation is led by a police detective who is unsuccessful. Oftentimes the villain gives the police a false lead. Then Dr. Watson tries to solve the crime and gets it all wrong. Finally the riddle is solved, let's say, by Sherlock Holmes.

Many of these detective stories are immaterial, insubstantial, so to speak; they are formulaic crosswords without any true content, that is to say—content that is typically found in the folkloric riddle. They lack in semantic nuance.

Anyone can be a murderer in Agatha Christie: the lines of investigation do not conflict, they are monosemantic, as it were.

But there are other kinds of ingenious riddle solvers. For instance, who killed Fyodor Karamazov—his eldest son Dmitri or someone else? Everyone is confused. It turns out that it was Pavel Smerdyakov but the middle son Ivan was somewhat guilty, too.

There can be yet another type of riddle. It is made known from the very beginning that Raskolnikov murdered the pawnbroker. It is described how he prepares for the murder and how he kills her. The reason why he kills her is unknown. That's explained in his article. Raskolnikov kills not because he is starving, although he *is* a poor, hungry student. He believes that there are certain individuals who have the right to commit crimes and be the judges of their own actions, and he wants to find out whether he is one of those extraordinary, willful individuals. And Raskolnikov's punishment is his inner disappointment. He solves his own riddle, simultaneously resolving the question whether there is a person who is allowed everything. His character is juxtaposed against Svidrigailov who doesn't even doubt that he is allowed everything, but who commits suicide nonetheless, not being able to withstand the uselessness of the answer. One can do anything, but there is no purpose.

Let's return to the folkloric riddle. The signs of an object are disassembled, analyzed, and after a few obstacles reassembled into a whole. But artistic compositions show the fallacy of simple solutions. The doors into the world are unlocked not as they ought to be unlocked. The world is unjust and mankind is too reserved.

Kafka has a short story about a man who is standing in front of the gates and is afraid to enter. He thinks that the entrance is forbidden. The gates finally close and the guard tells him: "These gates were intended only for you."

The man wasn't able to accomplish his main purpose. He is as though the opposite of Raskolnikov.

I would like to move on to a more complex phenomenon. Let me remind you of this book's subject: it is trying to prove that at the basis of every artistic work, every stage in artistic construction, lie similar principles of revealing the contradictions, that the artistic processes of various epochs and nations are universal in this phenomenon and hence comprehensible to us.

Let's turn now to Tolstoy's *Resurrection*.

I was a young man trying to publish my first poorly written stories. I went to a certain press where the old editor—his last name, I think, was Karyshev—told me how Lev Nikolaevich Tolstoy had offended him. Tolstoy published *Resurrection,* the plot of which he had borrowed, or according to Karyshev, had stolen from the unknown writer. He wanted to sue Tolstoy but all the courts refused his case. Those who had read both works—the work of Karyshev and the work of Tolstoy published in *Niva*—told him that they were very similar, but that his was bad and Tolstoy's was good.

I know, and evidently so does the reader, that Lev Nikolaevich Tolstoy took the main plot not from Karyshev but from Anatoli Koni who told him about a young man who, as a juror, was present at a trial and found out that the defendant, a prostitute, was a woman whom he had once seduced. The conflict here is the following: a person is judging another person whom he has ruined, in other words, he is judging the crime that he has committed—a rather ordinary crime.

The ordinary becomes tragic.

Tolstoy's characters have nothing in common with the Japanese. They belong to a different culture. What then amazed them in his book? Certainly not the fact that Katyusha was a prostitute, they have a different view on that subject. They were astonished that Katyusha loved Nekhlyudov yet refused to marry the aristocrat for the very reason that she loved him. The door unlocked for them at a different turn of the key, love turned out to be something else— something beyond possession.

The script for the film *Resurrection* was written by the talented screenwriter Yevgeni Gabrilovich and it was directed by Mikhail Schweitzer. The film in two parts included almost all of the action that took place if not in Tolstoy then in Karyshev. The actress playing the prostitute was a pretty young woman, and it was sad, even deplorable that she had been seduced. The film followed the novel's storyline. But in Tolstoy, Maslova's tragedy and the novel's conflict are not merely suggesting that Nekhlyudov seduced the girl and then gave her money.

After working hard on the Koni story, Tolstoy clarified for himself that Katyusha was the light and the rest were shadows. What helped him to enlighten the misconception of Katyusha and then grasp her character? What helped elucidate the shadows—the darkness of life, its falsehood?

Her fate represented the inhumanity of society in which Tolstoy lived.

I once coined and introduced the term *estrangement*.

In its construction, estrangement is similar to the riddle: it is based on the rearrangement of an object's signs. But in Tolstoy, the main function of estrangement is conscience.

Tolstoy often illuminates objects as if seen for the very first time not by naming them, but by characterizing them. For instance, in one of his descriptions he doesn't name the tree but writes: "a leafy tree with brilliantly white trunk and branches."[44]

He is talking about a birch tree—it can't be anything else—but it is described as if by someone who has never seen this kind of tree and who is surprised by its unusual form.

In February 1857, Tolstoy records in his diary: "Andersen's fairy tale about the new clothes. The task of literature and the word is to make everyone believe what the child is saying."

---

44   Lev Tolstoy, *War and Peace*. Translated by Louise and Aylmer Maude. New York: Simon and Schuster, 1958. All subsequent quotations from *War and Peace* are taken from this standard version.

He is talking about "The Emperor's New Clothes." The world must be shown without its familiar associations: the grandeur of ceremony must not hide the fact that a naked person is at its head.

The next entry is from the beginning of March. His diary entries are closely linked to one another: "One's pride and contempt for others, who has to carry out the vile role of a monarch, is similar to the pride and freedom of a prostitute."

This entry serves as a clue for understanding *Resurrection*. The question is not whether Nekhlyudov seduced the girl and turned her into a prostitute.

The implication here is that the so-called "decent" people surrounding Katyusha in Tolstoy's mind are much like the proud prostitute; this comparison with the prostitute allows us to perceive them differently.

Tolstoy writes about this very directly.

Nekhlyudov arrives at the prison to see Katyusha. He is shocked: "What astonished him most was that Katyusha was not ashamed of her position—not the position of a prisoner (she was ashamed of that), but her position as a prostitute. She seemed satisfied, even proud of it."[45]

Tolstoy develops the situation in great detail.

The prosecutor, superintendents, Nekhlyudov's mother, painted by the famous portraitist in her impressive décolleté, the ladies who flirt with Nekhlyudov, the pederast who sits in the governor gen-

---

45   Lev Tolstoy, *Resurrection*. Translated by Louise Maude. New York: Grosset & Dunlap, 1899. All subsequent quotations from *Resurrection* are taken from this standard version.

eral's office in Siberia, the lawyer, the people to whom Nekhlyudov appeals for help, the head of the prison, and the priest who performs an incomprehensible service, incomprehensible for everyone, including himself, but nonetheless a seemingly proper service, made proper by faithful habit—all of these people are the true Katyusha Maslovas—and she is perhaps the least of a prostitute compared to all of them.

These traits of prostitution are drawn to expose and condemn the world of banality.

The artistic image taken as something that we call "type" (*type* means impression, look up the word *typography* in the dictionary) is the keystone of the arch, marked with a special sign. The archetypal image of this novel is the falsehood of life, its illegitimate righteousness. The habitual is prostituted. The "lawful" becomes criminal in comparison with the ruined life of the prostitute, Katyusha, who was called Lyubov (Love) in the "house of tolerance."

Tolstoy was approaching the device, which I called "estrangement" in 1915, from afar. As early as in *The Cossacks*, Yeroshka dismisses the life of the Russian gentry, calling it "false." Lev Nikolaevich spent many years after that writing "Strider," in which human life is described from the perspective of a horse. And things such as property, love, man's right to hurt another man—all of it was strange and absurd. As a result, human life turned out to be a meaningless graveyard where people methodically buried decomposing corpses in splendid boxes.

A prostitute is the most abject creature in the world. She is the main hero of the book, the novel's love story is based on her. She destroys everything that surrounds her.

Katyusha Maslova is attractive. But in his initial sketches Tolstoy wanted to portray the prostitute with a deformed nose.[46] But he didn't. It was impossible. Besides, the details of her image, like the azure blue tint of the whites and the slight squint in her eyes, dark as black currants—had been decided from the very beginning. These features were necessary to recognize what is beautiful, poignant, and precise.

The image that a literary work is based on has multiple meanings and is contradictory like the image of Achilles who weeps for his friend: he plays the lyre, mutilates the dead body of his enemy, but then welcomes his enemy's father, offers him dinner, and mourns with him—this type of a stereoscopic, round character is more suitable for an epic than a one-dimensional character.

I am talking within the limits of a single, though broad, convention here.

For Nicolas Boileau-Despréaux, Achilles's tears after his first loss are only an excusable exception. Boileau-Despréaux never mentions any of the other contradictions.

Contradictions arise in Russian epics too, but not in fairy tales.

The heroes of Tolstoy, Dostoevsky, Gorky, and the foundations of their compositions are also based on contradiction. However, it is seldom in Gogol—he accentuates contradiction through the narrative voice.

Human beings are contradictory.

But Akaki Akakievich becomes human only in his delirium, after he turns into a ghost.

---

46   Alluding to the physical deformities caused by syphilis.

On the Relationship between the Laws of Image Construction
and the Laws of Plot Construction

I

I don't think that I have discovered anything new in the theory of poetic language.

Whatever was done in the field, it was formulated by Lev Jakubinsky and Yuri Tynjanov.

I noted in the beginning of this book that not every transfer of meaning is a trope, and it occurs not because "the image gets overused." I attempted to show how certain word formations that seem to work as imagery—metaphors—in reality emerge merely out of practical need and are never part of the poetic phenomena.

On the other hand, it can be observed that non-poetic applications can easily become poetic. The relationship of poetic language generally depends on the speaker's stylistic arrangement; this arrangement, of course, must be expressed in a form perceptible to the audience.

The most common technical phrase can become poetic if it is employed in an innovative way. For example, they used to write on the old railroad boxcars: "40 men or 8 horses." They were simple boxcars with two axels and could carry either eight horses, or forty people if you put two rows of planks around the sides of the cars.

Mayakovsky wrote in his poem "War and the World" (1916): "In the rotting boxcar four legs for forty men." The term "man" here implies a whole person, not disjointed but a two-legged man. A man without legs is a man in a different capacity, whereas a legless man is also a definition—not a poetic trope. But the boxcar carrying "four legs for forty men" introduces a conflict of concepts: man as a countable object and man as a certain whole.

Inserted in a description of war, the expression becomes poetic.

II

Metonymy is the selection of a part for the representation of a whole. In the usual sense, metonymy is a technical device: when we say "two hundred heads of cattle," obviously these animals cannot be without their heads. But this is not merely a technical simplification but also an awareness of the near equal worth of separate animals in a certain herd.

Metonymy has a different function in art. It's a convention that we have gotten so accustomed to that we use it without even noticing. One rare, albeit dislocated feature not only replaces the whole but also changes the quality of perception of the whole and renews the ways of drawing the whole into the focus of attention.

Stanza XV in Chapter Seven in *Eugene Onegin* begins like this:

> 'Twas evening. The sky darkened. Waters
> streamed quietly. The beetle churred.

The couplet is made of three phrases with two words per phrase; the fourth one with three words is enjambed. The abrupt full stops produce a sense of disjointedness.

The lines that follow slow down:

The choral throngs already were dispersing.
Across the river, smoking, glowed already
the fire of fishermen.

Tatyana walks pensively, immersed in dreams and as if unintentionally notices the surrounding details. She is absent-mindedly attentive. The fire is seen as glimmers of twilight in the mist.

In his response to a critical review, Pushkin wrote:

> I skimmed through the review of the seventh song in *Severnaya pchela* (The Northern Bee) at someone else's house and at such a moment when I had no time for Onegin whatsoever . . . I only saw very well written verses and a rather funny joke about a beetle:
>
> 'Twas evening. The sky darkened. Waters
> streamed quietly. The beetle churred.
>
> The critic was excited over the appearance of this new character and was expecting him to have a personality more vivid than the rest.

The critic deliberately breaks up the structure of the stanza and relocates the beetle into the list of characters.

In the meantime the beetle signifies silence, absent-mindedness, it replaces many things but it can't be a theme or a character on its own.

The choice of a beetle is intentional—it represents the sound of summer.

A literary work has its autonomous system in which the evaluation of parts is perceptible only within that structure.

There are simple metonymic constructions in art. In his essay "On Malo-Russian Folksongs," Gogol reviewed Cossack and women's songs:

> Their songs almost never become descriptive and aren't devoted to intricate depictions of nature. Nature in them merely slides through the couplet; nonetheless its features are so new, refined, and sharp that they represent the whole subject . . .
>
> Often instead of the whole external subject there is only one sharp feature, one part of the whole. You will never come across a phrase such as . . . " 'Twas evening," but what actually happens in the evening:
>
>> The cows came home from the woods, the sheep— from the pastures,
>> I cried my hazel eyes out, standing by my beloved's house.
>
> And because of that many critics, without understanding, thought such phraseologies to be nonsensical.

Gogol underscores the inconsistency of these songs, and how "usually objects that first grab the eye are the first ones to be included in the songs." But then he continues: " . . . some couplets that are knocked out from this variegated pile are simply stunning in their charming unaccountability of poetry."

The phrase "knocked out" appears to be a replacement for the verb "taken"; it creates a sense of the movement that dislodges one feature from the whole, as it were. The isolated ordinary or familiar feature becomes a "knockout"—something striking.

I am trying to compare the phenomena of different epochs and different genres in this little book by highlighting the features that connect them.

The artist does not and cannot transmit a phenomenon in its entirety. The common time with four beats already conveys a certain intermittence: "one—two—three—four." This intermittence is real and it allows us to show a single property common to a set of objects that we behold, and which is beyond their recognizable quality. Art always divides objects and offers a part instead of the whole, a feature of the whole, and no matter how detailed it is, it still is a dashed line representing a line. Art always separates the similar and unites the different. It is *stepped* (gradational) and can be montaged. But art is not a train connecting cars full of phrases. Connections highlight the ruptures. We isolate separate features in order to transmit the whole. If we develop a certain segment in great detail, then that segment replaces the whole, transmitting not so much its condition but the meaning of its condition. We divide narratives into separate chapters or paragraphs; we emphasize the distinction of separate lines through rhythm and rhyme. At the same time, we "repeat" and reinforce the previous word with the help of rhyme, as it were, forcing the reader to reread the preceding line.

Verse is characterized with a measure that returns. The return is the principle of versification; the construction recurs rhythmically. Human perception of the world as a whole is a recurring perception that compares and repeats the movement, and selects the familiar out of the unfamiliar. Whereas the first step is an initial evaluation, followed by a process of clarification: fitting the word into our knowledge, as it were.

Speaking of innovation in my old work, we should note how the concept of the evental was separated from the concept of plot. Plot is not the incident taking place in a short story or a novel. It is a construction which, through manipulation of events, characters, landscapes, and compression, magnification, or rearrangement of time, creates a certain sensibility, graspable and felt in the way that was intended by the work's author.[47]

The author creates a new model of the world. A model that is uniquely simplified because it is only but a part of the world, a part in which the interrelations of phenomena are seen and seemingly concluded.

The phenomena that are selected in a literary work are taken in certain developmental stages, like a change from happiness to unhappiness, a state of harmony to a state of chaos, or a feeling of solitude to a feeling of companionship. All of this might evolve differently in different works.

In Chekhov's "Misery," for example, a coachman is feeling lonely because of his son's death. Loneliness is shown against the backdrop of a city at nighttime. The coachman longs to share his melancholy

---

47   In *Theory of Prose*, Shklovsky compares a literary work to a battlefield. He writes: "The masks and types of modern drama correspond to the figures of chess. The plots correspond to the moves and strategies, that is, to the techniques of the game, as these are used and interpreted by the players. The tasks and the reversals correspond to the moves made by the opponent." Finally, Shklovsky compares the methods and devices of plot construction with the devices of orchestration, the arrangement or composition of music: "Works of literature represent a *web of sounds, movements and ideas.*"

with someone. But he is lonesome—he is nothing but a coachman to the passengers who sit behind him in the coach. In the end, the old man tells his grief to his mare: this is the kind of extreme loneliness that one feels in an inhuman society.

III

We often think that comparison brings more clarity, distinctness to an impression. But that's not true. Comparison in itself is always already incomplete.

In Tolstoy's favorite fairy tale, people try to explain what light is to the blind. They are told that light is like milk. They respond: does that mean it flows like milk? They are told that light is like snow. They respond: does that mean it is cold like snow? They are told that light is like paper. They respond: does that mean it rustles like paper?

Comparable things always coincide only partially. Moreover, in literary comparison and in metaphors the comparable things are dissimilar, meaning—their comparison appears to be utterly unexpected.

Let me give an example from Shakespeare. When Juliet is waiting for Romeo, she compares him with the sky and the stars:

> Come, night!—Come, Romeo! come thou day in night!
> For thou wilt lie upon the wings of night
> Whiter than new snow on a raven's back.—
> Come, gentle night; come, loving, black-brow'd night,
> Give me my Romeo: and when he shall die
> Take him and cut him out in little stars,

And he will make the face of heaven so fine,
That all the world will be in love with night,
And pay no worship to the garish sun. (Act III, Scene 2)

The comparison draws the world closer and the world as a whole
becomes unrecognizable. As a result of emotional immediacy, this
dissimilarity pushes, as it were, the comparable objects apart.

In the scene where Nozdrev, along with his servants, wants to
beat up Chichikov for cheating at a game of checkers, Gogol compares the conflict to an assault on a fortress. The attacking platoon is
rather small, while the fortress is enormous and indestructible:

> "Beat him up!" He kept yelling in much the same voice
> which some desperate lieutenant, whose harebrained brav-
> ery has already gained such a reputation that a specific or-
> der has been issued to hold him back by his arms during
> the heat of battle, uses to yell "Forward, lads!" to his pla-
> toon during a great assault. But the lieutenant has already
> felt the martial fervor, everything has begun going round
> and round in his head: Suvorov, that great general, soars
> in a vision before him; the lieutenant strains forward to per-
> form a great deed. "Forward, lads!" he yells, dashing ahead,
> without reflecting that he is jeopardizing the plan of attack
> already decided upon, that countless gun muzzles are
> thrust out of the embrasures of the fortress, the impreg-
> nable walls of which reach up beyond the clouds, that
> his impotent platoon will be blown up into the air like so
> much swan's-down, and that the fated bullet is already
> whizzing through the air, just about to shut off his vocifer-

ous throat. But if Nozdrev was portraying in his person the lieutenant attacking the fortress, desperate and at a loss, the fortress he was storming did not in any way resemble an impregnable one. On the contrary, the fortress was experiencing such fright that its heart was in its very heels.[48]

The similarity here is in the way Nozdrev explodes; he wants to do something he can't do no matter how much he wants to. Nozdrev cannot abuse his guest, though there have been similar incidents in the past. It is at this precise moment when the Captain of the District Police arrives with a commission to place Nozdrev under arrest for flogging someone with birch rods.

What is being insinuated here is the crime of violence against another person, a crime punishable under criminal law. And yet there is no similarity here. Instead, we have a conflict of renditions of tempers with an indication on their dissimilarity.

Let's look at similarities and contrasts, and particularly—the dissimilarity of the similar in *The Iliad*.

Ajax is a hero among the Achaeans, second only to Achilles in strength and courage. He lunges into the lines of the Trojans but Zeus engenders him with fear and Ajax is forced to retreat "pivoting, backpedaling, step by short step." The Trojans chase him away like angry hounds and brave settlers would drive out a lion. But then the tone of comparison changes, Ajax slowly draws back from the Trojans:

---

48   Nikolai Gogol, *Dead Souls*. Translated by Bernard Guilbert Guerney. New York: Random House, 1965. All subsequent quotations from *Dead Souls* are taken from this standard version.

> Like a stubborn ass some boys lead down a road . . .
> stick after stick they've cracked across his back
> but he's too much for them now, he rambles into a field
> to ravage standing crops. They keep beating his ribs,
> splintering sticks—their struggle child's play
> till with one final shove they drive him off
> but not before he's had his fill of feed. (Book 11, 656–662)

Ajax is a stubborn, proud warrior, yet the comparison with an ass that rambles into a field, of course, is incomplete and hardly ironic. The passage selects only the elements of inequality in strength and unwillingness to retreat.

Here is another example from Book 12 that is even more vivid. Nothing is quieter than falling snow. The Trojans want to burn the Achaeans' ships. The ships are on the shore, behind a wall made of logs and stones. Men are battling, hurling spears and arrows at each other. It is a hot battle. It's loud. The men are yelling like wild boars. And this is compared to a calm snowfall:

> Thick-and-fast as the snows that fall on a winter dawn
> when Zeus who rules the world brings on a blizzard,
> displaying to all mankind his weaponry of war . . .
> and he puts the winds to sleep, drifting on and on
> until he has shrouded over the mountains' looming peaks
> and the headlands jutting sharp, the lowlands deep in grass
> and the rich plowed work of farming men, and the drifts fall
> on the gray salt surf and the harbors and down along the
>   beaches

and only breakers beating against the drifts can hold them off
but all else on the earth they cover over, snows from the sky
when Zeus comes storming down—now so thick and fast
they volleyed rocks from both sides, some at the Trojans,
some from Trojans against the Argives, salvos landing,
the whole long rampart thundering under blows. (Book
12, 323–336)

The comparison is made between dissimilar things or, at least, things that are only partially similar.

Let's take one more example from *The Iliad*. The Achaeans are warring against the Trojans, it has been a long, desperate war. Some Olympian gods protect those under the siege, others side with those who are assaulting. The gods intervene in the war. They get hurt, they roar. The success reverts from one side to the other. What does the singer compare this oscillation in battle that appears to be a world war for Homer?

Everywhere—rocks, ramparts, breastworks swam
with the blood of Trojans, Argives, both sides,
but still the Trojans could not rout the Argives.
They held tight as a working widow holds the scales,
painstakingly grips the beam and lifts the weight
and the wool together, balancing both sides even,
struggling to win a grim subsistence for her children.
So powerful armies drew their battle line dead even . . .
(Book 12, 499–506)

At first we are told that the rocky bastion, ramparts, and breast-works are all drenched in human blood. But the Trojans are unable to rout the Argives; they hold tight as—and here is the comparison—a working widow holds the scales, painstakingly gripping the beam and lifting the weight and the wool together, balancing both sides even. In the midst of the roar of battle we are reminded of someone from a completely different world, someone who will never again appear in *The Iliad*, but will surface briefly in *The Odyssey*. Common people during the siege of Troy are only implied. In this passage they are represented through the working woman who is struggling to win a grim subsistence for her children, watching the scales, fearful of the movement of the beam, tired and anxious whether she has enough wool to balance the weight so that she can go home. This is what the thunderous battle scene is compared to, as if opening a door into a different world.

Exits into the "other" world are not so frequent in art.

These doors keep opening wider and wider. They are the doors of realism, the doors for expanding the realm of art.

And at the same time, the comparison in its confounding silence and calm strain gives a pause in the description of the battle, underscoring not the bitterness but the engagement of the warriors, their engrossment with the battle.

Later novels will portray the lives of aristocrats next to the lives of the poor, and the comparison of fates will connect the various levels of those novels. Take *War and Peace*, for example. A character will move from one state of mind to another.

Often a person is compared to grass. A battle is compared to a feast. In *The Song of Igor's Campaign*, for example: "Here was a want of blood-wine," the notion of blood is subordinated to wine—it becomes an adjective.[49]

Tolstoy in "Three Deaths" describes the death of a talkative lady who is frightened and talks too much, the calm death of a sick peasant, and the death of a tree that is cut down to be made into a cross for the peasant's grave.

Fighting against Shamil's army and Nicholas's empire, alone and mortally wounded, Hadji Murad is compared to a thistle, crushed by a cartwheel that rises up and even blooms. This is how Hadji Murad, wounded, but already not feeling his wounds, rises from among the dead bodies of warriors with a dagger in his hand.

He rises up, and his faith in the necessity of resistance embodies the power of nature's law.

This shifts the novella into a different realm.

Hadji Murad takes the wrong path, but for him *ghazawat* is a holy war for the liberation of peasant lands.

It is freedom from Shamil and Nicholas I.

Freedom is the law of human nature.

A man might be mortally wounded but he rises nonetheless for a new struggle. He rises up, or his son will rise up, or his neighbors, or even the neighbors of his nation.

---

49   *The Song of Igor's Campaign: An Epic of the Twelfth Century*. Translated by Vladimir Nabokov. New York: Vintage Books, 1960. All subsequent quotations from *The Song of Igor's Campaign* are taken from this standard version.

ON CONVENTIONS

On the Semantic Detail that Creates a Perception of Depth

Conventionality makes our perception dull when experiencing a literary work or painting relating to our epoch because we have become accustomed to it. We look at a painting that is rendered in linear perspective and not only interpret but also *see* the arrangement of parts in relation to one another, we *know* which object is behind what. This process is similar to how we speak in our native language—we are not conscious of the vocabulary or syntax that we use: this phenomenon is based on the fact that we "know" the language.

The decorative arts, like vase painting, for example, were highly evolved in ancient Greece. If we examine the drawings carefully, we will see that none of the figures overlap, they are in a somewhat easily perceptible space, but not in linear perspective to which we are accustomed in modern painting. This foreign convention is not so apparent to us because it is not applied onto a flat surface and is created for decorative purposes.

The Greeks knew, and so do we, that objects appear to get smaller in distance. This is not just the peculiarity of our vision but also a habit of perception that we take into account and apply in drawing.

But in order to introduce this perspective into our art, there has to be a certain convention, because we know that, while we see objects in diminished form, they don't really diminish in essence.

Modern man knows that the moon is a celestial body. But when he looks at the moon, it appears to be the size of a plate, in fact, the size changes according to the moon's location from the horizon. He unconsciously introduces the convention of common sense in the perception of cosmic space.

In ancient Greek novels (usually, at the beginning), the author depicted a landscape—often as a description of a painting.

But novels are more closely associated to our modern era, and it is quite impossible to grasp the laws of perspectival diminution from a description of paintings.

And yet philosophers argued about the problems of perspective. It was a contested subject. Let me quote from Plato's *Sophist*:

> [F]or if artists were to give the true proportions of their fair models, the upper part, which is farther off, would appear to be out of proportion in comparison with the lower, which is nearer; and so they give up the truth in their images and make only the proportions which appear to be beautiful, disregarding the real ones.[50]

The dialogue is about perspectival diminution and proportions of an edifice. The architect designed the building with particular

---

50   Plato, *Sophist*. In *The Dialogues of Plato*. Vol. III. Translated by Benjamin Jowett. Oxford UP, 1964.

proportions, particular relations of height and width in mind. The painter that Plato is referring to in his dialogue has diminished the proportions of the building to show depth. The philosopher argues because he considers the creation of the architect-artist to be truthful and authentic, while that of the painter-artist as replicated and false. The artistic reproduction of architecture elicits objection. Here the viewer hasn't yet accepted the convention of linear perspective.

Plato highly valued symmetry. In order to refute perspectival diminution, he chose paintings of architectural objects that had fixed proportions. The argument apparently went even further. The philosopher suggested depicting not what one saw but what one knew.

The old convention appeared to be effective and it took centuries for a replacement to evolve.

The Italian architect, sculptor and architectural theorist Antonio Averlino Filarete wrote:

> The ancients, even if they were cultivated and knowledgeable people, didn't know and never made use of this principle of perspective. And though they knew many good techniques in art, they depicted objects on flat surface without using this principle. One might say: "This method is flawed, for it shows something that does not exist." This is true, but at the same time this convention is useful in painting because the objects in the painting are not as they are in reality but as a representation of the things that you paint and wish to represent.

What we are observing here is the substantiation of a new convention in the old polemic. Objects in our consciousness exist independently and are associated with one another according to their differences. In painting, they appear in an altered relationship. The argument was about how to depict the parts of a distanced object.

The new convention is introduced into consciousness gradually, paragraph by paragraph, as it were. Finally, Leonardo da Vinci ends the debate. He states in his treatise on painting: "Perspectival diminution teaches that objects will be less discerned the more they are removed from the eye." He goes on to say that, "If you look at a man who is placed at the distance of a crossbow shot, and you hold the eye of a little needle close to your eye, you will be able to see through it many men, transmitting their images to the eye, and they can all be perceived at the same time in this opening. Therefore, if the man at the distance of a crossbow shot sends to the eye his image and it occupies a small part of the eye of a needle, how can you in such a small figure distinguish or see his nose or mouth or any detail of his body?"[51]

The debate seems to have ended.

But so-called "realistic" sizing and juxtaposition of objects according to their thematic importance still can be seen in children's drawings.

Seryozha, the seven-year-old boy in Chekhov's short story "At Home," draws a house, the roof of which has the same height as the soldier in the drawing. The boy's father says, "A man can't be taller

---

51   Leonardo da Vinci, *Leonardo on Painting*. Translated by Martin Kemp and Margaret Walker. New Haven: Yale UP, 2001. All subsequent quotations from *Leonardo on Painting* are taken from this standard version.

than a house." "No, papa!" Seryozha says, looking at his drawing. "If you were to draw the soldier small you would not see his eyes."

"Ought he to argue with him? From daily observation of his son the prosecutor had become convinced that children, like savages, have their own artistic standpoints and requirements peculiar to them, beyond the grasp of grown-up people."[52]

Children have their own hierarchies which can be seen through symbolization of objects in their drawings. This doesn't change and is true even today when they are exposed to photography, film, and television.

Children draw objects based on the convention of semantic hierarchy.

Professor Aleksandr Luria of the Psychological Institute in Moscow showed Eisenstein a child's drawing depicting a wood stove. Eisenstein writes:

> Everything is represented in passably accurate relationship and with great care. Firewood. Stove. Chimney. But what are those zigzags in that huge central rectangle? They turn out to be matches. Taking into account the crucial importance of these matches for the depicted process, the child provides a proper scale for them.[53]

---

52   Anton Chekhov, *Early Short Stories, 1883-1888*. Translated by Constance Garnett. New York: Random House, 1999.

53   Sergei Eisenstein, *Film Form: Essays in Film Theory*. Translated by Jay Leyda. London: Dennis Dobson, 1963. Quoted from the essay "The Cinematographic Principle and the Ideogram," which was originally published as an Afterword to *Yaponskoye kino* by N. Kaufman (Moscow, 1929).

The debate hasn't been resolved in literature either. Objects (their details) are magnified, isolated according to their semantic weight and according to their meaning in a given situation.

The "semantic center" is enlarged.

Gogol in *Taras Bulba* describes the Cossacks' passage through the boundless, desolate, beautiful steppe: "But once Taras pointed out to his sons a small black speck far away in the grass, saying, 'Look, boys! There gallops a Tatar!' The tiny mustached head fixed its narrow eyes straight upon them, from the distance, sniffing the air like a greyhound, then disappeared, like a stag, on perceiving that there were thirteen of them."[54]

The Tatar is Taras Bulba's rival. Noticing the rider's posture on the horse, the Cossack already sees the difference between them.

He paints on the invisible "mustache" and "narrow eyes" once he recognizes the rider.

Literature selects axial centers on its own by invoking their metonymic descriptions, or, in other words, by referencing objects or clues connected contiguously.

But in architecture, especially Baroque architecture, the space is interpreted not so much through visual perception as through recognition.

It is quite impossible to grasp the expansiveness of St. Peter's Basilica—it seems to have no scale. In the open space of the Basilica, far apart from one another stand the colossal statues of angels that one cannot see simultaneously at once.

---

54 Nikolai Gogol, *Taras Bulba*. Translated by Isabel F. Hapgood. New York: Alfred A. Knopf, 1931. Revised by Shushan Avagyan. All subsequent quotations from *Taras Bulba* are taken from this standard version.

This is how a good tour guide showed the Basilica—he told the tourist: "Close your eyes. Now open them and look over there."

The tourist saw the angel's small figure in the distance.

"Now turn around"—and the viewer was suddenly facing the colossus that completely barred his vision. Perspectival depth was perceived through the sculpture.

Apparently those who designed the Basilica had foreseen this impression. Baroque decor enhances the perception of the structure's actual depth. But there are instances when an element becomes the vessel that defines spatial dimension.

In late Baroque art, the relationship between architecture and perspective painting becomes illusory.

Chapels are decorated with plafonds composed of foreshortened mythological figures and side views of buildings. The painted figures sit on real cornices, and plafonds with artificial sceneries appear next to real windows. The viewer perceives two kinds of conventions and evaluates them on his own.

According to the Brockhaus and Efron Encyclopedia:

> It would have been strange to draw an oval shape on a flat surface in order to depict a sphere, since the drawing must work from any viewpoint and especially if it has large proportions. When depicting a sphere as a circle in painting, the artist departs from geometric perspective. In similar fashion, when depicting a colonnade parallel to the flat surface of the painting, the artist does not paint the columns on the outer periphery wider than the central columns, or when depicting a group of people—the periph-

eral figures are not larger than the central figures. If the group of people is depicted inside a building, the parallel lines (that are not parallel to the flat surface of the painting) converge at the vanishing point and, according to the convention of geometric perspective, the figures arranged along those convergence lines diminish as they get farther from the viewer. But the central and peripheral figures do not change in their appearance according to this convention, as they converge with the orthogonal projection of the flat surface.

The author of this entry, Fyodor Petrushevsky, was a Russian mathematician and physicist who wrote *Light and Color* (1883) and *Paints and Painting* (1891). He was friends with the Russian chemist Dmitri Mendeleev and the painter Ilya Repin.

The excerpt that I just quoted is common knowledge; it explains conventions that were so widely accepted that they were only mentioned in encyclopedias.

And so, academic painting imposed its own conventional rules on the difference of foreshortenings in the composition of a single painting.

We don't always inertly "see" the painting, but we also examine it, constructing as if the object with the movement of our examining eye. This is analogous to how a person examines a building when entering it.

In his drafts for *Montage* (1937), Eisenstein analyzed Valentin Serov's portrait of the actress Maria Yermolova. It was reprinted in a collection of his works and I am inserting here Eisenstein's "shot-by-shot" breakdown of the portrait. The actress is wearing a long dark-colored dress with its train spread on the parquet floor. The figure is juxtaposed against the background of the floor, the wall with gray panels and a mirror. The mirror reflects the opposite wall and ceiling of the empty room. The ceiling cornices meet right above her shoulders. The head is depicted against the background of the ceiling.

The painting gives an impression of total reality and its convention is experienced as something very simple. But, in fact, we are seeing the figure from a low angle view, we can see below her chin and face, nostrils and arched brows. Simultaneously, we are seeing her from above since we see the train of her dress on the floor. It appears that there are four angles in the diagram.

In his analysis, Eisenstein breaks down the portrait into individual shots: we are seeing the woman from above, based on the position of the train of her dress, and we are also seeing her from mid-torso level, and simultaneously from below, as we see the bottom of her chin and her head against the ceiling as a background.

It is a convention that we accept, submitting to the logic and will of the artist who has composed the painting—Serov, who has created a landmark for our path of examination.

The simplicity of the painting is intentional.

Perspective in Icons

It is also called *reverse perspective*, but its inventors didn't know about linear perspective at the time.

The old debate about perspective was either forgotten or it had not reached them.

Let's begin with perspective in icons as an introduction. We are entering the discussion from midpoint.

Old Russian literature, architecture, iconography, and folklore contain meticulously reproduced situations, speeches, and repetitions that are more noticeable to us than the repetitions of situations in contemporary art.

The integral feature of creative work in the antiquity lies in the constancy of situations and their verbal expression.

Once a certain "literary etiquette" has been formed, everyone is expected to follow the code: everything is described in such a way as it would have fit the actions of ideal characters. The behavior of villains also repeats particular situations that are usually nondistinctive. Perfectly expressed and even psychologized distinctiveness is revealed in its developed stages in the description of incredible villainy. We might even find some convincing details here.

Etiquette, or the established method of portraying characters and their dispositions, is perhaps observed even more strictly in iconography. As Dmitri Likhachov writes in *Poetics of Old Russian Literature*:

> The artist of the Middle Ages strove to depict all the properties of an object. He depicted the human figure in full frontal posture so that one could clearly see the symmetrical parts of the body: two hands, both sides of the face. . . . The artist did not seek an illusionistic portrayal of the human figure in unexpected turns, sudden postures, or ac-

cidental frames in the early stages of old Russian art. The appearance of profile depictions (including those of Satan, Judah in *The Last Supper*, and secondary figures) in the fourteenth century was a huge step toward a more accurate depiction of reality, a representation that transmitted movement.

The task of the medieval artist was to show an object with all its significant details. The top of the table was usually depicted from above so that every object on it would be visible. He also showed the legs of the table, if possible. The painter had to cut the number and size of individual objects in order to depict them in their entirety. So, for example, a building in the icon could appear smaller than a human figure. The foliage of a tree was depicted not as a whole crown but each leaf was painted separately and the number of leaves was sometimes reduced to only two or three.[55]

This implies that art is moving from conventional to more precise representation—it is perfected, as it were.

Yet we see in the same book that medieval art was not inferior to the art of the Renaissance, but that it was different and posed a different set of questions. The icons in a cathedral were arranged in a certain order and the viewer stood before them, as though, conversing with them and listening to their decrees.

---

55   A footnote by V. Shklovsky: Likhachov reiterates numerous times the interconnection between literature and painting in his *Poetics* (1967), stressing that the central object or figure in old Russian painting was depicted in its totality.

If the icon depicted an apostle writing something in a book, the pages were turned to the viewer, as if the figure wasn't really writing but pointing to the written message.

Any artistic representation as, perhaps, any fictional construction requires a skill to perceive the construction, an understanding of conventions between the audience and the author of the work. While studying Russian iconography, we must keep in mind that the viewer's perspective is from the position of those who are praying in the cathedral. The figures on the icons are not facing one another but directing their gaze toward the supplicant. It is as if they interact with one another through the praying person.

Painting in this period was part of architecture. It didn't have its own place except for its designated place in the interior of the cathedral. And that was deeply ingrained in human consciousness. When constructing Paradise in *The Divine Comedy*, Dante described a circle of spirits and a bowl in which water moved from center to rim and from rim to center, moving outward or inward according to how the bowl is struck, and he talked about cylinders—drums, the walls of which depicted saints (*Paradiso* XIV). Those were frescoes decorating the arches and drums of church domes.

The space of the world is made to fit in the space of the cathedral. It is not a realistic conception, but a defined one.

The main characters, the main objects of the imagery—Christ, the Virgin, and the saints—are placed on the iconostasis closer to the viewer, the cathedral is much farther, it is smaller than the figures due to its lesser significance. The edifice is often replaced with towers symbolizing a city, and the trees have a few, but elaborately painted leaves.

Whatever supposedly happens in the interior of the cathedral is shown outside of it.

Likhachov refutes the term "reverse perspective," saying that "The term isn't precise because there was no preexisting 'correct' or 'obverse' perspective before the medieval era."

This isn't necessarily true: the iconographer was conscious of obverse (or viewer) perspective and even emphasized it for the viewer. In the *Annunciation* by Andrei Rublyov and Daniil Chorny, the Virgin's face is turned toward us, the viewer, even though in reality the figures are facing one another: Mary is listening to the angel's revelation. We know that they are facing one another because of the position of her chair and parts of the building. The lower part of the building is depicted frontally but the upper part is turned diagonally so that the angel appears to be facing it. Details that are semantically less significant are rendered in linear perspective. Details that are admittedly significant appear in conventional (reverse) perspective and frontally, in façade. As a result the building in the icon seems to be swerving. This has been analyzed in Lev Zhegin's article "The Spatiotemporal Unity in Painting."

The verbal message wrapped in miniature drawings around the edges of the icon, showing separate moments from the holy day or from the saint's life, and at the center of the icon Salome dancing in front of Herod, the decapitation of John the Baptist, and the presentation of the head on the tray to Herodias—all of these are painted from various perspectives because they are unified by one and the same narrative.

Soon, as we shall see, a controversial argument will develop around this convention.

In his treatise on painting, Leonardo da Vinci considered the medieval conventions to be flawed:

> It is a very great vice found in many painters that they make the houses of men and other surrounding buildings in such a way that the gates of the city do not come up to the knees of the inhabitants even though they are closer to the eye of the observer than the man who indicates that he wishes to enter therein. We have seen porticos laden down with men, and the supporting column like a thin cane in the fist of the man who leans on it. Other similar things are to be disdained.

It would have been more accurate to say: "we ought to disdain."

The argument or, rather, the negotiations had already been going on for thousands of years.

When establishing the laws of linear perspective, da Vinci made no provision for cases where those laws were transgressed; vertical and horizontal foreshortenings were accomplished using different laws. The corners of the painting were rendered as though from different viewing angles than its central part.

Leonardo da Vinci removed the old methods of the portrayal of three-dimensional objects on a flat surface, as it were, and changed the conventions of Byzantine iconography.

Indeed, in old Russo-Byzantine iconography "the houses of men and other surrounding buildings" were often painted smaller than the human figures, so that the gates of the city indeed reached only up to their knees, but that was based on a specific semantic code.

Man and his actions were not supposed to be concealed by the wall. The main goal was to convey the human being. The flat surface was sometimes equated with the wall and it was treated differently—with conventional gold, for example, or in later icons it was covered with a *riza*, a decorated metal "robe." It was excluded from the "real" space.

Often there were several temporal and spatial realms simultaneously combined in a single icon. Various times were rendered to show the different moments of action during a specific event. On one panel you could see both the moment of beheading John the Baptist and presentation of his head on the tray that was not foreshortened but rendered as a metallic disc, as a halo around the head of the saint, seen from above.

Now, somewhat enlightened, let us turn again to the argument about apparency. Many people perceive academic perspective not as a conventional system but as a realization (and what's more—a full materialization) of geometrical perspective. This is a fallacy.

On Cinematic Conventions of Depth Perception

It was, in fact, another conventional system, just as the one we have in film today. Different camera lenses have different focal lengths, meaning different spatial distances. If we shoot the same object using different lenses, it will be arranged differently in space and in its distance from us each time. But lenses are interchanged so frequently that they are often combined in a compound lens, the turning of which immediately changes focus or, in other words, perspective.

Some thirty years ago, in order to change the shot, the angle, or to show a close-up, one had to show the change of perspective by reverting to the person who was looking. But already in Vsevolod Pudovkin's *Mother*, the camera angles depended on the importance of the image and there was no need to explain further why the system of perspectives had changed.

We go to the movie theater and perceive easily everything that we see there. We perceive things without interpretation, without the need of commentary. Meanwhile, individual frames—the montage pieces—are shot with different lenses: each lens has a different focal length; they depict the same objects at various distances though in reality the objects are in an unchanged spatial relationship with the viewer.

All of these *multidistanced* objects are rendered almost concurrently.

One frame follows another in a semantic or pictorial sequence. We assume that the frames in a single montage-phrase exist concurrently. There is no time to examine each frame, and instead we are left with a curiosity, a desire to examine. We accept the idea that the objects are in seemingly different distances in relation to us, because the semantically significant objects are closer, as though yielding to our attention. The viewer constructs the spatial realm based on the visual guidance of the film director.

But there is another convention beside this convention of bringing the symbolically significant closer to the viewer, while distancing the less significant. We usually use both eyes when looking at something, and we are able to interpret distance by switching between our visual axes. The camera uses only one eye. But we have conventionally agreed in cinematography to "see" depth. This depth is made perceptible either through changes in lighting, zooming in and out of variously lit areas, in other words, enlarging what in landscape painting was called aerial perspective, or by showing movement in the shot. Moving objects in the far background, along the mountain road, for instance, help us perceive depth on a flat screen.

We have already discussed St. Peter's Basilica through Gogol's method of portrayal—let's keep in mind the Baroque conventions of perspectival diminution. We should not react any differently when analyzing the conventions of cinematic space, even though we perceive it to be a real space.

One way to create a sense of depth in film is through an exaggeration of the size of detail appearing in the foreground and a reduction of objects in the background.

The famous set designer Vladimir Yegorov, who founded a new tradition in Russian film, used this method to create an illusion of depth. He would show an enlarged close-up of a detail—an eagle's foot, for example—and the frame was composed so that you could see only the foot and nothing else.

Or he would show the edge of a large flag. The eagle was positioned in the background. This allowed for recognition of the detail in the foreground and (illusory) perception of depth. Depth is usually created through an arrangement of recognizable details in the limited space of the shot, by forming a transparent, three-dimensional grid, as it were—doorways, stairs, gaps between buildings, bridges.

Another standard technique is to shoot a maquette of a building using a close-up. The viewer himself creates depth by construing the meaning of the maquette and arranging it in the allocated empty space. In *Minin and Pozharsky*, Pudovkin and Utkin used a maquette of St. Basil's Cathedral that was as tall as an average person and created depth by adding other conventional set decorations.

We perceive spatial depth in movies not because we are deceived but because we know how to read cinematic perspective.

The principle of cinematic space is no less conventional than the principle of reverse perspective. If traditional Chinese painters created the illusion of depth in the mountains by using the imagery of a flowing river and its winding paths, then today depth is created through the movement of caravans or cars, since the shot is not only a flat surface—but a flat surface seen through only one eye.

Conveying depth in sound film turned out to be somewhat different compared to depth in silent film.

The sound required a continuance in the shooting process; it expanded the length of takes, gave movement to the camera inside the set, and subsequently changed the set.

We are perhaps on the threshold of adopting a new cinematic convention of depth. Using distant sound effects, we can recreate what Tolstoy did in *War and Peace*: in his description of the battle of Borodino, the smoke coming from explosions and the sound validating the explosions are separated, and the delayed sound creates phonic depth in the scene.

This is an example of acoustic depth.

We shouldn't assume that there is only one system—the verbal—for transmitting thought, and that everything can be translated into the language of that sign system. And yet the process of thought, the juxtaposition of objects is possible only through the construction of sign systems, which the viewer or reader can perceive. This, in turn, occurs not through a mastering of conventions, but rather a change of conventions—a shift in systems that expand their own possibilities.

The new stereometric camera that Eisenstein was so excited about wasn't necessary after all.

The Convention of Time

Dmitri Likhachov, who understood perfectly the correlation between old Russian literature and painting, noted that time in the fairy tale is extremely condensed.

The action takes place during the day, questions are asked in the evening, solved in the morning—"the morning is wiser than the evening"[56]—and everything begins all over again. Moreover, the cycle of night and day is determined by the action. But here, too, we can make a clarification: incidents that predetermine the usual flow of events such as, for example, the attack of strange creatures, appearance of magical horses, theft of apples, and other incidents by the tomb of a parent—all of these things happen during the night. The main hero, usually the less powerful, acquires extraordinary qualities at nighttime. Nighttime in many fairy tales is a period of complications and a period that resolves many things for those who are awake.

A person is searching for something. He must keep searching for a long time. The search is like a job that requires food and clothing.

---

56 A Russian proverb often used in fairy tales, meaning that one may be able to solve a difficult problem by sleeping on it and thus delaying it until the following day.

The search in itself is always long. Time in the fairy tale is made of distinct moments and omissions. This time can be characterized as a *dashed line*, as a selection of moments that are marked according to the magnitude of their importance and as a replacement of the continuity of temporal reality.

Besides the dash-lined time, the fairy tale also incorporates conventional time. It is usually shown through changes in food or clothing.

Objectal time: the wearing of shoes, gnawing on iron bread—is a time of indeterminate length. It shows the indefinite period of metaphoric hardship because even in fairy tales it is almost impossible to gnaw on iron bread. It is used as a metaphor to convey a notion of time—"such a long time, that it might never happen."

In antiquity, this convention was underscored through an action or an act of cunning.

In the epic *Gilgamesh*, the main hero journeys to the underworld to bring back his dead friend. He must sail across the then-unconquerable sea and find the mysterious land. After Gilgamesh completes a series of tasks, he fails to carry out the last one: to stay awake for seven days. The hero falls asleep. The gods of the underworld bake a loaf of bread for each day he sleeps. Gilgamesh sleeps without waking up for seven days. When he awakens, he says, "I was almost / falling asleep when I felt your touch."[57] The gods show him the loaves, the first of which is rock hard and the seventh is still warm. Time here is shown through the quality of bread.

---

57   *Gilgamesh*. Translated by Stephen Mitchell. New York: Free Press, 2004. All subsequent quotations from *Gilgamesh* are taken from this standard version.

I don't think that the cunning of the Gibeonites who deceived Joshua was taken directly from *Gilgamesh* but it repeats the visual imagery of space and time in a new conceptualization.

When Joshua's armies conquer Canaan and slaughter the inhabitants of the neighboring city-states, the inhabitants of Gibeon, feeling threatened, decide to act with cunning: "They went and prepared provisions, and took worn-out sacks for their donkeys, and wineskins, worn-out and torn and mended, with worn-out, patched sandals on their feet, and worn-out clothes; and all their provisions were dry and moldy" (Joshua 9:4).

Later their deception is exposed but Joshua doesn't destroy the Gibeonites.

It's realism to convey the passage of time through an object's qualities as they change. This realism is exaggerated and distorted in the fairy tale. The hero sets out for a journey taking with him iron—sometimes cast-iron—bread and gnaws at it. He is wearing a pair of iron shoes. Everything is solid on him and everything wears away.

Both iron and cast iron are relatively new materials. We should have expected bread that was made of stone or bronze, but the antiquity of the fairy tale is the antiquity of an artistic composition that lives through renewal—changing its reality while preserving its structure.

The question here is not in the material that bread is made of, but in time, the passage of which can be shown in various ways.

Time in epic songs and epics is fluid and unrushed. The heroic warrior saddles his horse leisurely. It takes him as long as it usually takes to saddle a horse in real life. It's done with affectionate skill, with a description of the material that objects are made of—an explanation of why silk and gold are used.

Heroic deeds are committed at a faster pace.

In epic works such as *The Iliad*, the siege, consisting of a range of conflicts, is interrupted by quarrels among the gods who must decide which side should win.

Parallel timelines and alternate realities emerge.

The method of showing time in *The Odyssey* is somewhat different. We have the time when events take place—the time of action, and another time—the time of narration.

Odysseus narrates about his journey, how he tried to find his way back home.

There is also substitutive time, the time of Telemachus's journey—we called this cross-cutting in film, a cut to action that is happening simultaneously.

This method of showing time didn't change in the early European novel.

In the first realistic "adventures of the *pícaro*"—*The Life of Lazarillo de Tormes*—the main character narrates his life in segments. The segments are divided according to the time he spends serving a certain master in a succession of masters.

The segments are titled "treatises," each segment having its own subheading and a typographical layout that gives the appearance of individual booklets.

Descriptions of the hunt for employment are often cut down to a single phrase.

Time flows between the "treatises."

In the first volume of *Don Quixote*, the material was broken down into several sections, each section had its subheading and was laid out as a separate book. Even its end was designed so that the lines narrowed down and concluded in a conventional way.

The abruptness of transition from one event to another was marked typographically.

What we call today the second part of *Don Quixote* in reality would have been the tenth book of the novel.

The second part that was written as a separate book is not divided into any sections.

The convention of showing time in intermittent episodes is assimilated right before our eyes. When they bring Don Quixote back home, he is sick and as though under a spell, and when he recovers, his friends come to visit him.

They test to see if the hidalgo has regained his sanity. It turns out that Don Quixote continues to believe that he is a knight-errant.

He fully understands the insinuations made by his friends who consider him a madman, and responds to them with irony, as a sensible man.

Furthermore, it is not disclosed that during the three weeks that Don Quixote has been home, "almost a month," his history has already been published in a book originally written in Arabic. It has been translated into various languages and Don Quixote is now a legendary hero.

This convention is shown without a disguise. Nothing alludes to the fact that almost a decade has passed between the publication of the first and second volumes of the book. Historically Spain was going through a strained period but that's not mentioned in the book: the time in the novel is restricted. It is cut off from historical time.

Similarly, in *The History of Tom Jones*, time is conventionally predetermined. Fielding announces that the story is not going to be like a stagecoach that departs at a certain hour.

We might say that Fielding carries his characters in their own carriages, which are ready for departure whenever action is foreseen.

Time in the English novel is connected with a journey. Journeys back then were long: the road, the stops and conflicts in coachhouses were as common as the ticking of the clock.

I would like to point out how in *A Sentimental Journey*, the journey itself—the progress of the hero's movement, is slowed down and parodied. Sterne omits the parts where the hero is supposed to be sightseeing with the exception of Paris, but here, too, the city is described not through its architecture but its occupants.

He comments on the proliferation of dwarfs as a result of overcrowding in the city.

The state of affairs in France and, partly, the terror of the Bastille are depicted through metaphors.

The metaphoric landscape supplants the geographic one.

The hero-traveler, who is supposed to be traveling, stays instead in the same location for a lengthy period of time. Several chapters are meant to take place by the gates of a coachyard where his *chaise* stands waiting. The interior time prevails—the time of the hero's consciousness, his analysis of events. This type of interior analysis recurs in modern antinovels through the narrator's stream of consciousness.

Everything is done intentionally.

The novel introduces a new classification of travelers, the most innovative of which appears to be the "sentimental traveler."

The adventures are usually substantiated with a search and rescuing of a heroine, who is being forcibly married off.

Or, occasionally, an excursion to join the army of the pretender.

The older novels traditionally incorporated the motif of imprisonment.

"Prison time" sometimes provided a pretext for changing patterns in description.

This could have been realistic had it not been incessantly repeated. For example, the protagonist ends up in prison for a petty crime, usually for going into debt, and then isn't able to pay it back. The prison as pretext for stopping was used by Fielding, Smollett, and, in loosely parodied form, Dickens.

Mr. Pickwick goes to prison voluntarily. Even though he is a wealthy gentleman, Pickwick refuses to compensate a widow who has brought an action against him for breach of a marriage promise.

The text of *The Pickwick Papers* is intentionally and ironically conventional. This is evident from the route of Pickwick's journey. The purpose of the journey, and the actions during the journey and the club itself are all parodies.

It is the last will and testament of the old genre.

Let's retrace our steps.

By titling his book *The History of Tom Jones, A Foundling*, Fielding wants to emphasize his right to represent life "as it is" and not "as it should be." The word "history" here is the mask of reality.

The heroes of the novel are typically virtuous, reserved, and true to their women. Their loyalty is quite remarkable, and their temptations are varied.

Tom Jones is a historical hero, not fictional. He has a voracious appetite for good food, he drinks a lot, he is constantly disloyal to Sophia whom he nonetheless loves, and commits risky deeds such as accepting money from Lady Bellaston in exchange for his love.

Tom Jones is a foundling adopted by a distinguished country gentleman who doesn't know that the child is his own nephew. Later he banishes Tom from the estate, still not knowing the truth concerning his birth. And even though Tom Jones was brought up as a gentleman, he is forced to lead the life of a handsome rake who readily fulfills every stranger's request and is easily forgiven. He is on the margins of society and that makes him even more attractive.

Tom Jones doesn't live according to moral codes but according to the needs of a strong, handsome man. What we have here is a "true Work of a Historian" with a fictional hero.

In the first chapter of the second book, Fielding declares that he is the "Founder of a new Province of Writing," that he writes a selective history, which like a stagecoach—meaning, the plot of his book—travels at its own pace and time, and that he is not a historian but a writer—a master of time. "My Reader then is not to be surprised, if, in the Course of this Work, he shall find some Chapters very short and others altogether as long; some that contain only the Time of a single Day, and others that comprise Years; in a Word, if my History sometimes seems to stand still, and sometimes to fly."

But in the end, conventionality triumphs. The stagecoach of history arrives at the station of recognition. The hero acquires wealth, a wife, and legitimate children—the journey comes to an end.

The temporal flow in Fielding's novel is multiscaled. Years usually pass during intervals between the chapters and so-called "books" of the novel.

The novel is divided into eighteen books.

The omissions and cursory descriptions at the beginning allow the author to push aside the mystery of the foundling's birth. There are hints about his origins but these passages are separated from one another by such lengthy intervals that memory cannot retain the connections.

But they offer some plausibility for the traditional recognition at the end of the novel. The empathy for the infant intimated by Mr. Allworthy's stern sister—Miss Bridget (the boy's real mother)—is a clue to the mystery of his birth.

Until the very end of the novel we get consistent indications signaling that we are following a false clue regarding the hero's birth.

The history of Tom Jones develops parallel to another (rather dull) story—the adventures of his bride, Sophia.

The transition to Sophia's story serves also as a pretext for omissions.

I will give a few examples in order to show how time flows in *Tom Jones*.

The first book is an exposition: it is set outside of historical time and prepares us for the main action.

We don't really know the span of days or years encompassed by the first book; Fielding doesn't determine that.

The heading of the second book declares that it contains various transactions spanning two years. The third book acquires a faster pace: there are omissions and fast-forwarding of actions spanning five years. The fourth book accounts for events that occurred within a year. The fifth book—half a year. The sixth book—three weeks. The seventh book—three days. The eighth book—two days. The ninth book introduces new characters and the duration of action is twelve hours. In the tenth book the story moves forward by another twelve hours: it concludes with Sophia's escape, who quite rightfully suspects Jones of infidelity.

The eleventh book, spanning about three days, is dedicated to Sophia.

The twelfth book also spans three days.

The thirteenth book spans twelve days. The fourteenth—two days. The fifteenth advances about two days also. These time indications, as I mentioned before, appear in the heading of each book and their significance is determined by Fielding himself.

The sixteenth book contains a period of five days. The seventeenth book spans three days in which the author constructs the novel's culmination: Jones is imprisoned due to slanders. In the prison he finds out through Partridge, a barber, that his onetime mistress, Mrs. Waters, was in fact his mother, bringing him to the realization that he has committed the Oedipal sin. The eighteenth book unravels the whole intrigue. It is revealed that Tom's real mother is Allworthy's sister, who had bribed Mrs. Waters to claim the sin of giving birth to an illegitimate child. It turns out that Tom Jones is Allworthy's nephew.

It is simultaneously revealed that Allworthy's sister had confessed the secret to her brother, but the letter was confiscated by her second son—Tom Jones's rival, who also wants to marry Sophia.

Tom Jones is acquitted and after hasty apologies to Sophia, who readily forgives the handsome hero, marries her. Here the novel ends. It ends with where the nineteenth-century novel begins.

The History of Tom Jones succeeds in establishing the convention of realistic time and actualizing the convention of "a true history," but it concludes with a conventional ending.

Sterne's novel parodies realistic time. Barely having established its temporal laws, the genre immediately goes on to parody them. Sterne changes the material content and methods of analysis. He introduces a magnifying glass, as it were, through which he examines the emotions of his characters. The emotions are presented not realistically but in parodied form.

The parody is emphasized not only through the eccentricity of the analysis of the action but also the implied impediment of the event.

For instance, in chapters ten through thirteen the action takes place by the door of the *remise*. The author marvels at his own impediment: he has no clue how to end the conversation and ends it with what we would call today a "fade-out," breaking off the conversation with a numeral that signifies a new chapter.

Pushkin was well acquainted with Sterne's work, but his convention of time for the selection of material is purely his own and not Sternean. He cites Sterne quite explicitly though.

Time in *Eugene Onegin*, as Pushkin states, is structured according to the calendar. But the internal transformation of the heroes takes place outside of this time.

The omitted time is shown through the change of chapters, stanzas, or seasons, and commentaries by the author-narrator.

He enters the novel as an observer—a surveyor of the situation, events, and time. A surveyor of the significance of actions and emotions.

This narratorial time then becomes the means to not only fill in the omissions but also interpret them and move events forward.

The method of introducing a "personal hero" in the history of *The Captain's Daughter* is conventional.

Pushkin wanted to connect Pugachov's revolt to Catherine's palace coup, in which Peter III was assassinated and she succeeded him to the throne. The old gentleman, Grinyov, who stayed loyal to Peter III, was exiled to a far estate like Pushkin's ancestors.

The story is narrated from Pyotr Grinyov's perspective: "My father, Andrei Petrovich Grinyov, had in his youth served under Count Münnich and retired with the rank of first Major in 17—."[58] Since then Andrei Petrovich lived on his estate in the province of Simbirsk, where he married the daughter of a poor landowner of the district.

By mentioning the name of Count Christoph von Münnich, Pushkin gives away the actual date—1762—that was intentionally left out. This means that Grinyov's father, like Pushkin's ancestors, "kept his allegiance to the overthrown Peter III." This also means that Andrei Grinyov could not have married before 1762 and that his son was most likely born around 1763 or later.

The action in *The Captain's Daughter* is set in 1773. Consequently, the young Grinyov must have been ten years old during the Pugachovian revolt. He is seventeen in the novella.

I noticed this anachronism when reading the book. I also noticed that Pushkin mentions nine children, of whom only one has survived, taking it as his device to circumvent any age verification. My book on Pushkin's prose came out in 1937. The photo-reproduced edition of Pushkin's manuscripts from 1833–35 (edited by S. Bondi) was published two years later, in 1939. There are numeric calculations on the margins of the manuscript that work out Shvanvich's date of birth—Grinyov's historical prototype. In order for him to have reached eighteen in 1773, he must have been born in 1755, which is an impossibility.

Pushkin used this device, which remained unnoticed for over a century and rightly so, because fictional time is different from regu-

---

58 Aleksandr Pushkin, *The Captain's Daughter*. Translated by Natalie Duddington. London: J. M. Dent, 1961. All subsequent quotations from *The Captain's Daughter* are taken from this standard version.

lar time by the mere fact that it doesn't flow according to historical chronology. By speeding up and slowing down the action, rearranging the various parts, unraveling them or condensing in recapitulations, the author presents the events outside of regular time.

This should not be confused with temporal transposition, which changes the perception of the cause of action, forcing us to speculate about the causal circumstances in seemingly unexpected episodes. Pushkin does this in "The Shot" and "The Snowstorm."

Similarly, Lermontov impedes the analysis of Pechorin by transposing the events of his life. We are not allowed to see the hero close up, as it were; Lermontov slows down the narrative with descriptions of the landscape.

The action in one of the novellas in *A Hero of Our Time* takes place on the Georgian Military Road. The protagonists are traveling on a road that Pushkin had already paved in his *A Journey to Arzrum*. But they are moving toward Pushkin by changing the order of events.

The ground for the author's analysis has been scraped clean. Lermontov's descriptions of the local landscape coincide with those of Pushkin, but stylistically they diverge. We see the literary tradition that influenced Lermontov and the changes that he makes in that tradition.

The story about Bela, framed as a conventional conversation during a road trip, is narrated from Maksim Maksimych's point of view.

In this road trip story we are introduced to Pechorin who has been exiled to a remote fort for some misdeed.

The next story, "Maksim Maksimych," is the second meeting on the road. Here Pechorin appears not in Maksim Maksimych's narrative but in the account of the primary narrator. Their encounter with Pechorin leaves a cold impression. It turns out that Maksim Maksimych has been carrying Pechorin's diaries with him since they had parted. Now Pechorin's faithful friend feels hurt by him.

He gives the diaries to his casual fellow traveler, an exiled officer from Petersburg who oddly resembles the shadow of Pechorin.

The story of the primary narrator, who is traveling from some unknown place—heading into the unknown, to a certain degree repeats Pechorin's story.

The reading of found, abandoned, or handed-down diaries in a "tavern" is an old literary tradition.

But what's new here is that the hero of the road-trip story told at the Ossetian coachhouse, the person who chances on the secondary narrator (Maksim Maksimych), and the author of the accidentally acquired journals (Pechorin)—all appear to be the same but *differently* exposed person.

Time in the novel is rearranged. We don't know and can only guess about the successive stages of the hero's life.

Time is used here for the explication of the hero's mysterious psychology.

The reading of the diaries takes place as though at an accidental juncture. The first one is called "Taman," which according to Eichenbaum, is juxtaposed against "Bela."

We see Pechorin's first encounter with an ostensibly accidental woman, a woman not from his society. The encounter is understandably antagonistic.

But we are already familiar with the simple tale about the encounter of the "disillusioned" man with the "savage" woman; her love is now perceived anew from Maksim Maksimych's perspective who is almost in love with her but whom she hardly notices.

Bela's fate is inevitable.

In "Taman," Pechorin is absentmindedly searching for a love adventure.

He is searching for at least an accidental place in the world. And he ends up in a situation where the woman thinks he is a spy or an enemy. He escapes only by chance.

The narrator states in his introduction to "Pechorin's Journal":

> I learned not long ago that Pechorin had died on his way back from Persia. This news gladdened me very much, it gave me the right to publish these notes, and I took advantage of the opportunity to sign another man's work with my own name.[59]

This is an ironic statement. A man appears to be overexcited about the death of another man whom he appeared to like during their brief encounter. He bluntly declares about his appropriation of someone else's text. What we have here is an ironic refutation of authorship and its simultaneous affirmation.

Let me remind you: "Pechorin's Journal" begins with "Taman," a novella started as a travel sketch with a characterization of the hero, followed by "Princess Mary" and "The Fatalist." "Taman" is

---

59   Mikhail Lermontov, *A Hero of Our Time*. Translated by Vladimir Nabokov in collaboration with Dmitri Nabokov. New York: Doubleday Anchor, 1958. All subsequent quotations from *A Hero of Our Time* are taken from this standard version.

the journey to the Caucasus, meaning we enter a time that precedes the beginning of *A Hero of Our Time*. The action opens with Pechorin's arrival in a remote fort in the Caucasus where he was exiled. "Princess Mary" is the account of events that had caused Pechorin's exile.

"The Fatalist" describes one of Pechorin's adventures while stationed at the fort. The episode clearly precedes the events in "Bela" and exposes Pechorin's disillusionment with life: it is despair that leads the hero to—so frivolously—put his life at risk.

Evental time is rearranged.

We learn about the hero at different moments of his life either from the side—narrated in third person, or from his own accounts.

The evental sequence should have been like this: an exile from Petersburg travels to the Caucasus, arrives in Pyatigorsk, kills Grushnitsky in a duel, is sent away to the Caucasian border, meets Maksim Maksimych, risks his life during a fatal encounter with a Cossack who had killed another officer. Evental time is rearranged so that we can't ever fully examine the hero. We see him either in someone else's narration, in a lyrical outburst, or in a travel sketch.

It seems that the "hero of our time" has no time of his own, he has been thrown out of time. He lives "in the meantime" and doesn't wish to reveal himself to us.

*

With time, Tolstoy's work becomes less clear. Tolstoy comes to literature when the forms of the novel have been fully discussed and conceptualized. He is familiar with Sterne.

His first work, *Childhood*, is constructed covertly—in an intricate way. As the young Eichenbaum wrote in his book, we are looking at "the world through a microscope."

This method of examination resembles the Sternean technique, but the characters are not estranged, they are realistic, made closer to the narrator: he loves them, thinks of them as heroes who ought to exist.

He doesn't displace them even when examining from the side.

Childhood begins with a boy's awakening.

It gives a detailed account of the day and descriptions of a hunt, followed by the departure to Moscow, which concludes the first part. Chapters sixteen through twenty-four describe a single day—his grandmother's name day.

The mother's theme is central to the story, beginning with the boy's invented dream about his mother's death and ending with her actual death.

The evental episodes are disconnected from one another, and connect only through the narrator and his lyrical adages. The unity of the plot is achieved not through the unity of the events, but through the relationships between the characters.

The episodes are arranged in chronological order, though time progresses in a dashed line.

Tolstoy's breakdown of the novel into short chapters allows for an accurate portrayal of separate scenes and reduces the gaps of omitted moments. The events are expressed through their culminations.

Tolstoy doesn't "parody" time or juxtapose "narration" against the events themselves; he conveys time through detail and compares the temporality of individual life with the course of history.

In *War and Peace*, history disrupts biography. War is used as a motive for character transformation.

The characters appear as though in a new light—we examine them anew. The historical crisis changes their relationships. It renews the relationship between Natasha and Andrei. Between Natasha's decision to break off her engagement, which had embittered Andrei, and their new meeting passes a war, Andrei's wounding, the fire of Moscow, the Rostovs' loss of possessions, when in her selflessness Natasha leaves material things behind in order to transport the wounded.

The characters grasp the full extent of events through separation: history forces them to change abruptly.

The division into chapters and description of the return of the heroes are also interesting as they tend to reveal a person more explicitly when he appears and when he disappears.

This tendency has been around for a very long time and it fades away, dissolving in the noise of time instead of becoming its voice.

Which is why abrupt changes such as arrivals and departures are important in the formation of new insights.

Tolstoy needs Andrei Bolkonsky to leave his pregnant wife and return when she is in labor.

But in order for Bolkonsky to leave her pregnant, Tolstoy has to make the pregnancy visible.

In the beginning of the novel, the pregnancy of the young princess is shown through the remark that she doesn't go to any large gatherings, and that she walks "with quick, short, swaying steps." She is probably in her third or fourth month of pregnancy.

In the meantime, Tolstoy gives specific dates, describing the white night in Petersburg and pointing to events well known to everyone.

He needs to show how the young Bolkonsky departs, leaving his pregnant wife with his father and sister. To do this, Tolstoy has to emphasize the pregnancy, make it noticeable, showing the understandable discontent of the young princess, the legitimacy of her irritation, and Bolkonsky's indifference.

The birth required a juxtaposition: the birth of a son, the mother's death in childbirth, and the sudden return of the father. All of this had to happen after the Battle of Austerlitz. It was necessary to juxtapose the historical against the personal. The pregnancy timeline here is purely provisional. The factual miscalculation in this convention is ignored.

*

Evental succession in Tolstoy is often subordinated to compositional time. "The Death of Ivan Ilych" begins from the end, from the description of the dead man. *Hadji Murad* begins with an extended metaphor that describes the hero's death. Right before the chapter on Hadji Murad's death, his head is revealed to the woman who had been affectionate to him.

Anna is introduced in the novel not immediately but as a secondary character. Time in *Anna Karenina* is chronological but we enter Anna's life, her seeming prosperity, rather suddenly. We see the parodied, dry affection of Karenin, Anna's peaceful, falsely happy life and her superiority in comparison to everyone else. The story begins with an aphorism about happy families, followed by a description of a frivolous dream about singing female decanters. We enter the world of established relationships through a remark that those relationships are internally obsolete. Levin's remark about Russia—

that everything had turned upside down and nothing made sense anymore—also relates to the personal lives of the characters. It is in direct and unintentional contradiction with the novel's epigraph.

The epigraph ("Vengeance is mine; I will repay") professes the eternal law of God. But the criminality of Stiva Oblonsky (adultery against his wife) is disregarded, while the criminality of Anna Karenina (adultery against her husband) is refuted by way of analysis.[60]

Happiness and moral values in aristocratic families are inert and illusory.

Their morality has become obsolete; happiness is experienced in transient moments like, for example, Levin's blissful morning.

Life has completely disintegrated, though considering the novel's reality, it is still being idolized and people are still being sacrificed to it.

Those illusory morals suffocate Anna Karenina.

The novel begins with a positive affirmation of a moral life, then switches to the threats of mysterious and ruthless dreams.

In a sense, the novel has no closure. Vronsky goes to fight in a war that is meaningless to him.

Levin is depressed and only Kitty is conventionally happy, though, of course, we cannot ignore the fact that the landscapes in *Anna Karenina* and *The Devil* are nearly identical.

It seems to me that the hero in the contemporary novel, especially in the West, is becoming increasingly self-contained.

But occasionally, the novel will be constructed on the element of repetition (as in William Faulkner)—the same story is narrated

---

60 Lev Tolstoy, *Anna Karenina*. Translated by Louise and Aylmer Maude. New York: Norton, 1970. All subsequent quotations from *Anna Karenina* are taken from this standard version.

from rotating viewpoints. This technique can also be found in contemporary film.

The features of the "realistic world" are distorted in their fictional representation.

A good example of this is Nathalie Sarraute's nouveau roman.

The Golden Fruits is a novel about a novel and how we perceive narrative convention. The novel, in this case, functions as a "fictional reality" that allows for evaluative ruminations. We never get to the novel "The Golden Fruits" but only hear commentaries about it. The commentaries aren't attached to any character or action, but they exist independently, replacing and describing the characters and their development. The characters, or more accurately, the commentators, have separate, predetermined characteristics that are independent of "The Golden Fruits" and function solely as the carriers of a conversation about the art of the novel in general.

The order of each comment is predefined.

When one of the commentators says that "The Golden Fruits" is nauseating and vulgar, the other makes a traditional remark, if not a predictable one then at least an already existing, expected one: "But all that, you see, is done on purpose."

I will have to talk about many things, so pardon me for my ignorance.

*

Lev Nikolaevich Tolstoy liked to play solitaire while trying to determine the fates of his heroes. In his diary he wrote that he understood the Romans who resolved the most critical questions by drawing lots.

Tolstoy would have probably been very interested in contemporary game theory.

But there is the actual game, besides game theory.

There is chance—the danger of flipping the card. The game is based on the alternation between systems of interest; it holds and creates chance while devising combinations of cards.

Novels often contain a game deciding someone's fate.

The bet is on money—on interest.

We ought to include the analysis of interest in the theory of the novel.

My grandmother used to wear a small velvet hat with wide ribbons that tied under her chin. When I was seven years old, I was convinced that this hat constituted the structure of every grandmother. I had not seen other people's grandmothers, so basing my knowledge on my own grandmother I constructed a universal model of all grandmothers.

Later I found out that it was a hat from her youth.

These kinds of hats were called *toques* back then.

There comes a time in a person's life when he stops moving forward, stops following the general flow of time, and fixes surroundings through his sense of fashion.

Perhaps my attitude toward the new literary movements resembles S. A. Vengerov's attitude toward me, or my grandmother's attitude toward the new styles of hats.

Now I wear a fedora style hat and a fur cap, while my young colleagues walk around hatless.

Yet I perceive myself not only as someone from a different generation but also as a person who thinks less about his age and more about his epoch.

The Structuralists established the concept of structures—the idea of such an interrelation of elements that a change in one element results in a change of meaning and signification in all other elements. The most developed and refined structures are those of verbal language. We "grope" the world with words the same way as the blind grope with their hands, and unintentionally project the interrelations of our language structure onto the world, perceiving the world as a linguistic phenomenon, as it were. Perhaps this is a rational way of self-restraint.

But there is also a structure called art. I speak differently when I speak with a child, an old friend, an accountant, and even more so—a woman. I can change the structure of my language. But generally speaking, the structure of language is independent from me. It has existed for thousands of years. We were introduced to it in childhood, we grew up in it.

The structures of art are in some sense unique as the riddle proposed to the Philistines.

An artist creates his own structure of art. Consciously and sometimes unconsciously in his attempts to discern reality, he selects structures, defines the borders and interrelations of selected, juxtaposed meanings. He juxtaposes and compares the various structures of art, transferring the laws of one structure into the realm of another—let's call them substructures.

The structures of art are to a degree subjected to individual volition and they are correlated to other structures in intricate ways.

You will frequently come across the word "convention" in this book. It should not be confused with the concept of structure.

A convention is a set of conditions through which structures correlate with one another, and which the author involuntarily sets between himself and those to whom he is sending a message.

A convention usually includes several structures that obtain new functions through juxtaposition. Many years ago there used to be a single model of the physical world—the mill. Water flowed from one blade onto another. People harvested the energy of falling water. Today we don't project the experience of our common sense directly onto the life of the universe and we don't think that inner-molecular movement is equivalent to the movement of billiard balls.

There may be a correlation. They could be compared to one another, but they are certainly not identical.

PERSON OUT OF PLACE

Person Out of Place

I

In the *Symposium*, Plato constructs a conversation where the participants are only men. Here Socrates recounts what he has overheard from Diotima of Mantinea—he calls her a "stranger woman."

Diotima says that ". . . those who are pregnant in the body only, betake themselves to women and beget children—this is the character of their love; their offspring, as they hope, will preserve their memory, and give them the blessedness and immortality which they desire for all future time."[61]

The birth of Eros, the god of love, is introduced in Diotima's narrative rather abruptly and as if contradictorily.

On the day when Aphrodite was born there was a feast of all the gods, during which Poros (the god of resourcefulness) gets drunk and by accident sleeps with Penia (the goddess of poverty). Eros is born from an accidental affair. He is by nature neither mortal nor immortal. The story seems strange in the context of Greek mythology.

---

61 Plato, *Symposium*. In *The Dialogues of Plato*. Vol. I. Translated by Benjamin Jowett. Oxford UP, 1964. All subsequent quotations from the *Symposium* are taken from this standard version.

Eros usually appears as a fortunate god in myths; he is Aphrodite's son. He has a jealous mother who, according to one myth, is terribly jealous of the mortal woman Psyche. This is told in Apuleius's marvelous book. But Diotima tells a different story about Eros: "And as his parentage is, so also are his fortunes. In the first place he is always poor, and anything but tender and fair, as the many imagine him; and he is rough and squalid, and has no shoes, nor a house to dwell in; on the bare earth exposed he lies under the open heaven, in the streets, or at the doors of houses, taking his rest; and like his mother he is always in distress."

The myths contradict one another, and the genealogy of gods is confusing.

Aristotle believed that even the poet had no right to change existing myths. The poet selected myths and subordinated them to his will, which, of course, is the same as changing them.

The poet, to whose will I would like to be subordinated—Pushkin—said in *The Stone Guest*:

> Of all delights and joys in life
> To love alone does music yield in sweetness.
> Yet love is melody itself.[62]

One might argue that this is another description of Eros, who is not only the god of love but also the god of poetry and harmony.

Harmony is not repetition of the same thing but co-subordination of the divergent.

---

62   Aleksandr Pushkin, *The Stone Guest*. In *Little Tragedies*. Translated by Eugene M. Kayden. Antioch Press, 1965.

This is how Aleksei Losev described the essence of Heraclitus's fragment in his article "The Aesthetic Terminology of Plato":

> The content of the structural whole assumes not only the essence of the whole itself but also its separation and the opposition of elements against the background of a totality that unites them. A category of harmony emerges here, which is inevitably connected to the concept of the unity of opposites.

The same thing occurs in a literary work when evental structures are juxtaposed against one another.

If art describes happiness, then it is usually about a destroyed happiness, or a happiness that is about to be destroyed. It selects myths that narrate the destruction of happiness.

When they stopped using traditional myths in their direct form, tragedies changed to dramas, and the stage became a new platform for slaves and perverse youth. A new type of guilt emerged—not the familial or ancestral guilt, but the guilt of contemporary man who made a mistake or committed a crime and was called onto the stage by the dramatist. These were the laws in the plays of Menander and Terence.

Hegel marked a new collision emerging in "modern romances," meaning the novels of his time. On the one hand, there was the police, law courts, the army and political government, and on the other—the individuals with their subjective ends of love, honor, and ambition, or their confrontation with the existing order and ideals of world-reform. Hegel wrote:

But in the modern world these fights are nothing more than 'apprenticeship,' the education of the individual into the realities of the present, and thereby they acquire their true significance. For the end of such apprenticeship consists in this, that the subject sows his wild oats . . .[63]

The novel of Hegel's time ended with marriage, or rather, it was cut off by marriage. Marriage was supposed to break the hero's horns. The impact from lunging into the wall is later perceived in an entirely different way. As time passes, romantic conflicts are complicated with social ones.

In *The House of the Dead*, Dostoevsky describes the fate of criminals and insurrectionist soldiers who were sentenced to hard labor and sent to Siberia from the military divisions and prison barracks where they had revolted. These subversives become the leaders of the prisoners' movement, entering into a new conflict with the existing order and "lunging with their horns into the wall." The reason why one of the characters in *The House of the Dead*, Baklushin, ends up in prison is because of his unfortunate love for a young German woman who is to be married off to an old German watchmaker. The conflict of love shifts

63   G. W. F. Hegel, *Aesthetics: Lectures on Fine Art.* Vol. I. Translated by T. M. Knox. Oxford UP, 1975. All subsequent quotations from *Aesthetics* are taken from this standard version. The Russian version of Knox's translation "sows his wild oats," literally translates into "breaks his horns," which figuratively enhances Hegel's notion of the opposition between the subject and the unyielding order of civil society and the state. Shklovsky refers to this figure of speech in the following two paragraphs discussing conflict in the novel and Dostoevsky's *The House of the Dead.*

into a conflict with the captain who swears at Baklushin before the court. The conflict then is transferred to a new, broader domain—the prisoners' fight for their rights, a struggle for "normal prison conditions."

II

In a sad, sensible voice Tolstoy affirmed that marriage was only the beginning of conflict, and by this he meant other conflicts that expanded in his work and finally in *Resurrection* transformed into a conflict between the real truth and the falsehood of the pronouncements of a false government and religion.

When creating new models of art, humanity creates them not because the models themselves need to be renewed but because humanity fights for the expansion of its right to life, for the right to search and attain new kinds of happiness.

The realm of art is expanded with previously forbidden elements of life. The notion of hell changes. It becomes commonplace. The relationships between heroes change after death.

The old world explores the meaning of life before death. The Olympian gods and goddesses are examined with a critical eye. First, they argue with one another, then they are cross-examined and must answer new questions, as Cyniscus interrupts Zeus, exposing him in the contradictions of mythology.

New themes emerge. Lucian writes *Dialogues of the Hetaerae*. The dialogues are not cynical, they are rather ordinary. The hetaerae are supposedly the most liberated women but they live in the cellars of a forbidden world.

What once existed only in dreams and jokes, now, several generations later, becomes real in these illicit spaces.

The nature of recognition begins to change. Odysseus is recognized by his faithful slave. Electra recognizes her brother Orestes. The recognition of Oedipus is tragic: he is not only Jocasta's son but also her husband. The recognition is singular and tragic, but the Oedipal sin is redeemed through suffering. He is allowed to have a burial place. Gradually models of happy denouements begin to emerge. These are models of exceptional fortune, and fortune emphasized despair, as it were. Redemption in drama is ironic.

Recognition in Menander, Terence, Molière, and Cervantes is a compromisingly happy event. A young man wants to marry his beloved. His father wants him to marry someone else. But his beloved was once abducted, and suddenly the bride chosen by the father turns out to be the same woman as the young man's beloved.

In Longus's *Daphnis and Chloe*, two children are abandoned and become slaves. Their knowledge of love is self-taught, they are as if the first human beings, the first ones to experience human feelings, and hence everything is experienced in purest form. In the end Daphnis and Chloe find out that they are children of noblemen. This is revealed with the help of the tokens that were left with the newborns—a traditional device, the conventionality of which is not concealed any more.

In Menander's *Epitrepontes*, the shepherd Daos and the charcoal burner Syriskos argue over who should keep a foundling's tokens. Syriskos, to whom Daos has given the foundling, argues that the tokens belong to the baby, but Daos contends that he is entitled to keep them. The argument is taken to an arbitrator. Each party makes his claim. Daos states his sovereign right: the one who finds something is entitled to keep it and dispose of it as he pleases. He has given part of his find—the child—to Syriskos, and he is keeping the rest—the tokens—for himself. This is in accordance with the laws of antiquity. Syriskos claims something else: there is a difference—it's one thing to find an object, another to find a human being. He is here on behalf of the child, demanding that what belongs to the child must be returned to him. He argues in his speech that the tokens will help find the child's real father. If he loses his belongings, it would be impossible for the parent to recognize his child.

The basis of the argument is not social, but theatrical. Theatrical conventionality is confirmed here as an element of structure. The intrigue in comedy is now conducted by slaves. They reveal that the heroes of comedy are not condemned to the same bitter fate as people fighting for their rights in real life.

Menander, Terence, Plautus, and even the early Molière don't know of another method of how to escape prosaic life but to introduce a theatrical convention into the norm.

They need recognition as a myth about the possibility of happiness.

III

Let's follow the trail of Apuleius's hero in *The Golden Ass*. A curious young man mistakenly uses the wrong ointment made by an enchantress—thinking he would be temporarily transformed into a bird he's transformed into an ass.

He takes the roads made for asses. They chase him away, and he is kidnapped and beaten. He ends up in a den of thieves and overhears the tale about Psyche told by an old woman.

The ass is a person out of place because in reality the ass is a human being.

The perception of reality and daily misery is brought closer. At first, poverty is presented not directly but as a reason for adventures. Destitution is a pretext for showing exotic things. The typical cause for being thrown out of the world is poverty.

Lesage's hero, Gil Blas, is born into an ordinary petty bourgeois household that seems to be prospering on the outside. He is socialized into the world—he gets cheated and he cheats others. He lives a thousand lives and occupies a thousand places, passing through different circles and witnessing various crimes, and finally marries someone else's mistress. He is a mischievous rogue, though he never partakes in crimes.

The life of rogues is presented as though it were entertainment, something like watching a game of cards.

The interest of the audience shifts from the conventionally happy denouement to the exposition of an ordinary and ruthlessly inhuman life.

In *The Little Gipsy Girl* by Cervantes, it turns out that the girl was originally kidnapped from an aristocratic home. She has, of course, the trinkets of identification. As a result, she is identified and finds her happiness. It is perhaps the most conventional theme, but the Roma Theater in Moscow recently produced a play based on this novella.

IV

There are no places of escape in the nineteenth-century novel. One cannot return home without a compromise.

The old novels were based on the premise that a person accidentally falls out of his society. The nearly fatal condition of illegitimacy or loss of documents was a motive for the hero to wind up in a world that was the fate of millions. But the hero always escaped that world with the help of found documents. The hero of the old novel was a hero out of place, someone who belonged to a certain society but who has turned up in another one.

Love disrupts the hierarchy of people in a similar way.

Prévost's Chevalier des Grieux finds himself in a new situation as he forfeits his hereditary wealth to elope with Manon Lescaut. Above all, and unlike other heroes, he must forgive Manon who is constantly unfaithful to him. But des Grieux returns to her every time because he loves her.

Manon dies. Des Grieux buries her in the desert and then recounts everything that was then considered a crime. We are touched by these numerous betrayals.

We see that same love that Plato described to us through Diotima.

Eros is always poor, he sleeps in the streets or at the doors of houses. He is unkempt and miserable, always in search of what mortals and immortals desire.

Humanity seems to grow more and more melancholic, or perhaps we are perceiving grief in a more personal, profound way.

In the beginning of the novel, Anna Karenina is traveling in a train. The same train that later becomes the theme of her fate. She meets Vronsky's mother on the train, Vronsky follows Karenina's train in the snowstorm, and finally, in the end, Karenina dies under that same train.

Anna Karenina is coming home from Moscow to Petersburg. At this point she doesn't know yet that she is in love with Vronsky. She is only groping at her feelings as in a game when one is trying to find a hidden object and is told: "Hot, hotter, very hot!"

Karenina reads an English novel. But it's not pleasant to follow the reflected life of other people. She wants to take part in the action. She wants to experience everything. The hero of the anonymous novel was probably trying, with the help of a lawyer, to obtain documents for an estate and a title of nobility:

> The hero of the novel had nearly attained to his English happiness of a baronetcy and an estate, and Anna wanted to go to the estate with him, when she suddenly felt that he must have been ashamed, and that she was ashamed of the same thing—but what was he ashamed of? "What am I ashamed of?" she asked herself with indignant surprise. She put down her book, leaned back, and clasped the paper knife tightly in both hands. There was nothing to be ashamed of. She called up all her Moscow memories. They were all good and pleasant.

What was Anna Karenina ashamed of? Was she ashamed of the false happiness of the novel's characters or her future uncompromising fall? Her journey thus far is rather safe. She doesn't know yet that Vronsky will surge into the train, surge out of the storm that was "rushing and whistling between the wheels of the train," and that she will go to meet the storm.

Anna Karenina's story develops parallel to the story of Levin and Kitty. The families involved in the novel are the Oblonskys, the Karenins, the Vronskys, the Lvovs, and the Levins.

Levin is a good landowner: he knows that one must count the trees when selling a forest. Like all noblemen, he takes part in *zemstvo* elections, and though he has a few eccentricities, he is a man of his time and society.

But he belongs to a time where everything has been turned upside down and nothing makes sense anymore.

Tolstoy and Levin are somehow interrelated, though Levin's story is certainly not Tolstoy's memoir.

Tolstoy was a good landowner. Each time a daughter was born to him, he purchased land with a small forest, estimating that when his daughter reached marriageable age, the forest would also have grown, doubling in price—because a forest grows if you don't cut down the trees.

But Tolstoy was also a man out of place, though he acquired land and boasted of his ability to manage a household in front of another landowner, Afanasi Fet.

During those years when *Anna Karenina* was being conceived or, more precisely, when Tolstoy was just beginning to grasp the catastrophe of the woman who lost her place in society, or perhaps when Tolstoy saw the woman in the coachhouse by the railroad who threw herself under the train, he wrote to Fet in 1869: " . . . I finally decided to travel to Penza province to look at the estate in those backwoods that I intend on buying."

He wanted to buy an estate so that the price of the timber should cover the whole purchase price; a property with peasants living nearby, who owned next to nothing and would agree to work for any price.

In the meantime, there was a catastrophe already brewing parallel to this prosperous affair. It was maturing, but it seemed completely insane.

On September 4, 1869, Tolstoy wrote to his wife that he had spent the night in Arzamas: "It was 2 o'clock in the morning, I was terribly tired, I wanted to go to sleep and I felt perfectly well. But suddenly I was overcome by despair, fear and terror, the like of which I have never experienced before. I will tell you the details of this feeling later: but I have never experienced such an agonizing feeling before and may God preserve anyone else from experiencing it."

Tolstoy described the nightmare in *Memoirs of a Madman*. He mentioned Penza province and how the protagonist "looked out for some fool who did not understand business, and thought I had found such a man. An estate with large forests was being sold in Penza province. From all I could learn about it, it seemed that its owner was just such a fool as I wanted and the timber would cover the whole cost of the estate."[64]

The buyer is traveling with his servant, Sergei—most likely Sergei Arbuzov. He stays in a small room: "I remember that it tormented me that it should be square."

Through his whole being, the man becomes aware "of the necessity and the right to live and the inevitability of Death."

---

64   Lev Tolstoy, *Memoirs of a Madman*. In *Collected Shorter Fiction*. Vol. I. Translated by Louise and Aylmer Maude and Nigel J. Cooper. New York: Alfred A. Knopf, 2001. All subsequent quotations from *Memoirs of a Madman* are taken from this standard version.

Everything is written in a precise, disjointed, and unexpected manner for Tolstoy—"I found a brass candlestick with a burnt candle and lighted it. The red glow of the candle and its size—little less than the candlestick itself—told me the same thing."

"Always the same nightmare: red, white, and square."

This is how Anna Karenina dies. She falls into a torrent of memories, separates and registers individual features, perceives every movement that she makes, recalls that there is a little red handbag in her hand, feels how she quickly and lightly descends the steps that lead to the rails, and throws herself under the train: "A little peasant muttering something was working at the rails. The candle, by the light of which she had been reading that book filled with anxieties, deceptions, grief, and evil, flared up with a brighter light than before, lit up for her all that had before been dark, flickered, began to grow dim, and went out for ever."

This is how the novel, which had opened with a biblical epigraph about vengeance, ends.

What is forbidden? What ought to be punishable?

Anna Karenina was disloyal to her husband and loved another man; she was punished in the novel.

Levin is a faithful husband, a good family man, but at the end of the novel he is filled with melancholy and even despair.

Tolstoy, who created both threads in the novel, is also horrified at the thought of death; he tells about the "Arzamas horror," about the terrible square room and the dimming candle.

Dread and the feeling of approaching retribution lie beyond the events of the novel.

Eichenbaum thought that the image of the dimming candle seen by Tolstoy was poetic.

But rather, it was a sensation peculiar to Tolstoy—the "Arzamas horror."

The novel is full of realistic horrors.

Only Anna Karenina dies, but the horror is experienced both by Levin and by the person who considers that the path he has paved for Levin is the right path.

Tolstoy is a man out of place even in Yasnaya Polyana, the estate that he inherited.

He disliked Shakespeare and doesn't notice Hamlet's words that "the time is out of joint." Life goes on limping.

The reader might say: but the novel's hero is a typical person in typical circumstances; human beings are typically miserable.

This is true both in folklore and the novel when all circumstances appear to be crystal clear in the perspective of time.

But the hero of the fairy tale, as we have seen, is a person who has been slighted—the youngest son, the expelled daughter, or the banished wife.

The heroes of folklore are strewn with ashes of sorrow, they are sprinkled with the salt of difficult paths—journeys in the sea.

A typical person in typical circumstances is an unhappy person born in times of change, a person who is conscious of his loss of the place that he thought he had.

The hero is usually a person searching for his place because human beings change, they search for a place, want to become their own person, to triumph in the name of what they consider poetic and just. This was later called the prose of everyday life.

The heroes are people at the turning points of history; humanity perceives its changes through them, and the novel can't have a structure until it grasps the movement of history, the sudden change in relations. The stages of history are based on the disintegration of periods.

The poet is a person out of place, like Dante who is halfway across the world through the *Inferno* and *Purgatorio* to a faded *Paradiso*; he reexamines the past, turning over, overcoming the circles of hell.

One overcomes the past as he overcomes something very close to him, such as his own family, as Micah warned us: "For the son treats the father with contempt, the daughter rises up against her mother, the daughter-in-law against her mother-in-law, your enemies are members of your own household" (Micah 7:6).

Lev Tolstoy leaves his old house, which had lost its symmetrical harmony due to its hideous extensions; he leaves his wife, sons, daughters, daughters-in-law.

He had tested the route of escape in his stories and novels. He had studied the genealogies of aristocracy and searched for fellow-travelers for his flight.

Tolstoy parts with the past in *The Cossacks* (1852–1863), the unfinished novels "The Weary and the Burdened" and "The Decembrists" (1879–1884), *Memoirs of a Madman* (1884), *Father Sergius* (1890–1898), and *The Living Corpse* (1900). He wants to flee from home as Hadji Murad fled from Shamil, though Shamil holds his family hostage. Tolstoy describes the flight of Alexander I in *Fyodor Kuzmich* (1905), and the escape of a servant, Kornei Vasilyev, that same year.

In 1910 Tolstoy himself flees from home.

But they will tell me that I have chosen to write about a troubled man living in a country preparing for a revolution.

Is this applicable to the characters of Balzac?

It appears that Balzac tried to do everything that successful people do, but he certainly didn't flourish. How can we explain his failures? Is it pure coincidence?

Balzac supposedly did everything right. He was ahead of his time and outside of time, as it were. He bought land in the outskirts of Paris, tried his hand in the new field of typography. He was among those who knew that time was changing and people were starting to embody that change. But his consciousness was like a bird flying ahead of its time. And this famous writer with his famous walking stick, his famous novels, and his gorgeous suits was a man out of place in his own time, a failed businessman who saw what others couldn't possibly see.

As Marx said, the inventors and entrepreneurs who found new ventures in the name of new inventions are not the ones who become rich, but those who inherit the widowed ventures.

The inheritors too are participants in the movement—they are in the second row, marching after the first row of conquerors.

The construction of fairy tales, novels, short stories, the denouements of plays are all traditional, they are fixed, as it were, while consciousness constantly moves, it changes like the pathways of Don Quixote and the prudent Balzac, who didn't forget to change his name, adding the aristocratic-sounding *de* to help him fit into society.

Schemers, travelers, revolutionaries, women who leave their husbands—they all take action for different reasons. New countries are attractive, old lands are overused and begin to erode, old machines depreciate and stop generating profit, old moralities wear away, though their codes seem to be indestructible. But machines, systems will change, and so will the family structure, and soon priests will no longer unite the hands of couples in the church.

Humanity moves in contradictions, in its ascent, through the palpability of change, the change of systems, the change of functions in old rituals and social constructs. Humanity moves and consciousness changes. The history of literature is a record of the change in consciousness. We witness the creation of the world in the change of consciousness.

Man searches for his own place.

How did Marx evaluate Balzac and his characters? Paul Lafargue wrote in his recollections of Marx (1890):

> He ranked Cervantes and Balzac above all other novelists. In *Don Quixote* he saw the epic of dying-out chivalry whose virtues were ridiculed and scoffed at in the emerging bourgeois world. He admired Balzac so much that he wished to write a review of his great work *La Comédie Humaine* as soon as he had finished his book on political economy. He considered Balzac not only the historian of his time, but also the prophetic creator of characters who were still in the embryonic stage during the reign of Louis-Philippe I and did not fully develop until Napoleon III.

I am not insisting upon the universality of this definition, but I consider this observation to be substantially important.

Man as One of the Principles of Plot

Perhaps it would have been better to begin in the following way: "On plot as a method for studying man."

Tolstoy started *Anna Karenina* in the following way: "All happy families resemble one another, but each unhappy family is unhappy in its own way."

Happy families don't have a history. Or, more accurately, their history hasn't been discovered—there is no life without difficulty. Unhappy people are forced to recognize the cause of their misery.

A person struggles to attain happiness. Happiness is not stillness and tranquility, but a quality of consciousness. Happy people are kinetic, they are stable, but their stability is transient and there is no history there.

Abel was a keeper of sheep and Cain a tiller of the ground. Cain brought an offering to the Lord "from the fruit of the ground," while Abel brought "of the best firstlings of his flock." The Lord looked with favor on Abel and his offering, and rejected Cain.

In painting this was often depicted by showing the smoke from Abel's sacrifice rising to the sky and Cain's creeping on the ground. A conflict ensued: "The Lord said to Cain: 'Why are you so angry, and why has your countenance fallen? If you do well, will you not be accepted? And if you do not do well, sin is lurking at the door; its desire is for you, but you must master it'" (Genesis 4:3–7).

The conflict is detected, underscored by Cain's presumed guilt—his irritation with his brother. The conflict is resolved with murder.

Had Jacob not treated Joseph selectively, favoring him among his brothers, there would have been no conflict. The conflict arises quietly, it is accentuated through Joseph's prophetic dreams and maintained by the fact that Joseph is the only one among his brothers who receives a multicolored coat.

Achilles was famous and successful while fighting with other warriors, but the clashes between the Greeks and Trojans weren't material for the epic yet. When Agamemnon took possession of Achilles's beautiful captive, Achilles restrained himself from fighting back to avoid a direct confrontation, and only when he withdrew his troops from the battlefield did the scales begin to oscillate and the weighing pans lose balance. And then the epic begins.

The Iliad is about the events that take place after Achilles leaves the war. It's about the loss of his friend, his return to the battlefield to avenge for his loss, while already knowing that it would bring his own demise.

Had Odysseus not angered the gods, had Poseidon not prevented him from returning home, there would have been no material for the creation of the epic—the story of a person who can't return home.

He returns in the end disguised as a beggar.

He returns to a feast hosted by his wife's suitors—his rivals.

Aleksandr Veselovsky made a long catalogue of similar versions of the seemingly impossible scenario—a husband at his wife's wedding.

This scenario ended up in the typology catalogue of plots in Nikolai Andreev's companion to the fairy tales of Brothers Grimm.

That's how Odysseus the beggar sits on the ground among the suitor-rivals, the fake warriors, who fail to string his bow and make the bowstring resound with harmony.

That's how Dobrynia sits, disguised, at his wife's wedding with Alyosha Popovich.

The hero of the epic and the novel is a person out of place—a person with a broken state of affairs, someone who rebels, who changes everything.

Prometheus betrayed the gods and taught mortals how to make fire, thus changing the methods of sacrifice. He left his divine circle and aligned himself with a different system, for which he was chained to a mountain and tortured by an eagle—and hence the existence of the drama.

The unrecognized heir returns home where he finds that he has been replaced. He fights to regain his place. This story repeats with Orestes in Greece, Hamlet in Denmark, and in Russia.

In *The Seagull*, an innovative writer, Treplyov, is robbed of his place in the family; his mother has replaced him with the successful, and yet worthless, Trigorin. Treplyov's circumstances are worse than Hamlet's: his Ophelia—Nina Zarechnaya—is infatuated with Trigorin, too.

As in Shakespeare, Treplyov stages a "play within a play," but the new playwright is ridiculed in his mother's estate in the same way as Chekhov and Komissarzhevskaya were ridiculed in the Aleksandrinsky Theater.

A person out of place is someone who cannot actualize himself, who is fighting for his humanity and self-worth, for a place in history. This is the theme of art. It is an eternal conflict.

Art exposes the misrecognition of something new, and through misrecognition, one arrives at recognition. The son fights against his father and the father recognizes his son only in the final moment.

In *The Seagull*, the contender for the right to live is not acknowledged and dies. Incidentally, so does Hamlet.

The disinherited princes—Orestes, Hamlet, and the young prince in Mark Twain's *The Prince and the Pauper*—are the common heroes of art because they see differently from those chained by the habitual.

Art elevates and frees life, reexamining it anew because both the prince and his twin see the truth.

Voltaire's Candide, Fielding's Tom Jones, and Dickens's Oliver Twist all appear to be born out of wedlock. David Copperfield is a legitimate son but he is born after his father's death and his impoverished princedom—the house called "Rookery"—is seized by a gentleman with black whiskers, Mr. Murdstone, his stepfather.

Indeed, there were no rooks there. David's father had imagined that it was a rookery and everything was ghostly.

But people strive for the truth when trying to achieve justice, because the truth is not ghostlike, but it embodies the future to come.

Men who are declared dead in Dickens's novels live in the houses of their future brides unrecognized and pursue the hand of the woman who initially didn't love them.

The person out of place is perhaps an arrogant city-dweller, a young embittered man who rejects the girl who loves him, and later falls in love with somebody else's wife—the same girl who is now married to a nameless general.

Humanity is still on its way, which is why the person out of place is a traveler, a Robinson Crusoe on an uninhabited island, who must create all the elements of human civilization; Prince Myshkin, traveling in his mantle in late November, half mad; Dmitri Karamazov, deceived by his father; or the socially ambitious arriviste Rastignac—they are all heroes who transgress the ordinary. In art, the ordinary becomes visibly tangible, it is destroyed, ridiculed, and defeated.

For the old world, Pyotr Chaadaev, who was declared a madman, was a typical person in his typical place.

Gogol dreamed about a career in public service in order to restructure the world that had no place for him.

Tolstoy the landowner is a person out of place who builds a household and at the same time dreams of escape from home. His heroes left home too, they searched for another place in the world, tried to become Cossacks, were happy in prison where gunpowder tasted better than salt, became so undemanding that they thought the biting of lice helps to keep the body warm, as Pierre Bezukhov reasoned—one of the many illegitimately born heroes in Tolstoy's fiction.

The search for one's place in the world, restructuring of the world for oneself, war, heartaches, and false happy endings—this is the old history of literature and the biography of its heroes.

For a very long time this search seemed to have no end. The pretext for the search and attempts to overcome the Hegelian prose of everyday life were endless.

Menander, the most gifted Greek dramatist of the New Comedy, became the teacher of Plautus, Terence, Molière, and European comedy. The great master wrote apparently similar plays, the bases of which were identical as crystals, though we already have sixteen of his fragments now.

There were three recurring motifs at the center of all his comedies: violence, the abandonment of a child, and the recognition of the child by his parents.

People were out of place and the only way to escape their fate was through a new idenitification, a shift to another paradigm.

But their initial portrayal was like a veiled protest, since they existed as underprivileged subjects before the identification.

We will, however, begin not from Greek tragedy or Menander's comedy, but folklore.

A Note to the Chapter "Person Out of Place" and a Few Words on Ashes

Today we have such a multitude of fairy tales that it is quite impossible to try and make sense of them. We certainly can't retain them in memory, and there won't be enough index cards. We could create an enormous cybernetic machine, but what should it be programmed to do?

Of course, we shouldn't blame the fairy tales for this—there is no need to remember them all. One has to read and compare them, juxtaposing one against the other. Though the ideal task for me as a writer, not as an academician, would be to take a sample out of the barrel and make some general remarks based on that sample.

Knowing is equal to having foresight. Facts, multiplying, tear at their seams not only because the abilities of science are constantly growing but also because the seams are brought together with great difficulty. There are many similarities between fairy tale heroes from different nations far away from each other, and even time doesn't seem to change the fairy tales. Still, the fairy tale continues to live in reading and in theater.

Unlike other comparative works, Eleazar Meletinsky's *The Hero of the Fairy Tale* offers a broad overview of the the traditional fairy tale genre. In a chapter titled "The 'Low' Hero of the Fairy Tale," Meletinsky establishes two types of fairy tale heroes. A hero of noble birth, Ivan-Tsarevich, for example, and the low, "unpromising hero." I think it was Meletinsky who coined this phrase.

The low hero lives in abject filth. He is usually the youngest son, frequently an orphan, he may be half human and half beast. He is not handsome and he is typically bald-headed.

The hero's baldness is particularly emphasized in the East.

In the end, the bald-headed character becomes the lucky hero. He is the hero of the Karakalpak epic called *The Forty Maidens*.

I also want to mention another bald-headed hero who was not brought up in Meletinsky's book—the prophet Elisha. Not only was he bald but also quick to take offense.

When he was passing by a town one day, some small children jeered at him: "Go away, baldhead! Go away, baldhead!" The prophet was enraged: "When he turned around and saw them, he cursed them in the name of the Lord. Then two she-bears came out of the woods and mauled forty-two of the boys" (II Kings 2:23–24).

It is a grave insult to remind someone of his baldness. The slighted person can recover and avenge himself in such a terrible way only in a fairy tale, as did Elisha.

The low hero is excluded from the family hearth, as it were. He lives in the refuse where the ashes are still warm.

Hence the name of the heroine from a popular fairy tale—Cinderella. In an Azerbaijani fairy tale the hero rolls in cinders.

Another character related to Cinderella is Zapechnik, often called Ivan Popelov—he sleeps on or behind the stove. In a Karelo-Finnish fairy tale he cleans out the ashes.

The ashes and someone else's cooling stove have been the oldest sites associated with the wretched.

At the turn of the twentieth century in old Bukhara, the homeless tramps, who were often required to carry out executions and were given the clothes of the condemned, warmed up their bodies by the cooling stoves of the public bathhouse. The bathhouse, according to the Tajik writer Sadriddin Ayni, was adjacent to the town square where the executions took place.

Ash is the waste left after the fire. It is a sign of humiliation. And I think that lamentation—the strewing of ashes on one's head as an expression of grief, stems from here.

Abraham says in the Book of Genesis, "I who am but dust and ashes" (18:27). In the Book of Job, the afflicted sits among the ashes. In Psalm 102, the psalmist says, "I eat ashes like bread." In Ezekiel, the mourners strew dust on their heads, while the Prophet in Lermontov's poem says:

> I strewed my head with ashes then,
> Fled the black town, forlorn and bare.

This is an image that appears frequently. It goes back to the time when man was not allowed to go near the fire and he warmed his bones by the heap of swept-out ashes.

There are many explanations regarding the choice of such places: the collapse of primordial communism, the collapse of tribal relations, the so-called *minorat*—a long standing custom by which inheritance descended to the youngest male heir, the change in family relations, and so on.

But all of these causes led to one and the same condition, and fairy tales select from this differently originated but same condition.

So let's classify the bald-headed, the black sheep, the orphans, the cinderellas, and the ugly ducklings into a type of character who is out of place.

It is tragic when Monsieur Verdoux drinks rum for the first time before his execution and says that he doesn't like it.

It is tragic because he won't be able to try anything else in his life. It doesn't matter whether he likes something or not—his remark reveals the tragedy of a person who will be executed in a few minutes, yet who behaves as if he will be having many other drinks.

I discuss this in such great detail because art exists only through particularity, and behind all fairy tale devices and volumes of novels, behind all plot maneuvers and similarities in novels stands the storyteller, the person who narrates these things as if for the very first time, leading you through familiar pathways, as it were, and yet showing you new things.

And so—the person out of place is a common hero of art.

He is not settled in the old world.

The state of being out of place is the state of a typical person in typical circumstances. Werther, Don Quixote, and even Don Juan and Eugene Onegin are unhappy men and they are typical because despair and grief were typical in our past.

They might ask me: But isn't Hamlet, Prince of Denmark, a handsome man and an adroit fencer? We have seen him on stage—he is a real prince!

Yes, he is as handsome and good-looking as the biblical Joseph, and brave as Stepan Razin.

All the same, he must play the role of the madman and walk around in stockings that are "fouled, ungartered, and down-gyved to his ankle."

Prince Lev Nikolaevich Myshkin is another "unpromising hero" who suffers from epilepsy and later becomes an idiot. He is an heir to a large fortune, but travels by train in a third-class carriage at the end of November wearing a sleeveless mantle with a large cape and shivers from cold.

They will call him an idiot to his face, they will slap him, but in Dostoevsky's intention, he is not a funny Don Quixote but the bearer of a new truth.

Another "unpromising hero" is the young boy—the grandson of a ruined master dyer—a ragpicker, later a dishwasher on a ship—Aleksei Peshkov[65]—the real, documental hero of many books. And so is the homeless Mayakovsky, walking along the endless streets of the Garden Ring in Moscow, while the houses glare at him like angry dogs.

He is the man whom nobody wants to bet on, who doesn't have any practical skills, who isn't involved in the prejudices of his time, who tries to resolve things but often can't find new solutions to old debates.

---

65   Maksim Gorky, who was born Aleksei Maksimovich Peshkov.

I already mentioned the hero whom you know very well—Charlie Chaplin—the poor tramp in somebody else's suit and shoes that don't fit, but who always wins in the end. He defeats the giants and villains, transforming them into kinder beings. He always triumphs and then leaves. He is the forerunner of the Poor People's Campaign in America.

The man who rides in a car, yet picks up cigarette butts.

He is the Columbus of American poverty.

Everyone loves Chaplin. The actor who impersonates one and the same character—the person out of place, wearing someone else's clothes.

The failed hero is often a fool. He is lazy, he doesn't want to do anything. This type has been fully developed in the Russian fairy tale and, to a degree, in the Arabic tale (Aladdin, for example).

As a result it turns out that Ivan the Fool is not devoid of ironic ingenuity. He is brave, sometimes sly and inexhaustible in his efforts, only it seems that he doesn't notice any of his heroic deeds or isn't able to prove his authorship right away.

One can trace the characteristics of a former failure in Ilya Muromets, who spent his childhood on a stove. This dormant state on the stove—a place that excludes one from everyday life in the hut, is typical of the fool. Nothing, of course, suggests that Ilya Muromets is stupid. But he is unfortunate in another way—he was born a cripple who could not walk for thirty-three years, until one day men in old rags came to the house and gave him a magical drink of superhuman strength.

You always encounter the low hero in fairy tales. He usually has older brothers who detest him. In the end, he defeats them despite their tricks and crimes.

The older brothers cheat and betray the hero, sometimes they even kill him, but he resurrects and marries the princess.

I could go on with my list of low "unpromising heroes." Instead I suggest that we examine the fairy tale not from the perspective of historical antiquity, tracing it back to its primordial origins, but to analyze it through the laws of contemporary art by reversing our binoculars, as it were.

We can easily recognize the old failure-hero of the fairy tale who commits heroic deeds in contemporary novels, plays, and films. The low "unpromising hero" reappears in various periods and various places but differently each time. It seems to me that given the variety of the *causes* of this phenomenon, we should focus more on the causes of its *consistency*. It is important to establish not only *how* phenomena are determined by a particular situation but also *why* it is separated, with such consistency, from the vast repository of diverse phenomena. Structures of art go through processes of construction and selection. We must determine the laws of selection, find out not *how*, but *for what purpose* some structures get crystallized.

Let me remind you again that the "high" hero of the fairy tale—Ivan-Tsarevich—is depicted in a state of despair: he is searching for his abducted bride.

Recognition

Recognition is a motif that recurs frequently in Greek tragedy. A person turns out to be someone else—other than who people thought he was. He finds himself not in the kinds of relationships with others that he had anticipated. He looks closely and finds himself as if deluded.

Aristotle writes in Chapter 14 in *Poetics*:

> Let us then determine what are the circumstances which strike us as terrible or pitiful. Actions capable of this effect must happen between persons who are either friends or enemies or indifferent to one another. If an enemy kills an enemy, there is nothing to excite pity either in the act or the intention—except so far as the suffering in itself is pitiful. So again with indifferent persons. But when the tragic incident occurs between those who are dear to one another—if, for example, a brother kills, or intends to kill, a brother, a son his father, a mother her son, a son his mother, or any other deed of the kind is done—these are the situations to be looked for in myths.

In this case, *myth* means legend, a crystallized incident. It can also have another meaning—a story (*skazanie*), an oral account, or the essence of an act.

Aristotle continues:

> This, then, is why a few families only, as has been already observed, furnish the subjects of tragedy. It was not art, but happy chance, that led the poets in search of subjects to impress the tragic quality upon their plots. They are compelled, therefore, to have recourse to those houses whose history contains moving incidents like these.

Subsequently, many tragedians began to hold gatherings in the houses of those "few families." And as a result they created a relatively consistent model of action appropriate for tragedies. The model is selectively controlled, not everything that happens in life goes into it but only what is suitable for the representation in the action of what excites certain emotions.

Systems, selected from received myths that were somehow a reality for the author, become a tradition or a variety of genre, and various techniques of depiction emerge in each system, among which we will discuss recognition. It interests us not only as pure form, but also as an emergence of a model for the literary work.

And so, we know that during a certain period in the creation of classical tragedy it was essential to have a contradiction of action. A person thinks that he is acting in a certain way, while the meaning of his action is the opposite. Due to this, the action itself is reinterpreted; the object of the action is understood anew. A person intends to punish his enemy and he punishes someone from his own family or himself, because it turns out that he is the offender. This is the tragedy of Oedipus. There has to be recognition in order for a discovery to take place, which will lead to a reinterpretation of the action. For recognition, the person who appears to be the subject of recognition mustn't know at first about the details of his birth, or the others mustn't know of his origins, or they must think of him perversely.

Let's quote Aristotle once more, as he was the first to be interested in this question:

> What Recognition is has been already explained. We will now enumerate its kinds. First, the least artistic form, which, from poverty of wit, is most commonly employed—

recognition by signs. Of these some are congenital—such as "the spear which the earth-born race bear on their bodies," or the stars introduced by Carcinus in his *Thyestes*. Others are acquired after birth, and of these some are bodily marks, as scars; some external tokens, as necklaces, or the little ark in the *Tyro* by which the discovery is effected. Even these admit of more or less skillful treatment. Thus in the recognition of Odysseus by his scar, the discovery is made in one way by the nurse, in another by the swineherds. (Chapter 16)

Recognition was effected through body marks and objects—often a ring or medallion, and ocassionally documents.

In the following pages I will endeavor to show the seemingly autonomous development of the scene of recognition. But I will also show how that autonomy is, in fact, imaginary. In reality, it occurs because people, artists change. They don't repeat the past as much as they change it. Repetition is, to a degree, illusory. The purpose of change is to depart from conventions, widen the scope of the model's meaning, and at the same time bring it closer to reality. Different motives can be employed to achieve this purpose.

In *The Libation Bearers* (the second play of Aeschylus's *Oresteia*), Electra comes to the grave of her murdered father. She waits for her brother's return, hoping that Orestes will avenge Agamemnon's death. Electra finds a strand of hair on the tomb and footprints nearby. Next, the play unfolds in a dialogue between Electra and the sympathetic Chorus of her slave-women.

Electra: Someone has cut a strand of hair and laid it on the tomb.

Chorus: What man? Or was it some deep-waisted girl?

Electra: There is a mark, which makes it plain for any to guess.

Chorus: Explain, and let your youth instruct my elder age.

Electra: No one could have cut off this strand, except myself.

Chorus: Those others, whom it would have become, are full of hate.

Electra: Yet here it is, and for appearance matches well . . .[66]

Recognition is delayed with the help of conventional dialogue with the Chorus.

The strand of hair is thus discredited. But there is another sign—the footprints:

But see, here is another sign. Footprints are here.
The feet that made them are alike, and look like mine.
There are two sets of footprints: of the man who gave
his hair, and one who shared the road with him. I step
where he has stepped, and heelmarks, and the space between
his heel and toe are like the prints I make.

66   Aeschylus, *Oresteia*. Translated by Richmond Lattimore. U of Chicago P, 1953.

Now let's see how Sophocles reworks the same scene in his *Electra*. Electra's sister, Chrysothemis, recounts that she has seen their father's tomb wreathed in flowers, and—

> Right there on the edge.
> A lock of hair, fresh cut.[67]

Electra doesn't believe that it is the hair of Orestes and says to Chrysothemis, "Poor lunatic. I feel sorry for you."

She doesn't believe her sister because she has received news about their brother's death. Then Orestes reveals himself and it turns out that he is alive. To prove his identity, he shows a ring:

> Orestes : Look at this ring—our father's—
> Electra: Father's!
> Orestes: —and see what I mean.

At this point recognition, earlier refuted, becomes possible.

The peripeteia is still functioning here but it has become even more convoluted.

The scene of recognition has been preserved for thousands of years. It is necessary to free the person out of place.

Sophocles tries to complicate the old scene of recognition. The resemblance of hair is too conventional though. The footprints of the brother and the sister are probably not identical either. They most likely have different heights and have lived different lives.

---

67 Sophocles, *Electra*. Translated by Anne Carson. Oxford UP, 2001.

They may even be wearing different shoes—it is unlikely that both siblings are barefooted.

The scene is developed further and passed down to Menander. It is changed because the purpose of recognition has changed. Dramatists start to show ordinary life, the fate of the common man who is not a hero. It is a difficult fate. In order to unravel the knot they start to show a rare incident where the oppressed protagonist turns out to be of noble blood. Here is where the theme of freedom from captivity begins to emerge.

The works of Bret Harte and O. Henry preserve the ancient methods. A person is identified by his tattoo or a phrase such as "ticktock," which he used as a child to describe the clock. The character refers to the clock in his parents' house using that same phrase.

In later works, recognition plays as though a secondary role. Mark Twain has a short novel called *Pudd'nhead Wilson*: a mulatto slave, the wet nurse of her master's infant son, switches her own son and the master's son in their cribs. The slave's son becomes a respectable man, while the master's son is turned into a slave. There is a man in the same town who pursues such odd hobbies as palmistry and fingerprinting. He collects fingerprints from everyone, including the children. Consequently, when a murder takes place and the murderer leaves his fingerprints on the knife, Wilson is not only able to identify the criminal but also verify that he is the switched son of the slave. The novel repeats the intent of Menander's motif of recognition.

Art—fighting against the habitual and ascertaining the true qualities of man—makes repeated validations proving that man, in reality, is of noble origin. The need for such a model existed for a very long time, though of course today it has been almost completely abandoned.

What is the unifying premise of these endless recognitions and when do they end?

Let me remind you of the king's daughter who had to escape from home disguised in a donkey skin, or the princess whose tongue was cut off and who was forced out of her home.

At the basis of this motif, at least for the modern audience, lies the attempt to show the person *out of place* and to prove that every person is a human being.

Chekhov once said that he is tired of turning his works upside down as Levitan used to do. After finishing a painting, his friend Isaac Levitan would turn the canvas upside down and examine it in that position in order to see with fresh eyes the correlation between colors.

The scene of recognition has been employed in many different ways, but in Mark Twain the "white" master and the "passing for white" slave, who are returned to their proper places, are nearly identical. The true hero, it turns out, is the slave mother, who agrees to be sold once more in order to help her son repay his gambling debts. She is the most generous. The master's son is a slave like the rest.

The conventional scene of recognition has been refuted here. The true recognition in the novel is the revelation that Wilson, who was mocked in the provincial town as "pudd'nhead," turns out to be a great man.

The common motif has been rejected.

A Few Words about the New in Shakespeare

Shakespeare didn't create new plots. He took existing ones and re-interpreted them. His great plays were adaptations, deconstructed and reexamined versions of existing dramas and novellas.

In 1566, Giraldi Cinthio published *Hecatommithi*, which included a novella about a Venetian Moor.

The old novellas used to have "annotated" titles. We used to submit script proposals to the film factory in the form of those annotations. The annotation was supposed to include the situation, meaning an introduction of the sides that would be juxtaposed against one another in the film, and a description of the conflict. The following is an example of a script proposal for *Othello*:

> A Moorish general marries a Venetian woman. One of his lieutenants accuses her in front of her husband of adultery, and the husband orders his lieutenant to kill the man. The Moor kills his wife. The lieutenant denounces him. The Moor refutes the charges but due to convincing evidence is condemned to banishment. The criminal lieutenant, who masterminds the ruin of yet another man, eventually brings a wretched death upon himself.

The actions of the characters in this proposal seem to be recounted by a lawyer.

The novella doesn't make any pleadings but it contains a moral lesson. Only Disdemona is partially vindicated.

According to the novella, she falls in love with the Moor "not by a woman's whim but moved by his valor."

Let's try to differentiate the new application of the given situation and the change of its function.

The intrigue in the novella coincides with the intrigue in the play—Disdemona's intercessions on behalf of the captain, the involvement of the ensign's wife and the episode with the handkerchief. The story has a conventional moral, which is formulated through Disdemona:

> And much I fear that I shall prove a warning to young girls
> not to marry against the wishes of their parents, and that
> the Italian ladies may learn from me not to wed a man
> whom nature and habitude of life estrange from us.

For someone who knows Shakespeare's plays, the novella might seem like a retelling by a spectator who saw *Othello, the Moor of Venice* and, not understanding a thing, retold what he saw to his folks at home, while completely missing the point.

Shakespeare proved that Othello and Desdemona must love one another. Their love conquers all obstacles and the only thing that separates them is the crime. Iago isn't simply envious, he represents the ordinary. He is the one who tells Othello that Desdemona had betrayed her father when she fell in love with him, and thus could betray Othello, too.

The motive of action can be changed, but the motives of the function for which certain actions are described or performed are as if the essence of every composition. A change of those motives means a change of genre.

Motives can be parodied, but even the parodied motives can, in turn, change their own—non-parodic—action. For example, Don Quixote's actions imitate the actions of heroes from chivalric romances, and yet those heroes don't fight against useless things with useless weapons: Don Quixote's deeds appear to be comical, but the hero commits them with good intention and bravery. He has his own philosophy, his own conception of what the world should be like.

Which is why the externally parodic actions of the hero turn out to be tragic.

In the Italian novella, the Moor plans to kill Disdemona in such a way that the murder wouldn't be discovered. He is a criminal who is afraid of retribution. His despair in regards to his wife's "adultery" is accompanied with a feeling of self-preservation. He kills her with a sandbag to make sure that her body shows no signs of bruising. Then with the help of his accomplice he collapses a part of the ceiling in Disdemona's chamber, in other words—he stages her death so that it looks like an accident.

The ensign denounces the Moor and he is arrested. They torture him to obtain the truth, but the Moor denies everything. Then they condemn him to perpetual banishment, where he is eventually slain by Disdemona's kinsmen. The ensign is likewise tortured and dies a miserable death.

Cinthio's story is about crime, while Shakespeare's story is about love and the tragedy of love. Othello doesn't want to hide his crime. When right before her death Desdemona refutes Othello's murderous act, he reproaches her for her lie.

Desdemona, having a premonition of her own death, sings a song about a willow. It's a simple song. The daughter of a Venetian Senator, a woman belonging to the highest ranks of aristocracy, sings a maid's song before her death. The simplicity of the song is stressed; Desdemona explains where it came from:

My mother had a maid call'd Barbara:
She was in love, and he she loved proved mad
And did forsake her: she had a song of "willow;"
An old thing 'twas, but it express'd her fortune,
And she died singing it: that song to-night
Will not go from my mind; I have much to do,
But to go hang my head all at one side,
And sing it like poor Barbara. Prithee, dispatch. (Act IV,
Scene 3)

One involuntarily imagines Desdemona's posture as she sings a maid's song—it's the posture of an ordinary woman. She sings leaning her head against her hand.

There is an exquisite poem by Anna Akhmatova about jealousy and misunderstanding that leads to a catastrophe between a man and a woman. The poet describes a "silver willow" which has broken into the conversation. It is a remarkable willow but it's a quotation from high poetry.

The difference with Shakespeare, the difference with Cervantes is in the vast amplitude between the high and the low; they introduce a new kind of heterogeneity of episodes.

Structure subordinates a range of different materials. The laws of the literary structure demand variety in the material. Desdemona dies an ordinary death, she dies like any other woman, and she loves Othello as any woman loves a man, even if he is not in charge of fleets and isn't a conqueror.

Ophelia, having gone mad, comes to the castle and hands out flowers, which are probably imaginary. She sings popular folksongs and cites the symbolic and even cryptic meanings of the flowers. She comes to the castle as if from the woods or from the street, bringing with her popular sayings.

The world of Shakespeare is heterogeneous. Jesters talk to kings and win arguments; gravediggers aren't just servants who must bury corpses from the tragedies that transpire in the castle—they evaluate life.

The jesters appeared in comedy long before Shakespeare. They came to the stage with their own traditional forms of clownery.

Great art is contradictory, and this contradiction is expressed through the heterogeneity of materials that go into it.

Great art contradicts its own time by standing in the front lines, or more precisely, by moving forward.

The astonishing thing for Shakespeare is not that Desdemona fell in love with the Moor, but why the Moor didn't trust her love. Why did he believe in Iago's words, blindly accepting the petty rumor and its intended malevolence, yet didn't believe in simple love?

This new meaning of inequality is Shakespeare's own discovery.

Shylock is a villain to Shakespeare. But he sees in Shylock not just a covetous moneylender who loves only his money, but also a father and a sympathetic character who has emotions just as those who despise him and whom he himself hates.

The tragedy of Romeo and Juliet was modeled after Matteo Bandello's novella.

Bandello collected his novellas in the second half of the sixteenth century. The story about Romeo and Juliet had the following annotation: "The misadventures and sad death of two lovers: one dies after taking poison, the other dies from grief."

The author traces the incident that served as the novella's source to the beginning of fourteenth century. He retells something memorable, something that was universalized by antiquity.

The heroes in the novella have the same names as the characters in the future play. The difference between the play and the novella is not in the actions of heroes or what happens to them, but how they analyze what is happening to them, how they interpret their own fate. The interpretation is profusely metaphorical and heightens the tension of the events. This realistic profusion of emotion creates a tension in the action, which amplifies the meaning of hostility between the feuding houses.

The towered castles that stood in Verona were the houses of the city's nobility. There is an old Genoese fortress on the southeastern coast of Crimea, in Sudak—it stretches slantingly on the crest of a hill. Its towers have been preserved. Each tower, they say, belonged to a household that built it and defended it from invaders. The city united the factions, people's fates, households, guilds, and consecrated grounds. People fought for their own interests. Household feuds were anything but trivial, though they could be revealed through trivialities.

The conflicts are constructed in great detail. Romeo isn't just someone from a mutinous household (this isn't important to him yet: he is young and everybody loves him in the city) but he is also a loyal friend. He has no choice but to kill Juliet's cousin because his best friend had been killed. The feud between the households unfolds for him under a different pretext. He avenges not for his own kin but for friendship.

Romeo and Juliet are in love. They are still very young. But their love is so strong that it transforms them into eloquent speakers. Their eloquence exceeds everything. The love of Juliet and Romeo absorbs the whole world. The surrounding external world, as Hegel wrote in *Aesthetics*, finds "a counterpart to its own inner being."

Let's look again at Juliet's monologue,[68] which deeply fascinated Hegel:

> Come, night!—Come, Romeo! come thou day in night!
> For thou wilt lie upon the wings of night
> Whiter than new snow on a raven's back.—
> Come, gentle night; come, loving, black-brow'd night,
> Give me my Romeo: and when he shall die
> Take him and cut him out in little stars,
> And he will make the face of heaven so fine,
> That all the world will be in love with night,
> And pay no worship to the garish sun.— (Act III, Scene 2)

Hegel thought that metaphors and similes overburden the play, hindering the hero and distracting from the situation of the given act. He wrote: "Of course the images and comparisons in Shakespeare are now and then awkward and multiplied." But even so, by burdening the person, the comparisons lift him above the restrictions of life without tearing him from the things that are perceptible to his heart.

In *Hadji Murad*, Tolstoy describes an evening when the major's wife, Maria Dmitrievna, goes on a walk with a young officer, Butler, who is in love with her.

---

68 Shklovsky is citing this passage a second time, here in Boris Pasternak's translation. The first translation, cited in the chapter "Image and Riddles," was done by Tatyana Shchepkina-Kupernik.

The moon shines behind them and the shadows of their heads appear to be encircled with a halo. Apparently it is possible to have such a refraction of light—in any case, I believe Tolstoy. But this kind of separation of the hero, the underscoring of his exquisiteness—this is real. It is a sign of elevation, necessary for determining the human qualities.

In the novella, Juliet's cousin attacks Romeo. Romeo doesn't want to fight him. He is only spared thanks to the scale armor he is wearing. Tybalt dies by accident.

In Shakespeare, Tybalt assaults Mercutio and kills him. Of all characters, Pushkin liked Mercutio the best.

He described Mercutio as the spirit of the Renaissance—the buoyant, generously frivolous man whose life is full of joy.

It is Romeo's duty to fight Juliet's cousin. He has nothing in his defense. He finds himself in a situation where he must kill a man, knowing that his action will deprive him of Juliet forever.

As to the final scene of the play—Juliet's simulation of death and the events taking place by the tombs—it is all very traditional. The faked death of the hero and his reanimation is a common motif in the Italian novella. In the eighth story of the third day in *The Decameron*, Ferondo, having taken a certain powder, is interred for dead. Similar incidents occur in the tenth story of the fourth day, first story of the ninth day, and fourth story of the tenth day.

The motif is most effective when the simulated corpse is "resurrected" as a beloved person—that's the case in the last novella that I just mentioned.

The old models, old structures in Shakespeare's works were overturned, as it were. Tolstoy, a great critic of Shakespearean plots, criticized the dramatist saying that his tragedies were illogical compared to their novellistic sources. Indeed, the tragedies are contradictory and it was Shakespeare who engineered the contradictions.

But the same Tolstoy also emphasized the contradictoriness of the heroes' actions in Dostoevsky.

He argued that King Lear acted in a strangely irrational way. Lear gave away his kingdom and crown to his daughters. And yet he maintained some authority, keeping several of his loyal men. He wanted to rule as a king by giving away the fulcrum of his reign. He thought that reigning was natural to him, as feathers are natural to a bird. He was still a king from head to toe, though by giving away his power, he also forfeited his reign. His daughters undermined his authority and drove him away from his own house. He wandered in the storm, making eloquent speeches, arguing with his fool—all of this is strange for Tolstoy. His poetics is different, and he can't judge someone else's poetics better than us because he is partial to his own poetics. Time was up for the Shakespearean Lear, he had tired from the world. He wanted to pass his condition on to someone else, he didn't want to participate in the falsehoods of the world. Lear wanted to separate himself from everything. I will tell you what the actor Solomon Mikhoels said about Tolstoy's opinion of the Shakespearean tragedies.

Mikhoels played the part of King Lear. He read widely and it took him a long time to prepare for the role.

He read Tolstoy's pamphlet on Shakespeare. Tolstoy's objections sounded convincing to him.

But then he thought: Didn't Tolstoy also divide his property, give everything to his children and then leave home in late autumn?

While it's true that he didn't die in the steppe but in a train station, he wandered restlessly. The impossible turned out to be possible.

Sometimes the representation of great conflicts exceeds reality, as it were. But those conflicts are real.

They don't happen to everyone, but art lifts our heart to the level of tragedy.

Art evokes in us feelings that might seem useless. It makes a person worthy of its essence.

YURI TYNJANOV

The City of Our Youth

Petersburg wasn't known yet as Petrograd.

The tram cars didn't go as far as the seashore.

Nevsky Prospect was paved with wood blocks and ended not at Vosstaniya Square but at what was called Znamenskaya Square.

There used to be a Bityug in the square, standing on a wide platform with wide-spread hind legs as though he was suffering from kidney stones.

With a lowered head, the heavy built horse dug his front hoofs into the granite, his forehead as if propped against an invisible wall.

The stout equestrian looked cumbersome with his flat face, flat beard, and flat lambskin hat.[69]

The monument was erected as a symbolic beginning of the road to the Pacific, but what it really marked was the end of the Russian monarchy. The last imperial dynasty had already celebrated its three hundred years of rule.

It was sculpted, not without irony, by Paolo Trubetskoy of the famous Trubetskoy family.

---

69 The controversial monument to Alexander III, erected in 1909, was an open caricature of the counter-reformist and unpopular Emperor that caused an intense public scandal.

On the right side of the monument, along the canal track, stretched Ligovka Street with its narrow houses built on strips of land that used to be the coachmen's neighborhood. The village on the outskirts of the city was turned into a busy, loud, dirty station road. It used to have its own newspaper called *Malenkaya gazeta* (The Little Gazette), edited by Uncle Vanya—Ivan Lebedev—the well-known referee of French boxing.

Right behind the monument was the quiet neighborhood called Peski where functionaries lived. It had empty streets, a Greek church at the center, and a cheap apartment building with double gates, through which ran a railway to the industrial zone near Shlisselburgsky Prospect.

There were hospitals nearby.

Not too far away from the Greek church, on the third floor of the bleak building, in a relatively large and empty apartment that belonged to someone else lived the young poet and philologist Yuri Tynjanov. He was one of Vengerov's students from his seminar on Pushkin at the University of Petersburg.

It was a quiet neighborhood by the Smolny Institute, which used to be a school for noble girls. The ponds of the Tauride Garden pondered in silence around the Palace that housed the lethargic Imperial State Duma.

As a sign of its activity, the brick octagonal water tower reddened between the Duma and the Neva.

The barracks surrounding the Tauride Palace were mute. Sentries guarded the gates. The paved grounds were quiet. Everything seemed compressed like steam in a boiler.

Two gendarmes stood at every crossroad of the city, winter and summer, with rifles hanging over their shoulders. They wore pointed *bashlyk* hoods in the freezing cold to cover their ears.

The city was quiet, especially in the winter. It was gloomy in the autumn.

The university was a noisy place for us. It was often raided by the police. It stretched on the northern embankment of the Neva, which was famous for flooding the city.

Every person has a vivid picture at the bottom of his memory, like golden sand washed in a sieve.

That picture illuminates and colors one's life from below.

Dante, in *La Vita Nuova*, recollects himself as a boy when he was nine and saw Beatrice for the first time: "She appeared dressed in noblest color, restrained and pure, in crimson, tied and adorned in the style that then suited her very tender age."[70]

The memories and commentaries of the art theoretician in this book are interspersed with sonnets.

Years later, in *The Divine Comedy*, the poet describes a chariot similar to the one in Ezekiel's vision. Dante writes about his beloved:

> I found the gaze of her I had seen appear
> Erewhile, veiled, in the angelic festival,
> Toward me, this side the stream, directed clear. (*Purgatorio* XXX)[71]

She is still wearing the bright crimson dress—certain memories never fade away.

---

70   Dante Alighieri, *La Vita Nuova*. Translated by A. S. Kline.

71   Dante Alighieri, *The Divine Comedy*. Translated by Laurence Binyon. Viking Press, 1947. All subsequent quotations from *The Divine Comedy* are taken from this standard version.

Occasionally, the mind retains color as if it were a flag on the shore that one has left, or as if it were an oath.

Memory is always contradictory.

I remember the strange, angular ghost—a slanting angel in the mist, behind the Nikolaevsky Bridge.

It was the first crane that I saw then rising from behind the ship-building yard, across the big, clayey ripples of the Neva like an imprint of a cobblestone road.

Here Petersburg started with factories that got interrupted with palaces, and then again behind the Liteiny Bridge—right of Vyborgskaya Embankment and left of Shlisselburgsky Prospect—stood the red brick factory buildings, emitting smoke.

You could hardly ever see a blue sky above the city. But our student caps had bright blue bands.

Memories appear over the Neva in short spurts, between the smoke and the clouds.

There used to be a dockyard between the river entrances to the Admiralty decorated with anchors and wreathed spires. Now the open space has been crammed with a bank, a theater, and something else.

The yellow hands of the Admiralty jut out from the surrounding junk as the hands of a drowning person.

The low bent edges of the waves rock.

A person returns to his cradle and tries to rock it wanting to hear the old squeak.

The Neva rocked on its bluish clayey waves. Squeaking, the Palace Bridge (back then it was a temporary pontoon bridge) floated awkwardly on the river; its bank abutments and river supports were secured with thick yellow cables coated with rosin.

It smelled like tar. The bridge made a long, drawn-out bass sound.

The bridge moves, it squeaks. Behind it, leaning against the Spit of Vasilyevsky Island, stands the Petersburg Stock Exchange with its white Doric columns. The narrow red sidewall of the university building is further down.

The university cuts across the Vasilyevsky Island like a red line in a bookkeeper's journal.

Rattling with their oarlocks, green yawls built from Peter's sketches swim slantingly from the stony slopes of the Admiralty Embankment toward the university. Old steamships with low decks pass along the Neva.

The university building has two floors. The main corridor stretches over the arches of the ground floor and it's filled with light.

The barges by the Palace Bridge move slowly from side to side. In the winter, intercepting one another, violent blizzards whirl over the Neva.

In the evening, through the winter blizzard, students in visor caps with blue bands and old overcoats with raised collars walk toward the red building. They pass along planked walkways bordered with the double-dashed yellow lines of the kerosene lamps. The freezing bronze buttons rub against their cheeks. We didn't wear warm hats, our coats were rarely made of wadded cotton.

Blue caps, short *tuzhurka* jackets, fast paces, and loud animated voices.

The wide Neva is the heading line of the new history.

Somber palaces, the steep helmet of St. Isaac's Cathedral, the Admiralty, and behind the palaces—streams of smoke. The city of palaces stands on the palm of the city of factories. You can see the future: look around, you'll see the distant cranes over there, on your right, by the seashore, and the distant smoke of factories on your left. The

great, vast city engulfed in water—the city of poetic inspiration . . .
The city of white nights . . . The city of floods and revolutions.

The University

Fair- and dark-haired students crisscross the university corridor,
passing by the yellow ashwood bookcases.

Here you could run into a tall, nearly gaunt young man—
Vladimir Shileiko, who always separated himself from the rest.
I think he was one of the few scholars in the world who studied Sumero-Akkadian languages and translated the epic of Gilgamesh, which, compared to Homer's epics and the Bible, is a
much older book.

This is where the carefree law students who seemed unconcerned
with studies, the fretful and perplexing mathematicians, and we,
the philologists of all types, would gather.

This is where I first saw Osip Mandelstam—the poet with curly
hair and narrow face, who walked with his head thrown back.

Here, nearly half a century ago, I became friends with a youthful,
handsome man with dark eyes whose name was Yuri Nikolaevich
Tynjanov. He was participating in Vengerov's seminar.

The reputable professor Semyon Afanasyevich Vengerov, who
was not yet old and dressed carelessly in his long black frock coat,
looked dignified with his already graying beard.

Vengerov's method was empiricism. He tried to find out everything about the writer, especially about his biography, and to record
everything.

If he were to design a cathedral, bibliography cards would be its icons. When he started digressing, he couldn't stop. He kept starting one book after another. They would break off from the first letters because they were organized alphabetically, and there are many letters in the alphabet. He edited and published the works of classics, inserting in each volume miscellaneous portraits and pictures of the particular author as illustrations.

History for him moved alphabetically, and like the alphabet it was static.

It didn't ever need to move, it stood in place fixed like shelves in the library—everything repeated because everything was quoted.

Nonetheless, Semyon Afanasyevich had a few good traits. Desiring to know everything in literary criticism, he understood that a great writer was not isolated, as a tree can't be isolated in a forest.

He understood literature widely, yet he was unable to extract the important.

As a result of his extensive projects, he would end up publishing not a book but all of the material that goes into a book.

There were many talented people in Vengerov's seminar. They assimilated his wide knowledge, while also searching for something that he didn't have—a principle of selection. The literary critic Julian Oksman and the poet Georgi Maslov were among his students. The fair-haired Sergei Bondi studied Pushkin, too, and we anticipated that in a year he would publish a remarkable book.

In the seemingly uninterrupted flow of literature students saw the reality of conflict, the reality of literary schools, and how behind elusive, always experimental projects stood the changes in the relations of life.

The most interesting person among Vengerov's students was Yuri Nikolaevich Tynjanov. He wrote poems and they weren't bad at all. When doing research, he didn't just amass the facts, he was rather selective and knew how to see what others couldn't. He liked Derzhavin, read Kyukhelbeker, and he understood the meaning of being refused and not fulfilled in art.

Literary history in his view was not a history of changing errors but a history of changing systems through which one perceived the world.

The Polish linguist Baudouin de Courtenay was also among the lecturers at the university. He was a brilliant scholar of spoken language and speech phenomena—someone who knew how to select data. He unified Russian and Polish cultures, daily canceling out what had been previously discovered.

He worked with the private docent Lev Shcherba, who was perplexing even back then. Shcherba specialized in the logic of language and analyzed the system of thought beyond grammar, studying not only words but also the nature of semantic relations. He was a precursor of new philology.

Besides Shcherba, Baudouin de Courtenay had two other favorite students—Yevgeni Polivanov and Lev Jakubinsky.

Polivanov was a specialist in the languages of the Far East. He dreamt of creating a single system of grammar for all languages in which phenomena would not only be comparable but would also mutually elucidate each other's essence.

Yevgeni Dmitrievich was well acquainted with the Orient; he repudiated Nikolai Marr's monogenetic theory of language.

There was a scientific conference on Polivanov just recently in Samarkand and around forty papers were presented at the conference.

Lev Jakubinsky tried to prove the difference between poetic and prosaic language.

Both Polivanov and Jakubinsky were communists. Polivanov had become a communist before the October Revolution, Jakubinsky after 1917.

Boris Eichenbaum was a young docent who had already published some of his work. Viktor Vinogradov and Viktor Zhirmunsky also gave lectures at the university—they later became academicians.

There was a handsome man who used to come to Petersburg, he had a straight mouth, broad shoulders, his hair was always combed back and his voice could fill any valley. His name was Vladimir Mayakovsky. He used to argue with his audience. People learned from him, but nobody was studying his work yet. Mayakovsky himself was a great displacement in the world of the poem, born from the 1905 Revolution—a revolution that had failed but that had already moved the strata of consciousness.

After being admitted into the university, I submitted a very short proposal to Semyon Afanasyevich Vengerov: I said that I was going to found a new literary school, where, among its other goals, I would prove for the first time that Vengerov's work was obsolete. The great bibliographer, creator of incomplete masses of clouds—Vengerov—took the proposal, read it, and put it away in his folder. I saw it recently in the Museum of Literature. It smiled at me ironically—I looked at it with envy.

Still young and restless, we worked and went on strolls together. We walked our road together—Boris Eichenbaum, Yuri Tynjanov, and I—the only one alive today.

We strolled in the squares and along the banks of the Neva.

They had cut off the Senate Square with a small park a long time ago, blocking out the memory of the Decembrist revolt and disconnecting the buildings that were once interconnected.

Kyukhlya had walked through here, and probably Pushkin, too. The St. Isaac's Cathedral hadn't been built yet. Instead there were warehouses, piles of planks and stones, and the crowd—from behind the fences, hurled stones at the Tsar's loyal cavalry that had been sent to suppress the revolt.

The silent equestrian—Peter the Great, galloped in the square, his outstretched arm pointing toward the West. We could see our university's narrow side reddening behind the Neva, which wasn't gray or blue that night, but pink.

The night never came and it never passed.

It seemed as though the dawn would last all of our lives.

The young Pushkin, who had already authored numerous works and who was guilty of nothing, during such a night reproached himself for accomplishing too little, for not having lived right.

Responsibility has no boundaries.

Art resolves things differently.

In the light of the white night we reread the past without justifying ourselves.

The city of revolution, the city of Russian book printing, the city of Pushkin and Dostoevsky, the city of Blok, Mayakovsky, the city of Gorky, the city of quarrelling quarters, palaces and factories, the city of a river, the ice of which has been drenched in blood so many times—Petersburg, we love you as Leningrad in our lifetime, we love you till death! We swear by you in our books!

The world was young then. The ships stood on the wide Neva, ready to discover new planets. Everything was ready for sailing and for change.

Everything was in the future. Everything was half written and unfinished.

Everything was exciting.

The heavy St. Isaac's Cathedral was raising its glinting cupola above the city.

The years passed like the days of creation.

Yuri Nikolaevich's apartment in Peski was spacious, empty, and full of light. He didn't have any books yet. He had very few things in the apartment, and when I came to visit my friend, I would hang my coat on the light switch—there were no hangers.

Tynjanov worked as a translator at the Smolny Institute, then as a proofreader at Goslitizdat, the State Literary Press. He spent three years writing his first novel *Kyukhlya*, which he brought to Goslitizdat. The publisher looked through the first few pages of the manuscript and with an experienced, almost affectionate voice told him: "A work of fiction is a difficult thing. But you shouldn't be upset—you have your specialization."

He wasn't talking about literary theory, he meant proofreading.

Tynjanov lived with his wife, a cellist with overworked hands from too much exercise, and their daughter, who started writing amusing poems at a very young age. His sister Lida, who looked very much like Yuri, often came to visit them. Their apartment was always full of people: Veniamin Kaverin, a young student sporting long pants that still had the new smell of cheap fabric; Polivanov (I mentioned him earlier)—whom Kaverin called Dragomanov in his novel; the very young Nikolai Stepanov; and the even younger, irrepressibly cheerful Irakli Andronikov. I was there, too. With an amusing inaccuracy and thoughtful romanticism, Kaverin depicted me in his book under the name Nekrylov.[72] In the winter, everything grew stiff in this cold apartment.

The young Boris Mikhailovich Eichenbaum with his light, delicate hands talked about the *dominant*—the chief element in the hierarchy of compositional factors that determines, forms, and transforms meaning.

A Few Words On Theory

Today Tynjanov would have been seventy-five. "Dead people don't age, and not everyone lying in the grave is dead."

These are the young Chernyshevsky's words, when he was sentenced to the grave of exile.

Tynjanov—a student with a light step from Pskov and Rezhitsa, brought with him to Petersburg his views on art. He loved Derzhavin and Kyukhelbeker. Griboedov for him was in the circle of poet-friends.

Yuri read the kind of books that others only glanced over.

---

72   In 1928 Kaverin published a novel, *The Scandalist, or Evenings on Vasily-evsky Island*, in which he satirized Tynjanov, Shklovsky, and others from their circle of friends.

He wrote in his essay "On Literary Evolution": ". . . the study of literary evolution is possible only in relation to literature as a system, interrelated with other systems, and conditioned by them."

Tynjanov tried to understand the relationship between function and form—the purpose of a certain genre and the change of its meaning.

Every new community has its own tradition of discourse, its own methods of persuasion, and its own relation to facts. I am referring to the idea of community in a broad sense. In order to determine the meaning of details or pronouncements in a literary work, we must know the laws of that genre and understand its purpose. The same line, paragraph, or thought can be manipulated in different ways.

Poets call their works epics, epistles, poems, or parodies in order to fix the genre and the realm of its signification. But sometimes even they don't know where their train of thought is going. It is as though the system unveils itself, discovering its new possibilities.

The coexistence of several non-identical representations of life in a single work is common in literature.

The illusion of reality is already flickering in ancient Greek tragedy with the introduction of the Chorus.

King Lear, the Mayor in *The Inspector General*, the clerk in Ostrovsky's *It's a Family Affair—We'll Settle It Among Ourselves* address the audience directly, after which the illusion of the fourth wall is restored again.

The combination of two traditions can also exist disjointly; it can be divided among individual characters who have different styles, as it were.

The combination of high and low styles in *Dead Souls, The Overcoat,* and *The Diary of a Madman* is motivated differently in each work but it's certainly there. We can also find a combination of several genres in *Poor Folk.*

This shows that the subject of a story or its style of narration can incite different relations in a single work.

Interrelations are usually given as interrelations of styles, whereas one of the styles is taken to be traditional and the other as newly created.

This is why in literature it's important to study not the separate features of a certain work but the meaning of each feature in the system of that work, and furthermore to determine whether we are dealing with a monologic or a polyphonic work.

Archaists and Innovators

Tynjanov was beginning his work on *Archaists and Innovators.* I suggested a title that would express his ideas more clearly: "Archaists—Innovators." Akhmatova was about to agree with me. Tynjanov knew where his work was going. He studied the laws of the emergence of the new—the dialectic of literature—the revelation of reflection, which as though subverted the reflected object. Let me explain this in terms of the university.

The building of the university faced the Peter and Paul Fortress.

With years, new structures like the Stock Exchange and Rostral Columns emerged on the Spit of Vasilyevsky Island—this was a shift to another system.

The Stock Exchange and the fork in the river that was formed by it became the dominant in the construction of systems. By this time, the canals were already nonexistent and the island wasn't cut up into strips.

Various architectural ideas can coexist in a large city, and they are perceived in their contradiction.

Leningrad—and before it Petersburg—is a system of systems and it's more beautiful than the buildings built in it, because the city belongs to a different, much grander architectural design.

The exteriority of the city itself contains history—the change of forms in their simultaneous coexistence.

The journals of Russian aesthetes, such as *Apollon*, reproached bitterly but to no avail the architects who introduced disharmonious structures in the city's ensemble. But didn't the heavy helmet of St. Isaac's Cathedral clash with the high spire of the Admiralty? And didn't the sprawling Admiralty building, in turn, clash with the tightly assembled Cathedral confined to its quadrangular space in the square?

Generally in art, and that also means in architectural ensembles, collisions and transformations of the sign—the message—are important.

Let's imagine that the source of the message communicates an unchanging image or a sum of constant signs. We will lose our concentration and stop reacting to the system of identical signs. The mechanism of attention is built so that it grasps the sign of change of impression the quickest. Old systems are placed in parentheses, as it were, and perceived as a whole.

But great systems of architecture get supplanted, forcing one another out and then connecting in new, unexpected complexes.

That's how the Moscow Kremlin was built.

It is evident in architecture that the old remains because stone is everlasting. The old is preserved and revived in the new.

This is less obvious in literature.

In the meantime, old literary phenomena will be revived not only on the library shelves—as books, but also in the consciousness of the reader—as norms.

For his analysis of the relation of new genres to old ones, Tynjanov started from the simplest—by analyzing the literary fact. The literary fact—a semantic message or communication—is most clearly perceived at the moment of introducing the new phenomenon into a previously existing system, at the moment of change.

The most important feature in genre formation is the battle of systems, which enters the semantic meaning of the literary work and embellishes it.

As a system, genre constantly evolves, which is why all static definitions of genre must be replaced with dynamic ones.

Tynjanov wrote in the essay "The Literary Fact" (1924):

> All attempts at a single, static definition will fail. We have only to cast a glance at Russian literature to realize that this is so. All the revolutionary essence of Pushkin's *poema* (long poem) "Ruslan and Lyudmila" lay in the fact that it was a non-*poema* (the same can be said of his "Prisoner in the Caucasus"). This claimant to the genre of the heroic *poema* turns out to be a frivolous "tale" of the eighteenth century, one which, however, makes no excuse for its frivolity; the critics sensed that it was some kind of an exception to the genre system. In fact the work was a *dislocation*

of the system. The same can be said with regard to particular elements of the *poema*: the "hero," the "character" in "Prisoner in the Caucasus," was deliberately created by Pushkin "for the critics," the plot was "a *tour de force*." *And again the critics perceived this as an exception to the system, a mistake, and again this was a dislocation of the system.*[73]

The fact that *Eugene Onegin* was not a novel but a novel in verse made a "devilish difference" for Pushkin.

The ironic introduction through an unintroduced character was fortified with the intricate strophic structure of the novel.

Tynjanov generally argued that the literary genre dislocates itself; it evolves in a broken line. The dislocation takes place at the expense of the basic features of the genre.

What does it all mean?

The change of particular elements in a literary composition was analyzed by old theorists, including the prominent scholar Aleksandr Veselovsky. They studied changes in the methods of narration, creation of parallelisms, and evolution of the hero.

It is as though the history of literature was transformed into a bundle of separate multicolored threads and pulled through the eye of a specific literary composition.

They argued that art evolved independently from life, and didn't reflect or cognize life. It then appeared that art was as if static, that it could be repositioned, shaken up, as it were—senior genres became junior genres, but nothing new emerged.

---

73   Yuri Tynjanov. "The Literary Fact." Translated by Ann Shukman. *Modern Genre Theory.* Ed. David Duff. Harlow: Longman, 2000.

I read an article in the *Literaturnaya gazeta* (The Literary Gazette), which I think was titled "Realism Is Life." But what is life? Obviously it's something that constantly changes, or, to oversimplify—life is history, it is change. We must agree then that realism is the change of methods for cognizing the changing life, otherwise it will resemble the reality of the town of Glupov (Foolsville) depicted in one of Saltykov-Shchedrin's novels, where at a certain point "history comes to a standstill."[74] We ought to understand that Gogol's realism isn't the same as Dostoevsky's or Tolstoy's, and that Sholokhov's realism can't be similar to Tolstoy's realism, because the subject of cognition as such changes.

In literary theory, as in the history of literature, theorists studied any literary phenomenon through a historical lens both in relation to the concrete content of the phenomenon itself and in relation to other phenomena.

The battle for historical concreteness had to begin with the battle for precise definitions—what is literature? This was Tynjanov's method.

The change of separate literary facts in a composition was never as important as the change of systems that maintained an unchanging final purpose. That purpose could have been artistic eloquence which, in order to sustain, artists kept changing their methods of reflection.

We always knew that literature evolved but we never emphasized that this "evolution" moved through strange leaps and abrupt transitions, which left the contemporaries in awe and indignation.

---

74 Mikhail Saltykov-Shchedrin, *Istoriya odnogo goroda* [The History of a Town], 1869–70.

The classicists were replaced by the sentimentalists, they in turn—by the romanticists, and the latter—by the realists.

The transition from one system to another was always marked as a break, a turning point.

Inside these vast, transforming systems were individual authorial systems that kept supplanting one another.

The functions of the landscape in Turgenev, Tolstoy, and Chekhov, for example, are different. Some of the signs are partially (and deliberately) preserved, but their interpretations are drastically changed.

The so-called "art schools" are directions, alternations of systems of expression.

Pushkin's youthful poem "Ruslan and Lyudmila" incited both delight and resentment. You can already sense the clash of systems in this early work. His artistic conceptions that came after provoked even more objections. The tension of shifting systems grew. The reader didn't always want to know Pushkin's intentions, he was baffled by the author's voice as if it were the voice of a stranger.

In order to understand what is being said, it is critical to know who is speaking and what is being communicated to you. Sometimes when you hear the beginning of a telephone conversation, the words are incomprehensible at first, but as soon as you understand who the speaker is, the conversation shifts into the system of re-cognition, the system of your relations with that person, and everything becomes comprehensible, even though sometimes you are told things that demand effort to understand . . .

The seemingly pointlessness, hopelessness in Pushkin's "The Little House in Kolomna" appears to be a liberating fact from a semantic decision imposed from the outside, yet at the same time it redirects the attention to new spheres of reality. The paradox of the difficult and triumphant form of the octaves describing the everyday life in Kolomna prepares, as though, tomorrow's stage not for comedy but for tragedy involving new heroes.

Tynjanov was showing the purposefulness of art and the presence of history in the very process of artistic construction, thus asserting the eternity of a literary work.

This notion of the eternal does not suggest "eternal rest."

A literary work needs a pathway to slide through time, as it were, transferring the meaning of the events to a new realm.

Tynjanov deliberately wrote about the multifaceted nature of a literary work; it is even today not yet well understood.

They are now attempting to create a mathematical theory of aesthetics and its application to poetry.

Mathematical analysis grasps how a poem operates, shows the relation of a given poet's language to literary discourse and to conversational discourse.

But this raises new obstacles for us.

Language as such is not a unified system; it is an interrelation of several systems of verbal structures.

The word has its own history; it enters into new associations with other semantic constructions and refines verbal expressions through reinterpretation.

The poetic form is multi-layered and exists simultaneously in several temporal realms.

In *Archaists and Innovators*, Tynjanov elucidated one of the instances of the interrelationship of different systems. The system of Karamzin, Dmitriev, and Zhukovsky was not a wrong system but it wasn't the only possible one. The system of the archaists wasn't unified—the archaism of Krylov's fables didn't coincide with the archaism of Katenin's ballads. But archaism in general was opposed to the poetics of "Arzamas."

But when it turned out that the Karamzinian style failed to express or couldn't fully express the epoch of 1812, the archaistic moments intensified in their meaning.

Pushkin turned out to be a synthesizer of the two systems.

Forms that existed in the works of the archaists, or were accepted by them, acquired a new function in Pushkin.

There was a period when the Karamzinists absolutely rejected archaisms such as *sei* (this) and *onyi* (that). Decades later, Karamzin himself started *History of the Russian State* with the word *sei*.

Pushkin started *The History of Pugachov's Revolt* with *sei*, too, but this determined the importance of the event to the State; the book was originally titled "The History of Pugachov."

"*Sei* (This) Pugachov"—the Pugachov of *The Captain's Daughter*—was a ruler, tsar of peasant justice.

In his attempts to represent reality, in other words, to understand it, the writer creates a poetic model of reality. The model, of course, is not eternal because life keeps on flowing.

The writer might need reinterpreted elements from old systems for the construction of his new model.

Systems link up, they argue with and parody each other, entering the language of individual characters and acquiring new motives.

The political failure of Decembrism made it impossible for the Decembrist poetics to evolve any further, but it didn't disappear completely and continued to exist in the polemic.

Tynjanov chose Kyukhelbeker and Griboedov as the heroes of his prose works and subjects of critical study.

The General Meaning of Tynjanov's Pronouncements

Working on the interrelations of the Karamzinist and archaist poetics and studying the poetry of Kyukhelbeker and Griboedov, Tynjanov established first of all that the verse of Griboedov and Krylov was not accidental but governed by certain laws.

At the same time he showed, or he speculated, the law of dislocation—the battle of systems in a live composition.

He was able to see the drama—the drama of thought, the dialectic of history in art.

According to Friedrich Engels, "The first capitalist nation was Italy. The close of the feudal Middle Ages, and the opening of the modern capitalist era are marked by a colossal figure: an Italian, Dante, both the last poet of the Middle Ages and the first poet of modern times."[75]

By repeating this, we are asserting the fact of dialectical opposition and reinterpretation of poetic systems within the composition itself that is often felt by the poet himself.

Elements of a new poetics appear in the second book of *The Divine Comedy*. In the following lines from *Purgatorio* XI Dante is saying that new grass doesn't stay green for long:

---

75   From the Preface to the Italian edition of *The Communist Manifesto*, 1893.

O idle glory of all human dower!
How short a time, save a dull age succeed,
Its flourishing fresh greenness doth devour!

Dante's epoch marked various shifts of systems in the new culture.

Naught but a wind's breath is the world's acclaim,
Which blows now hence, now thence, as it may hap,
And when it changes quarter changes name.

Two systems of worldviews—dispositions—clash in this great epic poem: hell is constructed in the same way as the church used to construct it, but the Earth that is included in the Inferno already has a round form—it's a globe—dented from Lucifer's fall, and it is not America on the opposite side, but the mountain of Purgatory.

The sins are classified according to ecclesiastical tradition, but at the same time the Inferno is Florence. The symbolic city of hell with its battling factions is so crammed with Florentines that sinners from other parts of the extensive world are unable to get in. The Inferno represents a medieval understanding of history as the history of a city—one's own native city.

Confined in hell, the sinners are evaluated and classified according to their relationships in Florence. They are interested in poetics and their sins of lust are so enticing that after hearing a story about a couple's fall, or more precisely, Francesca's story about love, Dante faints.

The Inferno is Florence—it is the new debate of political factions, and at the same time Dante passes through hell guided by

Virgil, creator of the *Aeneid*, who sketched a map of another, antique underworld.

The contradictoriness of systems of thought, the clash of architectural designs created a great epic, as it were.

The monstrous ledges of Dante's *Inferno* are old and ancient—but they are populated with new residents.

Stories about visions of heaven and hell existed before Dante, Virgil, and Homer. Dante believed in the circles of hell, but he was also pushing down the present from the ledges of hell, knocking it down in the name of the future.

Innovation is battling against archaism here.

The fate of new art and new science, the fate of Dante's friends and famous lovers from that time, the fate of heroes from different factions, executed as a result of political arguments—everything is arranged on the shelves of the Inferno.

It is as though Dante is assigning his enemies to rooms in hell, which turns hell into a contemporary space. Next to his enemies in hell appear people who have violated the laws of the past, but who nonetheless are close to Dante.

The poet speaks with them as a friend, empathizes with them, and faints from grief.

Enemies turn out to be friends.

Farinata, for instance, chief of the Ghibellines, fought against the Florentine Guelphs, yet he loved his native city. He is the sworn enemy of the papacy and hates the Guelphs, but he appears in hell with head and chest erect—his spirit is not quelled, he is proud not only that he saved Florence but proud also of his fate. He rises up from his tomb, "as if of Hell he had a great disdain" (*Inferno* X).

The new epoch stands in its fiery tomb and argues with Dante, his family, his faction, and his religion.

The new, born out of the old, is regulated by *The Divine Comedy*'s architecture and at the same time triumphs over it.

Religious dogmas are refuted through the philosophy of the Renaissance. The very image of Beatrice embodies this polemic. Beatrice is on a chariot drawn by mystical creatures, which had appeared to the prophets earlier in their heralding imagery. Beatrice, nevertheless, speaks to the poet not as divinity but as a real, irritable woman, who accuses her admirer, perhaps even lover, of unfaithfulness. The poet listens to her as if she were alive and understands her accusations. Beatrice says: "If thou art grieving, lift thy beard and look" (*Purgatorio* XXXI).

The poet emphasizes the conversational nature of her tone:

> And when by "beard" she asked me of my face,
> The venom in the meaning well I knew. (*Purgatorio* XXXI)

The realism of the tone in this commonplace, almost domestic argument resounds from a prophetic chariot.

Purgatorio is even more biographical. It depicts love personified by Beatrice who guides the poet up along the terraces of the mountain, as Virgil had guided him down through the circles of hell.

The structure of Dante's underworld is shaped like a funnel that extends to the center of the earth and appears to be the matrix of the mountain of Purgatory.

The old does not disappear in poetry but exists in reinvented, altered form.

The *Divine Comedy* has its unoccupied place in Russian literature. Gogol, calling his composition an "epic poem," dreamed of creating a great trilogy: *Dead Souls*—that is, the dead souls of the Inferno, whom Russia did not resurrect. In the scene where Chichikov goes to the Administrative Offices to draw up the deeds to dead serfs, one of the clerks, a collegiate registrar, with a hint of irony is referred to as Virgil, who "on a time had served Dante." This new Virgil, whose back is frayed like an old straw matting, guides Chichikov to the Presence—the chamber of the Chairman. They find the Chairman in the company of Sobakevich, "who had been entirely screened by the trihedral symbol of authority." The trihedral object on the Chairman's desk is a prism encased in glass, framing the imperial decrees of Peter I on the new state reforms.

The rogues are gathered around the trihedral symbol, triumphing.

Gogol intended to write a second part—"Purgatory," which he had started in the book's second volume, and a third part—"Paradise."

But he destroyed "Purgatory."

It was burned, while the realistic vision for "Paradise" turned out to be insufficient. The circles of "dissimilarity" didn't materialize.

In art, it is nearly impossible to imitate a form completely—it can be accomplished only through parody. Absolute replication is impossible because history never repeats itself.

Gogol had wanted to guide the reader into another world with his "lyrical digressions" serving as gently sloping steps, but then he had to write that everything was understood "perversely."

He wanted to justify the epoch, showing not only the existing reality but also its rationality. He searched for an exit from hell without the agonies of a revolution, pinning his hopes on the internal reconstruction of the human soul without those dark transitions through the deep underworld through which Virgil led Dante—leading him to nowhere. This inaugurated a new beginning of a very long polemic in Russian social thought.

Blok and Mayakovsky embraced the new, refuting the old. In his play *Mystery-Bouffe* (1918), Mayakovsky led the Unclean, a group of working-class men, to paradise but was unable to build his paradise on earth. I have heard this sad conversation between Blok and Mayakovsky.

It was on Troitskaya Street, which is now called Rubinstein Street.

Memories of the past are retained in new, discerpted forms.

Yuri Olesha used to tell a parable that hadn't been written down. I will record it here, so that it doesn't get lost.

A beetle loved a caterpillar, but she died, wrapping herself in a cocoon. The beetle sat by his beloved and mourned her death. But soon the cocoon tore and a beautiful butterfly emerged from it. The beetle hated the butterfly for destroying and replacing the caterpillar.

I can't remember now—I think the beetle wanted to kill the butterfly, but as he flew up to her, he saw and recognized the familiar eyes of the caterpillar.

Her eyes had remained the same.

The old remains in the new; it is not simply recognized, but also reinterpreted. It obtains wings—a different function.

The eyes are now used not for creeping but for flying.

The range of poetic signs is perhaps reduced to a minimum. This is an example of a metonymic plot.

The Writer's Success

I am walking along the wide steps of the past, having chosen Tynjanov as my Virgil.

I go as a living man and as an echo of the past.

But the echo is not only a sound from the past—sometimes it predicts the formation of the bottom, which we still cannot reach, and the years that are ahead of us.

Terrestrial existence has been explored halfway a long time ago. Thoughts turn to memories.

But life becomes more meaningful when I recollect those whom I have seen alive, and those who died centuries ago and who, in their turn, remembered people who lived thousands of years ago.

And so, Mayakovsky will return to us as "a living man addressing the living."[76]

I must take a breath now. These ledges are difficult. There are no subway lines or pedestrian walkways between them.

From here it's uphill all the way.

The theorist became a researcher-novelist.

Tynjanov was not happy, though he had overcome many difficulties and knew what he was working for. He knew that he was a man of the revolution who studies the past in order to understand the present. His desire to make art purposeful and concrete, the desire to gain empirical knowledge on the literary struggle led him to continue his work as a writer.

---

76   Vladimir Mayakovsky, *At the Top of My Voice* (1930).

His novel *The Death of the Wazir Mukhtar* was a new circle, a new stage in *Archaists and Innovators*.

Tynjanov was attracted to Kyukhelbeker's bitter fate, the distinctive style of his creative work and theoretical views. The poet was Pushkin's most loyal friend and a revolutionary.

Kyukhelbeker had been completely forgotten.

In one of his letters, while doing research for Tolstoy (who was writing "The Decembrists"), Nikolai Strakhov reported that Semevsky's archive "includes a large number of unpublished poetry and prose by Kyukhelbeker, and his diary. The pile of notebooks made a striking and sad impression on me, but I had to conserve my labors and time demanded for the reading of those manuscripts. And yet you spoke highly of Kyukhelbeker." But Tolstoy wasn't interested in the archival material.

Life kept passing by Kyukhelbeker's manuscripts and nobody paid any attention to his work.

Even the memory of him as Pushkin's friend was overshadowed by Anton Delvig, also a close friend of Pushkin from the Tsarskoe Selo Lyceum.

Kyukhlya was written as a novel for children. This prompted the simplicity of the narration.

The novel was well received, widely read, and became an instantaneous success.

Scientific insight formulated itself into artistic discovery.

Young, persistent, cheerful, luckless, yet invested in the future that never materialized for him Kyukhlya became Tynjanov's most important friend. He resurrected Kyukhlya and showed that the conquered sometimes help their conquerors, enhancing their mastery.

Once Empress Catherine had helped turn the revolutionary scholar Vasili Trediakovsky into a laughingstock and even Radishchev was unable to resurrect the memory of the founder of Russian verse.

Kyukhelbeker, who had been turned into a laughingstock after the Decembrist revolt, was promptly revived by Tynjanov.

Tynjanov's apartment in Peski didn't change much over time, though it acquired some books and even a buffet table.

We will never be able to tell everything about our life and the lives of our friends, because we can't grasp the whole truth, and to relate something without fully understanding, well, it only leads to useless reproaches.

Tynjanov continued to write. A lot has been written about *The Death of the Wazir Mukhtar*, but I want to focus on two of his stories because the anecdotes and archeological observations made in these works transferred into the basis of new plots—and it is very seldom that new plots and conflicts emerge in the literary world.

A long time ago, *Russkaya Starina* (Russian Antiquarian) published an account about how during the reign of Emperor Paul I, a young regimental clerk made an error: instead of writing "and the second lieutenants . . ." he wrote "the second lieutenant Kizhe," which he was too frightened to correct and so created a fictitious person— Kizhe. He lived among other lieutenants and received a salary. For a long time they didn't know how to get rid of the nonexistent man.[77]

---

77 In this satire, an inexperienced army clerk accidentally makes a mistake when copying documents, and instead of writing "podporuchiki zhe Stiven, Rybin . . ." (and second lieutenants Stiven, Rybin . . .), writes "podporuchik Kizhe, Stiven, Rybin . . ." (second lieutenant Kizhe, Stiven, Rybin), putting the plural ending *ki* as the beginning of a new word and combining it with the emphatic particle *zhe*, thus inventing a new person, Kizhe, who is later in the story promoted in rank.

There had been very few descriptions of Emperor Paul in litera-ture, though Tolstoy had once considered him as "his own hero." Paul wanted the impossible: he invented an imaginary life and de-manded its actualization. He contradicted life by isolating, cutting himself off from it.

Lieutenant Kizhe became the symbol of this fantastic system of double life.

A nonexistent man has legitimate documents and undergoes suc-cesses and failures as a real, living person. He is flogged and sent to Siberia, then he is pardoned and allowed to return from exile. He is promoted to the rank of a general, even fathers children, and only dis-appears when they are about to make him a senior aide to the throne.

This is a new conflict—there had been nothing like it before. It is structured as a metonymic plot.

The other novella is *The Wax Figure*.

The work opens with the death of a great emperor, who had ea-gerly sought innovation, perceiving it as something good. He dies, drowned in hatred, having committed many old-fashioned evil deeds. But his great legacy continues to live on.

The will of the genius is materialized by inertia, in a contradic-tory way. His portrait—the wax figure—is sent to the Kuntzkamera as a curiosity.[78]

In essence, the post–Peter-the-Great epoch of the Russian em-pire is also an anti–Peter-the-Great epoch.

---

78   Founded by Peter the Great in 1714 and affiliated today with the Museum of Anthropology and Ethnography, the Kuntzkamera houses a collection of human and natural curiosities and rarities, such as, for example, human and animal fetuses with anatomical deficiencies. The irony in Tynjanov's story is that Peter's effigy is "exiled" to his own museum to be displayed among the most strange "monsters" and "anomalies."

The structure of this plot is allegorical.

Both novellas are realistic, they are based on historical facts and are very different from one another. The representation of the epochs of Peter I and Paul I required two completely different stylistic solutions.

Tynjanov wished to portray the bitter paradise of creative work in art, he wanted to write about Pushkin. His work was left unfinished—and not just because of his poor health.

The topic of the project was endlessly difficult and life was coming to an end.

They gave Tynjanov a large apartment on Plekhanov Street.

His rooms were now filled with books and furniture.

The street on which he lived was quiet and dark. His apartment, too, was dark and spacious. It was a typical old Petersburg apartment. Yuri Nikolaevich's office window looked out into a dark corridor-like courtyard.

One could see through the office window how early in the day people turn on the electric lights in their apartments.

His friends brought him illustrated publications so that the writer wouldn't have to go to the library, though the public library was nearby.

Tynjanov was friends with Nikolai Tikhonov, Anton Schwartz, Irakli Andronikov.

Arriving from Moscow, I would visit my friend. We would go for walks, but not too far, in the small park by the Kazan Cathedral. The park was enclosed in a wrought-iron fence designed by the architect Andrei Voronikhin. The fence was obstructed with a flower shop. We used to sit in the park, examining the details of the fence, or sometimes stroll along Nevsky Prospect. At the portal of the Kazan Cathedral, deceptively reconciled through fame, stood the statues of Kutuzov and Barclay de Tolley. Slightly diagonally, by the bridge on Griboedov Canal, towered the House of Books where not long ago Tynjanov worked as a proofreader.

The small cathedral safeguarded Kutuzov's tomb and the secret of the great Russian resistance. The colonnade of the cathedral, its steps were like an entrance into *War and Peace*, into the new truth of the new contradiction in the philosophy of life.

Tynjanov didn't get a chance to finish writing *Pushkin*.

Tynjanov's Illness

There is a disease called multiple sclerosis, the cure for which still hasn't been found. It impairs the functions of the central nervous system.

Tynjanov could still write but his legs were slowly starting to give in.

The progression of the disease was slow and sporadic—his one eye would move uncontrollably, he would start having double vision, or his walking pattern would change, then all symptoms would go away. He was under Dr. Dmitri Ivanovich Pletnyov's care, who examined him once briefly and suggested he live in the south.[79]

—Shouldn't I take off my clothes, doctor? Aren't you going to examine me?—Tynjanov had asked.

—I can tell you. Take off your left shoe. You have fallen arches,— Dmitri Ivanovich had replied.

---

79 One of the "enemy" physicians who during the Stalin show trials in the 1930s was falsely accused of traitorous activities, such as taking part in the poisoning and murder of Maksim Gorky, and was exiled to Siberia.

—Yes, I know.

—Then you don't need to take off your clothes.

I asked Pletnyov later on why he had received Tynjanov in such a way.

—I can't treat multiple sclerosis, I can only detect it. I usually ask questions, the patient answers and expects to hear a diagnosis. Well . . . I don't have anything to say. I'd rather have him think that I'm a careless doctor.

His symptoms would come and go. This held him back from work, taking away his confidence.

The need to follow his hero step by step, his hero's grandeur, and the challenge to represent him not only the way that others perceived him but also the way that he truly was perhaps were beyond the power of literature.

The theoretical part was moved aside, it remained unpublished. Academic titles aren't nearly as important for a person immersed in academic work as being in a working environment because it is extremely difficult to work in solitude. Productive work is also a conflict of ideas and systems of solutions; the work of a genius cannot be monological—it is dramaturgical and needs both conflict and agreement with his time and his friends.

During the war Yuri Nikolaevich was evacuated to Perm. There the disease took a faster course.

Time was palpable for the writer; he saw history unfold before his eyes and was unable to intervene.

I saw him in Moscow when they brought him back in a bad condition. He was placed in a hospital in the Sokolniki district with verdant groves and green, empty streets that branched out in a radial pattern. The city was still militarized, few people had returned from the war and those who did thought constantly about war—they were still mentally on the front.

I would visit my friend, but he wouldn't recognize me.

I had to talk in a quiet voice. Sometimes a word, most often the name of Pushkin, would revive his consciousness. He wouldn't speak immediately. First, he would recite verses. Yuri Nikolaevich knew Pushkin by heart, he recited the poems as though he was just hearing them for the first time, feeling completely stunned by their complexity, their inexhaustible depth.

He would start reciting the poems in a semiconscious state and slowly return to me, to his friend, along the path of the poem. His voice would become steadier, stronger, and he would finally regain consciousness.

He would smile at me and talk as though we were sitting in front of a manuscript, taking a short break.

—I asked for some wine, the kind they made me drink in childhood when I'd get sick,—he told me once.

—*St. Raphael*?—I asked him.

We were born around the same time and I remembered the sweet wine they occasionally made me drink, too.

—Yes, yes . . . but the doctor didn't remember. They brought me some pastry instead, and my daughter isn't here. Would you like to try it?

His consciousness would return. Then Tynjanov would start talking about the theory of verse and the theory of literature, about the inaccuracies of old definitions that carried us sometimes far away from the road.

Death and the Funeral

He was awake and cognizant when he was dying but without having the ability to work.

Few people came to his funeral, except they were writers and knew how difficult it is to write.

Yuri Tynjanov was buried in the Vagankov cemetery. It is quiet there. Almost nobody is buried there now. New houses and streets have been built near the groves on the edges of the cemetery.

The only sound that disrupts the calm is the train's whistle as it passes through Okruzhnaya Station.

There is a bifurcated tree by his grave—the heavy branch stretches over the grave like a mast without a sail.

The stone with Tynjanov's name lies on the snow-covered deck.

Tynjanov predicted the existence of new continents, understood the clashes of winds and streams. He was a great explorer, a great theorist who had not been fully understood yet. He recognized the usefulness of contradiction.

Now his books on theory are being published and reprinted.

I don't think that anyone has yet surpassed Tynjanov in the analysis of verse.

ON THE FUNCTIONS OF PLOT

About the New as a Change in Convention in General, and about Particular Conventions, Including a Change in the Method of Characterization

This is what one of the greatest contemporary composers, Igor Stravinsky, said about the conventionality of music. But first I need to make a short digression here. When musicians tried to play the earliest works by Stravinsky and Prokofiev, they kept getting out of time—they thought that their music couldn't have been written in notes. I heard these impressions from people who were at Prokofiev's graduation examination. But this music, too, that was supposedly disrupting established laws, was based on the deep knowledge of the laws of music. Stravinsky wrote about his own work:

> Just as Latin, no longer being a language in everyday use, imposed a certain *style* on me, so the language of music itself imposed a certain convention, which would restrain it within strict bounds and prevent it from overflowing and wandering into byways, in accordance with those improvisations of the author that are often so perilous for the composition. I had voluntarily subjected myself to this restraint when I selected a form of language bearing the tradition

of ages and was crystallized by them, as it were. The need for restriction, for deliberately submitting to a style, has its source in the very depth of our nature, and is found not only in matters of art, but in every conscious manifestation of human activity. It is the need for order without which nothing can be achieved and everything disintegrates. Every order demands restraint. But it would be wrong to regard that as an impediment to free will. On the contrary, the style, the restraint, contribute to its development, and only prevent free will from degenerating into full blown exorbitance.[80]

I was fortunate to hear the last speech of the great music theorist Heinrich Neuhaus. The old teacher of the renowned pianist Sviatoslav Richter and other great Soviet musicians came with one of his students to a meeting at the *Izvestia* newspaper office. We were discussing the question of innovation. Neuhaus was amusingly calm. He began to talk about "cacophonous music"—music that renounces ordinary devices of harmony—

> I had been unable to understand that kind of music, even though I have been immersed in music since childhood practically my entire life. When the Yugoslavian Symphonic Orchestra was visiting us just recently, they played a symphony, which I absolutely couldn't grasp before. After hearing their performance, I suddenly understood its laws.

---

80   Igor Stravinsky, *Chroniques de Ma Vie* [Chronicle of My Life], 1936.

Imagine a man who has lived in the same apartment all of his life and knows its corners by heart. And then suddenly he discovers that in the place where he had once thought was a wall there is a door there and other rooms behind that door where one can also live. I am speaking about this now, in such a way, because I am excited. I was able to understand the laws of other relations, other possibilities.

The unity of an artistic work is complicated.

Stravinsky appeared to be an innovator who negated everything

But he didn't negate for the sake of negating—he refused the old system in the name of the new.

The old norms still remained—the creator was simply pushing himself away from them.

An Evaluation of the Function of Parts in a Work

Stravinsky creates music based on a tradition that gives him his well-known "style." He is an innovator who is constrained by tradition and "the need for order."

Imagine a man who walks into the theater for the very first time: for him, the aesthetic structure of perception includes the layout of the auditorium, the stage curtains, and the process of raising and dropping the curtains.

In his autobiography *The Fairy Tale of My Life*, Hans Christian Andersen relates a story about a servant girl who sees a play for the first time.

Returning home, she recounts her impressions roughly like this: People came out and said "la-la-la."

Then "a lady fell down."

Then again "la-la-la" and she fell down again (the same lady).

Trying to make sense of this story, we realize that the stage curtain must have had an image of Melpomene, the muse of tragedy elegantly robed as a priestess. The "lady" must have been her.

The enormous picture—the curtain falling from above—appeared to the viewer as the most impressive dramatic event because she wasn't used to relating to people on the stage and being engaged or interested in their interrelations.

Andersen's fairy tales are well known today.

Yevgeni Schwartz would take Andersen's plots and reinvent them, often refreshing the conflicts and conveying them in common everyday settings. The audience, including children, perceived his plays, recognizing that they transgressed the tradition of the famous fairy tales.

Andersen, in turn, changed and revised folktales, and those changes became part of the structure of his own fairy tales.

There were writers in Chekhov's time who wrote sketches derived from the life of common people; there was much talk about how to "go to the people," and more often—how to approach the people.[81]

In "The New Villa," Chekhov tells about an engineer who is building a bridge over a river and his kind wife who convinces her husband to buy land and build a house on the bank of the river.

---

81 The expression "going to the people" gave name to Narodism or Narodnichestvo, a revolutionary movement in Russia among the socially conscious members of the middle class that arose after the emancipation of the serfs in 1861.

They encounter a range of conflicts. The basis of the main conflict is that the peasants and landowners are adversaries. The conflict is revealed in that they don't understand one another's behavior or even words.

Their worldviews are incompatible.

"We treat you humanely. You must pay us with the same coin."

The peasants misunderstand the expression and think that the gentleman wants money from them: the word "coin" is perceived as a synonym for ruble—there is no gold in the village. Annoyed, the gentleman threatens that he will treat them with disdain. But, again, one of the peasants mistakes the gentleman's words "look down upon you" for "look after you," thinking that the gentleman will care for him and his wife in their old age.

The miscommunication alone is a sign of a noncoincidence of interests.

Then the summer villa is sold to a government clerk, who restores the relations with the peasants and there are no more conflicts in the village. The kind lady was "a person out of place."

In order to laugh or cry, one must understand what is frightening or moving in a certain structure.

The young Mayakovsky wrote an autobiography titled *I Myself*. It begins like this: "I'm a poet. That's why I'm interesting. I'll write about that. About the rest—only if it can be defended with the word."

The autobiography is written in the form of a survey: there is a section with his place of birth, date of birth, and a list of family members. There is a short chapter called "The Roots of Romanticism"; it's about an ancient Georgian fortress. It depicts a certain way of life. There is a brief description of the mountains. This is followed by "FIRST MEMORY: Concepts of art. The place is un-known. Winter. Father has subscribed to *Rodina* (Motherland). It has a 'comics' supplement. They talk about what's funny and wait. Father paces and sings the usual: '*Allons enfants de la* po chetyre.'[82] *Rodina* arrives. I open it (a picture) and yell at once: 'How funny! The uncle and the aunt are kissing.' They laugh. Later, when the ac-tual supplement arrives and it's necessary to laugh, it turns out that earlier they were laughing at me. This is how my understanding of pictures and humor diverged from theirs."

The boy was prepared to laugh—and he laughed at something that wasn't funny, but perhaps, while aiming for the funny, the oddly dressed couple and their strange city behavior seemed funny to him. The adults who were observing the boy were also laughing. They, in turn, were laughing at the boy, who was laughing at the wrong picture.

I remember this petty magazine, *Rodina*, mentioned by Mayak-ovsky. It was a cheap quality magazine with illustrations printed on slightly reddish paper. The comics in the supplement were called, I think, "Gibes." There was hardly anything in it that was funny, and those who laughed were laughing as though out of duty, and were probably ridiculous themselves observed from the side—they were the most typical and complacent philistines.

It is important to know in this case not only *what* is being told but also *who* is telling it. Then we'll understand *why* it is being told, and what's funny to *them*.

---

82 The first line from the *Marseillaise*, the last word of which (*Patrie*, mean-ing "Fatherland") the father sings in Russian (*po chetyre*, meaning "four" or "in fours"), imitating the sound but not the sense of the French word.

The first memory is a reminder that in order to perceive one must know the "necessary conventions." This is followed by a reinterpretation of phrases such as "concepts of poetry," "roots of romanticism," "extraordinary," etc.

The old illustrated magazines don't make the same impression as they used to. The majority of people have forgotten them. What was considered inappropriate then—is appropriate now, what was funny then—it's not funny anymore, and it was probably not funny then either. It was habitual to laugh at certain postures, situations, and at certain people. Mayakovsky perceived this even more sharply. Vladimir Mayakovsky grew up in a small Georgian town or village called Bagdadi, near Kutaisi, in an extremely patriarchal environment.

The way of life depicted in that petty magazine was conceivable for him, yet ridiculous. He saw all of that in Kutaisi and it kept surprising him. In his laughter, Mayakovsky was right in his own way.

Let me move on to another story.

I will tell you a story from memory, or better yet, I will quote from Mark Twain. I remembered him because I told Vladimir Mayakovsky the following anecdote: a priest preaches in a village church and everyone in the congregation weeps, except for one person who sits in absolute calm. His neighbor asks him: why aren't you crying?—I am not from this parish—he replies.

Vladimir Vladimirovich thought that this was a correct response. The man in the audience didn't know the convention of what was moving or humorous in this parish, he didn't know how people related to things.

There was a time when people visited the insane asylum for entertainment. The madman was thought to be amusing.

I often notice how people in the audience laugh at parts that the director had not intended for humor; they are not prepared for that system of artistic vision. They don't know the local meaning of signs.

Mark Twain liked to read his stories and he traveled to various provinces to read. He would completely rearrange the piece for his presumed audience, adjusting the lengths of pauses. Once he came to a new town and doubting that his reading would be successful, hired claques. The rest of the story is conventional.

On the streets of the town Mark Twain meets his hero, Tom Sawyer. The boy is now a grown man. Mark Twain recalls that Tom has an infectious laughter. He says: "Tom, when I look at you and smile, I want you to laugh." Then he tells the claques, whom he has hired to appear in the theater with long sticks: "When the man in the straw hat—Tom—laughs, start laughing and make noise with your sticks."

Twain's fears were in vain. His reading went without a hitch. Signs weren't necessary at all, everybody was laughing.

Halfway through the reading, Mark Twain inserted a moving episode in his humorous story as authors typically do in American or English literature.

The audience froze. Mark Twain was telling them about a lonely, poor, homeless man.

The people in the audience followed every movement of the storyteller. Pleased with his ability to control the audience so well, Mark Twain met Tom Sawyer's gaze and smiled, inspired by the pleasure.

Tom Sawyer began to laugh, the claques started making noise with their sticks, and the audience exploded with laughter. And twenty-five years later, according to Mark Twain, he still can't dissuade people that this was his most successful joke.

The convention between the audience and speaker, in this case, was changed.

What was considered moving became funny due to the sign of laughter.

Mayakovsky had a lecturer's experience, he knew what was funny.

Plot Structures, the Change of their Meanings, and the Exploration of a Person's Place in the World

I am not going to hide from the reader the difficulties that stand before the writer. We have often discussed and talked in great detail about traveling plots. But it turns out that plots travel not only along roads but they also cross seas and inhabit islands where no ships have yet sailed. So, then, which plots travel and which ones repeat, and why do plots appear in places where it is impossible to drive, sail, or fly?

There is good weather and bad weather. There are patterns of cyclones. But seasons change. I envision spring in Crimea. It's still cold. There is a clear picture of bare oaks. The sea is hesitantly warming up. The line between light and shadow is signified through heat and cold. The cold air traces the sharp shadows of the cypresses.

We listened to fairy tales in childhood, they were repeated to us a plethora of times and, as Kipling noted, we would instantly wake up if the storyteller violated the structural laws of the fairy tale.

A child knows how a fairy tale is constructed, recognizes the new elements and can easily reconstruct a half-forgotten fairy tale. The structure of the fairy tale is sturdier than its elements.

I imagine spring in Crimea and simultaneously (and involuntarily) translate it into the phases of spring in the north, and I run up against the contradiction of evergreens next to the familiar picture of the oaks.

I have told many fairy tales to children. The fairy tales were easily formed and they easily disintegrated, but the laws of the emerging new on the background of the familiar were always observed.

Repetition in fairy tales is often based on a stepped structure. A knight fights with a three-headed, six-headed, or nine-headed snake. The obstacles keep getting harder. Similarly, the tasks given by the witch to the girl, whom she has captured, are gradually becoming impossible to accomplish. The same principle is used on the type of fairy tale in which the magic objects transform into something else, while retaining their original form—they are turned into a new obstacle for the hero to slow him down. So, for instance, the comb thrown on the ground turns into a thick forest, the towel into a river. The towel probably transforms into a river because its creases and folds resemble the movement of a serpentine river.

At the root of every artistic work lies someone's vision. That vision is connected with particular methods. A person learns how to see the world the same way he learns how to walk. But he walks without inventing legs. He already has legs.

A stepped structure can be constructed without a warning, unexpectedly. But as a rule, it is supposed to be gradual. For example, this is how materials are arranged in a stepped structure: silver–gold–diamonds, or copper–silver–gold. Normally there are three steps. The violation of this tripartite system, the transgression of boundaries is punishable, as it were.

There are a variety of exquisite fairy tales that might interest us among the old fables of the *Panchatantra*—the fairy tales and fables in the *Five Principles*, collected and transcribed between the third and fourth centuries.

Four Brahmin friends set out in search of wealth. One of them finds silver and goes home content. The second Brahmin finds gold, and the third diamonds. But the fourth Brahmin keeps going—he wants to find a higher reward and gets into trouble instead. A wheel whirling over a stranger's head, who is thus punished for a terrible crime, comes over the Brahmin's head and it is supposed to whirl around his head for millions of centuries.

In Pushkin's "Tale of the Fisherman and the Fish," the succession of rewards is presented in the following way: the old woman wants to get a new washboard, then a palace, to become the ruler of her province, and then the queen of her kingdom. The fourth reward that the old woman demands of the golden fish is to turn her into the god of sea, and to have the golden fish as her servant and messenger. She is punished by being returned to her old hut and broken washboard. The fairy tale is ironic, but it retains the traditional structure where three wishes are granted and the fourth prohibited.

Fairy tales disintegrate and are assembled anew. But the laws and processes, forming the crystal of the fairy tale, are retained. One might interpret them ironically, embellish or forget them, but even forgotten they still reemerge in the same form.

In Hans Christian Andersen's "The Tinder Box," a soldier travels underground to fetch a tinder box for an old witch. He first comes upon a dog with eyes as large as teacups. The dog is sleeping on a chest full of copper money. The soldier must seize the dog and place him on the witch's apron and then he can open the chest and take from it as much as he wants. The second dog sits on a chest full of silver money. Its eyes are as large as tower windows.

The third dog, with eyes as large as millwheels, sits on a chest full of gold. The soldier places the dog on the witch's apron. The dog obviously is much larger and taller than the soldier. But that's not taken into consideration here. What's considered is the structure-bearing sign, while the dog's size is apparently not increasing proportionately with the size of its eyes.

The fourth treasure is the tinder box. The soldier quarrels with the witch because of the tinder box and accidentally kills her—he doesn't like her temper.

Consequently, the materialization of the fourth wish, exceeding the foreseeable three wishes, is prohibited in Andersen as well. But in this case the violation is incited against the initiator of the search—the old witch. The witch is punished for her greed. She wanted to own the tinder box that summoned the dogs who would do anything at the owner's command. The tripartite system has been preserved, and the fourth element has acquired its traditional negative trait.

Plot in its construction can depend on several structures, which, when intersected with one another, create various turns, whereas the path to convergence of these turns cannot be explained by conglomerating but by unifying them into a single theme that has a constant and simultaneously different structure with a different solution.

Let's take, for example, a fairy tale that is popular in all cultures: several brothers have to complete a difficult task. The fact that they are brothers is not a requirement—they can be fellow travelers, but something has to unify them. Every one of them is skilled in his own trade. One of them is a carpenter and he carves out a woman's figure from a random piece of wood. The second is a tailor, he makes clothes for her. The third is a jeweler, he adorns her with jewels. The last one is a magician, he gives her life. They argue—who does the woman belong to? They go to court. The hearing takes place underneath a tree. The tree cracks open and takes in the woman—she had originated from the tree and naturally belongs to it.

The plot is based on the comparison of actions and the degree of their importance, and it is perhaps unusually varied. There is another denoucment (in a Scottish fairy tale, for example) where the woman is conceded to the father who has taught his sons the various trades.

There is a fairy tale in the *Panchatantra* that has a similar schematic structure. Four Brahmins were walking through a forest. Three of them were scholars, while the fourth was illiterate but had common sense. They came upon a pile of bones. One of them said that they were the bones of a lion and joined the bones. The second one, an anatomist, dressed the bones with flesh and skin. The third one, a magician, brought the lion to life. While the three men were fiddling with the bones, the fourth Brahmin climbed up a tree. The lion ate the three men, but couldn't get to the fourth man. This fairy tale leaves the fourth man unpunished. He was the person who wanted the least.

This plot, too, is based on the comparison of actions and the degree of their importance, meaning the actions are arranged in a certain order, ranging from the least important to the most important, so that in the end the last one is inevitably deemed as the most important (for example, the tinder box is more valuable than silver and gold, or common sense is more important than scholarship and magic, etc.).

The impediment formed through the stepped structure, signifying the meaning of the subject and action, creates suspense.

The argument is interesting in yet another way. Let's take this ancient construction that has been crystallized. A woman tells her husband on the wedding night that she has promised herself to another man. The courteous husband allows her to go to the anonymous rival in her wedding gown. On the way, the woman meets a highwayman. The robber doesn't touch her jewelry after hearing her story. The woman comes to her lover. When he hears her story, he tells her: "Return to your generous husband."

The construction has many variations. The development of this theme is discussed in detail in P. A. Grintser's *Ancient Indian Prose*. Quite often these tales ended with the question: Who is the most generous person among these men? Whereas if the answer was—the highwayman, who didn't take the woman's jewelry, it was immediately inferred that such an answer revealed repressed and illicit greed.

The structure of this tale has been intersected with the structure of another tale about a wise judge who uses a clever stratagem to determine the truth, tricking the parties into revealing their true feelings. It is the tale of how Solomon solves the argument between two women as to who is the real mother of a child; the true mother's instincts are to protect her child when the offered solution is to split the child in two, each woman receiving half of the child. In the case of the woman whom everyone generously cedes to another, if a person in the audience argued that the most generous man was the robber, he was considered to be a thief himself.

The form of inquiry has been used numerously. This story made its way into *The Decameron*. As in the ancient Indian collections, the stories in *The Decameron* are grouped according to the similarity of situations.

The theme of the tenth day in *The Decameron* is dedicated to those who "have distinguished themselves in the accomplishment of generous or magnificent deeds, in love or other fields."[83]

The fifth story of the tenth day is about a beautiful and respectable lady who is being pursued by Ansaldo. Getting weary of the baron's solicitations and love letters, the lady agrees to grant Ansaldo's wish if he presents her a garden in January, full of verdant lawns, flowers, and leafy shrubs, as it would bloom in May. The baron finds a necromancer who magically creates a garden. Curious to see the novelty, the lady visits the garden and is struck with awe at the beautiful sight. She tells her husband about her promise to Ansaldo. The husband tells her that she must keep her promise. The lady goes to Ansaldo's house and tells him about her husband's decision. "My lady," Ansaldo replies, "far be it from me to wreck the honor of one who is considerate of my love." The lady then is escorted back to her husband, who, from then on, becomes close friends with Ansaldo. After witnessing these generous acts, the magician refuses to accept his payment. The narrator asks: "What shall we say of this, tender ladies? Are we to place a lover's relinquishment of a lady well-nigh dead to him, and a love grown tepid with hope deferred, above the generosity of Ansaldo, who was much more ardently enamored

83   Giovanni Boccaccio, *The Decameron*. Translated by Frances Winwar. Random House, 1955. All subsequent quotations from *The Decameron* are taken from this standard version.

than ever and, in a way, stirred to new hope by the possession of the dear object he had so long pursued?"

The ladies' debate, deciding who had behaved more magnanimously—the lover, the husband, or the necromancer—is cut short.

The same story is given in the Franklin's tale in *The Canterbury Tales*. The question is well articulated:

> Lordinges, this question wolde I aske now,
> Which was the moste free,[84] as thinketh yow?

But structures can transform in much more complex ways. Let's take the tale about Paris, for example, who was supposed to give an apple to the fairest among three goddesses. He chooses Aphrodite, the goddess of love. For this, he is rewarded with Helen's love, and the Greeks with the Trojan War.

The argument about the apple can be parodied.

In O. Henry's *The Sphinx Apple*, three men and a woman get bored. The story is framed as a conversation between passengers stopped in their journey. The woman is given an apple, which she must promptly bestow upon the one who tells the most exciting story. They tell three stories, which I am not going to repeat. When the narrators turn to the woman for an answer, they see that she has fallen asleep. There is an apple core in her hand—she has eaten the apple herself.

The old question—who is the wisest, whose story is the best—is given an ironic twist at the end, since the person who was supposed to be the judge has given the prize to herself.

---

84 Noble, generous.

At the beginning of *The Arabian Nights*, a traveling merchant unintentionally kills the son of a jinn with a tossed date pit. For this, the jinn threatens to kill him. Then three old men appear. They proceed to tell their own stories, defying the jinn that their stories are more incredible than his own story about the murder of his son with a date pit. The stories are being compared as to which one is the most engaging. In reality, the theme of comparison is almost completely obliterated, it's used only to frame stories about incredible things.

I already mentioned that many novellas are based on a solution to a set of questions. Someone relates an incident and the listener must figure out the meaning, usually the moral, of that incident. It is as though the listener is included in the solution of the meaning of plot construction. Transformed, this method has survived until our times in detective fiction. The evidence is first collected by one detective, then by another. Sometimes even the murderers, trying to justify themselves or lead the trace away, assist in the gathering of the evidence. The crime is finally solved by an ingenious detective. Typically, the solution is almost always less interesting and terrifying than the riddle itself. But sometimes the solution is unexpected. For example, in one of Chesterton's stories, a high-ranking wealthy man goes fishing in the river and is later found with his own infallible fishing line twisted round his neck. This is clearly a murder. The man died suddenly. He was strangled, which means he was murdered. The investigation centers on those who are hypothetically interested in the prominent man's death. Further investigation reveals that the famous man's guests without exception were his enemies. Everyone is a suspect. But it turns out that the man had died of his own mistake—falling in the trap of his own fishing line. He is a common enemy, and though everyone had seen him dead, nobody resolved to declare it because secretly they all were potential murderers. In essence, he had persecuted himself. There is an analogical plot construction in Agatha Christie.

The multitude of solutions in detective fiction is based on the confession of the murder. The author tries his best to not allow the reader to glimpse into the last few pages. The question about guilt serves as the means of holding the reader's curiosity. The murder itself serves as pretext for the creation of a unique crossword.

Some authors of detective fiction change the names of their characters in the middle of the story in order to stop you from looking at the last page and solving the riddle without actually solving it. The list of versions is an inventory of solutions—every single of them negating the others—that gradually "intensify" in their horrifying nature.

I'll tell you an anecdote. In Italy, you can enter the movie theater at any time during the show. You buy tickets whenever you want and simply walk in. An usher will help you find a seat. People usually tip them for that. A man bought a ticket for a detective movie but forgot to tip the usher when he walked in. The annoyed usher told him: "Don't worry—the murderer is the accountant." The detective story is thus ruined.

Let me hold your attention a bit longer by saying that the multiplicity of evidences can destroy them if they are moving in different directions. There are many examples of this.

In "The Tinder Box," the soldier brings the king's daughter to his house with the help of the dog, while in the palace they have no idea where she has disappeared. The queen, though, is a very clever woman and ties a bag full of buckwheat flour round the princess's neck. She finds out where the dog has taken her daughter and marks the door with a large cross. The dog sees the cross and marks all the doors in the town with a similar cross.

In the second story of the third day in *The Decameron*, a groom commits a crime—he sleeps with the wife of King Agilulf, who, on discovering this, finds the man and cuts off a lock of his hair. The shorn man clips the hair of the rest of the servants; the evidence has been destroyed.

Convinced of the impossibility of finding the culprit, the king says: "Let him who did it, not dare to do it again. Now go, and God be with you."

I am not going to search for the origins of this fairy tale. It would be as difficult as finding the inventor of the wheel. What they kept finding was the principle of rotation—used, perhaps, for making fire in the Stone Age, or for drilling, or maybe even for spinning thread. Then, apparently, the wheel appeared. So it's almost impossible to find out when exactly this fairy tale appeared for the first time.

The fairy tale employs miracular occurrences, describing a certain violation of the ordinary, and we inadvertently come across sorcery.

There is a fairy tale with many versions in which two robbers are beheaded. With the help of sorcery their faithful wives reattach their severed heads but onto the wrong bodies. The question is: Who is whose *real* husband? In the simple version, the quandary is solved: the head is the most important—hence, the wife belongs to the man who has her original husband's head. This is a casuistic joke. But let's see how this is interpreted through various religious beliefs.

The members of a Jewish sect called the Sadducees, for example, rejected the doctrine of the resurrection of the dead. According to their beliefs, they denied this miracle not only because it was physically impossible but also because traditional practices wouldn't allow it. The custom of *levirate* marriage, for instance, rested on the principle that if a man died childless his brother should marry the widow. In the Gospel of Matthew, the Sadducees try to test Jesus Christ and ask him the following:

> "Teacher, Moses said: 'If a man dies childless, his brother shall marry the widow, and raise up children for his brother.' Now there were seven brothers among us; the first married and died childless, leaving the widow to his brother. The second did the same, so also the third, down to the seventh. Last of all, the woman herself died. In the resurrection, then, whose wife of the seven will she be? For all of them had married her."
>
> Jesus answered them, "You are wrong, because you know neither the scriptures nor the power of God. For in the resurrection they neither marry nor are given in marriage, but are like angels in heaven." (Matthew 22:24–30)

The representative of the new religious teaching must answer the question that split the old teaching into sects. The answer is formulated in such a way that it refutes the question: the laws of *levirate* and other customs are invalid in the "other world" where marriage also does not exist.

There are no "high" or "low" constructions in art.

It is not the heroes or their actions that lie at the basis of fairy tales and novellas. They aren't the links that connect plots to one another.

Plot constructions are diverse, and they are based on numerous methods that create suspense.

In *Crime and Punishment*, we are first told the "mystery" of the hero preparing for something, then the "mystery" itself, and why he is frightened when a passerby calls him a "hat."

All of Raskolnikov's actions are mysterious. Then everything is explained as he prepares for the murder.

Next begins the mystery of evidences: the inspectors are tracking down the hero. But as a result it becomes clear that the true mystery of the novel is based on the question of what is a crime and whether everyone experiences the feeling of guilt and confusion when committing a crime.

It turns out that Raskolnikov is trying himself. As a result, the novel's question is resolved in a different way. The principles of the solution are subjected to doubt.

The fairy-tale–parables repeat in various parts in the Gospels; they usually end with a question. They are riddles with a new solution because the principle of the solution—the moral—has been changed.

Dostoevsky, who often "placed suspense higher than the artistic," used the elements of the detective story in the philosophical novel. Thus, the origination of an element does not necessarily unravel for us the meaning of the novel. An element, a construction can be used in various ways and it might mean something entirely different in each system.

It has been frequently remarked that the determination of the genesis of a phenomenon and the analysis of its designation don't solve everything.

In the fourteenth chapter of the first book, Gargantua had read so many books that he could "recite every single line, backward," proving to his mother that "he had the whole thing at his fingertips," and that "designations were neither reasonable nor a science."[85] The irony here is that the book from which Gargantua quotes is dedicated to the question of designations.

The decisive factor is not designation, but rather how elements are employed in a work: the interrelatability of the elements—the structure (each element can be an individual structure) in a given work.

While writing *Resurrection*, Tolstoy kept rejecting the main idea of the construction, until he finally understood that Katyusha was the light, and the rest was darkness. He changed the function of his heroine in the plot composition and the novel was restructured.

When he was working on *Hadji Murad* he changed the principle of characterization, as he found something new in Chekhov. His journal entries from April and May in 1901 show attempts to grasp the new construction: "Dreamed about a type of old man (whom Chekhov forestalled me in describing) who drank and cursed—but he was a saint. I clearly understood the need of shadows in types."

From here on, "the shadow" gained a new function.

He wrote in his diary on May 7 of that same year: "I'll do this with Hadji Murad and Maria Dmitrievna."

---

85   François Rabelais, *Gargantua and Pantagruel*. Translated by Burton Raffel. New York: Norton, 1990. All subsequent quotations from *Gargantua and Pantagruel* are taken from this standard version.

The characterization and the language of the hero depend on the kind of function he has in the plot.

The Functions of Heroes in the Fairy Tale

I

Since its publication in 1928, Vladimir Propp's first work, *Morphology of the Folktale*, has received widespread recognition only in the past decade.

The epigraph to the second chapter, "The Method and Material," is from Goethe: "Anyone who pays a little attention to the growth of plants will readily observe that certain of their external members are sometimes transformed, so that they assume—either wholly or in some lesser degree—the form of the members nearest in the series."[86]

Goethe's prediction came true.

An epigraph usually indicates the direction of a book. In this particular case, the epigraph to the second chapter was the key to the theme of Propp's book.

The main idea in Goethe's essay of 1790 is that all organs of the higher flowering plants can be derived from a single model—the

---

[86] From Goethe's essay "The Metamorphosis of Plants" (1790). Translated by Agnes Arber. The epigraphs to every chapter in *Morphology of the Folktale*, which openly proclaimed indebtedness to Goethe, were omitted in the English edition of the book, first translated in 1958, which according to Vladimir Propp caused a misunderstanding of his methodology.

leaf. He based his theory on the study of both the cotyledons and parts of the flower—stamens and pistils. Everything was based on the principle of unity in the plant's structure.

Goethe tried to find a universal model expressed in the particular. This kind of a design would explain not only the elements of the whole, but would also open a path to the discovery of the origination of the whole.

Propp based his study of plot involving the functions of characters on the analysis of fairy tales. The experiment is quite new and it can be analyzed further, applied, and circulated.

The idea of creating a morphology of fairy tales is extremely important, as explorers perish in the material.

There are over a thousand titles compiled in the three-volume work by Johannes Bolte and Georg Polívka, modestly titled *Anmerkungen zu den Kinder- und Hausmärchen der Brüder Grimm*, whereas Afansyev's collection of four hundred fairy tales is referenced in it only once. *The Arabian Nights* takes up the same amount of space in the bibliographic index.

And now they are discovering materials from South America, Africa, and the Pacific Islands.

The question is drowned in the second ocean of information.

Scientific thought today is interested not so much in digging machines used for excavating new material, as in sieves for filtering and analyzing the material.

Attempts to explain the origination of fairy tales through mythology have been made a long time ago. According to the theories of the Mythological School, a myth reflected the primordial cosmogony of humankind and the first cosmographic observations.

For example, if the hero of the fairy tale "grew not by the day but by the hour," then this described the fast movement of the sun rising over the horizon.

One thing is left unclear: why don't we say "the hero shrunk not by the day but by the hour"?

Fighting against the ocean of material and arbitrariness of interpretation, Aleksandr Veselovsky divided the structure of fairy tales into motifs and plots.

A motif, according to Veselovsky, was the simplest narrative unit that could be created during the developmental stages of human consciousness in different places and independently from one another.

By plot he meant "a theme that is warped with various situational motifs."[87]

"Warp" here apparently means "that which is thrown across" or placed in tension like yarns on a loom before the weaving begins.

Veselovsky assumed that not only motifs but plots, too, migrate from one nation to another through a process of borrowing. He founded this on the fact that, according to mathematical calculation, it is impossible to have a random repetition of motifs with an identical sequence among a large number of elements of the repeating material.

If twelve stylistic motifs repeat, then the phenomenon cannot be explained either by chance or coincidence of laws of psyche, because "the probability of its independent formation takes on the ratio of 1 : 479,001,599."

---

87   Aleksandr Veselovsky, *Istoricheskaya poetika* [Historical Poetics], 1940.

In the chapter "The Ethnographic School" in *Theory of Prose*, I wrote:

> Besides, it is quite inexplicable as to why, in the act of borrowing, the *random* sequence of motifs should be retained. The sequence of events is distorted most of all in eyewitness accounts.

Propp objected in the second chapter of *Morphology of the Folktale*:

> This reference to the evidence of eyewitness accounts is unconvincing. If witnesses distort the sequence of events then their narrative is incoherent and meaningless. The sequence of events has its own laws. The short story, too, has similar laws, as do organic formations. Theft cannot take place before the door is forced.[88]

As we see, Propp considers that a literary work should follow the sequence of events. This view conflicts with such common phenomena as recollection, story within a story, prophetic dreams, and, generally speaking, I think that it rejects art as a system that has its own direction, its own laws, which illuminate reality without direct imitation but through reflection-investigation. Let's try to prove him wrong.

Quite often, in the detective story, the purpose of investigation is to establish the sequence of events—that is Chesterton's function.

---

88   Vladimir Propp, *Morphology of the Folktale*. Translated by Laurence Scott, revised by Louis A. Wagner. Austin: U of Texas P, 1968. All subsequent quotations from *Morphology of the Folktale* are taken from this standard version.

In his stories, Father Brown first of all tries to determine the actual sequence of moments during the crime, which is distorted first, unconsciously, by the witnesses and then, consciously, by the criminals.

There are stories that have been around for thousands of years, which are based on the theme of theft without actually containing any scenes of the door being forced.

In the second book of *The Histories*, Herodotus recorded the following story:

> Now, they say that Rhampsinitus had a huge fortune in silver, more than any of his successors, none of whom even came close. He wanted to store his money in a safe place, so he built a stone chamber as an extension off one of the outside walls of his residence. The builder, however, came up with the following crafty plan. He cleverly fitted one of the stones in such a way that it would easily be removable from its wall by two men or even one. Anyway, the chamber was finished and the king stored his money in it. Time passed. At the end of his life, the builder summoned his sons (there were two of them) and told them of the plan he had put into effect while building the king's treasure chamber, so that they would be comfortable for the rest of their lives. He explained precisely to them how to remove the stone and described its position in the wall. He told them that if they remembered his instructions, they would be the stewards of the king's treasury!
>
> He died, and his sons soon set to work. They went by night to the royal residence and found the stone in the

building. It was easy for them to handle, and they carried off a lot of money. When the king happened to go into the chamber next, he was surprised to see that the caskets were missing some money, but the seals on the door were still intact and the chamber had been locked up, so he could not blame anyone.[89]

Had the theft not occurred without the door being forced, it would have never become the subject of a story. The violation of habitual, predictable sequences and verisimilitude is more than common in literature.

Vladimir Propp's remark is rather naïve.

In the Chinese story "The Merry Adventures of Lazy Dragon," the protagonist—a thief called Lazy Dragon—makes a bet with a man that he can steal a winepot from his house without forcing open a door or window. The man sits by the table all night long watching his winepot, but falls asleep leaning his head on the table. Lazy Dragon removes a few tiles from the roof, then fastens a pig's bladder on to a thin, hollow bamboo, and lowers it slowly into the winepot. He blows through the bamboo and the bladder swells up to fill the pot and he pulls the winepot up through the hole in the roof.

Individual storytellers can also rearrange the obstacles that are experienced and overcome by the heroes of the fairy tale.

But this isn't important. The most important—interesting—thing is the professor's proposition in the analysis of fairy tales.

Propp proposed and substantiated his system of analysis: the method of selection of heroes' main actions and their functions.

---

89   Herodotus, *The Histories*. Translated by Robin Waterfield. Oxford UP, 1998.

The classification of actions, as a whole, is quite interesting.

What is function?

Propp explains in the second chapter: "Function is understood as an act of a character, defined from the point of view of its significance for the course of the action."

As far as I know, the application of the word "function" to literary works appeared in 1927 in Yuri Tynjanov's essay "On Literary Evolution." The term was scrutinized in his lectures at the Institute of History of Fine Arts, and years later the essay was included in his book *Archaists and Innovators*.

This is how he formulated it:

> The correlation of each element of a literary work, as a system, with other elements and with the whole literary system may be called the constructional *function* of the given element.
>
> On close examination, such a function proves to be a complex concept. An element is on the one hand interrelated with similar elements in other works in other systems (*auto-function*), and on the other hand it is interrelated with different elements within the same work (*syn-function*).[90]

After bringing numerous examples on the change of functions in different systems, Tynjanov concludes: "It is incorrect to isolate

90   Yuri Tynjanov, "On Literary Evolution." Translated by C. A. Luplow. *Readings in Russian Poetics*. Ed. Ladislav Matejka and Krystyna Pomorska. Dalkey Archive, 2002. All subsequent quotations from "On Literary Evolution" are taken from this standard version.

the elements from one system outside their constructional function and to correlate them with other systems."

In his book, Propp examines the functions of heroes in only one system, and besides he is using "a special class" of fairy tales that were previously classified by the Finnish folklorist Antti Aarne.

But the concept of function can be twofold. It can be: a) the self-contained actions of the heroes within a fairy tale proper—this is the hero's function as such; and b) the action of the hero as part of the fairy tale, taken as a literary work.

Besides, it is important to differentiate between the heroes and the basis for their actions. Characters might offer help out of gratitude or as a gesture in response to the hero's action. Help can be offered by a hired servant. In this case, the function of the hero is quite different.

But the help of the servant can be heroic in itself, as, in fact, the deed might be harmful to him: he was forbidden to offer that kind of help. He is punished for helping, and then the hero saves the servant by committing a heroic deed.

This isn't just a part of one and the same concept—it is, in fact, a change of artistic objective within the literary work itself. And from this point of view it's unfortunate that Propp, following many of Tynjanov's ideas, simplified the concept of function, reducing it to a mono-semantic notion. For instance, an action can be described as the performance of a certain custom.

The same action can be explained as a cunning stratagem.

The action, of course, doesn't change, but its function does.

The inability to grasp this led to misconceptions, and one such example is when Propp cites my analysis of plot structures and critique of descriptions without contextualizing any of my observations.

In the past, motives were explained historically, as they were considered to be traces of the past. Let's take, for example, the story of Dido's cunning. Dido takes refuge on the coast of North Africa and asks the local inhabitants for a small piece of land—as much land as could be encompassed by an oxhide. The clever queen cuts the oxhide into fine strips so that she has enough to encircle an entire hill and builds the city of Carthage. First she raises the city walls and then slowly starts to expand her lands. Vsevolod Miller analyzed this legend in an article in *Russkaya mysl* (Russian Thought, 1894). Let me quote from the second chapter of *Theory of Prose*:

> V. F. Miller traces the plot about the seizure of land using the method of cowhide strips in the following: the classical Greek legend of Dido retold in Virgil's *Aeneid*; three local Indian legends; an Indo-Chinese legend; a fifteenth century Byzantine legend and a Turkish legend that coincides with the building of a fortress on the Bosporus; a Serbian legend; an Icelandic saga concerning Ragnar Lodbrok's son Ivar; the twelfth century history of the Danes written by Saxo Grammaticus; the Gottfried Chronicle from twelfth century; a Swedish chronicle; the legend of the founding of Riga, as recorded by Dionysius Fabricius; the legend concerning the founding of Kirillo-Belozersky Monastery (with a tragic denouement); the folk legend from Pskov concerning the erection of the walls of Pechorsky Monastery under the reign of Ivan the Terrible; the Chernigovsky Malo-Russian legend about Peter the Great; the Zyriansky legend of the founding of Moscow; the Kabardinian legend of the founding of Kudenetov vil-

lage in the Caucasus (with a Jewish hero); and finally North American Indian tales about the deceitful seizure of land by European colonists.

Having thus exhaustively traced all versions of this plot, Miller directs our attention to the peculiar fact that the deceived party in these stories never protests against the violent takeover of land by the other party. This is possible, of course, due to the convention lying at the heart of every work of art, namely, that the situations in question depart from their interrelationships with reality and influence one another in accordance with the laws of the given artistic composition. In this story, according to Miller, "one has the sense of *conviction* that the act of covering a piece of land with strips of oxhide constitutes a juridical act that has the power of law."

The meaning of this act is conveyed in a Vedic legend recorded in the oldest Indian religious work entitled the *Catapatha Brahmana*. According to this legend, the Asuri spirits, who are hostile to the gods, measure out the land with bullhide and divide it among themselves. Correspondingly, the ancient Indian word *go* meant "land" or "cow." The word *gocarman* (cowhide) was used to describe a measured piece of land. In Miller's analysis, "The ancient Indian measurement (*gocarman*) can be paralleled with the Anglo-Saxon term *hyd* or "hide" in English, meaning, skin (*haut* in German) or a particular measure of surface, equivalent to forty-six morgens (old German measurement). This leads us to believe with a high degree of probability that the Indian term *gocarman* originally meant a piece of land that could be encompassed by the strips of a cowhide. And only later, when its ancient meaning was forgotten, did this word come to designate a measure of surface that can hold one hundred cows, a bull, and their calves."

As we see from this long quotation, the attempt to explain the "socioeconomic substructure" is brought not only to the bitter end but also to a certain level of absurdity. It turns out that the deceived party—and all versions of the tale are based on the act of deception—didn't protest against the seizure of land because land was generally measured by this means. This is complete nonsense. If, at the time of the supposed action of the tale, the custom of measuring land "by as much as one can encircle with cowhide strips" actually existed and was known both to the sellers and to the buyers, then there is neither deception nor a plot, since the seller knew what he was getting involved in!

Works of art, including folk art, have their own laws with the help of which they model the world and explore it. The repetition of these devices is an illusion similar to the illusion of the unchanging existence of the dogmatists of Christianity or the forms of Roman law.

Propp understands this but at the same time, after examining the particular phenomena of art, he still considers them to be universal and their functions both stable and unchanging.

In his grandiose attempt to write a historical poetics, Veselovsky at the same time saw art as something constant, ahistorical.

Propp paraphrases my analysis of the absurdities of the so-called genetic studies of the tale in his first chapter of *Morphology of the Folktale* and concludes: "Thus, the relegation of the story to historical reality, without taking into account the particulars of the story as such, leads to false conclusions, in spite of the investigators' enormous erudition."

Then Propp quotes Veselovsky: ". . . the phenomena of schematism and repetition will then be established across the total expanse."[91]

By "the total expanse" Veselvosky means "everything."

Veselovsky thinks that in the future "contemporary narrative literature, with its complex plot structure and photographic reproduction of reality," will change for us in the long perspective.

It is not clear here as to what changes in the "total expanse." Another thing that is not clear is whether anything new is born in art or whether it exists solely through transpositions.

It appears then that the phenomena of art are born singularly and reality, evidently, intrudes only as "photographic reproduction."

This isn't true for at least one reason: art is perceived only through, in Propp's words, "the synthesis of time, that great simplifier."

This is schematic and perhaps it was for this reason that Veselovsky was unable to accomplish his task.

My work is partly dedicated to the reexamination of such schemas, without, of course, pretending to give a final answer to the

---

91 Though Shklovsky makes it seem that Veselovsky's quote follows Propp's conclusion in the first chapter, it in fact appears in the final paragraph of the last chapter, "The Tale as a Whole," in *Morphology of the Folktale*, with which Propp strategically ends his study.

question. But I am trying to show that repetition of phenomena in art is illusory.

I am not going to trace each step of Propp's interesting work, partially following the author's advice, who states in a note to the third chapter, "The Functions of Dramatis Personae":

> It is recommended that, prior to reading this chapter, one read through all the enumerated functions in succession without going into detail, taking note only of what is printed in bold letters. Such a cursory reading will make it easier to understand the thread of the account.

Let's not enumerate the functions—there are thirty-one. This is an arbitrary number: the eighth function has nineteen subcategories, the twelfth and thirteenth functions have ten subcategories each.

We can take the simplest case. The initial situation with which tales begin is typically generic: they either open with a list of the hero's family members, or the hero is simply introduced by mention of his name or indication of his status.

Here Propp notes: "Although this situation is not a function, it nevertheless is an important morphological element . . . We shall designate this element as the *initial situation*."

Let's look at some other schemas.

Function 8a: One member of a family either lacks something or desires to have something. (Definition: *lack*.)

Function 9: Misfortune or lack is made known; the hero is approached with a request or command; he is allowed to go or he is dispatched. (Definition: *mediation, the connective incident*.)

Function 10: The seeker agrees to or decides upon counteraction. (Definition: *beginning counteraction*.)

Function 11: The hero leaves home. (Definition: *departure*.)

Function 12: The hero is tested, interrogated, attacked, etc., which prepares the way for his receiving either a magical agent or helper. (Definition: *the first function of the donor*.)

Function 13: The hero reacts to the actions of the future donor. (Definition: *the hero's reaction*.)

Function 14: The hero acquires the use of a magical agent. (Definition: *provision or receipt of a magical agent*.)

Propp elaborates further on this function: "Often the magical agent suddenly appears of its own accord, on the way, offering help and placing themselves at the disposal of the hero."

The catalogue of functions is interesting in itself. The key to its application was not to analyze the genesis of functions but to follow their transformations.

At the end of the book Propp included an eight-page appendix of diagrams and their symbolizations, which are quite impossible to read or understand.

But the book is interesting because it outlines the analysis of different plots and not just plots of fairy tales.

As it appears to me, the proposed method of analysis doesn't coincide with the subject matter of the analysis—it is much wider and not directly connected to the genesis of the fairy tale.

Propp's second book, *Historical Roots of the Fairy Tale* (1946), a 340-page study, traces the source or origins of the fairy tale to initiation rites, ceremonies marking entrance or acceptance into a group. Admission is accompanied with rituals: the novice is tested for his endurance of pain, deprivation of sleep, etc, and which, according to Propp, must have impressed our great ancestor (who lived before the pyramids were constructed, before Babylon was erected, and before the Pacific Islands were populated) so much, that he retained them in the ancient fairy tale.

The "compositional unity of the fairy tale," in Professor Propp's opinion, originated from here—"it is hidden in the historical reality of the past."

Art makes use of old, already existing constructions, and gives them new functions. The old is not only transposed but also reinvented by the new.

We recomprehend our history and alter the habitual.

Researchers, however, often study the ritual as a phenomenon that appears to be the source of social reality, since the ritual is a reminiscence, whereas social reality re-experiences that reminiscence, but changes it through the re-experience. Sometimes strange things happen in the works of very intelligent and independently thinking scholars. For example, in the chapter "Complication" of *Historical Roots of the Fairy Tale* (1946), Propp discusses the hero who leaves home and takes with him his horse, an iron club, and food.

Propp argues that the iron club isn't a club, in fact, but it is a wooden crook or a lance. He then argues that all the objects that were buried in the grave were subsequently transferred into the fairy tale from the traditional burial ceremony.

> The dead in ancient Bengal "were adorned in such a way as if they were going on a long journey." The Egyptians buried their dead with a sturdy crook and sandals. Chapter 125 in the *Book of the Dead* says: "This chapter must be spoken (to the dead) after his body has been washed in-

side and out, clothed, and after white leather sandals have been put on his feet . . ." The hieratic papyrus about Astarte (she is in the underworld) says: "Where are you going, daughter of Ptah, furious and terrifying goddess? Didn't the sandals that are on your feet get worn? Didn't the garments that were on you when you left and came back through the sky and the earth get torn?" These real, though durable sandals are gradually replaced with symbolic ones. In ancient Greece, they would find shoes made of clay and sometimes even two pairs of shoes in burial sites.

But in the fairy tale all of these objects are given to a living person for the purpose of going through a magical journey, in which, however, death appears only as a stopping place. After the magical resurrection of the hero, the objects are never mentioned again.

It appears to me that the underworld is modeled after our own world. The dead don't teach us how to eat bread or how to wear shoes, we are the ones—the living—who try to continue life for the dead. We still put shoes on the dead body before placing it in a coffin. This is the inertia of our relationship with the dead person—it's as if he were still alive.

People who buried shoes with the body were themselves wearing shoes. Those who placed weapons inside a tomb were armed, too.

Objects can be replaced with symbols. For example, the Chinese used to place offerings of paper at the gravesite representing money printed specifically for the dead. In Russia, they used to make special slippers for the corpse called *bosoviki*. Tolstoy mentions them in his tales.

The point here isn't that the fairy tale repeats old traditions, but that it conveys relations that are perceptible to listeners who are alive.

In cinematography, I often came across the question about how to convey time and space in film. And we would end up rendering those concepts through objects—there was no other way.

Propp believes that the iron bread and the iron boots, signifying fairy-tale time, have evolved from tradition and are retained as relics.

The question of generation—origins—is elucidated with great difficulty because it is necessary to find the reason of renewal of ancient traditions.

Propp's main achievement here is establishing the antiquity of the fairy tale. But the fairy tale is reborn every day. Fairy tale fantasy is always contemporary—iron and cast iron are relatively new, they are much younger than written language and literature.

The fairy tale is not so much a relic as an expression of new concepts using the old structure. The period of the origination of myths probably gave less plots than the conflict of myths. Plots use the contradictions of epochs. They insert in them new contradictions but maintain the old structures. We live simultaneously in multiple temporal realms. The present conquers the past, it swallows up the past as if it were bread.

II

Functions change. We need to clarify the meaning of function by linking it to the concept of evolution. As Yuri Tynjanov wrote in his essay "On Literary Evolution":

To summarize, the study of literary evolution is possible only in relation to literature as a system, interrelated with other systems and conditioned by them. The inquiry must move from constructional function to literary function, from literary function to verbal function. It must clarify the problem of the evolutionary interaction of functions and forms. The study of evolution must move from the literary system to the nearest correlated systems, not the disant, even though major, systems. In this way the dominant meaning of major social factors is not at all rejected. Rather, it has to be elucidated to its full extent through the question of the *evolution* of literature. This is in contrast to the establishment of the direct "influence" of major social factors, which replaces the study of *evolution* of literature with the study of the *modification* of literary works—that is to say, of their deformation.

Actually, the change of functions is synchronous with the change of the author's (or storyteller's) relation to reality.

First of all, the storyteller sympathizes with his hero and wishes that the hero would overcome the obstacles. If the initiate, usually an adolescent, strives to endure the trials in order to become a full member of his tribe, the hero of the fairy tale wants to escape from the witch, Baba Yaga; he wants to leave the underworld kingdom and return to his own world. Overcoming the obstacles, the hero marries his beloved, while his adversary—the king— dies. This has been preserved even in Yershov's fairy tale "The Humpbacked Horse."

The fairy tale in itself, as the epic, tells not only about the antiquity or about needs but also about the taming of nature, as if it were happening right now.

The hero experiences an extraordinary life—a life that is often foretold and complicated with forewarnings of hardship. This is a repeating life, shown in slow motion and as if simultaneously exaggerating the significance of its own events.

Death must be defeated, and the ordinary must be defeated, too; everybody dies, but the hero must conquer death. In order to do this he must go against the habitual—he must not sleep, not kiss the one whom he loves, not hurt the one whom he hates, not look at his wife. But it is impossible to conquer ordinariness. In the fairy tale, as in the novel, the person fights against the ordinary and he also fights against the impossible—he swims across rivers, climbs steep mountains. He defends himself from fear, turning objects into their likeness: a towel into a river, a comb into a thick forest.

The storyteller doesn't know where these magical transformations originate from, but he isn't the propagator of the fairy tale's life. He is the new creator, the one who narrates and surprises. Victory over impossibilities, finding a way out of difficult situations—these are the peripeteias of the fairy tale.

The fairy tale has a traditional opening; its forms are conventional, they combine the tension of a habitual victory over the impossible. The fairy tale as a phenomenon of art must be interesting.

The question of genesis of fairy tale motifs shouldn't be linked with the question of fairy tale construction.

The fairy tale has its own tasks, which are connected with the selection of elements of narration and their connection.

Time changes, the sails get bigger, the paths get longer, the horizon disappears, the earth becomes rounder, meridians and parallels appear on it. News about islands and continents, people of different color and customs travels across the ocean; goods with new smells, new tastes and new fabrics with new patterns appear from far places.

New plots get constructed about conquering obstacles on the way to these wonders and about fighting to obtain them.

The adventure novel appears. People learn about recent insurrections, imperial coups, and the arrival of new heroes.

The historical novel emerges or, at least, finds a place in human consciousness.

Forms of narration change. Some functions are preserved. If the functions, typical to fairy-tale heroes, depended solely on their origins or the conquering of old fears, if they were only reminiscences of customs that have disappeared, they wouldn't have migrated into the new novel.

In the meantime if we retell novels, simplifying their content, then their schemas would be similar to the schemas of fairy tales because they both incorporate coincidence and the change of the coinciding element—a coincidence of functions. The analogical function is necessary to show the struggle for life—the life that Gilgamesh fought for thousands of years ago.

In the fairy tale, the hero fights and overcomes fantastic obstacles with the help of magic devices. In the novel he overcomes realistic obstacles but often with the help of a traditional heroic deed, cunning or accidental luck, such as, for example, overhearing a private conversation, receiving an inheritance, or finding a lost document. Thackeray, as we have already noted, viewed this as a convention.

It might seem that in adventure novels, the functions of heroes are especially defined, and one might even say that they repeat the functions of fairy-tale heroes. We have already quoted Propp saying that "all fairy tales are of one type in regard to their structure." Here Propp draws a few fairy-tale sketches, one of which is the following: "One member of a family either lacks something or desires to have something" (Function 8a). This is defined as *lack*.

The misfortune or lack is announced, the hero leaves home, he receives a magical agent or helper, after which the hero is led to the whereabouts of the lost object, then he encounters the villain, the villain is defeated, the hero returns home only to find that a false hero has presented unfounded claims, the false hero is exposed and punished, the hero marries.

Let's take a look at the construction of Jules Verne's *In Search of the Castaways*: "On the 26th of July, 1864, a magnificent yacht was steaming along the North Channel at full speed." The yacht was called the *Duncan*, and the owner was Lord Glenarvan. The sailors capture a shark and in its stomach they find a strange object that turns out to be a bottle. They open the bottle and discover three documents that appear to have rotted from dampness. One is written in English, one in French, and one in German. Some parts of the documents are destroyed and others are intelligible. When they align the fragments from the different pieces of paper, they recover the message with some omissions. It states that a three-mast vessel called the *Britannia* foundered and a certain Captain "Gr" and two sailors were on that vessel. They entreat help and give their coordinates: latitude 37°11'.

Someone needs to be saved. It turns into a fairy-tale situation: "To go—not knowing where; to bring—not knowing what."

The captain's children appear and they think that their father, a fearless Scotsman, is dead. Lord Glenarvan is also from Scotland. They set out to find Captain Grant, but the longitude number in the coordinates found in the bottle is missing.

The problem is constructed in such a way that it foreshadows an adventure around the world.

A similar problem is posed in *Around the World in Eighty Days*.

Here, the motive for adventure is a bet placed by an eccentric English gentleman, Phileas Fogg.

But let's get back to the *Duncan*.

It turns out that there is a geographer, Jacques Paganel, on the *Duncan*—a helping character—who, being an expert in geography and geographical terminology, interprets the mysterious document variously throughout the novel. This sustains the need for a voyage around the world. Paganel's accidental yet helpful errors save the adventurers from danger.

In Australia, the adventurers meet with a mysterious character, who claims his name is Ayrton and pretends to be one of the shipwrecked sailors of the *Britannia*. In reality, he wants to seize control of the *Duncan*.

Ayrton is exposed, and an accident helps them find Captain Grant: Paganel had not taken into consideration the different names that an island might have. The account ends with two marriages. As a curiosity, the hero (Paganel) gets branded—the Maori tattoo him from the feet to the shoulders in New Zealand.

In *Around the World in Eighty Days*, the helper of the hero is his valet Passepartout. The antagonist is a detective named Fix, who mistakes the adventurer for a bank robber on the run and the hero almost loses his wager. The adventure ends with a marriage.

The functions of these characters are very similar to the functions of the fairy-tale heroes.

But the purpose of this novel, as other novels by Jules Verne, is different.

The actions of the heroes must create a desire in the reader to "see" various countries and experience, with the heroes, the various obstacles that hinder the journey.

The function of the hero is to illuminate the geographical landscape.

That's the main function of the hero in Pushkin's "Prisoner of the Caucasus"—to show, to describe Circassian customs.

Let's move to the analysis of *The Captain's Daughter*.

The Grinyovs lived comfortably, but one day the "father sat by the window reading the *Court Calendar*, which he received every year."

He repeats under his breath: "Lieutenant-General! . . . He was a sergeant in my company . . . a Companion of two Russian Orders! . . . And it isn't long since he and I . . ."

Grinyov wants his son to go into the Service: this can be defined as a "lack"—a desire to have a higher rank and orders. The young Grinyov is sent into the army escorted by his groom. On his way, he saves a wayfarer and gives him his hareskin jacket. Thus, he acquires a helper. Shvabrin turns out to be a villain, but Pugachov helps the hero and everything ends with a marriage.

How is this different from a fairy tale? The difference is in the purpose—to expose a national insurrection and its characters. The heroes have their own characters, they commit deeds, yet at the same time they help us see the Russian revolt in all its magnificence and contradiction.

The difference between Pushkin's novella and the novels of, let's say, Sir Walter Scott is that here a secondary character has the function of the main hero; he reveals the epoch, he is the main protagonist. In Scott, the function of an indebted robber or an accidentally rewarded gypsy is reduced to assisting the main hero.

Propp intentionally remarks that after going through an enormous amount of control materials, he has to limit his scope: "We shall use the collection by Afanasyev, starting the study of tales with No. 50 (according to his plan, this is the first fairy tale of the collection), and finishing it with No. 151."

The researcher thinks that such a strict limitation of materials can be theoretically justified.

But the research material that is actually being used is only the Russian fairy tale. The tales from *The Arabian Nights*, for instance, are organized quite differently and the functions of heroes in these tales are different. "Sindbad the Seaman," for example, includes information based on real journeys. The motivating prompts of the voyages and the actions of travelers (functions) in Arabian fairy tales are very different from Russian fairy tales.

Let me explain, through my analysis, the difficulty of the question about the relation between the fairy tale and the novel.

In Ivan Tolstoy's "Articles about Folklore," there is a fairy-tale object similar to the hareskin jacket that Grinyov gives to Pugachov—an act that predetermines his own fate.

Tolstoy traces the thread of the ninth story of the tenth day in *The Decameron*. He cites a German legend recounted by Caesarius of Heisterbach in the early thirteenth century:

There are two characters in this legend: a soldier and the devil. A soldier named Gerhard, who was an ardent devotee of St. Thomas, lived in the town of Hollenbach. He never refused a single beggar who begged in the name of St. Thomas. One day God permitted the devil in the guise of a traveler to come to Gerhard's door and ask for hospitality. Gerhard admitted the stranger immediately and, because it was cold outside, gave him his cloak to keep him warm through the night. In the morning both the stranger and the cloak were gone.

Then Gerhard travels to India to find the tomb of St. Thomas and asks his wife to wait five years for his return after which she might marry whomever she likes. He reaches the tomb of St. Thomas on the last day of the fifth year and laments that his wife would marry soon another man. Then Gerhard sees a passerby wearing his cloak. The devil thanks him for his hospitality and brings Gerhard back from India to Germany on time, just as his wife is about to get remarried.

Let us not bother with the question about the magical flight.

However, the tale in its entirety migrated into Russian folklore and was recorded in Perm.

The Russian version is called "Leshok."

The story of the devil who so marvelously commits an act of gratitude in exchange for a warm cloak is reminiscent of Pugachov's story. But we have the historical source of this episode: there is a reference in Pushkin's papers—"The register of Butkevich." A certain nobleman, Butkevich, had submitted to the government a long list of items that Pugachov had taken from him. The list includes a replica of the icon of *Our Lady of Kazan* with a frame of embedded pearls worth 330 rubles, thirty-eight stacks of hay, sixty-five mares, three pairs of cotton leg wrappings, and five pairs of wool stockings—these are incredible estimates of property value. Among these valuables, there also were "two jackets: one lambskin and one made of squirrel fur worth 60 rubles."

This catalogue is used in Chapter 9, where Savelyich presents a list of items to Pugachov during his takeover of the Belagorsky fortress. Savelyich's estimates are incredible! The catalogue is very detailed; it includes uniform coats, silk eiderdowns, and "also a hareskin jacket given to your honor at the inn, worth fifteen rubles."

The source of the novella turned out to be not a well-known fairy tale but a reinterpreted document. The function of the hero in this work dictated the need for a different material.

The Captain's Daughter is based on the story of Shvanvich, a gentleman who sided with Pugachov, and an actual document. The value of the jacket is maximally reduced in the novella—it is made of hare's skin, the cheapest and least reliable kind of fur. Pugachov remembers not the gift, but the endearments and hospitality.

Yuri Tynjanov discussed the change of function in a literary work in both his essays "On Literary Evolution" and "The Literary Fact." The friendly letter of Derzhavin was a social fact, whereas Pushkin's letter was a literary fact. The author related to it differently and the reader read it differently.

It is not enough to simply list the things that a fairy tale's protagonist is doing, it's important to also consider *how* he does those things and for *what* purpose. The helping agents, who are capable of transporting freezing air or heat in a stove, interest the reader for their exoticism. The helping animals, the cat and the dog, who steal a magic ring for the hero but who argue with each other on the way, have the same function as the main hero, but they are only *characters*; they are examined not only in relation to the fulfillment of the main quest of the fairy tale but also in relation to one another. It is and it isn't the same function.

It is important when something doesn't work in a composition. Sometimes behind the apparent error lies a new regularity (norm). Tynjanov would have explained this much better. The interesting morphological work done by Propp is too generalizing and it does not account for those instances where the schema doesn't coincide with the research material.

But in all likelihood, this daring project—Propp's *Morphology of the Folktale*, will aid us in the analysis of the formology of plot.

Historical Roots of the Fairy Tale is a different kind of work that, I think, is about something else and doesn't substantiate the first book.

We don't always explain the role of a phenomenon when trying to find its history.

I am not claiming that the adventure novel is *not* constructed in accordance with the archetype of the fairy tale, though it often ends with a wedding. It is quite possible that during the creation of the supposed archetype of the fairy tale the wedding ceremony, as a sophisticated custom, didn't even exist. The journeys and adventures, with their consciously disrupted course, in the basis of their movement carry the idea of an ordinary journey, which might appear variously difficult at various times.

The storyteller and the author of the adventure novel had different objectives.

The reader ordinarily doesn't know the foundations of art, and generally he doesn't care much about them. Moreover, he doesn't want to foresee the event, he wants to investigate it. He wants to delay the event, be held back by it in order to *really* experience it. Which is why happy marriages, described with such irony by Hegel in his *Aesthetics*, or stories about comfort and wealth, described so delightfully in the biographies of American millionaires, do not become the main material for art. Generally speaking and on the whole, the ships eventually reach their destination and deliver their freight. Adventures are disruptions of the ordinary. The word "escapade" includes in it the sensations of search, investigation, change in destiny—these become the elements of art. Art has its direction and purposefulness, which does not coincide with the aspect of how interesting the work is, but rather how skillfully the story is arrested or delayed. This is why Odysseus's journey home is not an ordinary voyage on a sailboat during the Trojan War. It is not an ordinary journey—it is a history of impediments.

Theoretically speaking, the discussion leads to the conclusion that art is selective and continuous; various adventures are continually being analyzed in a changing world.

The experience of old structures lingers but they don't repeat; they are used in collision for refuting one another.

It would have been strange to think that the initiation rite admitting a boy into tribal membership, the recognition of his manhood, and the torments that he had to go through were the only things to have survived not just the millennia, but also the period of tribal development and changes of social formations.

Life in itself repeats, since the world is based on an endless number of laws and which correspond to one another in different ways. Electric vibrations might correspond to the vibrations of the bridge through which a train passes, but the bridge is not vibrating because it remembers electricity. It is the unity of laws, not their memory.

The norms of the world are realized in art as the norm of art, which is connected with the laws of consciousness.

LANGUAGE AND POETRY

The Road into the Future and the Past
(An Unfinished Story)

I

In July 1856 Lev Tolstoy was ". . . writing a somewhat fantastic story."

He wrote only eight pages. They are inserted in a folio made of writing paper. Some of the pages contain separately inscribed phrases above the text representing the plan of the story and how it should develop.

The work was abandoned. Let's turn the pages and go over the typed text.

". . . Major Verein rode alone in the night on the road from the Belbek mill to the Inkerman position."

He was returning from a regimental celebration.

It was raining—gently sprinkling, then the drops would get larger, slanting with the wind, falling heavy and fast as though from invisible trees.

"On the road going south, over the horizon, the black sky often lit up with red streaks of lightning and Verein could hear the rumble of gunshots in Sevastopol. Wrapped in his army overcoat, heavy and reeking of soap from wetness, the major sat hunched on the damp warm saddle, pushing relentlessly his wet slippery heels into the sides of the tired bay cavalry horse."

Verein is a tall man with long legs and angular back. He is thirty-five and had served in the army for seventeen years, after which he was sent to Sevastopol where he maintained an impeccable record. He spoke perfect French and German, studied Italian, was always busy, and hardly ever had time to get bored. He didn't take part in the battles.

"The campaign in Crimea had moved him. He considered both sides of the situation: 1) his salary would be much higher during the campaign; 2) he could be killed or maimed for life. And as a result of the second reasoning, he thought about retiring and getting married. He thought long and hard, and decided that before retiring [and] getting married he first had to go on the campaign. From that moment on the dream of family happiness became an inseparable part of his memory and he contemplated it with an exceptionally unusual tenderness. He spent his leisure time in Crimea alone in his tent, smoking a pipe with a gloomy face, staring blankly at one spot and painting pictures of family happiness in his mind: a wife in a white bonnet, children playing in front of the balcony and picking flowers for papa."

Verein kept on riding.

It was still drizzling. Then the moon came out. The road turned whiter. Verein dozed off for a couple minutes, woke up, looked around and saw an entrance to an alley. The horse went on its own, as if going home. Verein looked at the horse—"It had changed. It was raven-black now, with a thick neck, pointy ears and a long mane." A dog with a high-pitched squeal started running around them in circles.

"—It's not good when you don't listen to your wife, Pyotr Nikolaevich,—a woman said,—I told you that it was going to rain.— Verein recognized the voice of M. N. and realized immediately that she was his wife, but oddly enough he wasn't surprised. He felt at home and it seemed as though he had been here a long time . . . He walked upstairs. Everything seemed new, yet familiar, awfully familiar and pleasant."

It appeared that he had had a recent argument with his wife, because she didn't want to stop nursing their youngest child, a girl who was already two years old. Now they made peace.

"They entered the living room where on the divan sat Verein's old mother, playing solitaire. She had died eight years ago, now she appeared very old. His older brother sat by the window. He was reading something out loud, by his side stood a boy with curly hair."

The samovar was waiting for Verein. Everyone else had had their tea.

Time is collapsed in this story.

Tolstoy didn't know how to move his hero along the grid of time that was both in the present and future. There were eight years between the time that the major had entered and "Sevastopol time."

Verein had appeared in the future.

I have lived a long life, I have seen crowds, been on many roads, and I know what a wet overcoat smells like.

I live simultaneously in the old world and the new.

I have been reading books by Structuralists with interest, difficulty, and benefit. I am getting acquainted.

I'm not surprised to appear in the middle of a conversation. Everything is interesting, but forgive the man who has long been absent from theory.

I was going my own way. I have seen my own cloudy sky.

Here, as before—forty years later—they are still primarily analyzing the poem; of course now they have applied mathematics to it, as it was expected a long time ago.

They still haven't weaned the child from the breast and she's already grown! The weather is pleasant, but everyone is walking dressed up in academic clothes.

But then again, a man who has just arrived mustn't argue or act surprised.

Ideas repeat—sometimes after fifty years, sometimes after one hundred years. It is good when they repeat with the knowledge that the path has been partially traversed, that there has already been a spiral turn.

It's worse when the repetition appears in the form of discovery.

What is even worse is when one cannot accept the discovery out of stubbornness.

Then what follows is something like an ordeal from an old adventure novel.

In a book that we have read in our early childhood—*The Adventures of Captain Hatteras* by Jules Verne—an expedition going to the North Pole gets lost in a thick fog. Let's keep in mind that the novel was written more than a century ago, which is why we mustn't be surprised to find a beautiful volcano in the North Pole. Here the achievements of old physics still invoke amazement, and the description of the winter camp is followed by a quote from the 1596 expedition led by Willem Barentsz. The most important thing for these explorers was always the discovery. The voyages cost a lot of money and, besides, many explorers never returned from the expeditions: Georgi Sedov, Captain Scott, Roald Amundsen, they all died.

Let's be tolerant toward each other, let's understand how difficult excursions, simple repetitions of circles, can be and let's see what innovation they have brought.

Now let's return to Captain Hatteras. The Captain is traveling with Altamont, an American explorer, Doctor Clawbonny, his loyal friend and an inexhaustible source of scientific knowledge, and his servant-companions, Bell, the carpenter, and Johnson, the boatswain. They get lost and find human traces in the fog, hoping that the footprints belong to Eskimos (because Eskimos don't count, since they are not discoverers). As they follow the tracks they find a lens from a telescope half-buried in the snow. It becomes evident then that they are following the footsteps of some European explorers. It is disappointing but they have to move forward. When they reach the coast, Doctor Clawbonny climbs a hill to examine the southern horizon and when he puts his telescope to his eye, he can't see anything. He studies his telescope—the lens is missing. He rushes down to his friends, yelling: "The footprints . . . the troop!"—"Well?" asks Hatteras. "Are they here?"—"No . . . no . . ." says the doctor. "The lens . . . My lens . . . Mine . . ." He shows them his broken instrument and explains that the footprints are theirs: when the men got lost in the fog, they walked in a circle, and came across their own tracks. "Let's go!" says Hatteras, as though crossing out his old tracks.[92]

II

I am convinced now that the very fact of perception of art depends upon a comparative juxtaposition of a work of art with the world.

92   Jules Verne, *The Adventures of Captain Hatteras*. Translated by William Butcher. Oxford UP, 2005.

The artist, the poet orients himself in the world with the help of art and introduces into what we call the surrounding world his own artistic perception.

There used to be an old term—*ostranenie* or estrangement. It is often printed with one "n," even though the phrase originates from the word *strannyi* (strange). The term came into usage in 1916 spelled in that particular way.

Often the term is mispronounced or mixed with the word *otstranenie*, which means moving the world aside.[93]

Ostranenie is the sensation of surprise felt toward the world, a perception of the world with a strained sensitivity. The term can be established only by including the notion of "the world" in its meaning. This term simultaneously assumes the existence of a so-called content, supposing that content is the delayed, close examination of the world.

Let me reiterate what Einstein wrote in his *Autobiographical Notes*:

> I have no doubt but that our thinking goes on for the most part without use of signs (words) and beyond that to a considerable degree unconsciously. For how, otherwise, should it happen that sometimes we "wonder" quite spontaneously about some experience?

That internal world, the model of the world, created by the artist in order to recognize the world, is formed on the basis of a strained perception, as if through inspiration.

---

93 The Russian prefix *ot* generally signifies a movement from or of something, establishing a relationship of something belonging to or originating from something else from which the first object is being pushed aside, removed, or separated.

The "act of wondering," in Einstein's words, occurs when "an experience comes into conflict with a world of concepts already sufficiently fixed within us."

Science avoids the act of wondering, it tries to overcome the element of surprise. Art preserves it. In poetry, art uses words and previously invented literary constructions—"structures." But it overcomes those structures, knocking them down, and renewing them through the very act of surprise.

The most important thing in the analysis of art is never to lose the sensation of art, never lose its palpability, because otherwise the very object of study becomes meaningless, nonexistent.

What OPOYAZ, the Society for Studying Poetic Language, worked on in a systematic yet contradictory fashion was an attempt to analyze, discover the universality of the laws of art.

I wrote in *Third Factory*:

> What is important about the formal method?
>
> Not the fact that the separate parts of a work can be given various labels.
>
> The important thing is that we approached art systematically. We spoke about art as such. We refused to view it as a reflection. We located the distinctive features of the genus. We began defining the basic tendencies of form. We understood that, in fact, you can distill from works of literature the homogeneous laws that determine their shape.[94]

---

94 Viktor Shklovsky, *Third Factory*. Translated by Richard Sheldon. Dalkey Archive, 2002.

I have clarified many things for myself, and I have rejected many things. Now I don't think that it is necessary to begin and end the analysis of a literary work with the study of language and rhythm. I don't think that definitions in and of themselves are a science.

It is imperative, for example, to approach the analysis of what Dmitri Likhachov modestly called "literary etiquettes" more boldly.

Today they hardly study what once was successfully or rather unsuccessfully called "plot composition"—i.e., the introduction into the analysis of art the study of comparative methods using events that exist outside the realm of art.

It is impossible to work only with structures of art, though the artist, the poet, constantly uses events or objects from real life, arranging them differently and unlike the way they are organized in ordinary life.

A long time ago I declared something rashly. I said that a work of art is the "sum total of its devices."[95]

I said it so long ago that I can only remember the refutation. Today I think that literature is a system of systems. It seems that the difference between the others in the field and myself is that I think the systems of art primarily reveal the contradictions in phenomena. The phenomenon itself, which exists outside of art, is experienced through the method of exploring various types of contradictions, whereas in art it is experienced mainly through the contradictory collision of structures.

I think that Sevastopol, which major Verein left, and the red streaks of lightning in the sky, the distant rumble of explosions, the

95   Viktor Shklovsky, "Art as Device" (1917), in *Theory of Prose*.

drenched horse, and the wet overcoat are just as real as the house, where the hero of the unfinished story arrived.

It seems to me that the artist first separates and extracts a certain set of phenomena from what we call reality, then he tries to newly experience the meaning of those phenomena in the totality of their construction, which must be understood in and of itself, although it is created and exists in the context of the "whole" reality.

I sit down again at the table from which many people have withdrawn. But they didn't disappear, they simply passed.

The man who has lived long, who has reconsidered many of his ideas, is not free from contradictions even now. Let's suppose that this is not his only fate.

On Roman Jakobson's Essay
"Poetry of Grammar and Grammar of Poetry":
New Tracks

I was saying that one doesn't need to return to the old tracks.

But one must use past experiences to strengthen and fortify minor observations.

We mustn't return to the beginning of the twentieth century, we mustn't pine for the fact that OPOYAZ once existed and that we used to publish studies on the theory of poetic language—*Poetics*. Those traces are still there but we aren't going to move forward by following them.

Speaking of the essential, we have already seen that there is a uniformity of laws that formulate a work. Now we know what that means.

It doesn't mean that we are given a particular problem and we put it in front of us, only then to formulate it. No, we build a composition, striving for a revelation of a certain essence, while staying the whole time in the realm of the same laws that get formulated variously in different materials. The priority of content is revealed precisely in the premise that laws are uniform because the problem is uniform. This doesn't mean that there are no contradictions in the composition itself, but they are not accidental—they are the contradictions of different perceptions of structures, their conflict and reinterpretation.

In a literary work, the writer, while moving forward, uses the past as a step—he uses the contradiction of the past. He lives both with his recollections from the past and memory of the future. By "memory of the future," Batyushkov meant hope.

But the memory of the future does not only signal hope but also invention.

Roman Jakobson's essay is elegantly titled "Poetry of Grammar and Grammar of Poetry." The title is its thesis.

The similitude of the left and right parts in the title is not complete—it is more like a mirror reflection of the right and left hands.

The word '*poetry*' stands on the outer edges of the title, while at its center the word '*grammar*' is repeated in different grammatical cases. The conjunction splits everything.

'*And*' is an ambiguous word. It is often used in the headings of scientific works. Yuri Tynjanov titled his thematic collection of essays *Archaists and Innovators*. At some point he was uncertain and wanted to title it "Archaists—Innovators." He was also going to write a special essay entitled "And."

Let's try to clarify what *'and'* means in headings such as "Shakespeare and His Time," or "Pushkin and Batyushkov."

'And'—this often exploited short word is used to signify either a link or juxtaposition, and sometimes—simultaneity.

The parallelism in the heading promises that the poetry of grammar will explain the grammar of poetry. Perhaps it asserts that language, its structure, gives birth to the grammar of poetry.

The assertion of this interpretation of the heading can be found in the essay's first part entitled "Grammatical Parallelism":

> During the late 1930s, while editing Pushkin's works in Czech translation, I was struck by the way in which poems that seemed to approximate closely the Russian text, its images and sound structure, often produced the distressing impression of a complete rift with the original because of the inability or impossibility of reproducing their grammatical structure. Gradually, it became clear: in Pushkin's poetry the guiding significance of the morphological and syntactic fabric is interwoven with and rivals the artistic role of verbal tropes.[96]

Parallelism is further defined in this essay as "the interaction between syntactic, morphologic, and lexical equivalences and dis-

---

96   Roman Jakobson, "Poetry of Grammar and Grammar of Poetry." Translated by Stephen Rudy. This section of the essay has been translated separately under the title "Two Poems by Pushkin." See Roman Jakobson, *Verbal Art, Verbal Sign, Verbal Time*. Ed. Krystyna Pomorska and Stephen Rudy. Minneapolis: U of Minnesota P, 1985. All subsequent quotations from "Poetry of Grammar and Grammar of Poetry" are taken from this standard version.

crepancies, the diverse kinds of semantic contiguities, similarities, synonymies and antonymies, finally the different types and functions of 'blank lines,' all such phenomena call for a systematic analysis indispensable for the comprehension and interpretation of the various grammatical contrivances in poetry."

We shall limit the scope of the essay's analysis to the material on Pushkin.

It is not coincidental that Jakobson takes the poem "I Loved You Once" as the basis for his analysis.

This eight-line poem has been cited sixty years ago by professor of Russian literature D. N. Ovsyaniko-Kulikovsky as a striking example of "lyric" and non-imagist poetry.

Let's look at the poem first:

> Я вас любил: любовь еще, быть может, / I loved you once:[97] love has not yet, it may be,
>
> В душе моей угасла не совсем; / Died out completely in my soul;
>
> Но пусть она вас больше не тревожит; / But let it not trouble you anymore;
>
> Я не хочу печалить вас ничем. / I do not wish to sadden you in any way.
>
> Я вас любил безмолвно, безнадежно, / I loved you silently, hopelessly,

---

97   Throughout the poem Pushkin uses the second-person plural pronoun *vy*, which conveys politeness, respect, and a certain degree of formality. In contrast, the second-person singular pronoun *ty* suggests familiarity and informality. The subtlety of this difference is lost in English translation.

То робостью, то ревностью томим; / Tormented now by
shyness, now by jealousy;
Я вас любил так искренно, так нежно, / I loved you so
truly, so tenderly
Как дай вам бог любимой быть другим. / As God may
grant you to be loved by another.[98]

As Ovsyaniko-Kulikovsky wrote:

The complete lyricism of the mood and expression in these
magnificent verses cannot be subjected to doubt and is
grasped by us immediately, without any effort . . . But where
are the images here? They are completely missing—not
only in the sense of cognitive images but also in the general
sense of separate, concrete representations.

So, to sum up, let's say the following: pure lyricism (verbal) in its essence is *imageless*. And though images often
appear in lyric works, they do not have cognitive power
and hence cannot be equated to real images in the artistic
sense.[99]

The analysis stopped there, it didn't go any further. It inherently
crossed out the old definitions but made no attempt to explicate
what exactly was being "grasped by us immediately."

---

98   Aleksandr Pushkin, "I Loved You Once" (1829). Translated by Stephen
Rudy as it appears in Jakobson's "Two Poems by Pushkin."
99   A footnote by V. Shklovsky: Professor D. N. Ovsyaniko-Kulikovsky. *Teoria
poezii i prozy* [Theory of Poetry and Prose]. 4th ed. Petrograd, 1917. The work
was used as a textbook in secondary school and was reprinted. A bad book.

Jakobson's analysis, on the other hand, gave a very concrete depiction of the linguistic structure of the poem:

> The very selection of grammatical forms in the poem is striking. It contains forty-seven words, including a total of twenty-nine inflectional forms. Of the latter, fourteen, or almost half, are pronouns, ten are verbs, and only five are nouns—moreover, nouns of an abstract, speculative character. In the entire work there is not a single adjective, whereas the number of adverbs is as high as ten. Pronouns—being thoroughly grammatical, purely relational words deprived of a properly lexical, material meaning— are clearly opposed to the remaining inflected parts of speech. All three dramatis personae are designated in the poem exclusively by pronouns: *ja* (I) *in recto*; *vy* (you) and *drugoi* (another) *in obliquo*. The poem consists of two quatrains with alternating rhymes. The first-person pronoun, which always occupies the first syllable of a line, is encountered four times, once in each couplet—in the first and fourth line of the first quatrain, and in the first and third of the second. *Ja* (I) occurs here only in the nominative case, only as the subject of the proposition, and, moreover, only in combination with the accusative form *vas* (you). The second-person pronoun, which occurs exclusively in the accusative and dative (in the so-called directional cases), figures in the poem six times, once in each line, except for the second line of each quatrain, being, moreover, combined with some other pronoun each time it occurs. The form *vas* (you), a direct object, is always dependent (di-

rectly or indirectly) on a pronominal subject. In four instances that subject is *ja* (I); in another it is the anaphoric *ona* (she), referring to *ljubov* (love) on the part of the first-person subject. In contrast, the dative *vam* (you), which appears in the final, syntactically subordinated, line in place of the direct object *vas* (you), is coupled with a new pronominal form, *drugim* (another). The latter word, in a peripheral case, the "instrumental of the perpetrator of an action," together with the equally peripheral dative, introduces at the end of the concluding line the third participant in the lyric drama, who is opposed to the nominative *ja* (I) with which the introductory line began.

It seems that this analysis didn't bring the poem any closer to the reader.

But here is a very interesting remark that Jakobson makes in the end:

> Here Pushkin, an unsurpassed master at utilizing the dramatic collision between verbal aspects, avoids indicative forms of the perfective aspect. The sole exception—"love has not yet, it may be, / Died out completely in my soul"— actually supports the rule, since the surrounding accessory words—"yet," "it may be," "perhaps," "not completely"— bring to naught the fictitious theme of the end.

This clearly indicates that the poem ends with a rejection and the words "As God may grant you" express the advent of something impossible. The lyrical hero thinks that his love cannot be replaced by another, and that it is higher than anything else that his interlocutor—the woman—might ever encounter in the future.

The poem "I Loved You Once" is a speech addressed to a single person and it is constructed according to the laws of classical rhetoric.

The classical traditions of rhetoric were thriving in Pushkin's time, though he claimed that he "did *not* read Cicero," preferring Apuleius instead.[100]

The laws of rhetoric are based on the particular construction of periods and the interrelations of their parts.

The analysis of the homophony and symmetry of clauses (*kola*) goes back thousands of years. Rhetorical systems differed in their styles; they were approximately classified as grand, elegant, plain, and forceful. Of all these styles, Pushkin's poem can perhaps be characterized as the "forceful type."

This is how the Greek rhetorician Demetrius defined a forceful speech in his treatise *On Style*:

> Conciseness is favorable to this style and a sudden lapse into silence is often even more forceful. And (strange though it may seem) ambiguity often produces force, since what is distantly hinted is more impressive, while what is plainly stated is held in contempt.

The use of the forceful style in this poem is rather unexpected. It seems as though it would have been more appropriate to use the elegant or embellished style for a conversation with a woman, but the styles have been displaced. Pushkin is not imitating the old struc-

---

100   From *Eugene Onegin*, Chapter 8, I.

ture but speaking as if overturning it. He speaks of the personal, about affliction, by suppressing his interlocutor and doing it as if involuntarily with the force of emotion.

At the same time he isn't speaking, as it were, but making a slip-up.

So genres usually exist in synthesized or contradictory forms. If they are given in their pure form, they too can resist ordinary speech. What we consider "imagist" is not based on the ordinary application of words. The poet's forceful, imageless, and as if unfinished address to the woman is an example of a unique negative form, which in this instance becomes especially powerful.

Jakobson's essay raises the question about figurativeness—about tropes—but in fact it analyzes rhetorical speech that has been elevated and made into a poem.

The fusion of poetic speech and verse epistle produces an exceptional literary form and, generally speaking, the structure of a literary work is always formed in correlation with other structures, which as a result furnish the given work with realistic precision.

Words exist in dictionaries, Pushkin reminds us. But they can create poetry only in combination with one another, because poetry is concrete and expresses a new quality of the transmitted message, or, as they say today—"information."

It seems as though we have come full circle in the study of poetics. In some aspects, the further elaborated theory has returned to its old rhetoric. This isn't bad if the fact of return is acknowledged and not turned into replication, and if one can see in it a new approach to the pulsation of the essence.

Plot and Trope

To become an ichthyologist, as they say, one doesn't have to be a fish.

As for me, I am a fish—a writer who analyzes literature as art.

I don't think that the dramatic collision in Pushkin is expressed "between verbal aspects."

It seems to me that the plotted finale is different from the other lines of the poem.

It is exhaled in one breath. It also seems that the dramatic collision is located in the word *you*, which always accompanies the word *I*.

In love poems, Pushkin often addresses the woman using the informal singular *ty* (you).

In rhetoric, litotes is a figure of speech that is the opposite of hyperbole. Pushkin spoke about a family, the members of which were becoming so small that soon one had to lick a finger in order to pick up one of them. That's an example of litotes.

But there is another kind of litotes that intentionally understates something or implies that it is lesser in significance than it really is. If you are freezing but instead you tell your neighbor (because you don't want to worry him) that you are cold, then that's a litotes.

The soldiers used to sing during campaigns in the Caucasus:

> In one word, it's hard,
> It's certainly not easy,
> By the way—it's fine.

This is a litotes.

When one is in love, one is often obliged to speak about love indirectly. If lyric poetry—all of it—is not a trope, then it is dissident speech.

The litotic plot in Pushkin's poem is that a man is trying to persuade himself that his love has faded. In reality, it hasn't. He talks about the various stages of that love, mentioning the changes, and hence gives the plot of analysis of his feelings. Beside the grammatical form this poem has a plot structure with complex peripeteias and characterizations of the qualities of relations.

It is a concise novel.

The number of correlated systems in a literary work, in general, constantly grows.

Compositional correlations get complicated, the meaning of the evental links are preserved but revealed less vividly.

The more the literary form evolves and the more the associative links get complicated, the less it is exhausted—exposed in the form—in its content by the linear, though brilliant, analysis.

This is why I am reviewing Roman Jakobson's excellent essay with such scrutiny.

A Witness from the Side

The prose and documentary writer Vikenti Veresaev translated Homer and was not particularly fond of poetry. His *Notes to Myself* was published posthumously in *Novy Mir* (New World). In essence it was an analysis of the meaning of trope in poetry, or more accurately—an assertion of the absence of that meaning.

Veresaev's claims are hasty, and there is perhaps nothing interesting in them except for the fact that they have been included in Roman Jakobson's research.

The *Notes* apparently interested the linguist as evidence of a disinterested witness.

Jakobson quotes from *Notes to Myself* with a sympathizing comment:

> Veresaev attested in his notes that sometimes he felt as if imagery were "only the surrogate of real poetry." As a rule, the so-called "imageless" or "cognitive" poetry employs the "figure of grammar" instead of repressing tropes.

In his *Notes*, Veresaev quotes a segment that got deleted from the published version of *Count Nulin* (without a mention that he is omitting the first two lines from the beginning):

> He boils as though a samovar . . .
> Or as a volcanic crater,
> Or—we have sufficient
> Similes at our disposal, and yet
> My staid genius has no taste for them,
> A simple story is livelier without them.[101]

Indeed, Pushkin's characteristic peculiarity is that he doesn't like images and comparisons. Because of this he

---

101 A footnote by V. Shklovsky: Veresaev misquotes Pushkin's poem; the second to last line should be "My humble genius is afraid of them."

seems to be particularly simple, and therefore his conquering force becomes markedly more mysterious. Sometimes I feel as if imagery were only the surrogate of real poetry, that when a poet lacks ingenuity to simply express his thought he turns to imagery. This opinion, of course, is heresy and it can be easily refuted. Then, apropos, we would have to cross out all of the poetry of the East. But, without a doubt, the use of imagery allows for all kinds of pretentiousness and affectation.[102]

Veresaev omits a substantial passage from the original text and, by doing so, changes its meaning. He probably would have eliminated those inaccuracies in a reprint. This is what Pushkin had after the uncut line—"But sleep just will not come to Nulin":

A fever runs through every limb.
The Devil fills his wakeful mind
With fancies of a sinful kind.
He boils as though a samovar
Before the hostess with her hand
Will gently turn the faucet off;
Or as a volcanic crater,
Or as a sea before a storm,
Or . . . we have sufficient
Similes at our disposal, and yet
My humble genius is afraid of them.

---

102   Vikenti Veresaev, *Zapiski dlja sebja* [Notes to Myself], 1960.

The stanza employs a "trope" that is rather bold. Pushkin rejected it because he knew that the epic, as it stands, would be criticized for its indecency—of course, later it was accused of "obscenity."

The comparison altered the meaning of the previous scene where Nulin is parting with Natalya Pavlovna:

> Rising, Natalya Pavlovna
> Declares the evening at an end,
> Wishes the count a good night's rest.
> The dizzy, disappointed guest
> Kisses her hand . . . And now, guess what!
> What end to coquetry? The tease—
> And may she be forgiven by God—
> Gives the count's hand a gentle squeeze.[103]

The movement of the "squeezing hand" was automatically being associated with the hostess's posture sitting by the samovar.

As a whole, it was a daring construction.

The "trope" here is certainly not ambiguous. The image of the "heating samovar" or the "boiling samovar," also the "faucet," had a broadly indiscreet meaning in oral folklore.

For example, here is a riddle from Arkhangelsk: "Between the hills, between the dales, a young lad malts a girl."

The hills and the dales are the sides of a traditional wide Tula samovar.

103   Aleksandr Pushkin, *Count Nulin*. In *The Gypsies and Other Narrative Poems*. Translated by Antony Wood. Boston: David R. Godine, 2006. All subsequent quotations from *Count Nulin* are taken from this standard version.

"To malt," according to Vladimir Dal's explanatory dictionary, means ". . . to sweeten up a bit with fermentation."

Here is another one: "Water plays against its sides, fire pushes deep inside."

Veresaev is a unique literary nihilist. I am familiar with his kind. He knows very well that what he is saying is heresy, but he wants Pushkin, too, to be a heretic of his (Veresaev's) own persuasion, so that he would be against what Veresaev considers "pretentiousness and affectation."

Veresaev understands that his statements are too general. The phrase "all of the poetry of the East" includes Persia, India, China, the Bible, and the poetry of the Romantic school. The witness, produced in this case by Jakobson, is testifying inaccurately, probably because he is making notes to himself. He is not a Pushkin textologist.

Some fellow travelers are there only by accident. Jakobson's remarks about Pushkin's poetics are important but they don't explain the main structure of his poetry. *The Prophet*, for instance, is in its entirety made of tropes.

So is the description of the flood in *The Bronze Horseman*.

Pushkin used shifting tropes that were seemingly contradictory and that switched in meaning:

> The mirth, now dead, that once was madly bubbling
> Like fumes of last night's cups is vaguely troubling;
> Not so the griefs that to those years belong:
> Like wine, I find, with age they grow more strong.[104]

---

104   Aleksandr Pushkin, "Elegy" (1830). Translated by Babette Deutsch.

The notion of aged wine doesn't cancel out the "fumes of last night's cups" of disillusionment, but it offers a new evaluation of the latter.

In their poetry, Mayakovsky, Khlebnikov, Pasternak, Tsvetaeva— and they were not poets of the East—often constructed the poem on the plot of an extended image.

All of this compels us to approach the question more seriously: one mustn't only see what one wants to see in the object of study.

Pushkin's mood in *Count Nulin* is complex.

Let's recall the parody chain included in the composition of the narrative poem. Pushkin makes direct references to Shakespeare's *Rape of Lucrece* twice. The second reference is in the scene by Natalya Pavlovna's bed:

> Then realization dawned upon her,
> And full of fury for her honor,
> Also, we may suppose, of fear,
> With sure and swiftly swinging hand
> She didn't hesitate to land
> A good hard blow on Tarquin's ear!

Tarquin's name is mentioned in an earlier scene where Nulin fumbles into her bedroom:

> Tarquin, in hope of sweet reward,
> Once more sets forth to seek Lucretia,
> Resolved to go through fire to reach her.

Pushkin had commented on this occasion:

> I found myself in the countryside at the end of 1825. Re-reading *Lucrece*, a rather weak poem of Shakespeare, I thought—what if it had occurred to Lucrece to give Tarquin a slap? Perhaps this would have cooled his enterprise and he would have been obliged to leave in shame? Lucrece would not have stabbed herself to death, Publicola would not have been enraged, Brutus would not have chased out the kings, and the world and its history would have been different.
>
> And so, we owe the republic, the consuls, the dictators, the Catos, and Caesar to a seductive occurrence similar to one that took place recently in my neighborhood—the Novorzhevsky County.
>
> I was struck by the idea of parodying both history and Shakespeare. I could not resist the double temptation and in two mornings had written this story.

In his "story," history is intersected with "a seductive occurrence." Pushkin loved images and comparisons, but he despised and parodied triviality by inserting a new meaning in the composition.

His structures are complicated and multilayered.

They resemble a forest. The forest is a structural system that links trees and mushrooms that grow differently and that can exist only in the following correlation—trees, undergrowth, grass, mushrooms—where everything is interconnected. The poet creates such forests and gives suggestive paths that lead inside.

Vsevolod Pudovkin used to tell me that a film director was someone who paved a path which one had to follow in order to see something exquisite.

The parody is carried out successfully, but the poet gives it a new reading. At first it seems that the honor of Natalya Pavlovna's husband is saved with the slap.

But then it turns out that the poet isn't defending the conceited husband at all. The story of the failed escapade is told to everyone. And though the husband is enraged, the poet continues:

> Lidin laughed most heartily,
> Their neighbor (who was twenty-three).

It turns out that Natalya Pavlovna has a young lover, and he is from their neighborhood.

He is laughing with Natalya Pavlovna.

The narrative poem incorporates tropes and repetitions of plot switching.

We mustn't separate the plot-evental structure of the work from its verbal structure. They don't coincide but they are correlated.

This is the forest, which Veresaev couldn't see beyond the first row of trees.

The poetry of Khlebnikov, Mandelstam, Tsvetaeva, and Mayakovsky isn't merely a collision of grammatical forms but it's also poetry with tropes. It is a collision of fates, the passage of a people through the edges of history.

Poets live a certain life, then they move onto another life, anticipating a third one. They anticipate as though by being resurrected in the future. Imitating biblical structures, Mayakovsky spoke about resurrection, floods, and new arks that go on journeys and arrive at new shores.

This evental structure, these collisions of meanings, the battle of meanings is subordinated to the universal laws of art. The poem cannot exist without it—the regenerating structure. It (the structure) has existed owing to its singularity.

Now I am moving on to recollections of life and poetry.

This is what writers do when they are not young anymore—they dream dreams.

Content and Conflict

Trying to refine their analysis, people search for examples of *single-layered* works, as it were.

That search is futile.

We can analyze the vocabulary of a composition, examine its prosody, syntax, and plot construction separately. This reminds me of my old, complicated, and somewhat perfected mistake. Half a century ago I wrote that a work of art has no content in itself and is comprised of the sum of its devices. That's precisely how I phrased it—the *sum*. If we agreed for a minute that a work of art has no content, then we would still encounter an understatement—why are the devices, the methods of artistic construction, summed up? Why aren't they being subtracted from one another, divided, or multiplied?

The notion of a literary work as a multistory construction with parallel, simultaneously existing floors (levels) or the idea that a literary work is comprised of a sum of artistic devices is incorrect. The floors are supported by walls and they often repeat one another in their design. They exist in simple relations with one another that don't require an overly complex analysis.

Do we have such a phenomenon in art?

The vocabulary of the separate parts of a work might already be contradictory by assignment.

If we take the basic rhythmic structure of a composition, the epic poems of Nekrasov and Mayakovsky, for example, often have a shifting meter.

In one of his epics Mayakovsky inserted a ballad containing elements from the vocabulary of the romance genre and the romantic eventality of a so-called "Gypsy romance."

A work of art almost always contains in itself a contradiction. The content of the work is often actualized precisely through those *palpable* contradictions. One can try and succeed in isolating the one side of those contradictions, but it's impossible to find a work, which in its composition would express a parallelism of different kinds of construction.

The conflict of the work itself is carried through rhythmically.

In the early 1920s, we were interested in montage. We thought that montage was the linking or connecting of pieces similar to the way bricks are assembled on cement to make a wall.

I refuted this view, too, in my essays of 1923 and 1924, pointing to the contradictoriness of montage.

Sergei Eisenstein acknowledged the primitivism of such artistic perception in a series of essays, among which he considered the essay "Vertical Montage" to be the most critical.

The concept of *vertical montage* is based on the orchestral score, where different lines indicate various possibilities of expression, all existing synchronously in their contradiction. Hence, in their first proposal to use sound in film, Eisenstein, Pudovkin and Aleksandrov insisted that sound, including the spoken word, should somehow contradict imagery. In any case, the word should be in a complex relationship with it—a kind of complexity that would be perceptible to the audience as well.

Sound film is not the same as silent film with sound that has been adapted to the image. Eisenstein achieved a lot in his study of the principle of montage and it's too bad that today they don't take his original assertions into consideration simply because they were preliminary and easily grasped.

Montage is an assemblage of variously expressed meanings that articulate a new content—the form.

Eisenstein wrote in his essay "Perspectives" (1929):

> "Content"—the act of containing something—is *a principle of organization*, as we would have said in a more flowing manner of expression.
>
> The principle of organization of thought appears to be the factual "content" of an artistic work.

So what is the main principle of organization in a work of art? The content is discovered in the organization of the composition. Sergei Mikhailovich wrote in that same essay:

> *There cannot be art without conflict.*
> Whether it is the collision of the acutely pointed lancet arch from the Gothic period with its inexorable laws of weight,

or the conflict of a hero in fatal peripeteias in a tragedy,

or the clash of a building's functional purpose with the conditions of earth, landscape, and construction materials,

or conquering the rhythm of a canonical poem with a mo-
notonously fixed meter.

The battle is everywhere.

A formation, born from the collision of contradictions,

the capturing force of which grows in its intensiveness
through newer and newer spheres of affective reactions
of the perceiver.

As a film director, Sergei Eisenstein had the opportunity to work
with a particular kind of material—a reel of film with fixed movements. The reel has its beginning and its end. The task was to link
the segments of the film.

At first the segments were linked according to a successive, chronological order. That was the sole function of montage. It was soon
discovered that this was not enough. And it was not only Eisenstein
who thought that this was not enough, but also other influential authors and well-known artists who didn't put forth analytical questions as theoreticians do, but who discovered through intuition.

Let's move on to Eisenstein's essay "Behind the Frame." Here is
its thesis:

The frame is by no means an *element* of montage.

The frame is a montage *cell*.

Just as cells in their division form a phenomenon of another order, the organism or embryo, so, on the other side
of the dialectical leap from the frame, there is montage.

By what, then, is montage characterized and, consequently, its cell—the frame?

By collision. By the conflict of two pieces in opposition to each other.

By conflict. By collision.

In front of me lies a crumpled yellowed sheet of paper. On it is a mysterious note:

"Linkage—P" and "Collision—E."

This is a substantial trace of a heated bout on the subject of montage between P (Pudovkin) and E (myself).

After several years of heated debates with Pudovkin, Eisenstein formulated a different theory: "I confronted him with my viewpoint on montage as a *collision*. A view that from the collision of two given factors *arises* a concept. From my point of view, linkage is merely a possible *special* case."[105]

The basis of every art form is always conflict—an exposure of the noncoincidence of the essence of a phenomenon. This is precisely why the analysis of a literary work is the analysis of conflicts in the very mode of expression.

Let's compare the lyrical hero's words from the poem "I Loved You Once" with Mayakovsky's fate. It is summarized and expressed in verse, and in general it is supposed to be analyzed as the fate of the poet. But, at the same time, it is the fate of the man of a new epoch who relates to people in new ways, and whose relationship to the woman must also be new. And Mayakovsky dedicated all of his work

---

105   A footnote by V. Shklovsky: With the invention of sound and color in cinematography, the analysis evolved in the direction of "vertical" montage.

to express the new sensation of that new life, all of it—the entirely new verbal instrumentation, the new rhythm and new methods of returning meaning through rhyme, and the new depth of rhyme that snatches the word from the middle of a previous sentence. This is how the infantryman used his halberd or glaive to snatch a knight from the row of knights, inventing thus his unique and fatal destiny.

"He" and "She"

Let's return once more to our discussion of pronouns.

Let's talk about lyric poetry.

One hundred and thirty-four years ago, Gogol wrote in an essay entitled "A Few Words about Pushkin" (1834) that Pushkin is "an extraordinary phenomenon and perhaps a unique manifestation of the Russian spirit: he is a Russian of the highest caliber, the kind that might appear perhaps only once in two hundred years."

Linguistic analysis is extremely important, as it is equally important that poetry is being studied scientifically, but let's not forget that the poet and his poetry are not only engendered by life but that they also engender life. One of the themes of the Russian folk song is love in the sense of the carnivalesque, so to speak, filled with springtime revelries. It is about the joys and miseries of marriage, about love and "bad" husbands.

The poet arrives and creates a new quality of love, he creates poems that surprise us—he foretells our own experience.

There are structures in the common work done by poets, artists and inventors who don't necessarily collaborate with one another.

Extracted from the ore, the sparks of the new are combined. A new composition emerges and it reinterprets structures through comparative juxtaposition.

It seems that in the poem "I Loved You Once" Pushkin surpasses himself. We don't have to look into his biography but we must think about the feelings created by this poet.

Let's compare the poem to Mayakovsky's poem "About This" (1923):

> It hurts?
>> So what . . .
>>> You live revering even pain . . .

I am not comparing the poets of the past with the poets of the present. Let's consider that the models of the world are created in poetry for the purpose of rebuilding the world. It's true, they use only words, but those are extraordinary words that are felt through the mouth, that renew thought and disrupt the sclerosis of concepts.

A lyric poem always contains a story, but it is not biographical.

The story of man is inscribed in the history of humanity.

It is universalized by other structures, for the poet—by structures taken from life.

Mayakovsky wrote to Tatyana Yakovleva who had been delayed in Paris. He called her to return to him as a man and simultaneously as a city:

> Come here now,
>> come to the crossroads
> of my great

and clumsy arms.
You don't want to?
Then stay and hibernate.
To old injuries
we'll add
a new one.
All the same
I will take you
some day
on your own
or with Paris too.[106]

He called her to return to "the crossroads" of his arms.

He felt as if he were a city—a citizen of his country.

In a letter to his friend Prince Vyazemsky, Pushkin wrote: "We know Byron well enough. We have seen him throned in glory; seen him in the sufferings of his great spirit; seen him on his catafalque at the heart of resurgent Greece."

Pushkin agreed with Thomas Moore's decision to destroy or bury Byron's letters. Pushkin continued: "The crowd eagerly laps up confessions, memoirs, etc., for in its baseness it delights in the degradation of the great, in the weaknesses of the powerful. It is overjoyed at the disclosure of any depravity. *He is as petty as we are, he is as vile as we are.* But you lie, scoundrels: He may be petty and vile— but not in the way that you are—in a different way!"

For Pushkin, Byron was "He" who had a complex destiny. The pronoun appears after a colon, and yet it's capitalized.

106   Vladimir Mayakovsky, "Letter to Tatyana Yakovleva" (1928). Translated by Peter Tempest.

Many of us are interested in the biographies of great figures. We publish countless books about their lives and consume them eagerly. But we should remember why they lived and why we are interested in them—Pushkin, Mayakovsky, Yesenin.

In an essay written after Yesenin's death, Mayakovsky crossed out a sentence from the draft. It said: "You have nothing left—no money in advance, no wench, no pub."

This was rhymed with the word "sobriety":

> What shall I do with these lines? How should I cut them down? I will leave out "no wench." Why? Because these "wenches" are living people. It would be tactless to call them that, when most of Yesenin's lyric poetry is dedicated to them with great tenderness. And that's why it is false, it doesn't sound right.[107]

One ought to talk poetically about love poems.

Boccaccio wrote that real women, not muses, compelled him to create the best in his work. One must be grateful for the inspiration.

Everything changes in the creative memory.

When the duchess asks Don Quixote about Dulcinea and whether she is a figment of imagination, the knight replies: "There is much to say about that . . . God knows if Dulcinea exists in the world or not, or if she is imaginary or not imaginary; these are not the kinds of things whose verification can be carried through to the end" (Part II, Chapter 23).[108]

---

107   Vladimir Mayakovsky, "How to Make Verse" (1928).
108   Miguel de Cervantes, *Don Quixote*. Translated by Edith Grossman. New York: HarperCollins, 2003. All subsequent quotations from *Don Quixote* are taken from this standard version.

With Sancho he speaks more poignantly: "In the same way, Sancho, because of my love for Dulcinea of Toboso, she is worth as much as the highest princess on earth . . . Do you think the Amaryllises, Phyllises, Sylvias, Dianas, Galateas, Alidas, and all the rest that fill books, ballads, barbershops, and theaters are really ladies of flesh and blood who belong to those who celebrate them?" (Part I, Chapter 25).

The women to whom Pushkin dedicated his poems, to whom Yesenin and Mayakovsky wrote poems, exist—they are real.

Don Quixote didn't allow the duchess—the mistress of the castle—to make fun of his love. Why is the knight so sensitive? He isn't—he is wise. Love, the love for a particular woman was never born easily. She was outlined, delineated in poetry: she was distinguished in the Bible in the way how Jacob didn't just want to become related to Laban, who was wealthy, through marriage, but he asked for Laban's youngest daughter's—Rachel's—hand in return for working fourteen years for him.

The academician Ignati Krachkovsky studied the theme of love in early Arabic poetry—and particularly the epic of *Layla and Majnun*. Majnun means "the madman." Fifteenth-century Uzbek poet Alisher Navoy wrote profusely on this theme. The epic's hero loves even the dog on the street where his beloved lives.

Majnun's name became associated with free, self-chosen love. It developed into a popular theme in poetry from Arabic countries, Iran, and nations living around the Caspian Sea.

A man falls in love with a woman and loses his mind. He searches for no other woman but Layla.

Majnun is more of a madman than Don Quixote. He is a man whose madness was imitated by the heroes of chivalric romances, such as Amadis of Gaul, who was in turn imitated by Don Quixote.

When Majnun met Layla and they kissed, the wild beasts gathered around them, the grass grew as tall as the trees and hid the lovers.

Love was maturing in poetry. The poets were inventing, composing, adapting the things that lovers said to one another about their love, the things that they promised to each other.

In his monograph *On Arabic Manuscripts*, Krachkovsky wrote about the search for Majnun's origins.

They tried to trace his lineage to a tribe, and not just Arabs—even Heine wrote about this.

Scholars of antiquity researched every tribe but couldn't find the birthplace of this madman whose songs were sung in every corner of the world.

We are all familiar with Hamlet's words about "the linkage of times that collapsed," which as a paraphrase renders the image of a breaking chain or string of beads. But in the literal sense, according to A. Anikst's afterword in his Russian translation of the play, the original text says—"the time is out of joint" (Act I, Scene 5). After which Hamlet states that he has "to set it right."

He is healing the time, reinventing it.

And it is Hamlet who, when asked what he is reading, replies: "Words, words, words."

Yet this is a trope—they are words, but they are different words.

One must achieve the correlation of various measures when analyzing. One ought to understand—by preserving the verbal gaps—that when creating them, the poet created new meanings that have to be conquered.

From one epic poem to another Mayakovsky dreamed about resurrection. He wished to be resurrected in the coming decades, centuries.

He pleaded with the future scientist, actualizing the idea of resurrection in the form of a request:

> Resurrect me
> > if only because
> > > as a poet,
>
> > > > I
>
> waited for you,
> > putting aside the daily nonsense!
>
> Resurrect me—
> > if only for that!
>
> Resurrect me,
> > I want to live my share!
> So that there won't be love—the servant
> of marriages,
> > desire,
> > > and breads.[109]

He was unhappy not because he wanted to build a new life for himself, and not because he was in love with the wrong woman, but because he wanted to see his life built into the life of a society that was not yet finished being formed.

It was his greatest desire, in the name of poetry. In the poem "Back Home," he wrote:

---

109 Vladimir Mayakovsky, "About This" (1923).

Proletarians

        arrive at communism

                from below—

by the low way of mines,

        sickles,

             and pitchforks—

but I,

      from poetry's skies,

          plunge into communism,

because

     without it

        I feel no love.[110]

This, too, is reality that needs to be analyzed. It is not only the reality of Majnun and Don Quixote, but also the reality of our present day that is moving into the future, that believes in the future and illuminates our present day with faith in the future.

The need to insert in the analyses the structures of evental facts created by the writer was obvious even to Roman Jakobson, but he didn't carry it out.

He admits this only laconically through half-phrases. This depletes the analysis and knocks it down to the old, already resolved argument about whether "image" is the basis of a literary work.

Plot is not the recording of fact. Rather, it is the artistic formulation of a chain of events—their collision, their comparison. Without understanding this, even through the most methodical

---

110   Vladimir Mayakovsky, "Back Home" (1925). Translated by Max Hayward and George Reavey.

analysis of the "grammar of poetry," we will arrive at the same old rhetoric.

We can't be indifferent to the old rhetoric, but we mustn't repeat it either—we must reinterpret it. We mustn't forget that rhetoric concerned itself with teaching persuasion and not showing how a writer creates a model of the world.

Oratorical poetics and the poetics of an artistic work are closely related but they are two different things.

The founders of rhetoric dreamed about creating a science of the word, just as Major Verein dreamed of a family life.

It is impossible to arrive into the future by skipping over the present and its new problems.

FRANÇOIS RABELAIS
AND MIKHAIL BAKHTIN'S BOOK

About Gargantua and Pantagruel,
and about Bakhtin's Rabelais and His World

Rabelais's novel has a strange and unique fate, starting with the way that it was published. The publication of the novel began from the second book, in which the author explicitly stated that he didn't write the first book. Here is what the author says in the prologue:

> You have recently read, fed, and taken to bed a book I did not write, *The Great and Absolutely Priceless Chronicles of the Great Giant Gargantua*. Like true believers you have swallowed literally every word written there, as if it were the text of the Holy Bible . . .

The book, which Rabelais refers to as the already finished book and which had captivated the readers, was published around 1532. It was a cheap illustrated mass edition depicting a parodied world of magicians, giants, and knights. Rabelais changed the surroundings of his heroes.

The first chapter of this book chronicles the origins and antiquity of Pantagruel's family.

It mentions the Bible and how Pantagruel's origins date back to the time when "Abel was killed by his brother, Cain."

The genealogy recorded in the Bible, besides listing names, also mentions the achievements of Adam's descendants: "Adah bore Jabal; he was the ancestor of those who live in tents and have livestock" (Genesis 4:20).

Then, "Zillah bore Tubalcain, who made all kinds of bronze and iron tools" (Genesis 4:22).

In Pantagruel's genealogy the remarks are made in the following way: "Goliath begat Eryx, the Sicilian giant who invented the shill game: which shell has a nut in it?" Or: "Caccus begat Etion, the first man to catch the pox because he didn't drink enough cool, fresh wine in the summertime." Or: "Oromedon begat Gemmagog, who invented those horrible pointed shoes they still wear in Poland."

The parody continues; for example, there is a line about an ancestor who was "the first in the world ever to play dice while wearing spectacles."

The parody here is explicit, as there are evident references to the Bible in the author's prologue—I will get back to it shortly.

In 1535, after the *second* book was published, Rabelais wrote the *first* book with which he obviously intended to replace that harmless book, which he parodically continued.

The title of the first book puts the emphasis on Gargantua, but it also mentions Pantagruel twice—first explicitly, then the book itself is characterized as "full of Pantagruelism."

Aside from that, the book is remarkable in its unusual audacity, which perhaps nobody has been able to surpass until this day. It underscores the antireligious sentiment of the novel, or I should probably say—its anti-Christian bias.

Gargantua's genealogy is very long and it goes back to Noah's ark. The author remarks gleefully:

> Let me explain that by a sovereign gift straight from heaven we've been given Gargantua's genealogy, right from the beginning of time, more complete than that of any man but the Messiah, of whom I say nothing, because it's none of my business. Also the devils (by which I mean slanderers and hypocrites) don't want me to. (Book I, Chapter 1)

The genealogy of "the Messiah" is narrated in the Gospel according to Matthew: "So all the generations from Abraham to David are fourteen generations; and from David to the deportation to Babylon, fourteen generations; and from the deportation of Babylon to the Messiah, fourteen generations" (Matthew 1:17).

Rabelais is mocking the length of this genealogy.

The source at which the parody is directed is masked by conversations about trivial things and references to great works by authors and scholars from the antiquity.

If we speak more generally about Rabelais's book as "carnivalized" literature, then we should mention that the participants of this particular carnival are extremely intelligent people who assume the readers to be ironic, erudite scholars.

The author's prologue is a parody of scholarly speech. The first chapter is antireligious. The second chapter is a parody about finding a little book with a treatise entitled *Antidotal Jokes* in an ancient tomb.

The jokes are written in verse and contain parodies of mythology and phrases that are grammatically correct but make no sense.

The fourth chapter chronicles the birth of Gargantua, which takes place during a banquet. After mowing the fields and killing the oxen, everyone overeats at the banquet.

Pregnant with Gargantua, Gargamelle is described as having eaten too much fatty beef tripe on the third day of February.

She overeats in the autumn—after the second mowing, when they were salting the meat so they would have plenty of pressed beef in the springtime.

Back then people didn't have refrigerators and they preserved meat by salting, curing, making sausages with various spices. Perhaps this can also explain the cost of spices in the Middle Ages.

After slaughtering the oxen, there was an excess of tripe that was bound to go rotten—they decided it was their duty to eat it all. Tripe is a type of edible offal from the chambers of the animal's stomach.

Rabelais connects all of these commonplace circumstances with the religious myths about the Immaculate Conception and the miraculous birth of the Messiah.

Chapter 6 is dedicated to the miracle of Gargantua's birth. This is how it happens: the mother gets an upset stomach, they give her a strong astringent, and consequently the birth is delayed.

> It made her womb stretch loose at the top, instead of the bottom, which squeezed out the child, right into a hollow vein, by means of which he ascended through the diaphragm up to her shoulders, where that vein is divided in

two. Taking the left-hand route, he finally came out the ear on that same side.

It would seem that all of this is a joke, an incredible joke at that, but Rabelais justifies himself by saying:

> I'm not sure you're going to believe this strange birth. If you don't, I don't give a hoot—but any decent man, any sensible man, always believes what he's told and what he finds written down. Doesn't Solomon say, in Proverbs 14, *Innocens credit omni verbo* ("An innocent man believes every word")? And doesn't Saint Paul say, in I Corinthians 13, *Charitas omnia credit*, ("Charity believes everything")? Why shouldn't you believe me? Because, you say, there's no evidence. And I say to you that, for just this very reason, you must believe with perfect faith. Don't all our Orthodox argue that faith is precisely that: an argument for things which no one can prove?
>
> And is there anything in this against the law? or our faith? or in defiance of reason—or Holy Scripture? Me, I find nothing written in the Holy Bible that says a word against it.

Other translations of the Latin quotes are: "The fool believes everything" and "Love believes everything." But if we take the version in the Bible, which Rabelais is so explicitly referencing, we'll see that Solomon says something else: "The simple believe everything, but the clever consider their steps" (Proverbs 14:15).

The apostle Paul was very influential among religious reformers; he wrote: "[Love] does not rejoice in wrongdoing, but rejoices in the truth" (I Corinthians 13:6)—and: "When I was a child, I spoke like a child, I thought like a child, I reasoned like a child; when I became an adult, I put an end to childish ways" (I Corinthians 13:11).

Rabelais then proceeds to list a plethora of incredible births in Greek mythology and the legends of Franks:

> Wasn't Bacchus spawned by Jupiter's thigh?
> And the giant Roquetaillade, wasn't he born from his mother's heel?
> And Croquemouche, wasn't he born out of his nurse's slippers?
> And what about Minerva: wasn't she born out of Jupiter's head—and through his ear?
> And Adonis, didn't he appear through the bark of myrrh tree?
> And Castor and Pollux, out from the shell of an egg laid and then hatched by Leda?

But the most important in all this game is the catechist phrase: "faith is precisely that: an argument for things which no one can prove."

The seemingly labyrinthine recounting and baroque overabundance of information given by Rabelais have a concealed purpose of diverting the reader's antagonism. The attention Rabelais received from his friends was different—the humanists were knowledgeable and knew, "like a dog," how to crack the bone open just to taste a bit of marrow. Here is Rabelais's characterization: "Just like the dog, you ought to be running with your educated nose to the wind, sniffing out and appreciating such magnificent volumes—you should be light on your feet, swift in the chase, bold in the hunt." Then he says, "by hard reading and constant reflection, you ought to crack the bone and suck the nourishing marrow" (Book I, Author's Prologue).

There is a passage in Genesis that mentions the following: "The Nephilim were on the earth in those days—and also afterward—when the sons of God went in to the daughters of humans, who bore children to them" (Genesis 6:4). I can't give extended commentaries here because it will break the content of the book.

It turns out that not all men are the descendents of Adam.

In the Book of Numbers we read about the twelve scouts whom Moses sends to explore the land of Canaan. They report back: "There we saw the Nephilim (the Anakites come from the Nephilim); and to ourselves we seemed like grasshoppers, and so we seemed to them" (Numbers 13:33).

Pantagruel, too, is a descendent of a race of giants, but these giants are parodied—they are what we call the "supernatural beings." In the antiquity, they used to tell about people with only one leg, or people whose faces were on their chests.

In Rabelais's world there are men with immense noses and hunched backs; they are just as real as the men with enormous ears who drink barley water—i.e., beer.

Their ears are so big that they could make a jacket out of just one of them, and a cape from the other one.

Then Rabelais continues with his version of the Bible:

> Others grew immense bodies. From them, finally, came the race of giants, from whom, ultimately, Pantagruel was born:
>> And the first of the giants was Chalbroth,
>> Who begat Sarabroth,
>> Who begat Faribroth,
>> Who begat Hurtaly, who loved bread soaked in soup: he reigned at the time of the Flood,
>> Who begat Nimrod,
>> Who begat Atlas, whose shoulders kept the world from falling,
>> Who begat Goliath,
>> Who begat Eryx, the Sicilian giant who invented the shill game: which shell has a nut in it?
>> . . . Who begat Aranthas,
>> Who begat Gabbara, who was the first ever to drink a toast . . .

Rabelais himself was a daring giant who was trampling on old science and religion.

If we were to crack the bone of the carnival, which he created, then it is a carnival of enlighteners—a carnival of humanists.

Empress Catherine II tried to establish something similar.

Mitropolit Yevgeni reports the following about Denis Fonvizin's *Message To My Servants Shumilov, Vanka, and Petrushka*: "The book first appeared in 1763, in Moscow, during Shrovetide masquerade when for three days the Moscow printing houses were permitted to publish freely."[111]

The epistle contains a master's conversation with his servants about the meaninglessness of human existence.

Nikolai Tikhonravov disagrees with Mitropolit Yevgeni, saying that *Message to My Servants* was published in monthly installments in *Pustomelia* (The Tattler) in July 1770. However, after the appearance of this work, the journal's publication was stopped.

I used to have a separate edition of Fonvizin's book in my own library, I don't know where it is now, but Mitropolit Yevgeni's report is accurate. I am more interested in the masqueraded liberties permitted by Catherine for only three days. Later many people repented for actually using this gift of freedom.

Rabelais was more fortunate in his ability to confuse his enemies. The excess of commonplace details, the realities of common people camouflaged the book; it appeared to be a book on trifles.

The carnival is realistically present in Rabelais but it has a purpose.

Obviously the Bible is in the background of Rabelais's work and is the main target of attacks. The chivalric romances are in the foreground. But in this novel the heroes are not ordinary knights, they are giant-knights who defeat everything and everyone. These giants can also be linked to the passage from Genesis (about the Nephilim).

Among Pantagruel's—and consequently his father's—ancestors are giants such as Atlas and Goliath, titans such as Briarus, who had a hundred hands, and Antaeus.

---

111 Nikolai Tikhonravov, *Sochinenia N. S. Tikhonravova* [The Works of N. S. Tikhonravov], 1898.

What we have here is a chain of insinuations and deriding caricatures—a parody of the Bible, which has been equated to Greek mythology and deliberate nonsensicality.

This is why I stopped on the birth of the hero and his ancestors. By reworking mass literature, Rabelais turns his parodic hero into a new messiah as well as a descendent of biblical heroes and giants of the antiquity.

A new savior is born. Instead of destroying the power of the devil or the original sin, he obliterates the faith in the devil and in miracles, the falsehood of the old mythology. A godlike giant is born.

Bakhtin's analysis of Rabelais's book is interesting and important. He selected this work from the rest of the literature, showed its connection to the carnival and folk parodies. But I don't think that he really showed who or what the parody was directed at.

The carnival was a place where everyone was given the right to clown and fool around: to speak the truth.

It seems as though whatever has been said at the carnival really means nothing, it's harmless, as it were. But Rabelais's carnival has a target and its parody is rather offensive. He isn't mocking or deriding isolated incidents during that period in France, he is actually parodying the church, the courts of justice, the wars and the made-up rights that gave certain people permission to oppress others.

Bakhtin connected Rabelais's method of description, the social reality of his heroes, and their ways to carry on a dialogue to the carnival and called it "carnivalization," but, as Bakhtin himself notes, the carnival in itself wasn't an aimless or harmless act; it was a return to the Golden Age—a life without constraints but also full of mischief.

Rabelais's carnival doesn't repeat the traditional folk carnival but rather redirects it, renewing the poignancy of the folk culture's first attacks on the dominant culture. The question is raised anew in Bakhtin's book, inspired by the extremity of its construction.

Carnival and Seasonal Work

We mentioned already that Gargantua was born right after the great mowing.

Agricultural work and harvesting is partially related to food: people celebrate the abundance of food and eat a portion of the harvest.

The carnival isn't merely a festival for all, it was initially meant for distinguishing those who labored.

Gargantua didn't work, but the table and the toasts that are pronounced during the banquet are those of the peasantry.

Rabelais's book is written by a highly educated humanist, but it widely employs the rituals of the carnival. During field work, especially during the sowing and cultivation of land, sexual taboos are typically removed and different laws are put into place. This is how the Polish anthropologist Bronislaw Malinowsky described field-work in *The Sexual Life of Savages in North-Western Melanesia* (1929):

> In the south of Kirivin Island and Vokuta Island the women who went out weeding in groups had the right to assault any man who did not belong to their tribe. According to local informants, the women actually undertook this with great zeal and enthusiasm.

The women of Kirivin Island, just as the slaves during the Roman Saturnalias, were exempted from prohibitions and norms reinforced by the existing authorities. This temporary shift in moral values can be traced in almost every nation a hundred years ago and, in the same way, it was observed in Russia, too.

During the sowing, morals also changed, sexual life was as if accentuated, brought to the foreground; it was presumed that the earth's fertility was connected with human sexuality. Christian ecclesiastics themselves often partook in such festivities.

> In various parts of Europe customs have prevailed both at spring and harvest which are clearly based on the same crude notion that the relation of the human sexes to each other can be used so as to quicken the growth of plants. For example, in Ukraine on St. George's Day (the twenty-third of April) the priest in his robes, attended by his acolytes, goes out to the fields of the village, where the crops are beginning to show green above the ground, and blesses them. After that the young married people lie down in couples on the sown fields and roll several times over on them, in the belief that this will promote the growth of the crops. In some parts of Russia the priest himself is rolled by women over the sprouting crop, and that without regard to the mud and holes which he may encounter in his beneficent progress. If the shepherd resists or remonstrates, his flock murmurs, "Little Father, you do not really wish us well, you do not wish us to have corn, although you do wish to live on our corn." In some parts of Germany at harvest the men and women who have reaped the

corn roll together on the field. This again is probably a mitigation of an older and ruder custom designed to impart fertility to the fields by methods like those resorted to by the Pipiles of Central America long ago and by the cultivators of rice in Java at the present time.[112]

Sexual intercourse during a particular season, performed as though by signal, was preserved in the carnival rituals of Rome as well.

Pavel Annenkov in his essay "N. V. Gogol in Rome in the Summer of 1841" recounts Gogol's dinner with his friend Aleksandr Ivanov:

> After emptying his plate, Gogol reclined and soon became cheerful and chatty, and commenced to joke with the servant whom he not so long ago reproached in a harsh manner. Hinting at the old custom of proclaiming the first day of May and arrival of spring with cannon shots from St. Angel Castle, which coincided with the familial customs, he was asking whether the venerable *servitore* was going to *piantar il Maggio* (literally—to plant May) or not? The *servitore* replied that he was going to follow Signor Nicolò's example, and so on.[113]

---

112   Sir James George Frazer, *The Golden Bough: A Study of Magic and Religion*, 1890.
113   Pavel Annenkov, *Literaturnye vospominaniya* [Literary Recollections], 1960.

They were sitting in a trattoria, talking and joking about an ancient custom.

The old tradition linking human sexual life to the arrival of spring was emphasized with a cannon shot that was audible throughout the world.

The cannon was shot from an ancient mausoleum towering above the Tiber, and upon hearing the signal the masses took action.

The form of the cannon represented perhaps a revival of the phallic symbol.

Generally speaking, there has been so much scholarship on carnival rituals and it has been so diverse that Bakhtin, of course, could not have reviewed even a tenth of those texts about the same motifs embodying ancient rituals, jokes that migrated into the realm of art.

It's a pity, though, that Bakhtin's book demonstratively says almost nothing about the festivals that originated Greek comedy and about Aristophanes.

Carnival and Carnivalization

The translator of Aristophanes, dramatist, and Soviet film critic Adrian Piotrovsky wrote in his introduction to Aristophanes's comedies:

> The spring celebrations of Greek farmers, vine-growers and wine-makers, and plowmen, the unruly and drunken processions—the phallic *Komos*—this is where "comedy"

originated from, according to the trustworthy evidence of Aristophanes, the father of ancient learning . . . "Comedy began with the phallic songs," he says, "and they sing them in various cities even today."

. . . the idea of conquering the dull routines of daily life was a certain fantastic reversal of social and natural relations, a reversal where the poor become rich, the "birds" and "animals" exchange places with "humans," the youth become the elderly, women become men—these types of performances served as basis for festivals in general and for theatrical masquerades. They equally define the tremendously popular May Games in medieval England, the Old Church Slavonic games, the Kemetic mystery system of ancient Egypt, and, finally, the Dionysia festival.

It is not without reason that the Komos is a festival of freedom, a celebration of the victory over everyday reality and conformity. Everything in the procession is reversed: the ones at the end come to the front line, women become masters and men turn into servants (*Assembly-Women— The Ecclesiazusae*), the birds become gods, while the gods lose their power (*Birds*), old men turn into boys and schoolboys become pedagogues (*Wasps* and *Clouds*). This reversal—the displacement in habitual relations is what endows the primitive carnival with a powerful *joie de vivre*, pathos of victory over ordinary life, lightness, and brilliance. The displacement is visually reflected in the fantastically magical costume of the Chorus, which turns humans into birds, wasps, and clouds; it permeates in every song and act by the Chorus. The part in the comedy which expresses this displacement with a great definition and force was called *parabasis* by the critics of the antiquity. The parabasis imperatively enters each one of Aristophanes's comedies. It wholly belongs to the people in costumes—the Chorus. Here the Chorus performs songs and "speeches" that eulogize the magical nature; the main motif of "displacement" or "transposition" is enacted in various ways.[114]

The carnival is experiencing changes—it's including history in itself.

This is formulated differently in Bakhtin's *Problems of Dostoevsky's Poetics*. The novelist is analyzed through the lens of carnival, as it were.

Let's take a look at the following passage from the fourth chapter in which Bakhtin elucidates the term "carnival":

> Carnival itself (we repeat: in the sense of a sum total of all diverse festivities of the carnival type) is not, of course, a literary phenomenon. It is *syncretic pageantry* of a ritualistic sort. As a form it is very complex and varied, giving rise, on a general carnivalistic base, to diverse variants and nuances depending upon the epoch, the people, the

114   A footnote by V. Shklovsky: I will not quote the entire Introduction to Aristophanes's *Theater* by Adrian Piotrovsky, but let me cite this final sentence: "Carnival, choral, and political comedy died along with the Athenian democracy and death of Aristophanes."

individual festivity. Carnival has worked out an entire language of symbolic concretely sensuous forms—from large and complex mass actions to individual carnivalistic gestures. This language, in a differentiated and even (as in any language) articulate way, gave expression to a unified (but complex) carnival sense of the world, permeating all its forms. This language cannot be translated in any full or adequate way into verbal language, and much less into a language of abstract concepts, but it is amenable to a certain transposition into a language of artistic images that has something in common with its concretely sensuous nature; that is, it can be transposed into the language of literature. We are calling this transposition of carnival into the language of literature the carnivalization of literature. From the vantage point of this transposition, we will isolate and examine individual aspects and characteristic features of carnival.

Carnival is a pageant without footlights and without a division into performers and spectators. In carnival everyone is an active participant, everyone communes in the carnival act. Carnival is not contemplated and, strictly speaking, not even performed; its participants *live* in it, they live by its laws as long as those laws are in effect; that is, they live a *carnivalistic life*.[115]

---

115   Mikhail Bakhtin, *Problems of Dostoevsky's Poetics*. Translated by Caryl Emerson. U of Minnesota P, 1984. All subsequent quotations from *Problems of Dostoevsky's Poetics* are taken from this standard version.

The general characterization is interesting but it becomes somewhat questionable when it is unconditionally applied to the book.

The dramatic theater's spectator, even today, is involved in the spectacle differently and on a deeper level than the reader in the process of reading.

Another clarification is that the inclusion of carnival elements in the pageant and literary work is still based "on the similarity of the dissimilar," the sensation of a reversal.

The carnival tsar or king implies the existence of a non-carnival king—he exists as a refutation just as the kings in the deck of playing cards didn't refute the existence of European kings. The existence of caricature engravings in medieval temples didn't refute religion, they existed alongside religion, and it was a coexistence of two different worldviews expressed through two artistic trends. This resulted in the creation of different sensations that are characteristic to art.

Utopia and satire are historical.

Separate structures that have already expressed the conflicts of society are either forgotten or they reemerge. It is similar to the recollection of something that came into memory unconsciously. Take the epoch of Aristophanes, for example, when a rural festival took over the city culture.

Aristophanes, who perceived the epoch in his own way, was one of the guests at Plato's symposium, but this didn't turn the *Symposium* into a carnival.

Rabelais's epoch is the epoch when memory was called to account for the canonization of new forms: the old was resurrected for the purpose of parodying the present. This duality gave reality to the present through an ironical examination.

Bakhtin himself thinks that antique literature entered Renaissance consciousness in its classical form, as he comments in a footnote:

> The authors of comedy, Aristophanes, Plautus, Terence, did not exercise any considerable influence. It has become commonplace to compare Rabelais to Aristophanes, but their resemblance cannot be explained by Aristophanes's influence on Rabelais. Although Rabelais was familiar with Aristophanes (among the eleven books preserved in his *ex libris* is a volume of Aristophanes in Latin translation), there are but few traces of his influence in Rabelais's novel. A certain similarity in the methods of treating the comic element can be explained by the resemblance of folkloric and carnival sources but should not be exaggerated. Euripides's only satirical drama which has been preserved, *Cyclopes*, was well known by Rabelais; he quotes it twice in his novel, as it must have, doubtlessly, had an influence on him.[116]

The footnote is rather lengthy but it's not fully articulated. It doesn't explain, for example, the nature of the "similarity in the methods of treating the comic element."

Rabelais certainly knew the French folklore of his time very well, but he filled it up with his own parodies of scholasticism, and

---

116   Mikhail Bakhtin, *Rabelais and His World*. Translated by Helene Iswolsky. Indiana UP, 1984. Revised by Shushan Avagyan. All subsequent quotations from *Rabelais and His World* are taken from this standard version.

through a new reinterpretation of Aristophanes, he attacked the aesthetics of high literature. Aristophanes is not Rabelais's source, but he is perhaps the director.

Maybe it would have been better to show how the aesthetic structures have been used broadly in different situations and employed in uniquely dissimilar ways. It's equally important to show the similarity of the dissimilar.

In Russia people celebrated the carnival of Maslenitsa. In the so-called "furnace festivities" some dressed as adolescents who were to be burned, others as Chaldeans who tried to destroy the followers of the true faith. They used pyrotechnic devices and explosives using the powdery spores of certain club mosses. After the Angel's victory over the Chaldeans, they would run out into the streets, raising havoc and setting their beards and carts on fire.

The carnival is an international festival. Carnival festivities in Rome were connected with the ancient Saturnalias where the slaves played the role of masters, while the masters served their slaves. The carnival, as Bakhtin argues, was a return to the Golden Age about which Don Quixote talked with goatherds, and to which Dostoevsky alluded in his drafts of *Crime and Punishment*. The Roman Saturnalias were not merely celebrations of food, but they were celebrations of social freedom; the premise of art here is in the principle that people, finding themselves in new social relations preserve the old relations by overcoming them. We see here a flickering double relationship to facts—to social relations.

It was improper to wear togas during Saturnalia. The city lived in an accentuated, double reality, as it were.

Let's turn now to some objections.

The carnival in its various manifestations is realized through the succession of millennia.

So what is it that differentiates the various manifestations of what Bakhtin calls carnivalization?

To begin with—not every conflict can be characterized as carnivalistic.

This can be argued by the mere fact that carnivals were timed and coincided with certain dates. The pathos of Bakhtin's books on Rabelais and Dostoevsky is in the generalization of conflicts beyond the conscious changes of literary forms.

But such generalizations often gloss over instances of realistic insight.

In his *Problems of Dostoevsky's Poetics*, Bakhtin sympathetically quotes from my book on Dostoevsky in which I was revising and supplementing the critical work done previously, primarily by Leonid Grossman, clarifying the problem of conflictedness in Dostoevsky and subsequently stressing the outstanding qualities of his work. I was saying that:

> As long as the work remained multilayered and plurivocal, as long as the people in it were still arguing, then despair over the absence of closure would not set in. The end of the novel signified for Dostoevsky the collapse of a new tower of Babel.[117]

Bakhtin agreed with most of my remarks in the first chapter of *Problems of Dostoevsky's Poetics*. It is important, I think, that the

---

117   Viktor Shklovsky, *Za i protiv. Zametki o Dostoevskom* [Pro and Contra: Notes on Dostoevsky], 1957.

conflicts which Dostoevsky exposed have not become obsolete and are experienced by humanity today precisely for the reason that they were fixed in a specific moment. I will repeat the observation, which Bakhtin quoted from my polemical note in the journal *Voprosy literatury* (Questions of Literature, #4, 1960):

> What distinguishes my study is not an emphasis on those stylistic characteristics which I consider self-evident—Dostoevsky himself emphasized them in *The Brothers Karamazov* when he titled one of the novel's books "Pro and Contra." I tried to explain something else in my book: what is it that provoked the debate, the trace of which appears to be Dostoevsky's literary form, and, simultaneously, what accounts for the universality of Dostoevsky's novels, meaning—who today would be interested in that debate?

By isolating the structure of historical phenomena, we can say that history repeats, yet at the same time we know that it moves. It moves in multidirectional, yet similar patterns of repetition, as it were.

Bakhtin blends repetitions into an immovable form.

The Rabelaisian carnival is a phenomenon of a particular period, created by people of a certain mentality; they are the ones who direct the carnivalized constructions that are as simple as a coat turned inside out at a Maslenitsa masquerade against the old. Rabelais's carnival is historical.

In a similar vein, Birnam Wood in Shakespeare's *Macbeth* is advancing on the criminal king's castle, but this wood has been cut

down—its trees and branches have been chopped from their roots—
and now it is functionally different, more current for Macbeth.

We cast phenomena into a murky future when we remove them
from their past, but separating Rabelais from the general study of
world literature is an accomplishment in itself, despite the conventionality of terminology and analysis of the carnival.

Inventions and discoveries are in essence failed attempts that
have been surpassed. But not all constellations are accessible. Even
coming up with a title is a difficult task.

An Attempt to Establish Gargantua's and His Son Pantagruel's Dates of Birth, as well as the Dates and Purpose of Their Deeds

Rabelais's epoch was a period of great discoveries and inventions.

In 1440, Gutenberg, who made polished metal mirrors, started
printing from movable type using the conventional screw press.

The first book by Aelius Donatus was published in 1456, which
was a historic event.

In the beginning of Rabelais's novel, Gargantua learns the alphabet
and reads Donatus's Latin grammar along with a few other books which
"took thirteen years, six months, and two weeks to accomplish."

His teacher, the great philosopher Tubalcain Holofernes, also
taught Gargantua to write in Gothic letters and he "wrote out all
his own books that way, since this was before the art of printing had
been invented."

This helps us get closer to deciphering the fictional dates in the
novel—we need them very much.

Undergoing transformations, these giants lived long lives, witnessing great events that happened during their lifetime.

Because of a complaint from his servants about an argument over flatcakes and gripped with thoughts of conquest, King Picrochole declared war against his neighbor Grandgousier, Gargantua's father. Then Picrochole had dreams to conquer the entire world, and capture French cities and castles starting with the provinces near Rabelais's hometown, then seize Germany, Tunis, Algeria, Sardinia, Bavaria, Corsica, Genoa, Florence, Rome, Palestine (here Picrochole wanted to rebuild Solomon's Temple), then finally conquer Asia Minor and reach the shores of the Euphrates.

The list continues for another two pages. It includes England, Iceland, Greenland, Poland, Lithuania, Russia, Constantinople, and, finally, Mesopotamia.

In order to defend the army from an attack from behind, Picrochole's captain suggests that the Muscovites should send four hundred and fifty thousand elite troops for mobilization. The question was about dictatorship over the world.

Gargantua's men surround Picrochole's army and the enemy troops surrender. Then, by the orders of his father, Gargantua pronounces a humanist speech that appears in Chapter 50:

> Our fathers, our grandfathers, and our ancestors from the beginning of time have all felt that, once battles were over and done with, the best memorial of their triumphs and victories should be trophies and monuments created in the hearts of those who had been conquered, brought into being by acts of kindness—and these, they were convinced, were better by far than any architectural symbols erected

in those conquered lands. It seemed to them that the living memories of human beings won by liberality were worth infinitely more than cold, silent inscriptions chiseled onto arches, columns, and pyramids, open to all the injuries to which stone and marble are subject, and forever liable to evoke jealousy and anger.

The enemy is conquered. "May God be with you!" pronounces the humanist. He releases all the prisoners of war, with the exception of the instigators of the rebellion: "But Gargantua did nothing more to any of them than to order that they run the treadles for the new printing presses he had just had installed."

In Book II, Gargantua sends his son Pantagruel to study at the University of Paris. Rabelais evidently assumed that the Sorbonne had carried out reforms to adopt a humanist philosophy, as Gargantua himself had to relearn everything in the school of humanists, where he trained in sports and read the ancient classics.

Gargantua writes to his son: ". . . But divine goodness has let me live to see light and dignity returned to humanistic studies, and to see such an improvement, indeed, that it would be hard for me to qualify for the very first class of little schoolboys—I who, in my prime, had the reputation (and not in error) of the most learned man of my day."

Let's make a note here: according to the encyclopedia, the first Greek text was published in France in 1507, and in 1539 Francis I facilitated the publication of Greek authors. Francis set an important precedent by embracing the new intellectual movement and by becoming a major patron of the humanists; he protected the movement from the Catholic censors at the Sorbonne.

Rabelais himself, while in the monastery, was condemned for reading the "profane works of Homer."

Gargantua's education was a topical issue for Rabelais. Rabelais was a polemicist who was interested in a vast range of questions—mostly in Greek literature, which today is part of the literary discourse. Here is another passage from the letter in which the old humanist addresses the young humanist:

> For now all courses of study have been restored, and the acquisition of languages has become supremely honorable: Greek, without which it is shameful for any man to be called a scholar; Hebrew; Chaldean; Latin. And in my time we have learned how to produce wonderfully elegant and accurate printed books, just as, on the other hand, we have also learned (by diabolic suggestion) how to make cannons and other such fearful weapons. The world is full of scholars, of learned teachers, of well-stocked libraries, so that in my opinion study has never been easier, not in Plato's time, or Cicero's, or Papinian's. From this day forward no one will dare to appear anywhere, or in any company, who has not been well and properly taught in the wisdom of Minerva.

Gargantua and Pantagruel was written by a cheerful humanist. Rabelais filled his book with allusions to classical antiquity. The allusions are, of course, parodies, but in this case the parody is used as a mask—it turns the sermon into a joke.

The ancient authors appear anew in Rabelais's company. The world celebrates their rebirth.

In the author's prologue, Rabelais quotes Alcibiades from the *Symposium* who praises his teacher, Socrates.

Socrates, according to Alcibiades, was ugly and bald-headed, walked barefoot, wore plain, peasant's clothes, was poor and "unlucky with women." But on the inside he was like a Silenus—a box full of rare medicines.

Rabelais is a defender of book printing and the new restored science—the philosophy that affirms the good nature of humans and death of old parochial beliefs.

He mocks Christian mythology. He takes the form of chivalric romance with its traditional adventures and deeds and uses it as a weapon in the war against traditions.

The carnival is the humanist's ally, not his master.

We mustn't think that Rabelais's jokes depict only the celebration of human flesh, even though this is certainly implied, as it was implied in the mischievous plays of Aristophanes, and later in Boccaccio's book about the plague that cleansed a mischievous city.

Rabelais's World

Rabelais's heroes—Gargantua and Pantagruel—are humanist giants and kings and people who are simply free. They defeat everyone, even the old-fashioned giants who came out of fairy tales wearing various types of armor, including armor made of stone, to fight against the humanists. The old giants are defeated by the army of humanists.

Brother John the monk, apparently a man of average height, fought against the enemies of the humanists with a cross-staff. It would have been obscene to use the whole cross as a club. After winning the battle, he was granted the right to establish an abbey on the land of Thélème alongside the river Loire, which would have an inscription on its gate that clashed with the rules and regulations of all the other abbeys or slogans of all coats of arms: "Do what you will!"

The splendid abbey of Thélème is inhabited by beautiful and free people, and is reminiscent of the abandoned villa in which Boccaccio's ladies and their gallant men used to tell each other stories.

To make sure that everything was perpetually in good order, the wood of Thélème was surrounded by a commune of goldsmiths, jewelers, embroiderers, tailors, upholsterers, and other craftsmen who worked only for the men and women who dwelled in that abbey.

The abbey made no exceptions for anyone who grumbled or complained, or was disposed to jealousy or conspiracy.

This was perhaps one of the first humanist utopias.

Centuries later Fourier would be unsuccessfully searching for financial support to establish his *phalanstère*.

In order to build and equip the abbey of Thélème, Gargantua gave millions in gold.

But the world of Rabelais gradually shrunk and became impoverished. The Reaction was already setting in.

At the end of the novel, after long arguments about whether Panurge should get married or not, Pantagruel and Panurge set sail to visit an oracle.

The islands that they visit cannot be found on geographical maps—they only exist on the pages of history.

The oracles living on those islands are not verbose, they are rather incoherent.

But the voyage equipped by Rabelais is one of the many journeys destined for the discovery of the Island of Utopia. The island was never found but this led to the discovery of the New World—full of anxiety and prepared for wars.

This was a period when the ancient oar-propelled galleys were being replaced with complex vessels with square-rigged sails and navigational tools. A period when the first merchant vessels set sail alongside the battleships.

The wind became a trade. During battles the adversaries tried to obstruct the wind from reaching the sails of the enemy.

It was the Age of Sail, a period of naval warfare, when the Anglo-Spanish war broke out and when the Dutch fleet fought against Spain.

Then came the glorious epoch of the naval fleet.

The more Rabelais wrote his novel, the more it appeared to depart from the triumph of reason. And the search went on.

The abbey of Thélème will not be erected alongside the Loire—there will be ruins and remnants of other abbeys and castles there.

Happiness seemed possible to Pantagruel and Brother John. The Golden Age was ahead of them and the only thing that they hadn't figured out yet was how the humanists of the abbey were going to pay their workers. So far they had Pantagruel's contribution—he had invested his money to build a utopia.

Rabelais's chivalric romance is a novel about the grandiose power of man.

Brother John, the monk who led the peasants to revolt, is resurrected by Sir Walter Scott as the friar in the band of Robin Hood.

Gymnast conquers the giants, he is a poor student, starving humanist, and scientific skeptic who at the beginning of the novel doesn't believe in victory, because the giants are gentle monk philosophers.

Don Quixote's world plays chivalric romances just as it plays shepherds and shepherdesses. In the second part, Don Quixote is constantly fooled. In the duke's palace he finds himself in a grand spectacle about "the deceived madman."

Even when trying to realize the short-term program, the impartial governor (or rather, the impartial leader) and judge Sancho Panza, who uses folkloric wisdom to solve difficult cases, survives on the *ínsula* not more than a few days.

Though it's true that Sancho has his own folkloric time, his own history and future; he isn't just a body, he embodies irony and trust.

A person who is perceived solely as a body has no history—history is created by humanity.

Rabelais parodies the court and judges in order to raze the nonsense of petitions incomprehensible even for the plaintiffs.

He parodies the scientific methods used at the Sorbonne and the old conventions of marriage.

But he still believes in the kind philosopher king who will reform everything, because the meaninglessness of the old world is obvious to the humanists.

They eat a lot and drink a lot—they feast at the banquet of the future. The carnival is thus reinterpreted.

What's new about them is that they are conscious of the passing time.

For Rabelais and for Gargantua and Pantagruel the Silver Age has already begun.

The doors to the antiquity have been opened. We can muster and reinvent medicine, geography, jurisprudence. We can build new buildings.

The Golden Age will arrive tomorrow.

The Golden Age—is an age of uncensored publishing and free speech. Scholasticism will be defeated. The power of religion will be limited and the Sorbonne will be reformed.

Only hardworking and courageous people will live in the Golden Age.

It will be a time when people will work, love and revel.

This age is reminiscent of the triumphant ending of Aristophanes's *Birds*.

Men, with the help of birds, have blocked the space between the earth and the sky. A plebeian marries Zeus's daughter. The Chorus sings:

> Move back, make room, make space for him!
> Fly round the jubilant man with jubilant cheer.
> Behold his bride: how fresh and lovely!
> This marriage means felicity to our city.[118]

The new city, which they found in the sky, is called Nephelococcygia, which translates to Cloudcuckooland. This is the name of the bird camp that has blocked the sky of the ancient gods, intercepting and obstructing the flow of the sacrificial smoke that rose up from the earth to feed the gods. We are the descendents of that great city.

---

118   Aristophanes, *Birds*. Translated by Stephen Halliwell. Oxford UP, 1997.

We need a wide world and a high sky for the flight, but we know that besides air castles and satiating dreams there is the long process of laying the foundations of the abbey of Thélème. The path to Dostoevsky's planet will be paved by Tsiolkovsky's grandchildren.

The Breadth and Historicity
of the Construction of *Don Quixote*

The chivalric romance existed alongside the fairy tale and tried to supplant it. Thanks to book printing, the chivalric romance became a popular genre and so provoked the writing of Rabelais's novel.

Appearing in prose and verse parodies, the chivalric romance became renewed in high literature and simultaneously infused it with popular elements.

We have paid very little attention to the fact that Don Quixote, dressed in his ridiculous armor from different periods, lives and commits heroic deeds among the readers of chivalric romances.

They are the heroes and the first readers of the picaresque novel.[119]

In the third chapter of Part I, the innkeeper proposes his brief biography: he has traveled through many parts of the world, committed countless wrongs, seduced a few maidens, deceived several orphans, and now lives in this inn on other people's account.

This rascal and antipode of the knight is, at the same time, an admirer of chivalric romances. People who laugh at Don Quixote are laughing at their own dream.

---

119   A footnote by V. Shklovsky: *The Life of Lazarillo de Tormes: His Fortunes and Adversities* appeared in 1554 and was mentioned in *Don Quixote*.

It is strange for the innkeeper that the chivalric romance might be harmful to anyone. He says:

> I don't know how that can be; the truth is, to my mind, there's no better reading in the world; I have two or three of them, along with some other papers, and they really have put life into me, and not only me but other people, too. Because during the harvest, many of the harvesters gather here during their time off, and there's always a few who know how to read, and one of them takes down one of those books, and more than thirty of us sit around him and listen to him read with so much pleasure that it saves us a thousand gray hairs; at least, as far as I'm concerned, I can tell you that when I hear about those furious, terrible blows struck by the knights, it makes me want to do the same, and I'd be happy to keep hearing about them for days and nights on end. (Part I, Chapter 32)

Other heroes in the novel also defend chivalric romances; the innkeeper's daughter and his wife are among them.

The innkeeper recites passages from those books by heart. He recounts about the valiant Don Cirongilio of Thrace who, "when he was sailing down a river a fiery serpent rose up from the water, and as soon as he saw it he attacked it and straddled it, right across its scaly shoulders, and with both hands he squeezed its throat . . ."

These deeds remind me of Fantômas from the French science-fiction television series about gangsters and super-intelligence officers—everyone watched those series, but the chivalric romances, I think, were nobler, more humane, and more scientific for the time than the Fantômas sequels.

The reign of knight-errantry continued for centuries.

Russian *lubok* literature[120] contained elements not only from Russian fairy tales and heroic epics about Ilya Muromets, but also Byzantine chivalric romances, which is how Bova Korolevich became a legendary hero in Russia.

In *Three of Them*, published between 1900 and 1901, Gorky describes a tavern in which, quivering with curiosity and a strange, warm feeling of delight, three boys enter a new magical world, where great evil monsters fall under the mighty blows of brave knights.

They are huddled in a small, dirty garret separated from the tavern by thin boards; someone is playing on the harmonica and singing a dance tune in the noisy room next door. The two boys are bending low over the book, and one of them reads in a quiet, whispering voice: "Then the knight hugged the monster in an iron clasp and it roared in a voice of thunder from pain and terror."

One of the last remnants of this genre—*The Legend of Saint George*—was being rewritten and reprinted right up to the Revolution of 1917.

Cervantes's novel depicts a knight, an ascetic and a pauper who must try to preserve external decency and not mend his black

---

120   The *lubok* was a mass-produced illustrated broadside that enjoyed popularity among diverse strata of the rural and urban population in Russia beginning from the last half of the seventeenth century. Combining a lively image with a brief text, the *lubok* depicted contemporary, historical, or fairy-tale themes, most of them secular in the nineteenth and early twentieth centuries. Cheap *lubok* prints and chapbooks served as one of the most effective means of conveying government-sanctioned ideas in imperial Russia.

stockings with green thread. But the difference between the actions of Don Quixote and Sancho Panza is social. Sancho Panza is a peasant. The difference between Don Quixote's deeds and the deeds of Rabelais's giants is in the change of historical perspective. The writer invents something else because he has seen other things and the future seems dark to him.

Don Quixote is a poet, an excellent critic who knows Spanish history very well. He is in the midst of people who, as we noted before, know the structure and common themes of chivalric romances. He is "venturesome," according to Sancho Panza. He might decide to fight against lions. Don Quixote is a utopian, and Dostoevsky remembers his utopia in the drafts of *Crime and Punishment*.

Following the myth about the Golden Age, eulogized in Ovid's epic poem, and picking up a handful of acorns, Don Quixote talks about a time when "justice stood on her own ground, and favor or interest did not dare disturb or offend her as they so often do now, defaming, confusing, and persecuting her. Arbitrary opinions formed outside the law had not yet found a place in the mind of the judge, for there was nothing to judge, and no one to be judged" (Part I, Chapter 11).

In the second part of the book Don Quixote is constantly falling prey to cruel jokes. People laugh at him after having read the first part of the book.

Don Quixote is traveling now as a famous yet humiliated man. People remember his failures but they don't remember his wisdom.

The knight unintentionally walks into a print shop; printing and typesetting had become one of the common trades. The first part of *Don Quixote* had already been reprinted several times, and now some literary corsair was printing the second part. Don Quixote must now defend Cervantes as well.

There was an abundance of books, but Gargantua's and Pantagruel's belief that books would conquer the cannons did not materialize.

Cervantes had seen cannons as a soldier in a Spanish infantry regiment and on board a military galley.

Though printing had become a common trade, it seems that Don Quixote knew little about the business of printing. They show him the type drawer as something exotic. He gets excited that good books are being translated into the Castilian language; he even checks the translation to see if it's good. But Don Quixote knows that the translator's art "is not well-known in the world, which is always unwilling to reward rare talents and praiseworthy efforts. What abilities are lost there!" (Part II, Chapter 62).

As any literary hero, Don Quixote is contradictory—he is simultaneously a knight from a small village and a writer with a great deal of experience. He advises the publisher not to print the translated book at his own expense.

The publisher will nevertheless undertake the printing of the book that is bound to incur losses.

Literary publishing didn't resolve anything.

The humanists don't assign imprisoned interventionists to run their printing presses as they did in Rabelais's novel.

It was the entrepreneur who took over the printing press.

About Repetition
About Sancho Panza, Aristophanes, Gogol, and Faust
About the Fact that There Are No Repetitions

In *Rabelais and His World*, Bakhtin transforms "the poor farmer" (this is how Cervantes introduced Sancho Panza) into a mythic figure:

> The fundamental trend of Cervantes's parodies is a "coming down to earth," a contact with the reproductive and generative power of the earth and of the body. This is a continuation of the grotesque tradition. But at the same time the material bodily principle has already been reduced. It is undergoing a peculiar crisis of splitting; Cervantes's images of bodily life have begun to lead a double existence.
>
> Sancho's fat belly (*panza*), his appetite and thirst still convey a powerful carnivalesque spirit. His love of abundance and wealth have not, as yet, acquired a basically private, egotistic and alienating character. Sancho is the direct heir of the antique potbellied demons of fertility, which decorate the famous Corinthian vases. In Cervantes's images of food and drink there is still the spirit of popular banquets. Sancho's materialism, his potbelly, appetite, his abundant defecation are on the absolute lower level of grotesque realism of the jovial bodily grave (belly, bowels, earth) which has been dug for Don Quixote's abstract and deadened idealism . . . (Introduction)

The Knight of the Sorrowful Face must die in that grave, as it were, in order to be reborn a better and a greater man.

I decided to end the quote at the ellipsis—it's too long, anyway.

Here, in Bakhtin's analysis, Sancho Panza's image at times acquires an extremely fixed and simplistic form. In Chapter 6, Bakhtin discusses the dialogues of Don Quixote and Sancho Panza, saying that, "in reality, it is a dialogue of the face with the buttocks, of birth with death."

There is no deliberate degradation here—"buttocks" and "death."

Bakhtin perceives life and death in an ambivalent duality. It is the disagreement of opposites that always exist in conflict with one another. But the general in art exists in a concrete, new, dissimilar embodiment.

Today, in theory, we are experiencing the exhilaration of the discovery of the similar. I will have to talk about repetitions in Thomas Mann. Gods from various epochs and cultures recur; wise slaves and patriarchs reappear among newer generations without any differentiation.

The well by Jacob's house appears to be a foreshadowing of the pit into which Joseph will be thrown by his brothers.

The dry well is described as if it were a grave.

The image of the grave repeats again in the form of imprisonment in Egypt.

Mirrors reflect one another. The angle of incidence equals the angle of reflection. But the angle of refraction doesn't exist.

There is no movement in history, just as there is no solidity in the self-abnegation of generations.

Rabelais is against war; it detracts from work and generates poverty.

For Gargantua, the abbey of Thélème, built with funds donated by patrons, was the threshold of the Golden Age.

For Don Quixote, over half a century later, the duke's palace is a place where he is mocked and where Sancho Panza is washed in a tub of dishwater. The writer realizes that the duke's court for Don Quixote the humanist is, in reality, a prison. And his hero pronounces the great words as he leaves the castle: "Freedom, Sancho, is one of the most precious gifts heaven gave to men!"

The Golden Age is in the past. One must endure the cruel and long Iron Age.

Sancho Panza lives in the present.

The Golden Age for Sancho is when one overcomes hunger.

Sancho's appetite is the appetite of a simple man. It was Hercules—the hero of the mobs—who was a glutton.

Sancho Panza is not a clown, in any case, he is not Ryzhy the circus clown. He is a peasant, "working in the fields" since he was young.

He is a strong, clever, naïve man who has seen a lot.

The duchess doesn't understand why the sly Sancho Panza tolerates the mockery and follows Don Quixote, to which Sancho replies with poignant simplicity that they are from the same village, whereas Don Quixote says about Sancho that "he doubts everything, and he believes everything" (Part II, Chapter 32).

Sancho Panza is a miller, who is wiser than the abbot; a potter, who is smarter than the *boyars* of Ivan the Terrible; a seven-year-old, who can answer the question his father cannot solve; Mark Twain's Tom Canty, who is more sensible than the imperial council; Jeanne d'Arc, the maid of Orleans, who knows how to use artillery.

Sancho is greedy, but as the novel progresses and according to Don Quixote, he becomes "more wise and less foolish." Don Quixote advises his squire how he should behave as the governor of Barataria; when Sancho hears the advice about the responsibilities of leadership he is ready to step down from his governorship. Sancho is a virtuous judge and he won't accept any bribes.

By the end of the novel Don Quixote acquires some of Sancho's traits, while Sancho adopts some of Don Quixote's traits.

Rabelais's carnival is not a mystery or a pageant of popular merriment. He sees in the carnival the victory of François Villon, Brother John, Gymnast, and Panurge over old France along with its university, court, and church.

Panurge is a scientist: he knows every language including Basque.

But that's how they joked in the popular Athenian theater, where they intermixed various languages including Scythian, Persian, and even the language of the birds.

Similarly, Molière intermixed dialects in his comedies.

The novels of Rabelais and Cervantes are separated by only half a century, and one can learn by studying them that the reader isn't just interested in the disagreement of the "upper parts" with the "lower parts."

I will remind you of another disagreement: of the young Franz Berthold, the knight who is seized and imprisoned for stirring up a peasant revolt. The prison sentence is: "Until the walls of my castle are blown up . . ." Franz busies himself in prison with alchemy—discovers gunpowder. He invents a new type of weapon and blows up the castle. The knight ("mediocrity personified") is killed by a bullet. At the end of his outline (written in French), Pushkin wrote: "The play ends with reflections and the arrival of Faust on the devil's tail (discovery of book printing—a different type of artillery)."[121]

Let me repeat what Gargantua wrote in his letter to Pantagruel: "And in my time we have learned how to produce wonderfully elegant and accurate printed books, just as, on the other hand, we have also learned (by diabolic suggestion) how to make cannons and other such fearful weapons."

Many people believed that it was Faust who invented book printing.

Pushkin was an attentive reader of Rabelais.

Bakhtin's Theory of the Grotesque

Rabelais's books are historical; they were produced by a great epoch of great hopes that never materialized. Cervantes is also historical. It doesn't seem right to me to show Rabelais and Cervantes outside humanism and reactionism—outside the drama of human history.

A literary work already contains in itself an element of contradiction; development and contradiction should not be perceived as purely internal. The model of man, which Rabelais created, which Victor Hugo found and Mikhail Bakhtin developed, exists in constant transformations.

We must pay attention and take into account the peregrinations of Don Quixote, the wars and journeys of Pantagruel, Gulliver, the life of the archpriest Avvakum, the suffering of heroes and their

---

121 An unfinished historical drama by Aleksandr Pushkin, which has been titled by scholars *Scenes from the Times of Chivalry*.

authors, the prisons in Fielding and Dickens, and the penitentiaries in Dostoevsky when examining a literary work.

Man doesn't live alone—he is part of the human race.

The shortcoming of the world model proposed in Bakhtin's work is that it doesn't show the thousand-year-old history of art. According to Bakhtin: "Rabelais's illuminative role in this respect is of the greatest importance. His novel must serve as a key to the immense treasury of the creative work of folkloric laughter, which as yet has been scarcely understood or analyzed."

The concept of "folkloric laughter" is new here.

But what serves as material, which in turn becomes humorous? What conflict or conflicts provoke this laughter?

What are the temporal changes of this tradition? Which elements repeat in its reemergence?

Which Birnam Wood, that terrified Macbeth, is advancing on the old sorcery?

Rabelais's epoch was a period when art was being reinvented.

In *The Psychology of Art*, Lev Vygotsky first outlines Freud's theories, then polemicizes against them:

> The effect of a literary work and versification is wholly derived from the most ancient instincts which remain unchanged throughout the entire span of culture, and artistic effect is completely limited to the narrow realm of individual consciousness. Needless to say, this is a serious contradiction to all the simplest facts of the actual condition of art and its actual role. It would suffice to say that the very questions of repression—what exactly is being re-

pressed and how?—are always conditioned by the social environment in which both the poet and the reader must live. And hence, if we look at art from the viewpoint of psychoanalysis, the historical evolution of art and the changes of its social functions would be incomprehensible, since from that perspective art has always and consistently, from its beginning to our present day, served as an expression of the most ancient and conservative instincts. If art is any different from dreams or symptoms of neuroses, then, as Otto Rank correctly noted, its difference lies in the fact that it produces artifacts that are socially conditioned. But Rank doesn't offer any conclusions from this finding and he doesn't evaluate it properly. He doesn't show and explain what exactly art does with the socially valuable and how, through this social value of art, the social gains power over our unconscious.[122]

The unconscious becomes conscious in art. Sometimes it passes through the phase of the grotesque.

The grotesque concealed in itself a revolt.

One of the first theorists of the grotesque, Victor Hugo wrote in this genre.

In 1862, Dostoevsky wrote an enthusiastic foreword to Hugo's *Notre-Dame de Paris* in the September issue of *Vremya* (Time). He wrote that the novel contained the formula for all works of art of the nineteenth century: ". . . its formula is the rehabilitation of the

---

122   Lev Vygotsky, *Psikhologia iskusstva* [The Psychology of Art], 1917.

fallen man, crushed unjustly by the weight of circumstance, by the stagnation of centuries and by social prejudice. It is the exoneration of the social outcasts humiliated and rejected by all."

Dostoevsky thinks that it is useless to search for allegories in art, but still: "Who wouldn't see in Quasimodo the personification of the oppressed and reviled populace of medieval France, deaf and disfigured, who only has its terrifying physical strength, but in whom love and desire for justice finally awaken, and with it—the consciousness of its own truth and yet untapped, limitless power?"

Hanging from the bell and metaphorically embodying the sound of the bell, Quasimodo calls in the voice of history, but he doesn't know who his friends or enemies are and kills the people who want to save Esmeralda. He avenges his beloved by killing the traitor priest and dies clutching Esmeralda's dead body.

Hugo wrote the theory of the grotesque and applied it to his art. Dostoevsky admired Hugo's work; he expanded and developed it further because Hugo's grotesque is historical—it links the lower with the higher.

According to Hugo, every genius has his invention or artistic discovery; Rabelais has made his—the belly. He wrote that ". . . this universe, which Dante put into Hell, Rabelais confines in a wine cask."[123]

In his book *William Shakespeare*, Hugo places Cervantes and Shakespeare next to Rabelais. This is not only in chronological order but it's also historically correct. In the Rabelaisian grotesque Hugo sees the argument against ordinary perception.

---

123   Victor Hugo, *William Shakespeare*. Translated by Melville B. Anderson. Chicago: A. C. McClurg and Company, 1887. All subsequent quotations from *William Shakespeare* are taken from this standard version.

Dante walked through hell, illuminating the history of his time. Rabelais confined his world in a wine cask.

In a metaphor, one object is compared to another, but it's not confined in it as in a prison and it doesn't replace the other.

The metaphor turns our knowledge of the subject as a stoker turns pieces of coal in a firebox with his tongs.

Rabelais's "wine cask" is juxtaposed against the church, restoring man in his flesh but without cutting him out of history.

The characters, the schemas of construction, change through repetition and renew the contradictions within them. The carnival is contradictory in itself, which is why it employs the mask: a person behind a mask is only partially recognized. He is a person whom you both know and at the same time don't know.

They used to parade monkeys at the mask festival in Japan. The monkeys wore masks that were replicas of a monkey's static face— they were not just monkeys anymore, but masked monkeys, and so they were introduced into art.

The first stage of the ancient comedy was probably the wooden cart used as a platform. This already separated the actor in costume from the people in the audience, who could also be in costumes. But the stage allowed the actor to play, to switch off and disconnect from the ordinary world, so that it would become visible.

Theatrical illusion flickers, it appears and disappears, generating new insights of the ordinary through art.

"Corporeality" in Aristophanes, Rabelais, and Shakespeare is not a juxtaposition of the "top and bottom," or "front and back." It is a method of renewing insight and broadening the frequency of perception. It gives the elements of displacement in Aristophanes, Cervantes, and Rabelais.

Greatness is corporeal. Venus is imbued with corporeality. And Homer probably ate like Sancho at the symposia.

Aristophanes was no less frank and no more obscene than Rabelais. The women in *Lysistrata* withhold sex from their husbands. The theme is composed with a phallic frankness; it unfolds in a chain of erotic scenes. But the women are on a sex strike because they want to end the Peloponnesian War and secure peace.

The comedies of Aristophanes as well as the novels of Rabelais and Cervantes are proposals for a reconstruction of the world; these proposals are shrouded in the vestments of "folkloric laughter"—a coat turned inside out. The old can also be destroyed through humor.

A critical work about Rabelais could have included an analysis of Aristophanes's comedies. They preserve the link to rural festivals celebrating the cultivation of land. The essence of these comedies is dislocation, transposition, and conquering of the ordinary. The women are not only arguing with their husbands, but Euripides, too, thinking that he has misrepresented them.

The works of Aristophanes are full of political debate and erotic self-willfulness. The comedies include philosophical arguments— they are the first examples of new literary criticism.

Changing the course of art in Russia, Gogol recalled Aristophanes.

The Author of the Play in *Leaving the Theater After the Presentation of a New Comedy* lingers in the lobby of the theater after the performance and overhears how two dilettantes discuss his work. The First Person says: "I merely wish to make the point that the play has no complication." The Second Person disagrees with him, saying: "Well, yes, if by complication you understand what it is usually taken to mean, that is, a love story, then, you are correct, there isn't one." After a few remarks the First continues: "But the result of all this is to give comedy a more universal meaning." The Second replies: "Well, isn't that its true, primary meaning? Comedy was originally created from social and national elements. At least, that is the form its father, Aristophanes, gave it. Afterwards it fell into the narrow crack of individual concerns and introduced the course of love as the one and only inevitable complication."[124]

We shouldn't suppress Rabelais's cheerfulness, the geographical breadth of his novel, or the time of laughter's battle against stagnation and standstill.

The grotesque coexists with utopia.

It would be wrong to think of the carnival as merely a celebration of physiology. The carnival marked a change in social relations: slaves were the equals of their masters, there was freedom of speech.

The argument about the fate of art in *The Frogs* becomes a debate about the fate of Athenians and simultaneously an examination of the creative work of dramatists.

The main contrasting juxtaposition in the stream of stepped juxtapositions in Rabelais's novel appears to be that Pantagruel is a great inventor, commander in chief, and representative of new morality. Man, according to Rabelais, is naturally virtuous if we don't

---

124   Nikolai Gogol, *Leaving the Theater after the Presentation of a New Comedy*. Translated by Isabel Heaman. *Hanz Kuechelgarten, Leaving the Theater & Other Works*. Ed. Ronald Meyer. Ann Arbor: Ardis, 1990.

count religious prescriptions as virtue. Human vice emerges as a perversion of tendency.

Panurge calls that society the kingdom of Saturn—meaning, the Golden Age. He recalls the Roman festival of the slaves, the week-long festivities with its rituals expressing freedom. The paths of Rabelais, Cervantes, and Dostoevsky are not identical but they move in the same direction.

About the Menippea

Bakhtin discusses the combination of the serious and "folkloric laughter" as a special genre, which he calls "Menippean." None of Menippus's satires have survived. We don't even know the exact dates of his life. According to a legend, Menippus was a philosopher from the Cynic School and was originally a slave who had been freed. They also say that he was a moneylender.

The Roman writer Marcus Terentius Varro of the second century BCE wrote about Menippus's satire and from him we know that Menippus fused verse with prose in his writings.

In Lucian's dialogue *Menippus, or The Descent into Hades*, Menippus appears wearing a chiton and a hood, a lyre in his hand and a lion-skin draped over his shoulders. The clothing was apparently the exact reproduction of the theatrical costume of Dionysus as he arrives at the gates of Hades in the first act of *The Frogs*. I should also mention his slave, riding behind the god on his donkey.

Obviously Lucian's knowledge about Menippus traces back to Aristophanes. It appears as though Menippus had been in Hades and witnessed the conflict between Aeschylus and Euripides; his costume is the costume of Dionysus—the judge presiding over the contest of the tragedians in *The Frogs*.

Lucian's Menippus is a Cynic who is skeptical about everything. *The Satyricon* is occasionally classified as a Menippean satire.

In the winter of 1593, the name of Menippus was unexpectedly used in an argument between French jurists and philologists of the Catholic League. Legal advisers, parliamentarians, and chaplains rediscovered Varro's *Menippean Satires* and wrote their own version. Marx writes about the satire:

> *Satyre Ménippée de la vertu du Catholicon d'Espagne* (Menippean Satire about the Powers of the Spanish Catholicon) is an amusing story about the Estates General, convened by Charles de Guise, the Duke of Mayenne in Paris in 1593, in the hopes of electing himself to the French throne and replacing the pretender to the throne, Henry IV of France. The satire helped Henry IV immensely. The title derives from the name of the Cynic philosopher Menippus. The work was conceived by Pierre le Roy (canon of Rouen and chaplain to the cardinal of Bourbon); he wrote the first three parts of the satire, which are probably the weakest: Catholicon, *Tapisserie* of the League (an ekphrasis of the rugs that decorated the main room where the meeting was taking place), and its Procession in Paris. The most important section of the text was co-written by Pierre Pithou, Jacques Gillot, Jean Passerat, and Florent Chrestien. During the winter of 1593, the friends wrote and

revised the work that satirized the debates of the representatives of the League. Most of the poems were written (anonymously) by Passerat, to whom belongs the quatrain that explains the double cross on the coat of arms of the League:

> Mais dites-moi, que signifie
> Que les ligueurs ont double Croix?
> C'est qu'en la Ligue on crucifie
> Jésus Christ encore une fois.[125]

Marx examines the satirical piece as a political pamphlet. In another article published in 1853 in the *New York Daily Tribune*, Marx writes: "The English Capitalist League of the nineteenth century is yet to find its historian, as the French Catholic League did in the authors of the *Satyre Ménippée* at the end of the sixteenth century."

Bakhtin applies the term "Menippean satire" to an incredibly broad spectrum of works, including texts from the antiquity as well as modern works. He even ascribes the Menippean genre to Hemingway in one of his notes in *Problems of Dostoevsky's Poetics*.

There are no "pure" genres. However, occasionally a certain genre is fixed as a classical type, meaning it becomes canonized.

Generally speaking, all types of genre contain in themselves a movement, which makes them contradictory. It is this contradictoriness of genre that Bakhtin defined as "Menippean."

As a result, the concept of the "menippea" in his analysis overtook almost the whole range of literature.

---

125   But tell me, what does it mean / That the Leaguers have a double cross? / It means that the League has crucified / Jesus Christ all over again.

The term "menippea" was necessary for Bakhtin as he was dealing with something new and undefined, but because the scope of its use was so broad, the term lost its definition.

In *Problems of Dostoevsky's Poetics* (Chapter 4), Bakhtin expounds the Menippean satire in these broad terms:

> At the close of classical antiquity, and again in the epoch of Hellenism, a number of genres coalesced and developed, fairly diverse externally but bound together by an inner kinship and therefore constituting a special realm of literature, which then the ancients themselves very expressively called σπονδογέλοιον, the realm of the serio-comic. It included the mimes of Sophron, the "Socratic dialogue" (as a special genre), the voluminous literature of the Symposiasts (also a special genre), early memoir literature (Ion of Chios, Critias), pamphlets, all bucolic poetry, "Menippean satire" (as a special genre) and several other genres as well.

The genres are listed without any reference. Menippean satire is placed in quotation marks as an isolated case in literature and unrelated to the more solid genres.

Then, in the next few pages, the meaning of the term changes.

Bakhtin refers to the *Satyricon* as a "Menippean satire" in the form of a novel. Then he mentions *The Golden Ass*.

About the works of Lucian and Seneca, Bakhtin writes: "This line of experimental fantasticality continues, under the defining influence of the menippea, into the subsequent epochs as well—in Rabelais, Swift, Voltaire (*Micromégas*), and others."

Bakhtin then observes that the menippea may have influenced the *Soliloquies* of Augustine and writes: "We should mention in passing that Dostoevsky too, when representing the phenomenon of the double, always preserved alongside the tragic element an element of the *comic* as well (in *The Double*, and in Ivan Karamazov's conversation with the devil)."

A few pages later, Bakhtin states that, "Essentially all of the defining features of the menippea (with, of course, the appropriate modifications and complications) we will find also in Dostoevsky."

Bakhtin knows that Dostoevsky could not have emerged directly from the ancient menippea (even if it existed), but he thinks that, "it was not Dostoevsky's subjective memory, but the objective memory of the very genre in which he worked, that preserved the peculiar features of the ancient mineppea."

I am afraid that these statements are too general, just as the claim that carnivalistic license "was very well illustrated by Goethe in *Wilhelm Meister's Apprenticeship*, and in our time by Nemirovich-Danchenko in his memoirs."

All of these claims, of course, are made with reservation, but the menippea is increasingly becoming associated with the carnival: "Carnivalization permeates both its external layers and its deepest core."

Gradually, the Menippean genre unifies a most variegated array of exemplars, and though the name, or, more accurately, the term "Menippean satire" was recovered in 1594, it was a unique and singular instance. The assertion that during the European Renaissance "the menippea infiltrates all the large genres of the epoch (the works of Rabelais, Cervantes, Grimmelshausen, and others)" is not accurate. In the next paragraph Bakhtin adds Hoffmann to the list. And a few pages later he includes "the highly original dream lyrics" of Heinrich Heine, and also mentions George Sand and Chernyshevsky.

The expansion of the term escalates at high speed, whereas at one point it is elucidated illusorily, at another—blurred once again. Bakhtin's suggestions regarding Dostoevsky's descriptions are rather interesting but they are not fully elaborated.

Meanwhile, the book is dedicated to Dostoevsky and it must create an opportunity to study and understand how those concepts apply to his texts. Consider the following statement: "The combination of carnivalization with the adventure plot and with pressing social themes of the day was found by Dostoevsky in the social-adventure novels of the nineteenth century, primarily in Frédéric Soulié and Eugène Sue (also somewhat in Dumas *fils* and in Paul de Kock)." Dostoevsky, too, is associated with carnivalization and the menippea.

The terms "menippea" and "carnivalization" are used in various polyvalent combinations. And yet Bakhtin asserts that, "Two 'fantastic stories' of the late Dostoevsky—"Bobok" (1873) and "The Dream of a Ridiculous Man" (1877)—may be called menippea almost in the strict ancient sense of the term, so precisely and fully manifest in them are the classical characteristic features of the genre."

There is no need to elucidate Dostoevsky through unknown sources, especially if they don't give the genesis of the methodology of Dostoevsky's work.

"Bobok" and "The Dream of a Ridiculous Man" are two completely different works, moving in two different directions. A man lies down on a tombstone and hears the dead talking to each other.

There have been many conversations of the dead in literature, take *Gilgamesh*, for example, or the works of Homer and Lucian, the Bible, or even eighteenth-century Russian literature and Mayakovsky's epic poem "Man."

We hardly ever finish our conversations with those who are living; we never want to part with those who are dead.

But "Bobok" is an extraordinary story—it's important not only in its divergence from the other conversations of the dead, but also in its place among Dostoevsky's works. It turns out that the dead don't pass away immediately; they have a few weeks during which their consciousness slowly fades away. We hear petty conversations—the voice of the decaying waste.

This is a rejection of immortality.

"The Dream of a Ridiculous Man" is constructed in an entirely different way.

A man dies and becomes indignant in his coffin. He is resurrected by his rage and transported to another planet—the planet of the Golden Age.

The people living on it are free of envy, jealousy, and material desire.

And though the Ridiculous Man—Dostoevsky's contemporary—was a kind person, he changed the morals of the planet's inhabitants. They became like the people living in the nineteenth century. The Ridiculous Man pleads with the people on the planet, he begs them to kill him, to crucify him on a cross. He even shows them how to make the cross.

The story elucidates Dostoevsky's relationship to religion and socialism, as well as Christ.

The names of genres do not change the destinies of books, but the concept of the menippea, as well as the concept of carnivalization, disconnects us from Dostoevsky, disinherits him from his historical essence, his tragic nature.

And I think that the researcher has failed in this aspect of his project in the *Problems of Dostoevsky's Poetics*.

Bakhtin possesses the attributes of a discoverer and an inventor, but the scope of his generalizations sometimes turns into a sea, engulfing the already-found specificities.

"MYTH" AND "THE NOVEL-MYTH"

About Myth

Myth was believed to be the prototypical poetic genre; they asserted that philosophy and science emerged from myth. Schelling wrote about this in his *Philosophy of Art* over a hundred and fifty years ago.

For a long time they thought that fairy tales were the echoes of myths, that they deified celestial phenomena. They explained the similarity of fairy tales by their origination from a singular (usually Aryan) source. Myths were restored and connected to one another in various ways.

The Russian folklorist Aleksandr Afanasyev studied fairy tales and his definitive work on the subject, *Poetic Views of the Slavs on Nature*, was published in three volumes between 1866 and 1869. The influence of Afanasyev's work can be seen in the works of many writers; I remember how Yesenin was enamored by this book and how he wrote a tract on literature, "Maria's Keys."

This fascination and burgeoning curiosity for myths has returned, or reemerged today in the form of neo-mythologism. The recurrence is marked by a great change and enrichment in theory.

Carl Jung wrote on psychological archetypes—primordial generic models produced by the collective unconscious of mankind.

To be sure, mythology precedes literature and defines it in many ways.

Myths in human memory are like tools in a smithy—they are meant for work, not for storage. Myths are selected for the construction of a new aesthetic structure.

Greek mythology invented the tools and methods of their use in the construction of Greek art. It found the laws of art in mythology. But there are many myths in the world and they are more diverse than the tongs and hammers in a smithy. Different poets, while working on the history of one and the same hero, chose various myths as material and sometimes were reproached for this. The myth of Medea who takes revenge against her husband by stabbing their children to death was not the most well-known story. It was selected from the ancient material by a man who passed through the school of the great Greek tragedy and who, while contesting that tradition, was trying to end it.

Mythology defines many realms and it has achieved a lot; we return to mythology as we would return to an ancient tool or weapon. Mayakovsky hoped that the communist society would return to his poetry. But future art will not approach Mayakovsky with that same old perception; he will be read anew. Mythology is not a place for leisurely walks; it's a battlefield.

The Scottish inventor, James Watt, was given the task of improving the steam engine. He discovered in the steam engine the elements of the universal engine, which was later noted by Marx.

The ingenious discovery was the change of the instrument's function.

From this moment on, the steam engine entered a new phase in its history.

But myths, while they repeat, are never the same; they are like footsteps on an ever-changing road.

Thomas Mann's novel, which we are going to discuss, is a classic example from the neo-mythological school. Mann connects all myths that are alike and ties them all into one, as it were. But in each reference Osiris, Adonis, Hermes appear as separate phenomena with different functions. Sometimes it is easier to connect Hermes to Figaro, with his devious servants from the Italian comedy, than it is to the crowd of gods.

The Bible uses a mixture of techniques—it unifies a broad range of genres. It is a chrestomathy of genres.

Every single book in the Bible is written in a different style. The tale of Joseph is nothing like the story about the flood or any contemporary novel.

I agree with the comment of Tolstoy, who taught peasant children and assigned them to revise the tale of Joseph, but dreaded the fact that the story would be reinvented in the tradition of the European novel:

> Let's take the tale of Joseph, for example, which moves me even today, as it moves all of mankind. Give it to Boborykin and let him compose it. Would he not ruin everything with his technique and his awful descriptions: "He said, raising his left leg, while it was half reclining . . ." or: "The gray paint on the door was faintly illuminated by the small lamp"?

. . . The tale of Joseph lives and will live for many centuries, while Boborykin's writings will only last a season.[126]

Mann's novel belongs to the neo-mythological school and simultaneously marks the end of the historical novel. I am not comparing Mann to Boborykin, but Mann is so interested in costumes, personal attributes, landscapes, and sceneries, and knows everything so well that it is somewhat contradictory to the theory of myths (that endlessly mirror one another and thus conquer time) to which Mann adheres.

The tale of Joseph is more connected to its own time than it might seem to Mann. It is an invented biography, which nonetheless appears to be true. The tale contradicts mythology even in the number of its pages, its detail and scope as a different genre of creative thought. Which is why, while working on the details of Joseph's tale and enriching it with archeological facts, Mann is forced to throw out some lively passages from the biblical text that emotionally correspond to that epoch and to those interrelations of tribes and nations in which Joseph's tale takes place.

The Smoke of Millennia

Let's retrace the path.

Mann writes in the prelude of his multivolume work *Joseph and His Brothers*: "Our historical records date back approximately seven

---

126 Lev Tolstoy's remarks, recorded by the Russian composer Ilya Satz (1875–1912). *Ilya Satz*, 1923.

thousand years—during this period, at least, not a single wild animal has been domesticated to serve us. All that lies beyond memory."[127]

The epic of Gilgamesh was originally titled *He Who Saw Everything*. According to the clay tablets, the epic was recorded by the exorcist and scribe Sin-leqi-unninni. Evidently, it is about five thousand years old. The text was formed in a precise way; it is neither myth nor history. Rather, it is one of the very first records about the inexplicability of death, the difficulty of digging wells, the incomprehensibility of good and evil, the hardships of distant journeys, and the high cost of weapons.

It is not a myth, though the characters in the epic talk and argue with the gods, swim across the ocean using logs made from the tallest cedars to push their raft forward, journey to the underworld, and return from there.

The epic is full of events the credibility of which is difficult to prove.

According to the Russian linguist, historian, and translator of the epic of Gilgamesh, Igor Dyakonov:

> The period between the fourth and third millennia BCE marked the end of the Stone Age and beginning of the Iron Age. The vast forests of Europe, Asia, and Africa were inhabited by half-savage hunting tribes, while the steppes of the dry subtropical zone between Spain and China were

127 Thomas Mann, *Joseph and His Brothers* (*The Stories of Jacob*; *Young Joseph*; *Joseph in Egypt*; *Joseph the Provider*). Translated by John E. Woods. New York: Alfred A. Knopf, 2005. All subsequent quotations from *Joseph and His Brothers* are taken from this standard version.

populated by goat-herding tribes (they didn't have horses or camels then, so they weren't nomadic yet).

The farmers . . . tilled the fields that they irrigated by blocking streams, grew and harvested half-wild barley, wheat, and spelt with the help of wooden or clay sickles with flint teeth.[128]

This was an era when bronze weapons were a novelty. Some time later: "A famous warrior rode in his chariot: it was a two-wheeled cart with solid wheels, a saddle-like seat for the driver and a small platform in the back for the spear bearer. Or it was a four-wheeled car . . . with a central axis and reins between the 'horns' from which hung the quiver with arrows and darts."

The military chariot was typically drawn by donkeys, rarely by mules. The mule was a rarity—it was the offspring of a female donkey and a wild male horse that roamed in the steppes or mountains. It was a hybrid of two creatures from different species—wild and domestic.

Mules were very expensive. According to the Second Book of Samuel, David's son Absalom rode on a mule.

Let's take, for example, a description from one of Sindbad's voyages in *The Arabian Nights*. The material of this fairy tale reflects the tales of ancient travelers and legends about them. In his first voyage, Sindbad survives a shipwreck and swims to the shore clinging to a wooden tub and discovers an island on which he sees a mare, "tied on the beach." He goes up to her, but she cries out with a terrible cry. Then a man appears from under the earth and tells the following:

---

128 Igor Dyakonov, Introduction, *O vsyo vidavshem* [He Who Saw Everything: The Epic of Gilgamesh], 1961.

Every month, about new-moon tide we bring here our best mares which have never been covered, and picket them on the seashore and hide ourselves in this place under the ground, so that none may espy us. Presently, the stallions of the sea scent the mares and come up out of the water and seeing no one, leap the mares and do their will of them. When they have covered them, they try to drag them away with them, but cannot, by reason of the leg-ropes; so they cry out at them and butt at them and kick them, which we hearing, know that the stallions have dismounted; so we run out and shout at them, whereupon they are startled and return in fear to the sea. Then the mares conceive by them and bear colts and fillies worth a mint of money, nor is their like to be found on earth's face.[129]

There are some fairly accurate details in this tale about the stallions that emerge from the sea and about the price of their offspring: the stallions scent the mares that are deliberately brought to the shore during their heat cycle.

The scent, of course, cannot penetrate the water, but the wild stallions, which were once called wild donkeys, would scent the female donkeys and descend from the mountains.

The archetype of this tale is derived from reality. It is the reality of a domesticated mare mating with a wild stallion of a related kind.

This is how dogs sometimes give birth to wolf cubs.

We shouldn't think that the archetypes of myths are myths only: they might transfer not only old rituals but also old techniques.

---

129 *The Arabian Nights' Entertainments or The Book of A Thousand Nights and a Night*. Translated by Richard F. Burton. Random House, 1997.

Sometimes myths originate like a new kind of grain culture about which Thomas Mann thought mankind could never know anything, and that man sowed the same kind of seed throughout the centuries.

The new grain cultures appear in high mountainous areas where the genes of plants survive mutation under the influence of cosmic rays.

These new cultures are hardier and susceptible to change.

According to the Soviet geneticist Nikolai Vavilov's theory of the origin of cultivated plants, cultivated flora appeared and was developed within relatively few geographic centers located mostly in mountainous regions.

It is possible to trace the existence of repeating analogical patterns in various types and species of plants.

The evolution of plants has its own purposefulness and direction, which one can study and change for different purposes.

Myths do not flow through the pipes of history; they change and splinter, they contrast and refute one another. The similar turns out to be dissimilar.

Thomas Mann asks in his essay "The Sufferings and Greatness of Richard Wagner": "That Astarte of the Second Empire, Nana, is she not symbol and myth?"

Zola's Nana is not mythical. She is the embodiment of Napoleon III's empire.

Nana's repulsive death from smallpox foreshadows the defeat and capture of Napoleon III at Sedan. She is mediocre like Napoleon. She is the ghost of a fake and fatal attraction.

Katyusha Maslova is not mythical either. She is the record of one of the structures from the old system of the Russian Empire. The church, the courthouse, and the homes of aristocracy are exposed as brothels. Katyusha is not a prostitute among other prostitutes—she is the sign evaluating this world. She appears to the young Tolstoy in the Caucasus as an answer to the world which he had left behind.

She is a method of comparison.

Katyusha's "resurrection" is manifested in the fact that she leaves the lifestyle to which she is doomed, she prevails over the design of her life. She is the scale of all constructions of the novel.

They are all measured by this criterion—her fate—the basis of the structure.

Nana is a harlot of her epoch and the symbol of its destruction; she destroys the men who love her. The harlot in the epic of Gilgamesh is not the archetype of all harlots—she is a woman of her own epoch, and she is blessed and cursed by it.

We will analyze Thomas Mann's novel in order to show that myth is not sowing the same seed in the same soil. It does not replicate the archetype, but rather recalls the archetype for the purpose of refutation.

It might seem that art moves through repetitions but those repetitions are only illusory. We do not simply assess the pulsation of the changing essence, but rather cut and carve steps in those seeming repetitions and compare them.

New Elements in the Old Epic
(The History of Gilgamesh)

Let's renew our path with examples.

Gilgamesh is the hero of the Akkadian epic—of the multi-characteristic stage—who was apparently a historical figure, living nearly three thousand years before the Common Era, at a time when in the lower parts of the Tigris farmers had already learned how to build irrigation canals and had domesticated the donkey but hadn't yet tamed the horse. Gilgamesh and his friend Enkidu journey on foot to commit heroic deeds.

The great king and warrior Gilgamesh lives in a city with strong walls:

> See how its ramparts gleam like copper in the sun.
> Climb the stone staircase, more ancient than the mind can imagine,
> . . . inspect its mighty foundations,
> examine its brickwork, how masterfully it is built. (Prologue)

Fired brick was a new invention that was a source of pride.

Gilgamesh, who owns an ax and a knife made of bronze, hears that the gods have created a new hero, Enkidu, who is as strong as himself.

Enkidu, with long hair covering his body, roams all over the wilderness, eats grass, and, when he is thirsty, drinks water from the waterholes kneeling beside the wild animals. The hunters are terrified of this savage man. Enkidu destroys the traps and frees the trapped animals from the hunter's holes.

Enkidu's story is repeated twice.

The unhurried pace of art was not yet burdened by experience. First, the story is told by the narrator, then it's repeated by the person who has witnessed it: the impediment here is tautological.

Gilgamesh sends the hunter with Shamhat the harlot to meet Enkidu. He instructs Shamhat to strip off her robe and lie by the water-hole.

When Enkidu arrives to the water-hole, he sees her and approaches:

> She used her love-arts, she took his breath
> with her kisses, held nothing back, and showed him
> what a woman is. For seven days
> he stayed erect and made love with her,
> until he had had enough. (Book I)

At last, when he gets up, he realizes that all the animals have left him forever. He realizes that he can no longer run like an animal, his mind "had somehow grown larger."

Then Shamhat gives Enkidu one of her robes and leads him to a shepherd's hut:

> "Go ahead, Enkidu. This is food,
> we humans eat and drink this." Warily
> he tasted the bread. Then he . . . drank seven
> pitchers of the beer. (Book II)

Enkidu is gradually introduced to human civilization, he becomes the protector of hunters and best friend of Gilgamesh. Together they travel to the Cedar Forest where terrible monsters live.

Intimacy with the woman humanizes him. She gives him the knowledge of life, the foreboding premonition of sorrow and death. She tears him away from his flock.

I am reading the epic of Gilgamesh, rereading it and analyzing the repetitions, and I am filled with awe at how people perceived themselves and how they told stories about themselves.

Everything is valued—both Enkidu's battle against Gilgamesh, and the friends' journey to the Cedar Forest. They walk side by side, they dig wells, they eat their bread sparingly.

Then they commit deeds and see dreams—the dreams foretell their actions. They commit deeds and then reinterpret them.

And though Shamhat civilizes Enkidu, he curses her for that. He assigns her to live under the shadow of a tavern wall, warm her body by the hearth.

Sleeping in the ashes for warmth is the last place for refuge, it is a place for paupers.

Enkidu curses the harlot with the ultimate curse of homelessness: to become the lover of a homeless man, to roam the streets without a place to rest. But Shamash, the god and protector of Uruk, interjects: "Enkidu, why are you cursing / the priestess Shamhat?"

The god reminds Enkidu that it was Shamhat who gave him beer and bread fit for a king. And Enkidu blesses the harlot.

Scholars have finally learned how to touch and understand the clay tablets that bear the cuneiform script, which appears to have retained the hammered nail marks.

The tablets signified a shift in the change of human relations.

The wedge-shaped impressions on the tablets are arranged differently; sometimes they look like traces left by birds, but in reality they are traces of changing structures.

This is how man's relationship to the world, the various segmentations of the visible realm change: it is the knowledge of the world through labor and disillusionment.

About Tolstoy's Favorite Tale

By this I mean the biblical tale of Joseph.

There are no miracles in this tale: check it for yourselves.

The story occupies less than half of the Book of Genesis.

It impedes the flow of the narrative.

The story seems to be outside the genealogies of the Bible.

Joseph didn't become one of the founders or patriarchs with a long line of descendents. It is possible that when the story was added to the Book of Genesis, the names of the patriarchs were already set in stone.

Joseph's tale is separate from the other narratives.

This episode is current even today.

It takes up twenty pages in the Bible, printed in two columns and in small type. A hundred years ago, following Lev Tolstoy's instructions, the pupils in Yasnaya Polyana composed their own versions of the old novella. Their compositions were no longer than two pages. The best writers were Fokanov, Tolstoy's follower (later he dug a grave for Tolstoy and became its first guardian), and Morozov, a talented boy who later became a hopeless failure.

Jacob the shepherd had twelve sons—some were born from his first wife Leah, others were born from concubines, and two—Joseph and Benjamin—were born from his second and beloved wife

Rachel. Jacob's marriage to Rachel was difficult. He had to serve seven years for her, but his uncle Laban duped Jacob into marrying the oldest daughter Leah instead. After a week of wedding festivities Jacob was allowed to marry Rachel in return for another seven years of service with Laban.

It wasn't Leah's fault, of course—she had frail eyes, she wasn't beautiful and was coerced into marriage, thus becoming the unloved wife who gave birth to strong sons.

Joseph, the son born to Jacob's beloved wife Rachel, was handsome and shrewd. He was Jacob's favorite son, the child of his old age. Jacob gave Joseph a colorful tunic for which his brothers envied him and wanted to kill Joseph. This is how the older sisters in a fairy tale kill their youngest sister for receiving a golden apple and a silver tray.

Joseph had dreams that foretold the future. The first retardation in the story is designed around the two dreams in which Jacob and his sons bow before Joseph.

This forewarning exaggerated the tension caused by envy.

In his first dream Joseph saw him and his brothers binding sheaves in the field, when suddenly "my sheaf rose and stood upright; then your sheaves gathered around it, and bowed down to my sheaf" (Genesis 37:7).

Then in a second dream Joseph saw the sun and the moon and eleven stars bowing down to him.

Jacob was not pleased when he heard about these dreams; he rebuked Joseph by saying, "Shall we indeed come, I and your mother and your brothers, and bow to the ground before you?"

There is an anomaly here: Joseph's mother, Rachel, had died in childbirth when giving birth to Benjamin. The second dream does not take this into consideration.

Stories have their own laws and don't merely repeat what has already been said.

In Joseph's dream a dead person bows down to a living person. Jacob doesn't notice this in the Bible.

Dreams in ancient novellas and novels are as if the first illusory step toward the realization of an action. They increase the suspense and, by foreshadowing the course of events, enhance their importance.

It was Thomas Mann who noted that Joseph didn't become the progenitor of any of the tribes of Israel.

Only a part of Joseph's descendents are mentioned in the Book of Numbers (34:23). We learn in the Book of Joshua (14:4) that the descendents of Joseph formed two tribes, but the Book of Psalms says something different: "[The Lord] rejected the tent of Joseph, he did not choose the tribe of Ephraim" (Psalms 78:67).

I won't quote every single reference to Joseph, but my impression is that this hero has a special, venerable, and simultaneously contested place in the Bible. It is probably for this reason that Mann chose Joseph as the main character for his novel.

Jacob's sons tended their father's sheep in the valleys of Palestine. Some of them were born of Jacob's lawful wives, others were the sons of concubines who had borne children by the wives' orders. These were coarse people living in the wilderness.

They pastured their flock by the roads going to Assyria and Egypt, along which traveled caravans of traders. However, Joseph was different—he wore a special tunic that his father gave him because he was Rachel's son and because he was his father's spy. Joseph's relationship with his brothers was competitive: "Joseph brought a bad report of them to their father" (Genesis 37:2).

Joseph was gifted and wise. He was the chosen one and his far-sightedness is expressed through his prophetic dreams that foretell the future and ability to interpret the Pharaoh's dreams.

Wisdom couldn't have been expressed more clearly in the Bible.

The biblical story of Joseph could have been an ordinary story about a successful household, but Joseph isn't merely successful, he has the gift of prophecy—he saves the Egyptians from famine. The fact that Joseph does this by acquiring all the farmland for the Pharaoh is an attempt to explain the system of land acquisition in Egypt.

Joseph is a good man, though he is also treacherous. He forgives his brothers for their desire to kill him and for selling him into slavery. He forgives them first of all because they are his kin and also because they don't betray their youngest brother, Benjamin. The kindness of this powerful man attracted many people to Joseph's character.

There is a description of Joseph in Jacob's testament, which I will not quote in its entirety because it is very long. The first person mentioned in the testament is Jacob's firstborn son Reuben, who pitied Joseph and tried to save him from his brothers' wrath. Here is what Jacob says to him:

> Reuben, you are my firstborn,
> my might and the first fruits of
>   my vigor,
> excelling in rank and excelling
>   in power.
> Unstable as water, you shall no
>   longer excel

because you went up onto your
  father's bed;
then you defiled it—you went
  up onto my couch! (Genesis 49:2–3)

Then Jacob talks about the acts of his two sons who avenged for their sister Dinah's rape—their punishment was ruthless and severe. Jacob pronounces:

Simeon and Levi are brothers;
weapons of violence are their
  swords.
May I never come into their
  council;
may I not be joined to their
  company—
for in their anger they killed men,
  and at their whim they
  hamstrung oxen. (Genesis 49:5–6)

Jacob lists the names of his other sons—the names of fierce and terrible men. One of them is described as someone who has been enslaved:

Issachar is a strong donkey,
lying down between the
  sheepfolds. (Genesis 49:14)

Another son is described in the following way:

Dan shall be a snake by the
    roadside,
a viper along the path,
that bites the horse's heels,
so that its rider falls backward. (Genesis 49:17)

These are ruthless men who are unrelenting to one another; they are condemned by their own father. Joseph, on the other hand, is characterized differently:

Joseph is a fruitful bough,
    a fruitful bough by a spring;
        his branches run over the wall. (Genesis 49:22)

This shifts comparison into a different realm. The tree in the garden is by the water, it is a mighty tree visible from afar, existing not only for itself but also for the welfare of others.

Mann recognized this uniqueness of Joseph's humanism and used the biblical legend in his novel.

During those difficult years of World War II, the Fascists preached cruelty as a religion. They believed that they were God's chosen people in a chosen nation, contrasting their race against all other races, and priding themselves in their cruelty.

It was necessary to give a lesson to the nations based on a model that everyone knew—an old model that would be envisioned anew.

Joseph's compassion is humane and it does not reduce his power, but rather elevates it. His kindness is extended to other nations as well.

Mann created a remarkable image of a dreamer, a leader, a person whose bitter fate led him to tenderness, forgiveness, love, and understanding of the future.

Kind, though humanly or rather boyishly boastful, Joseph is not depicted as a saint, but he changes in the way others perceive him and acquires a certain gentleness. The people in his life change in the course of the novel, too.

Joseph is thrown into a well, then he is sold to Egypt. There he rises to success, but because of the rumors spread by his master's wife Joseph is thrown into jail. While in prison Joseph is treated kindly by the chief steward who puts him in charge of all the prisoners.

Joseph interprets dreams even in confinement. The first dream foretold that the imprisoned royal cupbearer would be freed in three days and restored to his post, while the second dream signaled the death of the baker. The man who was restored to his office and promised to help Joseph forgot all about him.

But after some time the Pharaoh himself has two dreams—about ugly and gaunt cows, and about thin and blasted ears of grain.

None of the magicians or sages in Egypt were able to interpret the dreams. Then the chief cupbearer spoke up and told the Pharaoh about the enslaved youth. Joseph was summoned to the Pharaoh and the dreams were interpreted: both dreams foretold the seven years of great famine that would ravage Egypt. Joseph was put in charge of collecting and storing the grain in preparation for the famine.

The novella includes foreshadowing dreams about the envy and hatred of the brothers; confinement in a dungeon; exile in Egypt; slander; and newly interpreted dreams.

Joseph's brothers are compelled to come to Egypt to buy grain. There is no grain in any of the neighboring lands, and the brothers' journey is prompted by necessity.

Joseph, empowered by the Pharaoh, could have contacted his father earlier to let him know that he is alive, but novellas have their own conventional laws—they exclude the evident and include that which must impede or delay the story's (*fabula*) progression and ensure its self-containment.

Joseph meets his brothers. They come to Egypt without Benjamin. Joseph could have rebuked them, he could have at last revealed himself.

But he doesn't. He controls himself, leaves the room, weeps in a private room, and after washing his face, returns back. He demands that the buyers bring their youngest brother, Benjamin, to him. He tortures his brothers with threats, which they don't understand, and orders that they leave one of the brothers, Simeon, with him in Egypt: "And he picked out Simeon and had him bound before their eyes" (Genesis 42:24).

The least guilty of the brothers is Reuben, who is under the constant weight of his unconscious remorse and says in front of Joseph, whom none of the brothers recognize: "Did I not tell you not to wrong the boy? But you would not listen. So now there comes reckoning for his blood" (Genesis 42:22).

Notice how delicately the action is being delayed and retarded in this famous novella, how it inscribes impediment and recognition, which later the Greeks would call *peripeteia* in their drama, and notice also how it is not mythological.

Recognition takes place later in Chapter 45, when Joseph decides the time for the revelation of truth. He delays recognition because, as it appears, this impediment is also the punishment of his brothers who wanted to kill him and realize their guilt only now. Joseph himself reveals his name to the brothers:

> Then Joseph could no longer control himself before all those who stood by him, and he cried out, "Send everyone away from me." So no one stayed with him when Joseph made himself known to his brothers. And he wept so loudly that the Egyptians heard it, and the household of Pharaoh heard it. Joseph said to his brothers, "I am Joseph. Is my father still alive?" But his brothers could not answer him, so dismayed were they at his presence. (Genesis 45:1–3)

This passage also reveals Joseph's character. His cry and his desire to know about the well-being of his father—all of it is inscribed through artistic signs of that era.

The arrow of intensified emotion is released from the bowstring.

The events of the novel—and not only the events but all the features of this artistic composition—are constructed in such a way that, through incomplete repetitions and retardations, it compels us to slowly move along the stages of the marvelous fate of Joseph, the man who rejected vengeance but not his pride.

The significance of moral decisions and their contradiction within the composition become synchronized.

The basic law of harmony is actualized here.

The story (*fabula*), images, and characterization of heroes all separately contribute to this harmony.

The origin of the supposed impossibility of problems proposed in the fairy tale is different from the shrewd actions of Joseph that impede recognition for the purpose of his own transcendence.

These are interchanging techniques of retardation and they can be explained and explicated not through history or prehistory, but through the laws of artistic construction that desires to give man "the bulging joy of recognition" (Mandelstam), to transmit the author's philosophy of life.

This is why the novella turned out to be immortal. It was included in the Book of Genesis as a new voice. It is not just a story about crime, but also about forgiveness.

The favorite son of a prosperous shepherd was sold into slavery by his own brothers. The slave—Joseph—was given the assignment to manage Potiphar's household, who was the courtier of the Pharaoh and almost the second-most powerful man in Egypt.

Three times the man ends up in a place that is not his own. He is the man who swiftly changes his position in society.

This is the difference, the elasticity and strain of the wooden staff, which pulls the string of plot and shoots the arrow.

In Mann's novel this tension is replaced with a chain of contrasts, a series of ironic turning points in historical perception.

And as a result, everything in his novel becomes ordinary, too liberal, I would say, and less tragic.

The Novel and the Novella

The past lives in us through refutation or simply reconceptualization.

Shakespeare dramatized Italian novellas, which simultaneously contained in them recent events, recollections from past events, and echoes of myths. But a new work always demands a new space for itself.

The problem is that pyramids are almost entirely constructed from stone. The capacity of the interior space in them is actually not bigger than a hole in a stump made by a worm. That's how narrow those compartments are in the pyramids, which hold the sarcophagi.

Thomas Mann expanded the space of the novella about Joseph. He took this simple novella—a story about decency and success, and rewrote it as a myth. He wove the myth into endless comparisons of legends about gods and heroes, algebrizing their contrasts, as it were.

But Joseph's brothers didn't simply abduct him from Palestine; they tore him away from his family and from the world of myths. The motives in the novella are socially realistic and concrete.

Mann's Joseph is the inheritor of many names; he remembers and knows everything, and he quotes everything as a pedantic dogmatist.

Mann's novel is a composition constructed not only as an overview of the past but also departure from the past. The story of Joseph in the Bible is like a breach into the future, it's like a reconstructed street in an old city—it's a masterpiece.

The model of the world in which Joseph lives is scrutinized in Mann's novel through mirror-like repetitions.

The world of repetition is stagnant and, hence, pessimistic, even though the hero is kind.

It is perhaps possible to parody the construction of this biblical novella, but rewriting it is simply an impossible task.

There is a reason why Goethe refused to do it, and not just because he was too young.

The impulse behind his last novel, according to Mann, was in part Goethean. In his autobiography *Poetry and Truth*, Goethe wrote that he had always wanted to work out the history of Joseph in prose, to create a fully improvised story, but then after writing his biblical prose-epic he destroyed it because it lacked an "underlying meaning" (Part I, Book 4).

Goethe had wanted to complete the artless tale with an amplified account of characters and events. In 1942, Mann, too, thought that the entire biblical story was written "sparingly, almost as a reportage."

In his old age, in Munich, Mann set out to write his tetralogy, saturated in reminiscences about myths, Goethe, and Sterne, as well as echoes of early German Romanticism.

Mann's novel is massive and polemical. The history of Joseph is consciously separated from the rest of the Bible.

In his book *What Is Art?* (1897), speaking about what makes art universal, Tolstoy wrote:

> In the narrative of Joseph there was no need to describe in detail, as is done nowadays, Joseph's blood-stained clothes, Jacob's dwelling and clothes, and the pose and attire of Potiphar's wife when, straightening a bracelet on her left arm, she said, "Come to me," and so on, because the feeling contained in this story is so strong that all details except the most necessary ones—for instance, that Joseph went into the next room to weep—all details are superfluous and would only hinder the conveying of the feeling,

and therefore this story is accessible to all people, it touches people of all nations, ranks, ages, has come down to our time, and will live on for thousands of years.[130]

This is why I am not completely convinced that Mann did the right thing by repeating Goethe's attempt and hence stepping over Tolstoy's interdiction. But it's a fine novel. There is a remarkable, perhaps even ingenious chapter called "Account of Mont-kaw's Modest Death" that recounts the friendship between the young Jew and an old Egyptian. This is a chapter about solidarity, equality, and acceptance of someone else's grief.

The novel grows and achieves high levels of magnitude when Mann departs from the biblical story and creates new fields for analysis.

Mont-kaw was Potiphar's overseer—he was a kind and unhappy man. Joseph's feigned tenderness toward his master was probably new for Mont-kaw; he had never known any tenderness. The account of human relations is masterfully executed here. The deference of the steward transforms almost into a son's love.

Joseph was eloquent in his speech: he knew how to deceive others, prompting them his own decisions as though they were made by them. Joseph knew how to say gentle, kind words before someone went to sleep. But Mont-kaw was dying, and here the mastery of the novelist, who constructed and prepared the scene, reaches its pinnacle. Joseph says to the dying man:

130   Lev Tolstoy, *What Is Art?* Translated by Richard Pevear and Larissa Volokhonsky. Penguin, 1995.

Is it not with *must* and *may* today just as always, just as when I took leave of you with my evening blessing, saying you need not think that you must rest, but that you may? Behold, you may! Here is an end to problems and plagues and every vexation. No more bodily pain, no choking constriction, no fear of cramps. No loathsome medicines, no burning poultices or sucking, wriggling worms at your neck. The dungeon pit of your troubles is open wide. You walk out of it and stroll whole and free down the paths of consolation, which with each step lead deeper into consolation. For at first you move through fields you know well, those that received you each evening with the help of my blessing. Yet without your knowing it, there is still some heaviness and shortness of breath in you, in your body, which I hold here in my hands. (*Joseph in Egypt*, Part V)

This depiction of the two men's relationship engages the reader. But the novel has very few successful moments like this one. The descriptions of characters and circumstances repeat to no end.

Potiphar's wife slanders Joseph and he is thrown into prison. The prison warden, Mai-Sakhme, is unlucky in love and he is a bad writer. He writes sketches about his unsuccessful encounters with women. Joseph's relationship with Mai-Sakhme is identical to his relationship with Mont-kaw. Gradually he takes control over his master as he did with Mont-kaw. The roles are almost reversed and Mai-Sakhme becomes Joseph's steward, and he is the one who escorts Joseph to the Pharaoh's palace.

In ancient dramas the heroes had confidants and they told their confidants about their intentions in front of the audience. Apparently this was a motive for an internal monologue.

During a conversation, Joseph and his former supervisor Mai-Sakhme improvise the future recognition scene. Joseph worries. His master, whom he now simply calls Mai, prompts him how to act: in what language to speak with his brothers, perhaps use a translator, employ various kinds of tricks, and impede the moment of recognition.

This conversation takes up an entire chapter.

But here is the actual recognition scene:

> And Joseph? He had risen from his chair, tears sparkling as they ran down his cheeks. For the slanting shaft of light that had previously fallen on his huddled brothers had silently wandered to the last opening at the end of the hall, directly opposite him—that is why the tears running down his cheeks sparkled like gemstones.
>
> "Let all Egyptians go out from here," he said, "everyone out. For I invited God and the world to be guests at my game, but now God alone shall be its spectator."

This passage is followed by a long paragraph about how Mai-Sakhme helps the scribes and servants to clear the doorways, after which Joseph reveals himself, "ignoring the gemstones on his cheeks . . ."

The episode is treated rather conventionally. It's inaccurate. It has been needlessly prolonged and it lacks in emotion.

It is extremely difficult to recompose an old song using a new melody. One must change the method of instrumentation.

One must present the world as it is—adopting that vision as a writer.

Let's talk about contemporary writers. When, in Valentin Kataev's novel *A White Sail Gleams*, the young Gymnasium student who plays "lugs," a game with buttons, loses and becomes his friend's slave—a childish yet brutal game, and has to smuggle cartridges in his satchel—we believe it. When in *The Cottage in the Steppe* the children are eating jam without permission and trying to make sure that it isn't noticeable when looking at the jar—we believe this, too, and we get anxious.

We feel sad for the boy when he is hunting for money to buy an electric machine and they sell him a battery instead (*The Electric Machine*, 1943).

The electricity of anticipation flows through these descriptions—we feel the electric voltage.

When the boy in *Kubik* is looking for forty kopecks to build an air balloon, when he repeats the invention, we are as curious as he is. When he imparts his recollection about the lightness felt in the water, the sensation of weightlessness—we experience it with him.

We become like children again, we recollect our childhood, when we leaf through Mark Twain's book and read about the argument of the two boys by the Mississippi.

But when we find ourselves in a world suffering from an excess of things, a world of thick soles and garish objects that have different prices, when we try to live depending on the emotions of excitement from the quality of material objects, the entry through the gates of life becomes unbearable.

The episodes of a narrative can be linked variously, in any case, they don't have to be assembled around a unified hero, but the writer must be able to convey his relation to objects.

The old novel is alive in the ancient scriptures, but the experiments to create a new novel have survived in only a few pages of the new books.

The pathos of Thomas Mann, the pathos of a creator of new mythology is understandable to us, because he has lost the old anticipation in the present day.

There was a sudden need to support the weakened plot of the novel with scaffolding, which tied the body of the narrative to the old post thrust into the ground.

Sometimes Mann's novel succeeds, other times it fails. Occasionally it is hard to turn the pages. But the path that Mann chose is the path of a person who carries with him not objects but ideas, who does not want to lose the magnitude of the past.

I am trying to show that doubling or tripling the length of the narrative, introducing a mythological thread, or splintering the hero is only a preliminary path. Mann finished the old novel. We don't know what will happen next, because the most difficult thing is to understand the present, to evaluate it, to see the essence through its appearance, in other words, *to remontage your perception* while passing through a familiar street, to learn to select the important and elevate it into plot, i.e., the cognition of the narrative's subject.

History in the present moves in contradictions.

What seems standing is, in fact, flowing.

That's how the glaciers of Central Asia irrigate our cotton fields. One must learn, by directing his willpower, how to use water and silt when diverting the flow of the Nile.

History and Time

Mann's smart novel is ironically constructed according to the laws of architecture using the method of non-identical repetitions of the European novel. If the brothers are going to throw Joseph into a well, then at the beginning of the novel he must be sitting beside the empty well under the moon and his father, Jacob, will be fearing for his son, that either a lion will tear the boy apart, or he might fall into the well.

This primary scene is a foreshadowing of the brothers' actions. Here the well signifies death and resurrection, and so does the episode of Joseph's imprisonment.

The heroes of the new novel have read all the European novels and live, rejecting national enmity and revising the Freudian understanding of life.

Mann is a great novelist but he colonized the ancient novella with skeptical, modern-day heroes, dialogues, and narrator's commentary.

Mann is looking into history as if he were looking into a deep well, at the bottom of which is yet another bottomless well.

There is a Central Asian joke that in order to build a minaret, one should build a deep well and then turn it inside out.

In Mann's novel history, having been forced inside, turns into a well with ledges.

The novel's style is ironic. Its architectural design, it seems, is repeating the structure of myth. The author believes in myth by refuting history.

He believes, perhaps, only in Atlantis.

Everything there leads into salt water.

It is the same flood, only here it's the ocean not the rain that destroys everything. Those who survive the flood live by memories.

The construction of the biblical story is amplified in Mann's epic; it is extended with descriptions of details, dialogues, and correlations to other so-called "pre-flood civilizations."

The nature of the stratum of broken pottery, found in the cultural layer on which cities and dwellings stand, systematically changes. The broken pieces are stronger than the newer pots, they are almost flat and they aren't easily broken or crushed. They characterize the layer, assisting the observation of changes of cultures without turning succession into a blended mix.

Humanity moves, changes its morals, invests *new things in the old.* We are not merely taught by the past. We, too, revise the past by re-comprehending it. We use our inheritance differently—by refuting it.

But in Mann's novel the parable sometimes prevails over history.

The cultural layers in the novel are correlated in such a way that they often seem to be either synchronous or diachronous. The pace of time in separate parts of the novel transmits the present—our calendar and the dial of our clock.

Biblical time moved in conventional cycles of seven. This was the pace of life back then.

Real time was tracked by the cattle-breeder. It was determined by the alternation of generations of men and cattle.

By rewriting the biblical story that was told in less than twenty-five chapters into a novel of more than a thousand pages, Mann inscribes in it our own time and our way of tracking the flow of time. His perception of "short" and "long" is different from the perception of the cattle-breeder's "short" and "long." In Mann's novel Jacob's consciousness retains the hours and minutes that existed only in a different culture—where people perceived them merely astronomically.

It's true, though, that the debate about determining the accuracy of the dates of the events is ironical.

The world in the Book of Genesis is familiar only with goats and donkeys.

Later on they will learn about camels and insert memories about them in the old stories.

The smoke of millennia is permeable, and time didn't just increase the depths of the well. Life doesn't roll like a ball in which it is impossible to distinguish the top from the bottom, but rather changes through wars and inventions.

Humanity broadens its experience, moving forward. Myths change as a word changes its meaning. Inventions move upward in spiraling circles without constricting the spiral. They only "seem to" repeat, emerging in new constructions.

Rejecting the flow of time in the very beginning of his novel, and repeating it "over and over again," Thomas Mann asserts that humanity doesn't realize its antiquity, that during the historical epoch man didn't domesticate a single animal, that antiquity was stagnant, devoid of the movement of time.

This is not true, as we have already said.

The horse and the camel had already been domesticated in the Sumerian, Hittite and Egyptian cultures.

Today we know our past better than our antecedents, we are aware of time and we are learning that the representation of that time and its perception are multifarious and different.

Let's emphasize, though, returning to Mann's conflict with history, that his argument is noble in its purpose.

Mann is fighting for humanism, presenting it as an almost eternal phenomenon.

An arrogant boy, spoiled by his father's favoritism, a tattletale and a dandy, learns how to forgive through fear and labor; he learns that sometimes one ought to seek the fault in oneself.

Tolstoy and his pupils understood this in Joseph's story very well.

All of this is clear in the voluminous novel, too, but it has been stifled by archeological detail. The initial delay in the process of humanization in the novel is presented as an immobility of time.

This is a misinterpretation of the past. Potiphar's household didn't live according to our laws of love and jealousy, and not because Potiphar was a eunuch.

Humanity sometimes was not capable of understanding.

It perceived its past in its new reality, in the present.

Now it is the future that foresees, analyzing the present through art and computing it through science.

Everything is prepared in Mann's novel craftily, with an inspired talent; everything is revealed and motivated with detailed resentment.

Joseph's master Potiphar, a royal official, an excellent hunter, turns out to be a eunuch who was castrated by his own parents in order to facilitate his royal career. He is a disfigured man. This makes him more gracious in his treatment of Joseph for the supposed sin. He gets a chance to say to his parents: "If you are old and senile and must die, then you may die now."

It is the parents' fault who, by castrating their son, have caused the imaginary betrayal of his wife. The brilliantly reinvented Potiphar throws the slave out of his house half-accusing and half-acquitting Joseph of his crime.

Even if there had been a betrayal, he was not the one who had been betrayed.

In the brief biblical tale, Joseph is understood even without this incident. The old books weren't supposed to explain who Joseph had slept with because virginity was quite simply forbidden. It was only tolerated as an offering to God.

Mann wrote a novel full of wondrous details, splendidly characterizing Leah and Rachel, the gentle giant Reuben who left home and who was guilty not just for being born to the unloved wife.

But the world does not roll like a wheel. Nothing repeats; the mystical associations and the name Osarsiph that Joseph took in Egypt recalls the name Osiris, and Joseph's situation, who in the bedroom of Potiphar's wife recollects Gilgamesh when Ishtar besieged him, and the imaginary yet precise repetitions are all quotations. Humanity carries history in itself—it does not quote history. Those who quote history are the ones who can't create anything new.

Grieving over Joseph's bloody robe, Mann's Jacob quotes from the Book of Job. But Job's grief is much deeper, he revolts against the structure of the world. This revolt helped Dostoevsky when writing *The Brothers Karamazov*.

A Few Remarks on the Novel-Myth

One must not return to the past, but one can be enriched by the past as Goethe was when writing his *Faust* while making use of the Bible and, perhaps, the tradition of puppetry.

Mann's novel was written by a great author who had a full grasp of the material from the past and who treated novelistic technique with a certain irony. There is a reason why in one of his articles Mann mentioned Sterne's name in relation to his own novel.

Joseph and His Brothers is not a return to the past—it is a defense of the present. Mann was defending humanism, while fighting against the Fascists.

But the method of selection of the essential for description, the method of articulation of the object, the method of alternative linking changes with time.

The success of the novel, the author's mastery is perceived through the relationship between the novel and the short biblical story that Tolstoy was so fascinated by.

The story of Joseph could have been published today in two feuilletons.

Rachel's death—the death of Jacob's beloved wife is narrated in just a few terse sentences.

Joseph's biblical biography conveys the peculiarities of his behavior—he is a big-hearted trickster.

Joseph's story was widely used in Eastern literature as a story about temptation and faithfulness. All of the redundant elements, even if chronologically necessary, were left out. It was a simple tragedy about jealousy and devotion. The parents and brothers appeared in the narrative only in relation to the conflict.

Even though Rachel's death is chronicled in Chapter 35, Jacob still talks of her in the biblical story as if she were not dead. The words "mother" and "father" are fused in a single word—"parents," which is why when confronting his son, Jacob refers to Rachel as though she were still alive.

The descriptions in Mann's novel are too wordy and the characters are too eloquent.

The novel gives a full account of Rachel giving birth to Benjamin. It says about Jacob that "he had two passions: God and Rachel."

The woman's death is slow and moving.

Mann's novel is approximately 150 or 170 times longer than the original tale.

Every epoch has its conventions of representation that must be followed. The new emerges in the old—it appears suddenly, as if rejecting the old perception but without obscuring it.

In the epic of Gilgamesh, the hero argues with the goddess as if she were his equal. Then his best friend Enkidu dies.

The living man tells his dead friend about their past deeds. Everything is expressed laconically but with an impeded flow of time:

> For six days and seven nights I mourned him,
> until a maggot fell out of his nose.

Then I was frightened, I was terrified by death,
and I set out to roam the wilderness. (Book X)

The detail that can be called naturalistic invades the myth, which simultaneously embodies history (including the name of the historical king who reigned in the Mesopotamian city of Uruk).

The elements of past, present, and future perceptions of life co-exist next to each other in art.

The epic precedes the novel. The myth precedes the epic.

The novel cannot, though it unbearably wants to, return to the epic form.

We can trace the difference between the methods of showing the passage of time in the novel and in the Bible.

Joseph's story in the Bible, as we have been discussing, is composed as a novella packed with genealogies. These genealogies fortify the novella's link to the other parts of the Bible and show the passage of real time.

The story doesn't show the transformations taking place inside the hero.

He is beautiful and good, and he never changes. He doesn't get fat, doesn't get old. He perfectly fits the requirements necessary for the narration.

In Mann's version, Joseph is described as a young man, then as an adult, and finally as a portly man.

Even his beloved Benjamin, who had also become a portly man, doesn't recognize his brother despite the obvious signs when the great Egyptian treats his guest in a special way.

It is as though Benjamin has a presentiment of recognition, but still doesn't recognize the man with whom he spent his childhood. None of this is in the Bible. The biblical motivation is magical. As in fairy tales, the hero returns home, having committed heroic deeds and without having aged. Old age in *The Odyssey* is employed so that the hero can return home unrecognized.

Athena doesn't magically transform Odysseus—she simply returns him his youth. The old nurse recognizes Odysseus by the scar on his leg that he had gotten from a wild boar.

Mann introduces real time to the biblical story: the precise number of years. This is impossible, because the story was written by someone who had no need to precisely mark and subdivide the passage of time.

Mann simultaneously gives a characterization of time in general and comes to the conclusion that it is unfathomable:

> When as adventurous storytellers we plunge into the past, we taste death and the knowledge of it—that is, the source of both our desire and our ashen-faced apprehension. But desire has more life—nor do we deny that it is bound up in the flesh. But the object of desire is the first and last of all our remarks and inquiries, of all our zeal: humanity— for which we shall search in the underworld and in death, just as Ishtar had searched there for Tammuz, and Isis for Osiris, in order to know it there where the past is. (Prelude: Descent into Hell)

The past of history and mythology for Mann is an idiosyncratic state of immobility.

In the next page he says: ". . . three thousand years down—and what is that compared to fathomless depths?"

Mann's time is populated with myths but, repeating one another, they don't transmit the various states of human consciousness.

Joseph is simultaneously Tammuz, the god of spring; Osiris, the god of resurrection; Hermes, who tricked Apollo and stole his cattle; and Gilgamesh, who surpassed everything, except for sleep.

The hero is construed repeatedly in half-quotations.

The quotations do not give the epic any temporal depth—they are like a gilded literary *riza* embellishing an icon, turning everything into a replicating ornament.

Potiphar's wife, Mut, while trying to seduce Joseph, is ashamed of her own desire and, at the same time, invents various pretexts to offer gifts to her beloved. He rejects the woman, as Fielding's quasi-parodic hero Joseph Andrews would have rejected her.

She speaks with Joseph as a knowledgeable woman.

She says: "I lack cleverness because of my unbound desire for your flesh and blood, but I will do what I say. I am the loving Isis, and my gaze is death. Beware, beware, Osarsiph!"

Consoling Mut who has gone mad, Joseph recalls Gilgamesh, who had rejected Ishtar's love and she had led the Bull of Heaven to destroy Gilgamesh. He was not a quotation then.

Human nature is simple and predictable.

The harlot turned the beast into a man and sent him to commit deeds.

The act that the Bible called fornication was perceived as a new way of life in the epic of Gilgamesh. Examples and parallels brought into the story of Joseph diffuse the fictional time, wash it away like Indian ink.

The act that the Bible called fornication was considered a crime in Goethe's *Faust*.

The angels believe that Margaret must die.

The important thing is not repetition, but dissimilarity born from the experience of new knowledge.

Tolstoy characterized and described his heroes differently than how Chekhov had started characterizing his heroes.

He considered Chekhov to be not only a great writer but also someone who had attained new mastery.

Time was assessed by the genius through the changing methods of representation.

Conflicts, reinvented numerously through mythologization, stop being conflicts in a certain work.

In the archaeological sense, Mann's novel is precise as a museum, but archaeology is perceived outside of chronology.

The novel contains a large number of disputed triumphs.

It is like arranging new furniture in an old apartment.

Mann wrestled with the old biblical myth while admiring its antiquity.

The desire to enter such a crusade is understandable. The young Goethe dreamed about it. Not having lost his battle, Mann emerged limping much like Jacob, when he wrestled with a stranger who, seeing that he could not prevail struck his opponent on the hip socket to leave a sign that Jacob had fought with one who was more powerful than him.

Mann's ironic heroism does not resurrect his novel as a universal structure of prose.

When a child is born, the midwife ties a firm knot and then cuts the umbilical cord that connects the fetus to the mother.

Art is discontinuous. It is born for new knowledge, new investigation, new articulation of perception and creation of new structures.

Yesterday is still there—we can hear the sound of it, but its echo should only be regarded when recording the new sound.

John Updike's *The Centaur*

In *The Centaur,* the story develops as though in two parallel threads: first—in the United States in the present, and second—in Greece during the conventional existence of antique heroes and gods. Updike is apparently Mann's disciple.

The simultaneous actions are comparatively juxtaposed and interweaved in a complex fashion. Cruel boys throw arrows at their teacher: one of the arrows strikes the core of his shin. He limps out of the classroom, clanking with his three remaining hooves:

> He tried to keep that leg from touching the floor, but the jagged clatter of the three remaining hooves sounded so loud he was afraid one of the doors would snap open and another teacher emerge to bar his way. In this crisis his fellow-teachers seemed herdsmen of terror, threatening to squeeze him back into the room with students. His bowels weakly convulsed; on the glimmering varnished boards, right in front of the trophy case with its hundred silver eyes, he deposited, without breaking stride, a steaming dark spreading cone. His great gray-dappled flanks

twitched with distaste, but like a figurehead on the prow of a foundering ship his head and torso pressed forward.

The American high school teacher, Caldwell, is simultaneously a poor man in a knit hat and the wise centaur Chiron, the contemporary of Prometheus. The characters in the novel are both modern-day Americans and mythological heroes at the same time, whereas the initials of their American names correspond to the initials of their mythological names. They are endowed with a second life.

The story is narrated from the perspective of the teacher's son, Peter, who has psoriasis.

In Greek mythology, Chiron was kind, he had a disputed lineage that was lost in the contradictoriness of myths. We only know one thing for certain—he was the guardian and instructor of Achilles, Asclepius, the god of healing and medical arts, Apollo, Jason, and many others. Chiron was immortal, but he sacrificed his immortality so that Prometheus could live. He had a painful death, poisoned with an arrow, and was honored with a place in the sky as the constellation Sagittarius. He is one of the most humane centaurs and, perhaps, heroes in the myths. Unlike Updike's portrayal, Greek vase paintings depicted Chiron with human forelegs.

The impoverished American Centaur drives an old car, which is being fixed up by his friend Hummel, who also limps. In the world of myths Hummel's name is Hermes, though Hermes had never met Chiron in Greek mythology.

The mechanic has three workmen in his shop—it appears that they are all Cyclopes, the helpers of the limping Vulcan-Hermes, whose smithy was once situated underneath Mount Etna.

This isn't the first time that blacksmith Cyclopes are appearing in literature.

It is said in *Eugene Onegin* about how:

> . . . the rural Cyclopes
> in front of a slow fire
> treat with a Russian hammer
> Europe's light article. (Chapter 7, XXXIV)

Caldwell's old car is being similarly "treated" at Hummel's Garage. When humanity is utterly miserable, it returns to old but restored and newly woven myths. The Centaur's ailing son is simultaneously the author of the book, or, at any rate, the narrator of the story.

The women who love or desire the Centaur are gifted with heavenly beauty and sophisticated, divine morality. In Chapter 6, this morality is juxtaposed against a technical American imitation of love—a simple affair, as simple as a model of an engine made for a child. The morality of centaurs is much higher, though it's melancholy.

Centaurs appeared in pre-revolutionary Russian literature, as well. In Andrei Bely's first work, *Second Symphony, the Dramatic*, the centaur has the traces of ironic origins. He is married to "a fairy tale": "She had coral lips and blue, blue eyes—the eyes of a fairy tale." The democrat, who is most likely the prototype of the author, is in love with her.

She is the wife of the gentle sea-centaur, "who was a citizen since Böcklin's time. He used to snort and dive among the waves, but then decided to change his seafaring lifestyle and live on the land. He gave up his four hooves for two legs, put on a tailcoat and became a man."

The centaur appears frequently in the *Second Symphony*; he is hapless, plain, fairly rich, and he even buys paintings.

Symbolist poems about centaurs were so banal they were turning into platitudes. Andrei Bely had a poem entitled "The Centaurs' Games," in which he invoked: "O where are you, Centaur, my vanished brother—" and wrote in another poem:

> The old man snorted anxiously, swinging his truncheon,
> and galloped off into the dark woods,
> swishing his gray tail.

In his tragic memoirs *The Beginning of the Century*, Bely wrote: "Seeing the mummified human horde, whom you have chosen as your own, seeing your close ones, for whose sake you broke away from the past, become distant—is a bitter thing. But it's even worse not to recognize the purpose of your own dawn's rebirth: in ashes and in cinders. If you appear in these pages as an object of memoirs (not as a judge or critic, but a self-sentenced man), then I can say this: I was reflected in them only as I once felt about myself."[131]

The great Russian philosopher Vladimir Solovyov, who was already dead then, walked over this presentiment of another world on the roofs and "pulling out a little horn from his pocket, trumpeted over the sleeping city."[132]

This was said in irony, of course. It was self-consolation—a projection of grief and inadequacy onto other objects and conflicts existing in art, as it were.

---

131 Andrei Bely, *Nachalo veka* [The Beginning of the Century], 1933.
132 From Andrei Bely's *Simfonia 2-ya, dramaticheskaya* [Second Symphony, the Dramatic], 1902.

The ancient birthplace of humanity's philosophy of life—mythology—wasn't turning into a myth, but becoming a replacement for reality. The grotesque was a motivation for the break from reality.

Updike's hero is a realistically decent and unhappy man. He rises above what they call reality, above the mediocrity of life and intellectual poverty of the average American philistine.

Caldwell's life is all too realistic: the miserly salaries of the teachers, the threats of losing a job, the debts that are impossible to pay off are very real.

A correction by the author (not the hero)—it is the birth of humanity's consciousness in mythology—humanity takes pride in itself.

In art, humanity often thinks through comparisons. It searches for truth, like artillerists at war get close to hitting their target—they shoot, missing the target, then they try again.

Hitting the target seems to be accidental.

It's a pity that I have to part with the noble centaurs.

They lived in Russia before Andrei Bely.

There used to be a Slavonic compendium of myths from sacred texts, the Bible, Greek mythology, and the Talmud, called the *Paleya*.

There the religious scribes engaged in harsh polemics with Jews and Muslims, who in the end were deemed heretics.

In old Russia we also had Jewish sects and dualist heretics—they appear in the apocryphal legends about Solomon and Kitovras. The legends were partially discussed by Aleksandr Nikolaevich Veselovsky in his work titled *Slavic Legends about Solomon and Kitovras*.[133]

---

133 Aleksandr Veselovsky, *Sobranie sochinenii* [Collected Works]. Vol. VIII. 1921.

Evidently these legends were connected to the old chivalric romances—the most ancient ones, such as the Western European legends of Merlin and the Holy Grail.

Kitovras is a centaur. In wisdom he equals Solomon. He participated in the construction of the Temple in Jerusalem. He was kind and gentle, but due to his nature Kitovras walked only in a straight line, even when there were bends in the road, and so he destroyed buildings. Once a widow asked him not to destroy her home. Kitovras tried to go around and broke his ribs, and said: "A gentle word will break the bones." According to Veselovsky, the painting above the doors of the Cathedral of St. Sophia in Novgorod depicts the following: "On the first level, the gigantic winged figure of the Centaur-Kitovras holds in his hand a small figure wearing a crown, probably Solomon, whom he is about to overthrow."

Art often thinks through juxtapositions.

Updike's novel is one of the attempts of a double, symphonic representation of reality, so to speak, an attempt to humanize the habitual, the magical-heroic.

Chapter 5 in *The Centaur* is an actual four-page "obituary" of George Caldwell, the tortured teacher, who had accomplished a few good but insignificant things in his life. Here is an excerpt from the end of his obituary:

> In addition to a full load of extracurricular school activities, including the coaching of our gallant swimming team, the management of all football, basketball, track, and baseball tickets, and the supervision of the Communications Club, Mr. Caldwell played a giant's role in the affairs of the community. He was secretary of the Olinger Boosters' Club,

Counselor to Cub Pack 12, member of the Committee to Propose a Borough Park, vice president of the Lions and chairman of that service club's annual lightbulb-selling campaign for the benefit of blind children.

In this American novel, too, man is not understood. It is as though he doesn't fit in the pages of the novel: the parodied everyman intentionally cannot be suited to the heroic irony of the novel.

The tormented Centaur dies on the road by the broken-down Buick, in the midst of a brutish landscape:

> Chiron came to the edge of limestone; his hoof scratched. A bit of pale pebble rattled into the abyss. He cast his eyes upward to the dome of blue and perceived that it was indeed a great step. Yes, in seriousness, a very great step, for which all the walking in his life had not prepared him. Not an easy step nor an easy journey, it would take an eternity to get there, an eternity as the anvil ever fell. His strained bowels sagged; his hurt leg cursed; his head felt light. The whiteness of limestone pierced his eyes. A little breeze met his face at the cliff-edge. His will, a perfect diamond under the pressure of absolute fear, uttered the final word. *Now.*

Here Updike includes an untranslated Greek passage from *The Library* of Apollodorus. The translation is as follows:

> The wound refused to heal and Chiron entered his cave, wishing to die. Since he was immortal he could not. Zeus

permitted Prometheus to become immortal in his place and so Chiron died.[134]

The novel ends with the words: "Chiron accepted death."

As I was reading Updike's novel, I kept thinking how the juxtaposition of several threads is a commonplace occurrence in art. In most cases, the evental basis for juxtaposing is usually (but not always) explained.

Victor Hugo wrote in his treatise on William Shakespeare:

> All Shakespeare's plays, with the exception of *Macbeth* and *Romeo and Juliet*—thirty-four plays out of thirty-six—offer to the observer one peculiarity which seems to have escaped, up to this day, the most eminent commentators and critics; one which is unnoticed by the Schlegels, and even by M. Villemain himself, in his remarkable labors, and of which it is impossible not to speak. It is the double action which traverses the drama and reflects it on a small scale. Beside the tempest in the Atlantic is the tempest in the teacup. Thus, Hamlet makes beneath himself a Hamlet; he kills Polonius, father of Laertes—and there stands Laertes over against him exactly as he stands over against Claudius. There are two fathers to avenge. There might be two ghosts. So, in *King Lear*, side by side and simultaneously, Lear, driven to despair by his daughters Goneril and Regan, and consoled by his daughter Cordelia, is repeated in Gloster, betrayed by his son Edmund and loved

134   Apollodorus, *God and Heroes of the Greeks: The "Library" of Apollodorus*. Translated by Michael Simpson. U Massachusetts P, 1976.

by his son Edgar. The idea bifurcated, the idea echoing itself, a lesser drama copying and elbowing the principal
drama, the action attended by its moon—a smaller action
like it—unity cut in two; surely the fact is a strange one.
(Part 2, Book IV, Chapter 1)

"These double actions are," according to Hugo, "the sign of the
sixteenth century."

He talks about mirrored plots in sculpture and in painting from
that period.

Hugo is right in his observation, but double (parallel) action was
not just the mark of the sixteenth century. It went beyond the Renaissance.

Good and evil brothers appear frequently in novels and plays.

Parallels in family histories recur in the novels of Tolstoy.

What Updike did in his book was nothing new. The only innovation appears to be the absence of a motive in the use of the parallel
structure.

One and the same character is simultaneously not that same
character. The shift from one narrative thread to the other is always
abrupt and unexpected.

There is not a single form in the history of art that disappears,
and neither are there pure repetitions. The old form returns anew
in order to express something new.

The old form throws a colorful, often ironic, shadow on the
new one.

THE NEW GENRES

Genre
Once More about the Same Thing

The permanent links that emerge are joined so tightly that the soldered joints become as if atrophied, reduced, and the whole process appears in unified form. But we can test the exact meaning of the function by turning the whole structure upside down. Then the distinctness is restored.

Human consciousness examines the external world without restoring the whole system of search each time.

The internal links become so habitual, so routine, that they are as if absent, but the whole chain is tested by the very law of reflection—the law of testing consciousness.

Except genre is not only a trace.

Genre is not just an established unity but also a juxtaposition of contrasting stylistic phenomena that have been experientially tested as being successful (possessing emotional nuance) and have been perceived as a system. This system is defined at the very beginning (of assignment) through naming: such and such novel, or such and such elegy, or such and such epistle.

This general definition introduces the reader into the world of the story and warns him beforehand—how, in what system the soon to be analyzed phenomena are arranged.

In the process of its formation, the genre-type already assumes the existence of *other* type-systems.

The permanently established customs—the etiquettes of the order in which the world is examined (as it appears to me)—are called genres. They don't change gradually, and they often don't change in separate features but the whole system collapses and reassembles as a new flight of stairs, as it were.

An innovator is a guide who changes the tracks but who also knows the old pathways. He knows the old experience as if by absorbing it.

Nikolai Vilmont quotes Dostoevsky's words in *Great Companions*, recounted by Nikolai Strakhov: "*He* (not clear who this "he" is—N.V.) accuses me of exploiting the great ideas of world geniuses. Why is that wrong? Why is it wrong to sympathize with the great past of humanity? No, my lords, a good writer is not a cow that regurgitates the cud of everyday reality, but a tiger that devours the cow and everything else that it ate!" Having said this Dostoevsky abruptly got up and prepared to leave, as though he had come only to throw this replica at the anonymous accuser . . ."[135]

He thought of himself as the new realist, who destroyed the old representation, while at the same time feeding on it.

The Debate about the Novel

The debate about the novel has been tediously prolonged and continues not without irritation.

---

135   Nikolai Vilmont, *Velikie sputniki* [Great Companions], 1966.

By "novel" we usually meant a multifaceted work the aim of which was to correlate its various facets.

But there are many different kinds of novels and novellas.

The link of the thread between Pirogov and Piskaryov isn't a link at all. Rather, it is a perpendicular collision of relations of two different men in a chance meeting on the street. One man kills himself, while the other spends an evening dancing after having been thrashed.[136]

The rationale—the motivation of the link is that these men met and bowed to one another.

The Russian novel is unusually kaleidoscopic and it doesn't carry on the tradition of the European novel, rather—it refutes the structure of the European novel.

Tolstoy wrote in his diary on April 4, 1861:

> On the road, as I was throwing pebbles, I thought about art, too. Is it possible to have as one's sole aim only situations and not characters? I think it is, and that's what I have done, and that's where I have been successful. Only it is not a universal issue, but mine.

The character's unity in Russian prose, as Tynjanov pointed, often has a paradoxical nature. In Gogol's *The Nose*, Major Kovalyov's nose turns up in a newly baked bread. That same nose is seen promenading in a gold-braided uniform on Nevsky Prospect, and when the Major approaches it, the nose tells him that there can be

---

136 Nikolai Gogol's "Nevsky Prospect" (1935).

no close relations between them, since the buttons of Kovalyov's undress uniform are different from its own and, hence, they serve in different departments. The nose prepares to leave for Riga. Then the nose is found and returned to Kovalyov but he is unable to stick the nose in its old place. Tynjanov wrote in *The Problem of Verse Language* (1924): "It is absolutely remarkable how in this grotesque the equivalence of the hero—the equality of the nose to *The Nose*—doesn't falter for even a minute."[137]

"Situations" might demonstratively not coincide with the character and not create characters if that was not an issue put forth by the author himself.

According to Tynjanov: "The hero is never static, he can only be dynamic. And it would suffice to just have the sign of the hero, his name, so that we don't have to keep an eye on him the entire time."

More about the Hero

I am trying to remain within the limits of a single work, but the purpose of my book is an attempt to grasp the mobility of the literary work and the multiplicity of its meanings.

There are two heroes in the world of Russian literature—Eugene Onegin and Tatyana Larina. Though Eugene Onegin lent his name to the epic novel, his life didn't fit into it because Pushkin was unable to narrate Onegin's meetings with the Decembrists.

---

137   Yuri Tynjanov, *The Problem of Verse Language*. Translated by Michael Sosa and Brent Harvey. Ann Arbor: Ardis, 1981.

The Decembrists were expurgated from the end of *War and Peace* and they were expurgated from *Eugene Onegin*. Despite these omissions, the artists were able to create unified works.

Andrei Bolkonsky's son Nikolenka's dream is the prophecy and analysis of the Decembrist revolt.

The unity of *Eugene Onegin* is much more complex.

It has numerous branches and it is dense in its foliage. It grows into Russian literature, as it were, but it has no denouement, and this is emphasized when Pushkin mentions the unfinished novel ("who never read life's novel to the end") and the half-empty goblet ("not having to the bottom drained / the goblet full of wine").

It is wrong to talk about heroes as though they are real people. They become acquainted with one another differently and they stop loving one another in a different way. And besides, they have the right to depart from life without dying. But Tatyana's judgment— that, too, is literature. Dostoevsky judged her in his speech about Pushkin when speaking about the fate of the Russian person.

So what is it that I want to remind you from Tatyana's story?

Pushkin abandoned Onegin in a bitter moment, and in the last stanza Onegin lost his social environment. I will quote only three lines from that last stanza:

> "Some are no more, others are distant,"
> as erstwhiles Sadi said.
> Without them was Onegin's picture finished.

He is cut out of time.

There are certain etiquettes in any given epoch, certain morals, not in the sense of negating the concept itself, but in the sense that they belong to different lifestyles: some have disappeared, others will persist.

Pushkin solved the fate of love differently each time.

So what is Tatyana's fate in the novel's system of images?

She must leave home, her "familiar woods." It is time to depart:

> Nature, tremulous, pale,
> is like a victim richly decked. . . . (Chapter 7, XXIX)

Then winter arrives: "Tatyana dreads the winter way" (Chapter 7, XXX).

What is awaiting her? Marriage is deliberately constructed as something dull and unexciting.

A certain imposing general at the ball does not take his eyes off her. Tatyana doesn't notice him in the crowd. Her two aunts spot him, describe him to her—where he stands. Tatyana sees her fate and is surprised, as it were: "Who? That fat general?" (Chapter 7, LIV).

This important, esteemed man is Tatyana's future husband.

Pushkin sees Petersburg through his own and simultaneously Tatyana's eyes. He is not Onegin, and Tatyana is the fate that he can't have.

The structures of art are naïve sometimes, they grope for happiness or replace it with an equally interesting despair. The characteristics of the heroes change. The fat general acquires a name—Gremin, a voice, and sings an aria in Tchaikovsky's opera. We see his love for Tatyana—their new relationship—expressed through music.

Dostoevsky saw her as a victim and wasn't wrong either.

The hero's transformation isn't always the result of a personal transformation catalyzed from within. This change often takes place with the author's discovery and increased understanding of the hero. Occasionally, the hero is designed with an intentional duality, as we see in Hoffmann.

Maybe Chichikov's ruminations about the list of purchased dead souls, which also included names of escaped serfs, is not a slip made by the author, as Belinsky had once thought, but perhaps a grain of truth through which Gogol wanted to articulate a different essence in Chichikov.

Herzen is a brilliant writer, whose artistic experiments are extremely interesting, yet not fully explored, and whose work still hasn't been understood in our time.

In 1866, Herzen wrote in his foreword to the fifth part of *My Past and Thoughts*: "As I started printing another installment of *My Past and Thoughts*, I stopped once again at the fragmentary nature of the stories, pictures, and the *footnoted* contemplations, so to speak."[138]

Herzen continues to talk about the ambiguity of the work's genre: "*My Past and Thoughts* is not a historical monograph, rather it is a reflection of history in a person who has appeared on its pathway *by chance.*"

The endless flow of articles in *Kolokol* (The Bell) represents art based on documentation, yet at the same time it's a kind of art that proffers generalization. It is a judgment on time, as it were, with an inclusion of documental data.

Trial scenes have often appeared in literature, for example, in *The Brothers Karamazov* or in *Resurrection*.

---

138   Aleksandr Herzen, *Byloe i dumy* [My Past and Thoughts], 1856–68.

Yet art doesn't merely depict a trial, it *is* a pleading and it *is* a trial over life.

Herzen's line of thought continued in Dostoevsky's *Diary of a Writer*.

Of course, Tolstoy thought jubilantly that the structure of the old European novel was not universal.

He negated the Western European novel, while acknowledging its capability. Here is what he wrote: "Russian [literature] artistic thought doesn't fit inside that mold and searches for something new . . ."

In the margin he wrote: "Remember Turgenev, Gogol, Aksakov."

Turgenev happened to come first due to his *Notes of a Hunter*, the structure of which defined *The Sevastopol Sketches*.

What exactly was Tolstoy not satisfied with in the European novel? I think that, first of all, he has a different way of particularizing his hero and separating him from life in general.

The fates of the heroes in *War and Peace*, their temperaments and relationship to life change with the advent of war. Pierre Bezukhov returns from war completely cleansed as if in a bath—or at least that's how Natasha perceives him. The war has cleansed the future Decembrist.

Pierre and Natasha's marriage does not conclude the novel. Nikolenka's dream is prophetic—it foretells the failure of Pierre's mission and the beginning of a conflict between the aristocrats such as Pierre and those who follow Arakcheev, such as Nikolai Rostov.

The novel doesn't have a conclusive end and this was marked by the fact that the first sketches of the novel began with a description of the defeat in Sevastopol and the return of the Decembrists to their fatherland.

In *Anna Karenina*, nothing is concluded for either Levin or Vronsky.

Anna Karenina dies, but her question still persists.

Tolstoy moves on to new works, such as *The Forged Coupon*, where the heroes change yet the situations remain the same.

Classic Russian prose is innovative not only in its plot formation, but the hero, too, is new or the concept of the hero is revised, refined in this tradition.

Eugene in *The Bronze Horseman* is named the "hero" of this Petersburg tale in the twelfth line of Part I and he doesn't have a surname. The author says about the hero's name: "It needn't the special commendations . . ."

In his unfinished poem "Yezersky" (1832), Pushkin makes a provision that the main character in his work might provoke some objections from the critics. They will tell him that:

> It would be best if the poet
> Takes a subject more sublime,
> That no translation can be offered
> To unembellished heroes . . .

Eugene is not a hero—he is a wood chip floating on the waves of the flooding river. He is the victim of history, incapable of protest. He is practically the neighbor of Akaki Akakievich, only the latter is completely devoid of any romantic intelligibility, and yet their protest is not a chance occurrence.

The title of Lermontov's *A Hero of Our Time* establishes the new condition of the "hero." Pechorin is a hero deprived of the possibility to commit a heroic deed, and the whole structure of this work, beginning with the sketch-like notes of the anonymous man, disrupts the novelistic tradition and, while changing our perception of Pechorin, allows us to determine his significance.

Pechorin is established as the "hero of our time." Lermontov writes: "Perhaps some readers will want to know my opinion of Pechorin's character. My answer is the title of this book. 'But this is wicked irony!' they will say.—I wonder." Even to Lermontov Pechorin is not a hero—he is merely a character who might become a hero.

The Hero in Dostoevsky

In *Crime and Punishment*, Porfiri Petrovich says to Raskolnikov in the second chapter of Part 6: "It's not time, but yourself that will decide that. Be the sun and all will see you. The sun has before all to be the sun."[139]

But in which planetary system must the hero become a sun?

Handsome, intelligent, perhaps even a genius (the sun)—Raskolnikov is not a hero not only because he commits a crime in a setting that conflicts with the aesthetics of the novel.

Returning home after Porfiri's interrogation and meeting with the petty bourgeois, Raskolnikov thinks about the so-called "heroes":

---

139   Fyodor Dostoevsky, *Crime and Punishment*. Translated by Constance Garnett. Bantam, 1996.

No, those men are not made so. The real *Master* to whom all is permitted storms Toulon, makes a massacre in Paris, *forgets* an army in Egypt, *wastes* half a million men in the Moscow expedition and gets off with a jest at Vilna. And altars are set up to him after his death, and so *all* is permitted. No, such people, it seems, are not of flesh but of bronze! (Part III, Chapter 6)

For Dostoevsky, Raskolnikov, in fact, is not a "hero." He is not a Napoleon, though he is portrayed as a compelling person. The moral characteristic of Napoleon, the main motive for his actions rest on the fact that he doesn't have any moral dilemmas, unlike Raskolnikov, whose essence demands the examination of moral problems.

The essence of Dostoevsky's novels differs from the essence of old novels in the way in which Dostoevsky examines moral problems in their contradiction and doesn't treat them as something concrete and unchanging.

It is the concept of the hero that is being scrutinized here.

The methods of knowledge—of exposure of the world's contradictoriness—lie at the basis of art structures, which is why the history of art is also contradictory. On the one hand, it is uninterrupted; we see how plots and themes live for thousands of years. We see how old works get resurrected. We realize that Aristotle's poetics hasn't expired yet and that Greek mythology was not only the basis for art in the antiquity but also the bread off which contemporary art feeds. On the other hand, we see that art is discontinuous; schools alternate; we learn about breaks, debates, negations—it reminds me of ice floes that collide and crush against each other, breaking the ground, and creating new mounds.

So what is genre from our point of view?

Genre is a convention—an agreement of meaning and synchronization of signals. The system must be understandable to both the author and the reader. This is precisely why the author often announces at the beginning of his work that it is a novel, a tragedy, a comedy, an elegy, or an epistle. He indicates the mode in which the reader must perceive the work and recognize its structure.

The structure that emerges often takes the form of something not quite anticipated, surprising, something that appears to be within the realm of analysis and yet retains an "otherness."

Once More about the Horizon

When *The Song of Igor's Campaign* was written down, Russia already had a great culture, its own canons of organization and relationship of parts to each other, and its own selection of objects for description.

How does *The Song* begin?

> Might it not become us, brothers,
> to begin in the diction of yore
> the stern tale
> of the campaign of Igor,
> Igor son of Svyatoslav?

Let us, however,
begin this song
in keeping with the happenings
of these times
and not with the contriving of Boyan.

Art never passes but it always negates itself, changing and renewing its mode of expression—not merely to alter the form, but to find a perceptible and precise expression of a new reality. The bard Boyan created the old form. Now the new author—the author of *The Song*—proposes a new form on the template of the *bylinas*[140] from that time, using them as documents.

But first of all, we must understand the ancient words.

Let's take a look at these lines from *The Song*:

O Russian land,
you are already behind the culmen!

Scholars have spent a great deal of time trying to figure out the meaning of these words. They interpreted "culmen" as hills. They tried to understand it by studying and finding examples in the old Russian Chronicles. Izmail Sreznevsky gave the following example: "The enemy went around Suzdal—behind the culmen." The city of Suzdal stands above the river, on an

---

140 A traditional form of Old Russian and Russian heroic narrative poetry transmitted orally, still a creative tradition in the twentieth century. The oldest *bylinas* belong to a cycle dealing with the golden age of Kievian Rus in the tenth to twelfth centuries.

elevated landform. Maybe the word "culmen" meant scope or horizon. The old Russian sphero-conical helmet sloped as a human skull.

Remember how Taras Bulba and his sons leave their native home—the steppe behind them turns into a hill, concealing the roof and the trees:

> Their farm seemed to have sunk into the earth. All that was visible above the surface was the two chimneys of their modest cottage, and the crests of the trees up which they had been wont to climb like squirrels; before them still stretched the meadow . . . And now only one pole above the well, with the cartwheel fastened on top, rises solitary against the sky; already the plain across which they have been riding appears a hill in the distance, and has concealed everything. Farewell childhood, and games, and everything—farewell!

"Culmen" means new horizons that are conquered by the new forms of art; behind them is the new perception of the world.

And so—art is constantly in front of a new horizon. It never passes but it always negates itself. It continuously replaces itself, changes the modes of expression—not simply to alter its form, but to find an expression for reality, to secure the derivation of knowledge about the very existence of the object. The renewed form sharpens the efficacy of perception.

The Shifts in Genre

There are footlights, curtains, or their replacements in theater.

There is a "theatrical language."

In 1880, Ostrovsky remarked that one must write for the people not in the language that they speak, but in which they desire.

Pugachov's language in *The Captain's Daughter* and in Yesenin's "Pugachov" is not merely conversational.

The new "harmony" is the new transformation of "its own."

Mayakovsky's language isn't merely conversational, but it's conversational as a negation of poetic language.

The history of the novel is continuous in its negation. It negates "its own other."

What changes, in particular, is the insight into the psychology of the characters.

The psychology of Robinson Crusoe in Defoe's novel is as clear as the records in an accountant's ledger. It is divided into two columns—debit and credit. Good. Evil. It projects clerical logic. Courage and despair are explained and substantiated; only the things that have proof are thought to exist.

There are various conventions for studying the psychologies of characters in the novels of Turgenev, Tolstoy, and Dostoevsky. They can be juxtaposed for comparison but they aren't identical, nor should they be equated.

The psychology of Turgenev's heroes must explicate and substantiate their actions. The substantiation of the heroes' actions in Tolstoy isn't stemming completely from their psychology. Psychologically, the heroes later make slips regarding their actions, while the reasons for those actions lie in the collective unconscious, or in what Tolstoy called "preconscious movements" in his youthful work "A History of Yesterday."

In this short story, the young writer emphasized the illogicality of our everyday behavior, the contradiction between our psychology and actions.

Here is an excerpt from this little-known work:

> "Do stay and have some supper," said her husband. Since I was busy pondering the matter of third person forms of address, I failed to notice that my body, having made the politest possible excuses for being unable to stay, had put down my hat again and sunk calmly into an armchair. It was evident that the intellectual side of me was taking no part in this folly.[141]

The etiquette is violated.

Tolstoy tried to solve the complexity of the hero's stream of consciousness on numerous occasions. The way that he came to perceive the psychology of his heroes led him to the discovery of a contradiction between the analysis of the cause of action, both one's own and someone else's, and the true origins of the action, sometimes lying beyond the character's consciousness. This is not an introduction of ambiguity to clarity. Tolstoy discovered that it is wrong to search for an incentive based solely on what people think

---

141   Lev Tolstoy, "A History of Yesterday." In *Collected Shorter Fiction*. Vol. II. Translated by Louise and Aylmer Maude and Nigel J. Cooper. Alfred A. Knopf, 2001.

of themselves. Psychologization as an explanation of heroes' actions in Tolstoy is pure illusion:

> This illusion is caused by two things: first, due to the psychological property to forge *après coup* of intellectual reasons for what is inevitably happening, just as we forge past dreams as a fact that happened in the waking moment; and second, due to the law of coincidence of countless reasons in every catastrophic event, and due to the law that any fly can justifiably think of itself as the center of everything and its needs—the goal of the entire universe, and also due to the law according to which a person might think that a fox is tricking the dogs with its tail, while it's merely using it to make a turn.[142]

The psychologism of Tolstoy's mature novels is juxtaposed against the psychologism of the old classical novel.

The bared psyche of the hero doesn't explain any of his actions but rather accompanies his actions and justifies him, as it were.

Dostoevsky's psychologization is conventional in its own way and elicited protests in Turgenev.

There is an archival record in which Sergei Lvovich Tolstoy wrote down Turgenev's remarks: ". . . everything happens in reverse in Dostoevsky's work. For example, a man meets a lion. What will he do? He'll naturally turn pale and try to run away or hide. That's exactly how it would be in any simple story, for in-

---

142   From an earlier version of *War and Peace*.

stance, in Jules Verne. While Dostoevsky will say the opposite: the man turned red and didn't move. This will be an inverted common place."

Of course, we shouldn't forget here that the biased observation that demotes Dostoevsky's work ought to be explained with the existing tension between Dostoevsky and Turgenev—not only in everyday issues, but also in their literary relationship.

Turgenev wrote: "That's a cheap trick for earning a reputation of an original writer."

The oppositeness of the heroes' behavior in Turgenev's novels and the novels of Dostoevsky is marked with a vigilance of rage.

But Dostoevsky's construction was the one that prevailed for a long time.

About Content

I refuted the idea of content in art when I was young, thinking that it was pure form.

My comrades in the Moscow Linguistic Circle, led by Roman Jakobson, argued that literature is a phenomenon of language, they repeated the same thing in Prague, and they repeat it now in great detail in articles on Pushkin's poetry.

I can repeat again Einstein's words from his *Autobiographical Notes* about the creation of the scientific model of phenomena: "I have no doubt but that our thinking goes on for the most part without use of signs (words) and beyond that to a considerable degree unconsciously."

We used to think in OPOYAZ that literature was a phenomenon of style and form, that literature was not cut off from other forms of art, that the elements of myth could be used in painting or sculpture and could be returned and reused in literature, that the structure of Dante's *Inferno* is not only verbal but also geometrical. We ascertained that language is only one of the structures used in art—that art used other structures as well, other systems of signs that had different modes of interrelationship.

Back then I used to say that art had no content, that it was devoid of emotion, while at the same time I wrote books that bled, like *A Sentimental Journey* and *ZOO*. The latter was also called *Letters Not about Love* because it *was* a book about love.

Love in it is articulated through various allegories, illuminating all of the phenomena. The dialogue that occurs between the man and the woman sheds light on that time period.

The dialogue is rich in content, and the people that are mentioned in it are not only real but they are alive even today.

The tile that I knocked out of the furnace with my fist during an argument was real too, though it wasn't mentioned in the book.

People can be reflected in art, but the course of perception is transformed as the ray of light is refracted in a prism. The optics of art deflects the rays in order to make them visible in a different way—to make them palpable.

When creating artistic constructions, artists first of all create models of the world, which then they study through the methods of art in the work itself. They make use of personal experience, but they also connect to the universality of human experience. This human experience helps us perceive the subject on a much grander scale.

The strange notion that art never ages, and that we can still read Homer, the Bible, and the epic of Gilgamesh that was written thousands of years ago anew, is based on the fact that comparative juxtapositions reveal the essence of phenomena. The author enters the world as a youth or a child, but then he begins to examine the world using the human experience, he compares everything, becomes wiser. He is in awe.

The author's astonishment changes the human experience. Chinese poets think similarly; they are astonished at the juxtapositions.

*

Epochs collide in art. They foresee themselves in art and at the same time outlive themselves in art. What we call genre is in reality the unity of conflict.

I think that every work of art, as a link in a self-abnegating process, is juxtaposed against other works of art.

Don Quixote is juxtaposed against the chivalric romance. Sterne's novel is juxtaposed against the adventure novel. Diderot's *Jacques the Fatalist and His Master* is juxtaposed step-by-step against the novel that preceded the pre-revolutionary epoch.

In the latter, the structure of the old novel was obliterated from the very beginning; there wasn't even a hint of an introduction. The heroes didn't have full names. The book opened like this: "How had they met? By chance, like everyone else. What were their names? What does it matter to you? Whence had they come? From the nearest possible spot."[143]

143   Denis Diderot, *Jacques the Fatalist and His Master*. Translated by J. Robert Loy. New York UP, 1959.

This work is based on the negation of elements from old structures.

All the chance incidents and conventional elaborations that form the old novel are rejected here, and the book announces that the characters whom you expect to encounter are nothing like the characters from previous adventure books.

Diderot's book is an antinovel. Chernyshevsky's novel (*What Is to Be Done?*) with its constant argument with the reader continues Diderot's experiment and is juxtaposed against the traditional novel. It will be practicable in the future. Today it is antirealistic and therefore it's made of dreams.

The films of Eisenstein, Pudovkin, Dovzhenko (with his use of slow motion), that changed the law of montage, were perceived as a negation of old structures.

There comes a time in every man's life when he renounces whatever is fashionable, considering it a mistake, and stays in his old, narrow pants and old-fashioned hat.

I have been studying the history of art for a long time now and I know.

The new skirts are too short for me.

Art is a means for experiencing the world. And for that purpose it constructs its own contradictions. I didn't understand this, and that was my mistake. The contradiction lies within the construction itself, but I wasn't able to notice it back then.

On the one hand, I asserted that art is devoid of emotion, that it is only a collision of elements, that it is geometrical.

And on the other hand, I spoke of *ostranenie* (estrangement), that is to say—the renewal of sensation. In that case I should have asked myself: what exactly are you going to estrange if art doesn't express the conditions of reality? Sterne, Tolstoy were trying to return the sensation of *what*?

The theory of estrangement, that became widely accepted and applied by many, including Bertolt Brecht, conceptualizes art as a mode of cognition, as a method of investigation.

Art transforms. Genres collide in order to preserve the sensation of the world, in order to prolong the flow of information from the world, and not to perpetuate the sensation of the already traditional form.

I think that Dostoevsky's path is much more contemporary than the path of the contemporary Western novel. In his notes to one of his books, Dostoevsky wrote that he was the first one to have understood "the inevitability of the impossible." The inevitable to him was the social revolution that was supposed to bring back the Golden Age.

There is a continuous discussion about the Golden Age in his notes and sketches, from the conflicts of which evolved *Crime and Punishment*.

Social revolution is illusorily impossible, but it's truly inevitable.

A revolutionary who is disillusioned with the revolution but who won't abandon it—Dostoevsky perceives both its impossibility and its inevitability. The suspension of the inevitable—that's the true embodiment of *dostoevshchina*—that's the main conflict in Dostoevsky and in the contemporary Western novel. Man, like a frightened horse, balks at the impossible, freeing his neck from the yoke, but the inevitable cannot be avoided, and the impossibility overpowers the effort.

The writers of the contemporary antinovel are also searching for new artistic possibilities. But the hero, in this case, has been cut off from the world. He has been sealed in a barrel, like Prince Gvidon, and cast into the sea. He feels the cadence of the waves but he can't see anything. The waves brought Prince Gvidon to the shore.

In the contemporary world we see the illusory nature of the consciousness that has been severed from the world. The antinovel is like a radio that only receives inner interferences.

But new forms of the novel that reject the old, of course, do exist and they will exist in the future as well.

The "Literature of Fact"

There has been a systematic interest in documentary literature in Russia for a long time. Pushkin published *A Journey to Arzrum* in *Sovremennik* (The Contemporary) along with the notes of Nadezhda Durova, Denis Davydov, John Tanner, Turgenev, and others.

He motivated his friends (especially Pavel Nashchokin) to write literary notes.

Belinsky spoke about the connection between art and science and welcomed the sketches by Herzen, who created new documentary literature. Herzen's experiment was used by Tolstoy, and not just in the form of essays. Tolstoy began and ended his grandiose literary path with documental prose—*The Raid* (1852), *The Sevastopol Sketches* (1855), and *Three Days in the Village* (1910).

Soviet prose and many of Gorky's later works are documental. When Ilya Gruzdev started writing Gorky's biography, Aleksei Maksimovich would send his additions and photographs of some of the heroes from his books. Arguing in a mock-angry tone, Gorky would ascertain the strict documental nature of his memoirs. In the appendix to *Gorky and His Time*, Gruzdev quotes from Gorky's letters that document his own biography over a couple dozen times. It's done rather intelligibly, but without any precise dates.

Forwarding a letter by a certain Slastushensky, who was familiar with Aleksei Peshkov through work at the Dobrinka Station, Gorky wrote to Gruzdev: "Yesterday I sent you a letter from the Dobrinka Station telegrapher. . . . The letter proves that I, in fact, am a real person, and not invented by Gorky, as Bunin has tried to assert."[144]

Isaac Babel also wrote documentary literature. Even poetically described phenomena in Babel are documental: comparatively juxtaposed by the author, these phenomena elucidate one another, creating a new plot.

The ordinary is presented as the emotional: emotionalism was real in the epoch of the Russian Revolution.

Prishvin and Paustovsky, too, are documental.

Soviet prose was changing, and literary criticsm still hasn't been able to fully grasp or acknowledge those changes.

Take, for instance, Yuri Olesha's *No Day without a Line*. This multifaceted work was conceived as a realist book without any evental links between its parts.

Its new nonevental unity is intentionally bared.

The principles of how to construct a work of prose or a poem vary. In *Eugene Onegin*, for example, the evental links don't prevail over the associative links—they only organize them.

Pure formal solutions, like altering a poem's meter through the elimination of caesuras, can give the reader a sensation of denouement—resolution.

---

144   Ilya Gruzdev, *Gorkii i ego vremya* [Gorky and His Time], 1962.

The future charts new pathways, canonizing what once was considered insignificant and worthless.

It pushes aside denouements and reinterprets them by colliding their structures.

But even Dulcinea del Toboso couldn't exist for Don Quixote without an exact address. Even dreams must be concrete; satire and fantasy must all lean on the past and the future.

RETURN THE BALL INTO THE GAME

Return the Ball into the Game

The absurdity of the world was depicted in old literature as well. Dickens shows the meaninglessness of the trial process in *Bleak House*: the long trial ends with the revelation that the disputed estate has been wasted on the legal fees accrued from the case. In *Dombey and Son*, the company goes bankrupt and it's left unclear as to what exactly caused the collapse. Dombey's dream to establish a dynasty is also nonsensical. Similarly, Merdle's fraudulent dealings in *Little Dorrit* lead to the collapse of his bank and, subsequently, the loss of people's life savings. But what was he doing? Why did they believe him? What was the swindled money for? These questions are purposely left unanswered.

Meanwhile, the swindler is terrified of his wife and the chief butler and timidly drinks two-penny-worth of tea in a corner.

The forces that move the world are portrayed not so much in an antagonistic light as in absurdity. The only affairs that are more or less rational are those of the secondary characters, but their rationality is illusory in their reflection of love schemas of old novels.

The world of individual fates—of a divided sky—was not always content with conventional endings.

There are endings that are demonstratively not concluded. They negate the idea of closure. This is how Sterne's novels end. In *A Sentimental Journey*, his sentimental traveler stops at an inn that doesn't have enough beds for all the guests. He agrees to share his bed with a stranger lady and her servant-maid, whereas they come to a mutual agreement to sleep in their clothes. The journey ends rather abruptly. The maid gets herself between the traveler and his accidental companion and this is how the novel ends:

> So that when I stretch'd out my hand, I caught hold of the Fille de Chambre's
> END OF VOL. II.

This isn't the strangest ending in Sterne.

One of Pushkin's and Tolstoy's favorite books, *The Life and Opinions of Tristram Shandy, Gentleman*, which was published in nine volumes, doesn't have a conventional ending, and this demonstrative absence of an ending is intentional. In Chapter 33 of the last volume, Tristram Shandy's father, as an impropriator of the great tithes, was obliged to keep a bull for the service of the parish. This was a form of estate tax, as it were.

During one of the mating bouts, the bull fails to impregnate a cow. At the same time, one of the housemaids is giving birth.

The comments about the housemaid and the cow are mixed up: this confusion is deliberate and comical.

Finally, the conversation is interrupted by Mrs. Shandy:

> L - - d! said my mother, what is all this story about?——
> A COCK and a BULL, said Yorick——And one of the best of its kind I ever heard.
> END OF VOL. IX.

The cock-and-bull story belongs to the series of never-ending tales featuring extensive narration of typically irrelevant incidents. The shortest Russian version of these tales goes like this: "There once was a birch on which hung a washcloth. Shall we start from the beginning?"[145] This next one is a bit longer: "A priest had a dog, and he loved his dog . . ." Then the priest kills the dog and writes on his grave: "A priest had a dog," and so on. The inscription on the grave recursively repeats the whole story.

Sterne, a brilliant writer, doesn't have evental endings. Instead, he leaves the reader with circumstances that transition from one into another, demonstrating the absence of logic in the new but already meaningless life and signaling its discontinuity.

There are literary works the last pages of which are declared to be lost, such as, for example, Gogol's *Ivan Fyodorovich Shponka and His Aunt*. There are others in which the ending is demonstratively absented, but its absence—the interruption—is disguised.

In *A Hero of Our Time*, the unnamed narrator receives from Maksim Maksimych the journals of Pechorin. At the end of his introduction to Pechorin's journals, the narrator states:

> I have included in this book only that which refers to Pechorin's sojourn in the Caucasus. There still remains in my possession a fat notebook wherein he narrates all his life. Some day it, too, will be presented to the judgment

---

145 Involving a high degree of wordplay, these tales are constructed on the element of repetition: separate words and phrases, that often may use rhyme and echo (*mochala* / *s nachala*), are repeated in their entirety without any changes, or with minor changes, producing a comic or rhetorical effect: "There once was a birch on which hung a washcloth [*mochala*]. Shall we start from the beginning [*s nachala*]?"

of the world, but for the present there are important reasons why I dare not assume such responsibility.

Lermontov belonged to the post-Decembrist generation—people with difficult fates. The narrator is in the Caucasus "with government property," he is evidently in exile. We are told everything about Pechorin, what he did in the Caucasus, but we must infer how he originally got there. His death was foretold. There is nothing in common here with Sterne.

Eugene Onegin has an equally remarkable ending, which is worth to recite if only for the purpose of reading these remarkable lines once more and thinking about them one more time.

There are many omitted stanzas and unfinished chapters in *Eugene Onegin*. Onegin has seen and experienced a lot between the interval of his separation from Tatyana and their new meeting.

The following fragment was preserved from Chapter 10:

> [H]ere Lunin daringly
> suggested his decisive measures
> and muttered in a trance of inspiration;
> Pushkin read his noels;
> melancholy Yakushkin,
> it seemed, silently bared
> a regicidal dagger;
> seeing but Russia in the world,
> in her caressing his ideal,
> to them did lame Turgenev hearken . . .[146]

---

146 Aleksandr Pushkin. *Eugene Onegin*. Vol. III. Translated by Vladimir Nabokov. New York: Pantheon Books, 1964.

The deleted lines mentioned Turgenev, Pestel, Muravyov—Pushkin's generation had been interrupted, cut down.

How does the novel end?

Onegin meets with Tatyana. She tells him despondently: "Yet happiness had been so possible, / so near!" Whose happiness?

> [A]nd here my hero,
> at an unfortunate minute for him,
> reader, we now shall leave
> for long . . . forever. . . . (Chapter 8, XLVIII)

Happiness, like the idea of an ending, was impossible.

The arrival of Tatyana's husband—the general, is a deceptive ending.

> But those to whom at amicable meetings
> its first strophes I read—
> "Some are no more, others are distant,"
> as erstwhiles Sadi said.
> Without them was Onegin's picture finished.
> And she from whom was fashioned
> the dear ideal of "Tatyana" . . .
> Ah, much, much has fate snatched away! (Chapter 8, LI)

Sadi's words are repeated here as a reminder of the epigraph to "The Fountain of Bakhchisaray."

They are as if saying that not only did she, the prototype of Tatyana, disappear, but that society itself disappeared.

But the ripples of the novel are endlessly wide. Onegin's picture is finished without them, apart from the collective fate.

The meaning is ambiguated with these forceful and somber words:

> Blest who left life's feast early,
> not having to the bottom drained
> the goblet full of wine;
> who never read life's novel to the end
> and all at once could part with it
> as I with my Onegin.
>
> THE END

The goblet of life was not pushed aside, but it was taken away from Pushkin. It was taken away from Russia.

This is the history of the absence of closure in *Eugene Onegin*.

The Sternean ending is the rejection of the principle of closure.

Pushkin's ending in *Eugene Onegin* is the sad mark of the impossibility to tell the rest of the truth about the fate of the hero among his friends.

In comparison, these books "without an ending" are dissimilar, as one has no ending due to an impossibility of expression, while the other—due to an attitude toward the laws of construction.

The general was Onegin's companion; they recollect "the pranks, the jests of former years"—conceivably not only with women.

My Parting with Tolstoy

The history of the writing of *War and Peace* breaks up into several separate questions that require separate answers.

We meet with a few unexpected things here.

In a draft preface that was meant to introduce the novel "1805," Tolstoy wrote: "In 1856 I began a novel with a clear sense of direction and a hero who was supposed to be a Decembrist returning to Russia with his family."[147]

A part from this early version came out in 1884 in the collection *XXV Years: 1859–1884* under the title "The Decembrists," published by the St. Petersburg Literary Fund and introduced by Tolstoy with the following note: "These three chapters from the novel entitled "The Decembrists" were written before the author began writing *War and Peace*."

War and Peace was conceived from its end. The novel begins with a depiction of Russian aristocracy after the Crimean War.

This conception completed *The Sevastopol Sketches*, as it were.

Tolstoy kept retreating from his analysis of the causes of Russia's defeat, and the heroes who appeared in 1856 as old men, were depicted as youths in "1805."

The conflict stayed the same, the situation changed, but it did not disappear as it reemerged again in the first drafts of *War and Peace* and in Nikolenka Bolkonsky's dream at the end of the novel.

The novel's conflict resided in the failed insurrection, inevitably destined to repeat itself again in some unpredictable manner.

Tolstoy said that Decembrism passed over the Russian society as a magnetic storm, extracting all the iron from the waste.

---

147   Chapters from the first part of the novel, then entitled "1805," began to appear in 1865 in the periodical *Russkii Vestnik* (The Russian Herald). Tolstoy was increasingly dissatisfied with this version, although he allowed several parts of it to be published (with a different ending) in 1867 still under the title "1805." He heavily rewrote the entire novel between 1866 and 1869, eventually publishing it under the title *War and Peace* in 1869.

So how does the silver summit of "the universal novel" by Tolstoy end?

Pierre is already part of the "conspiracy," considering it inevitable. He talks about it openly with Denisov and Natasha in Nikolai Rostov's presence, who retorts that his duty is to obey the government and he would not even hesitate an instant if Arakcheev ordered him to lead a squadron against his best friends and destroy them.

Later downstairs, in his bedroom, Nikolenka Bolkonsky awakens from a terrible dream, which ends the evental thread of the novel. The episode is followed by an epilogue that discusses history in general terms.

But the dream is terrible:

> He had dreamed that he and Uncle Pierre, wearing helmets such as were depicted in his Plutarch, were leading a huge army. The army was made up of white slanting lines that filled the air like the cobwebs that float about in autumn and which Dessalles called *les fils de la Vièrge*. In front was Glory, which was similar to those threads but rather thicker. He and Pierre were borne along lightly and joyously, nearer and nearer to their goal. Suddenly the threads that moved them began to slacken and become entangled and it grew difficult to move. And Uncle Nikolai stood before them in a stern and threatening attitude.
>
> "Have you done this?" he said, pointing to some broken sealing wax and pens. "I loved you, but I have orders from Arakcheev and will kill the first of you who moves forward."

Seized with terror, Nikolenka awakens. He recalls the noble Roman youth Mucius Scaevola and how he thrust his hand in the fire: "Why should not the same sort of thing happen to me? . . . I only pray God that something may happen to me such as happened to Plutarch's men, and I will act as they did. I will do better."

Having been pardoned by the old man, Pierre might die or survive, but his friends will certainly die.

Andrei Bolkonsky's son, Nikolenka, is headed toward death.

This is another example of an ending without closure. In Tolstoy's work, Russia destined to lead the histories of nations—makes a new step for all of humanity. Lenin wrote in an essay titled "L. N. Tolstoy": "The epoch of preparation for revolution in one of the countries under the heel of the serf-owners became, thanks to its brilliant illumination by Tolstoy, a step forward in the artistic development of humanity as a whole." It was in 1910. Everything was only beginning—repeating in a changed and dissimilar way.

It seems that we have already discussed how *Crime and Punishment* and *Resurrection* have parallel yet differently motivated endings—the return to religion.

An impoverished gentleman, Raskolnikov tries to pave a Napoleonic pathway to the Golden Age by trampling over moral interdictions.

He doesn't want to accomplish this pompously, as a conquest of worlds, but rather through the banal, yet, at the same time, terrible crime of murder and robbery.

What interests him more isn't even the result of his crime but the verification—is he human or a "trembling beast"?

The question is about the universality of human morality. In Dostoevsky it is constructed as Christian morality.

The crime crushed Raskolnikov and that was his punishment.

Sonya, who loves Rodion, brings him the New Testament. After recovering from his fever, Raskolnikov begins to read the Bible. He knows that he still has seven years of hard labor:

> He did not know that the new life would not be given him for nothing, that he would have to pay dearly for it, that it would cost him great striving, great suffering.
> But that is the beginning of a new story—the story of the gradual renewal of a man, the story of his gradual regeneration, of his passing from one world into another, of his initiation into a new unknown life. That might be the subject of a new story, but our present story is ended.

If we apply the concept of "vertical montage" to *Crime and Punishment*, in other words, if we retrace the interrelationship of structural constructions, we will first of all reveal the multiplicity of conflicts:

—the conflict of hunger and the feeling of guilt regarding one's family;

—the conflict of human degradation and the awareness of one's worth;

—the conflict (most importantly) of the answer to the question, "What is a crime?" Is everyone susceptible to repentance? And, conversely, are there people (such as the old pawnbroker) who don't have to abide by moral codes?

Externally, these conflicts are structurally framed as a detective novel, in which secrets and mysteries are revealed one by one.

The conflicts that are revealed in *Crime and Punishment* become apparent to Dostoevsky only gradually, and as we know from the publication of the novel's drafts, the author hesitated in his selection of conflicts and even tried to eliminate some of them.

At the end of the novel, the deeply realistic conflicts are resolved only conventionally, without fully manifesting all of their inter-contradictions. Dostoevsky promised to write a new book but he never did.

Tolstoy completed *Resurrection* thirty-three years after *Crime and Punishment* was published.

Katyusha Maslova leaves with the political prisoners. She doesn't accept Nekhlyudov's life, offered to her. She leaves with the exile Vladimir Simonson and the party of revolutionaries.

Nekhlyudov leaves on a ferry, looking at the fast-moving, wide river that separates him from Katyusha Maslova, Kryltsov who is dying, and Simonson whom Katyusha loves. Nekhlyudov returns back to his hotel and, unable to sleep, picks up the Bible. He is supposed to be resurrected—that's how the novel was initially conceived.

Then begins Chapter 28. It is only a few pages long and mostly consists of quotations from the New Testament. Nekhlyudov concludes:

> "And so here it is, the business of my life. Scarcely have I finished one and another has commenced." And a perfectly new life dawned that night for Nekhlyudov, not because he had entered into new conditions of life, but because everything he did after that night had a new and quite different significance than before. How this new period of his life will end time alone will prove.
>
> *December 16, 1899*

THE END

The novel ends as if with a reiteration of the epigraphs, alluding to the forgiveness of sins.

The novel opens with four epigraphs from the New Testament and ends with quotations from Matthew. In reality, the quotations are paraphrases and had Tolstoy quoted them in entirety, they would have taken up more than a page.

The epigraphs and the quotations at the end of the novel form a circle, as it were, but Nekhlyudov's fate is outside of that circle, while Katyusha's—breaks it.

The function of the epigraphs and conclusion is the dissimilarity of the similar.

The novel is restructured and refutes itself by changing the meaning of Katyusha's fate—the function of the hero. There is a solution but it is based on the necessity of an outcome promised by Tolstoy: "How this new period of his life will end time alone will prove."

The outline of the book had been written before the novel had been started.

The original conflict in "Koni's story"—that would evolve into *Resurrection*—was that an affluent gentleman seduced a poor girl and she became a prostitute. Some years later, the gentleman had been summoned for jury duty and, coincidentally, the woman on trial turned out to be the same girl whom he had seduced. He repented and married her and this was supposed to be *his* resurrection.

In the process of his analysis Tolstoy realizes that the question was not in Nekhlyudov's misdeed or in the fact that the woman ended up in a brothel. Rather, Katyusha's fate for Tolstoy turns into a lighthouse—a source of light that condemns the whole life of Tolstoy's contemporaries. It is a *terrible verdict*.

The rest of the heroes (besides the revolutionaries), and this was done unconsciously—it was not Tolstoy's intention—are "shadows." Only Nekhlyudov is not elected, not resurrected from these shadows. He understands the illegality and corruption of life in general, sees the prostituting nature of the entire system.

Chekhov argued against the idea that Tolstoy tried to end the novel with evangelical aphorisms, that he left all the occurrences intact. He wrote in a letter to Mikhail Menshikov (January 28, 1900): "The novel has no resolution, whatever is at the end can't be called a resolution. To write all that and then to throw everything on passages from the Gospel—well, that's just too theological!"

Tolstoy wished to save only Nekhlyudov, or to be sure—Nekhlyudov in marriage with Katyusha. But in the end only Katyusha is resurrected because she leaves Nekhlyudov's world along with that phase.

This was also the conflict of Tolstoy's life: he tried to resolve it by fleeing from home.

Briefly about the Antinovel

Kafka in his antinovels attempts to show the absurdity of life as a whole; nothing is alive in this world or, at least, nothing makes sense. The processes are meaningless, authorities are incomprehensible. Chancelleries and institutions have no boundaries—it is as though the intestines have ruptured and the feces have moved into the peritoneum. The meaninglessness of life has become total. The world is in lockdown. It is like a clock with a bent dial.

This notion of the death of time persists in the work of a contemporary artist.

In the beginning of Fellini's *8 1/2*, the camera shows a city tunnel for motor vehicles. Trapped inside their cars, behind windows, people are suffocating from the smell of burning gasoline and lead salts emitting from their idling engines.

The world has come to a contradiction with itself: both the tunnel and the cars are made for speed, so that people can leave the city quickly, but some are suffocating as a result of an adverse effect.

The hero wants to fly away, but his friends and the producer capture him with a lasso and drag him back down into the city.

The hero searches for an escape in rural Italy, Catholic Italy, Garibaldi's Italy.

Everything has been destroyed.

One of the love scenes in the film is enacted by the hero—the film director—for himself. He creates a scenario of a sudden, estranged love affair.

Everything that's straightforward, ordinary has been exhausted by newspapers and the art of the past.

The heroes of the film are very different, but they are all frightened, they predict the destruction of the Earth, as it were.

The main hero—the film director—is waiting for the end of the world. He builds a huge rocket that is supposed to fly over the Earth, saving a group of chosen individuals.

The rocket cannot go up. There are no cosmic Mountains of Ararat. These are unattainable things, and the film returns to self-replication, popular circus, farce, and old conventional heroes with whom the man who can't finish his work leaves and passes through the frames of his own film.

I am talking about simple things—about how the construction of books, the construction of old oral stories, not yet bound in books, depends on the paths of humanity, the direction in which humanity moves and what it wants to achieve.

I have seen many films with different endings. I have worked with many film directors. Once in a trattoria in Rome, I met with a well-known film director. He told me that he had been writing that same day (not knowing I was in Rome) on Mayakovsky talking about my path. I have seen many films and I know how difficult their denouements can be, how they are becoming even more complicated, and I know the doubts that Tolstoy expressed at the beginning of the writing of *War and Peace*, that neither death nor marriage of heroes can serve as an ending. Even the death of one of the heroes can't be an ending, because the story shifts to the life of other heroes.

In one of the remarkable films by Antonioni, *L'Eclisse* (*The Eclipse*, 1962), a man and a woman cannot figure out their relationship. The scenes evolve around the stock exchange, where we see the outcomes of bank operations, decisions that have been made and not been carried out. The world of material things has devoured the living beings. The film ends with a shot of water slowly running out of a leak in a barrel.

But this isn't his most melancholy work. Antonioni has another film that's more well-known—*Blow-Up* (1966), or it can be translated in Russian as "A Shot in Large Scale." If we were to give a simple synopsis of the film, then this is how it would unfold (keep in mind that the evental path, along which I'll take you, will bring us to a dead end).

A young talented photographer is in search of something sensational. He walks into a park and takes a photograph of a strange woman. Later he makes many blow-ups of the photograph. Suddenly he notices a body lying in the grass under the trees. Then the woman appears again and wants to buy the photograph. A plan is devised to steal the photograph. Everything is disconnected and complicated. Then the photograph disappears. The photographer returns to the park but the body is gone. He goes to see his friends, but they are busy with their own affairs—something that today the film industry calls "sex" for short.

They don't pay any attention to him and they don't care about the blow-up—the attempt to sensationalize ends in failure.

On the way, the photographer sees a group of university students dressed in masquerade costumes.

They are playing a game of tennis: we clearly hear the fast, staccato sounds of the ball hitting the racket.

Then we realize that we are watching a mimed match—it's a game without a ball.

There is no sense, no ball in the game—only the ghost of sound.

Its purpose—the ending has disappeared. Nobody cares about the murder mystery and its solution. It can be used in a newspaper article or in photography, but nothing more. The denouement has vanished. There is no ending . . .

Pasolini's films end differently. In *Uccellacci e uccellini* (*The Hawks and the Sparrows*, 1966), for example, the story evolves around Francis of Assisi who sends his friars to preach Christianity to the birds. The Franciscan friars turn up in the contemporary world.

They successfully preach the commandment of love to the hawks and to the sparrows separately and convert them to Christianity.

But the Christian hawks hunt the Christian sparrows—that's their nature.

The friars pray. A monastery, involved in the hectic activity of buying and selling of faith, appears around them. The friars leave.

They see terrible things—the meaninglessness and futility of birth and death. They see a Chinese man for whom a beggar woman gets a swallow's nest from the roof of an old house. Their guide through the world of miserable lawlessness of strange tangled pathways is a crow, who has been sent to them by fate. The crow walks sideways, he is searching for something. In the end, the travelers get hungry and they eat the crow.

We have survived millenia, it was not for nothing. We don't think that crows taste good in soup, we don't believe in the height of irony of the denouement.

But individual denouements, the denouements of specific incidents change against other juxtaposition-denouements, as it were.

We think more and more expansively.

Conflicts occur not only between separate individuals but also between generations, social systems. Irony doesn't help any more. It doesn't save Antonioni, Pasolini, or even Fellini—a talented artist, whose entire film is about how man builds a rocket that is supposed to carry him out of this world into another one.

The journeys of Gilgamesh, who crossed the ocean with a pole, seem difficult to his descendents.

People write poems about writing poems.

Writers write novels about writing novels, film scripts about film scripts.

They are playing a tennis game without a ball, but the journeys of Gilgamesh, Odysseus, Pantagruel, and even Chichikov must have a purpose.

Return the ball into the game.

Return the heroic deed into life.

Return meaning to the movement—and not to the record of achievement.

EPILOGUE

I remember the anchors on the bands of the visorless sailor caps.

They probably stayed only on those caps: children's games preserve many things from the past.

Ships—growing, changing their dimensions and names—sail away.

The lowered anchors in the ports connect them to the underwater side of the Earth.

The ports are the libraries of the sea. How many books, how many ships corrode and rot away unclaimed.

But the sign of the anchor—signifying hope—has persisted in memory and technology.

Youth!

The coat of arms of Leningrad depicts two intersecting anchors: a sea anchor with two flukes and a river anchor with three flukes.

Don't change the coats of arms, made glorious with inspiration.

On the sandbanks of the wide river, where the seals basked in the sun, rose a great city that today has been renamed after Lenin.

The intersecting anchors remind me of the dialectical method, of the overcoming of contradictions. There is a connection of already-treaded and new pathways in the very essence of art.

One should learn to understand the particular as part of the whole; the port stop as part of the ship's journey. The concept of the anchor includes in it the concept of the oar and the sail.

The structure is a demarcated part of the movement; the movement, which is a change of conditions, switches structures.

Art moves and simultaneously stands still. It moves in front of you in a poem, a work of prose, or picture.

It moves, overcoming contradictions, while simultaneously creating new ones.

The dissimilarity of the similar is part of the laws of art. It includes maturing, attainment of love, adventure, and unification of the present with the past and the future.

The city of Venice stretches above the flat waves of the Adriatic Sea.

At some point in history some tribes moved here to escape from the Huns and they became seafarers, merchants, and travelers: they built pile-dwellings on the sandbanks, anchored their vessels. They sat by the fire, mined salt, made glass, painted paintings, loved, betrayed, and were deceived.

The threatening sea also protects the city.

There isn't much sunlight in Venice. The canals breathe with antiquity. The sea tides bare the old walls. And I won't hide that I have seen rats calmly walking along the narrow ledges.

The sea returns with the tidal flow. The water rises, its reflections wash the walls. The moored gondolas raise their noses and look at the city of Venice across the embankments.

Perhaps someday the sea will wash over Venice, but people will continue to live—uniting the sea with the land. Perhaps they will build underwater cities or cities that fly. They will build new cities, overcoming the contradictions.

There used to be a printing house in Venice called Aldine Press that operated for several centuries. It published good books, artisti-

cally stylizing the black, slender letters slightly slanted to the right in cursive type.

I used to have a few books from Aldine Press—they're gone now. I read other books.

The publishing logo imprint on Aldine books was a dolphin around the anchor.

Then, unlike today, there were many strong, cheerful dolphins on the waves of the wide sea, by the shores, where the crests of waves grew thick shrubs of foam. The happy rivals of ships competing in speed: maybe at the bottom of the sea, whistling to one another, they tended their schools of fish.

One of the dolphins rescued the Greek poet and musician Arion— Pushkin's brother-in-arms, the hero of his poem. Perhaps the dolphins are musical creatures.

The anchor is a symbol of strength, hope, and stopping. The dolphins symbolize movement, buoyancy, speed.

I would have liked this book to be published by Aldine Press, but it's impossible: the house stopped publishing, I think, five hundred years ago.

Please reprint the logo of Aldine Press here, in this book.

Let it not be a melancholy book, but a cheerful one.

Regarding the ending—

I don't like that word.

There will be no ending.

JOHN F. BYRNE LITERATURE SERIES

The John F. Byrne Literature Series is made possible through a generous contribution by an anonymous individual. This contribution allows Dalkey Archive Press to publish one book per year in this series.

Born and raised in Chicago, John F. Byrne was an educator and critic who helped to found the *Review of Contemporary Fiction* and was also an editor at Dalkey Archive Press. Although his primary interest was Victorian literature, he spent much of his career teaching modern literature, especially such writers as James Joyce, Samuel Beckett, and Flann O'Brien. He died in 1998, but his influence on both the *Review* and Dalkey Archive Press will be lasting.

SELECTED DALKEY ARCHIVE PAPERBACKS

ARNO SCHMIDT, *Collected Novellas.*
   Collected Stories.
   Nobodaddy's Children.
   Two Novels.
ASAF SCHURR, *Motti.*
CHRISTINE SCHUTT, *Nightwork.*
GAIL SCOTT, *My Paris.*
DAMION SEARLS, *What We Were Doing*
   and Where We Were Going.
JUNE AKERS SEESE,
   Is This What Other Women Feel Too?
   What Waiting Really Means.
BERNARD SHARE, *Inish.*
   Transit.
AURELIE SHEEHAN,
   Jack Kerouac Is Pregnant.
VIKTOR SHKLOVSKY, *Bowstring.*
   Knight's Move.
   A Sentimental Journey:
     Memoirs 1917–1922.
   Energy of Delusion: A Book on Plot.
   Literature and Cinematography.
   Theory of Prose.
   Third Factory.
   Zoo, or Letters Not about Love.
CLAUDE SIMON, *The Invitation.*
PIERRE SINIAC, *The Collaborators.*
JOSEF ŠKVORECKÝ, *The Engineer of*
   Human Souls.
GILBERT SORRENTINO,
   Aberration of Starlight.
   Blue Pastoral.
   Crystal Vision.
   Imaginative Qualities of Actual
     Things.
   Mulligan Stew.
   Pack of Lies.
   Red the Fiend.
   The Sky Changes.
   Something Said.
   Splendide-Hôtel.
   Steelwork.
   Under the Shadow.
W. M. SPACKMAN,
   The Complete Fiction.
ANDRZEJ STASIUK, *Fado.*
GERTRUDE STEIN,
   Lucy Church Amiably.
   The Making of Americans.
   A Novel of Thank You.
LARS SVENDSEN, *A Philosophy of Evil.*
PIOTR SZEWC, *Annihilation.*
GONÇALO M. TAVARES, *Jerusalem.*
   Learning to Pray in the Age of
     Technology.
LUCIAN DAN TEODOROVICI,
   Our Circus Presents . . .
STEFAN THEMERSON, *Hobson's Island.*
   The Mystery of the Sardine.
   Tom Harris.
JOHN TOOMEY, *Sleepwalker.*
JEAN-PHILIPPE TOUSSAINT,
   The Bathroom.
   Camera.
   Monsieur.
   Running Away.
   Self-Portrait Abroad.
   Television.
DUMITRU TSEPENEAG,
   Hotel Europa.

   The Necessary Marriage.
   Pigeon Post.
   Vain Art of the Fugue.
ESTHER TUSQUETS, *Stranded.*
DUBRAVKA UGRESIC,
   Lend Me Your Character.
   Thank You for Not Reading.
MATI UNT, *Brecht at Night.*
   Diary of a Blood Donor.
   Things in the Night.
ÁLVARO URIBE AND OLIVIA SEARS, EDS.,
   Best of Contemporary Mexican
     Fiction.
ELOY URROZ, *Friction.*
   The Obstacles.
LUISA VALENZUELA, *Dark Desires and*
   the Others.
   He Who Searches.
MARJA-LIISA VARTIO,
   The Parson's Widow.
PAUL VERHAEGHEN, *Omega Minor.*
BORIS VIAN, *Heartsnatcher.*
LLORENÇ VILLALONGA, *The Dolls' Room.*
ORNELA VORPSI, *The Country Where No*
   One Ever Dies.
AUSTRYN WAINHOUSE, *Hedyphagetica.*
PAUL WEST,
   Words for a Deaf Daughter & Gala.
CURTIS WHITE,
   America's Magic Mountain.
   The Idea of Home.
   Memories of My Father Watching TV.
   Monstrous Possibility: An Invitation
     to Literary Politics.
   Requiem.
DIANE WILLIAMS, *Excitability:*
   Selected Stories.
   Romancer Erector.
DOUGLAS WOOLF, *Wall to Wall.*
   Ya! & John-Juan.
JAY WRIGHT, *Polynomials and Pollen.*
   The Presentable Art of Reading
     Absence.
PHILIP WYLIE, *Generation of Vipers.*
MARGUERITE YOUNG, *Angel in the Forest.*
   Miss MacIntosh, My Darling.
REYOUNG, *Unbabbling.*
VLADO ŽABOT, *The Succubus.*
ZORAN ŽIVKOVIĆ, *Hidden Camera.*
LOUIS ZUKOFSKY, *Collected Fiction.*
SCOTT ZWIREN, *God Head.*

FOR A FULL LIST OF PUBLICATIONS, VISIT:
www.dalkeyarchive.com

My Life in CIA.
Singular Pleasures.
The Sinking of the Odradek
    Stadium.
Tlooth.
20 Lines a Day.
JOSEPH McELROY,
    Night Soul and Other Stories.
THOMAS McGONIGLE,
    Going to Patchogue.
ROBERT L. McLAUGHLIN, ED., *Innovations:*
    An Anthology of
    Modern & Contemporary Fiction.
ABDELWAHAB MEDDEB, *Talismano.*
HERMAN MELVILLE, *The Confidence-Man.*
AMANDA MICHALOPOULOU, *I'd Like.*
STEVEN MILLHAUSER,
    The Barnum Museum.
    In the Penny Arcade.
RALPH J. MILLS, JR.,
    Essays on Poetry.
MOMUS, *The Book of Jokes.*
CHRISTINE MONTALBETTI, *Western.*
OLIVE MOORE, *Spleen.*
NICHOLAS MOSLEY, *Accident.*
    Assassins.
    Catastrophe Practice.
    Children of Darkness and Light.
    Experience and Religion.
    God's Hazard.
    The Hesperides Tree.
    Hopeful Monsters.
    Imago Bird.
    Impossible Object.
    Inventing God.
    Judith.
    Look at the Dark.
    Natalie Natalia.
    Paradoxes of Peace.
    Serpent.
    Time at War.
    The Uses of Slime Mould:
    Essays of Four Decades.
WARREN MOTTE,
    Fables of the Novel: French Fiction
    since 1990.
    Fiction Now: The French Novel in
    the 21st Century.
    Oulipo: A Primer of Potential
    Literature.
YVES NAVARRE, *Our Share of Time.*
    Sweet Tooth.
DOROTHY NELSON, *In Night's City.*
    Tar and Feathers.
ESHKOL NEVO, *Homesick.*
WILFRIDO D. NOLLEDO, *But for the Lovers.*
FLANN O'BRIEN,
    At Swim-Two-Birds.
    At War.
    The Best of Myles.
    The Dalkey Archive.
    Further Cuttings.
    The Hard Life.
    The Poor Mouth.
    The Third Policeman.
CLAUDE OLLIER, *The Mise-en-Scène.*
    Wert and the Life Without End.
PATRIK OUŘEDNÍK, *Europeana.*
    The Opportune Moment, 1855.
BORIS PAHOR, *Necropolis.*

FERNANDO DEL PASO,
    News from the Empire.
    Palinuro of Mexico.
ROBERT PINGET, *The Inquisitory.*
    Mahu or The Material.
    Trio.
MANUEL PUIG,
    Betrayed by Rita Hayworth.
    The Buenos Aires Affair.
    Heartbreak Tango.
RAYMOND QUENEAU, *The Last Days.*
    Odile.
    Pierrot Mon Ami.
    Saint Glinglin.
ANN QUIN, *Berg.*
    Passages.
    Three.
    Tripticks.
ISHMAEL REED,
    The Free-Lance Pallbearers.
    The Last Days of Louisiana Red.
    Ishmael Reed: The Plays.
    Juice!
    Reckless Eyeballing.
    The Terrible Threes.
    The Terrible Twos.
    Yellow Back Radio Broke-Down.
JOÃO UBALDO RIBEIRO, *House of the*
    Fortunate Buddhas.
JEAN RICARDOU, *Place Names.*
RAINER MARIA RILKE, *The Notebooks of*
    Malte Laurids Brigge.
JULIÁN RÍOS, *The House of Ulysses.*
    Larva: A Midsummer Night's Babel.
    Poundemonium.
    Procession of Shadows.
AUGUSTO ROA BASTOS, *I the Supreme.*
DANIËL ROBBERECHTS,
    Arriving in Avignon.
JEAN ROLIN, *The Explosion of the*
    Radiator Hose.
OLIVIER ROLIN, *Hotel Crystal.*
ALIX CLEO ROUBAUD, *Alix's Journal.*
JACQUES ROUBAUD, *The Form of a*
    City Changes Faster, Alas, Than
    the Human Heart.
    The Great Fire of London.
    Hortense in Exile.
    Hortense Is Abducted.
    The Loop.
    The Plurality of Worlds of Lewis.
    The Princess Hoppy.
    Some Thing Black.
LEON S. ROUDIEZ, *French Fiction Revisited.*
RAYMOND ROUSSEL, *Impressions of Africa.*
VEDRANA RUDAN, *Night.*
STIG SÆTERBAKKEN, *Siamese.*
LYDIE SALVAYRE, *The Company of Ghosts.*
    Everyday Life.
    The Lecture.
    Portrait of the Writer as a
    Domesticated Animal.
    The Power of Flies.
LUIS RAFAEL SÁNCHEZ,
    Macho Camacho's Beat.
SEVERO SARDUY, *Cobra & Maitreya.*
NATHALIE SARRAUTE,
    Do You Hear Them?
    Martereau.
    The Planetarium.

SELECTED DALKEY ARCHIVE PAPERBACKS

CARLOS FUENTES, *Christopher Unborn.*
Distant Relations.
Terra Nostra.
Where the Air Is Clear.
JANICE GALLOWAY, *Foreign Parts.*
The Trick Is to Keep Breathing.
WILLIAM H. GASS, *Cartesian Sonata*
and Other Novellas.
Finding a Form.
A Temple of Texts.
The Tunnel.
Willie Masters' Lonesome Wife.
GÉRARD GAVARRY, *Hoppla! 1 2 3.*
Making a Novel.
ETIENNE GILSON,
The Arts of the Beautiful.
Forms and Substances in the Arts.
C. S. GISCOMBE, *Giscome Road.*
Here.
Prairie Style.
DOUGLAS GLOVER, *Bad News of the Heart.*
The Enamoured Knight.
WITOLD GOMBROWICZ,
A Kind of Testament.
KAREN ELIZABETH GORDON,
The Red Shoes.
GEORGI GOSPODINOV, *Natural Novel.*
JUAN GOYTISOLO, *Count Julian.*
Exiled from Almost Everywhere.
Juan the Landless.
Makbara.
Marks of Identity.
PATRICK GRAINVILLE, *The Cave of Heaven.*
HENRY GREEN, *Back.*
Blindness.
Concluding.
Doting.
Nothing.
JIŘÍ GRUŠA, *The Questionnaire.*
GABRIEL GUDDING,
Rhode Island Notebook.
MELA HARTWIG, *Am I a Redundant*
Human Being?
JOHN HAWKES, *The Passion Artist.*
Whistlejacket.
ALEKSANDAR HEMON, ED.,
Best European Fiction.
AIDAN HIGGINS, *A Bestiary.*
Balcony of Europe.
Bornholm Night-Ferry.
Darkling Plain: Texts for the Air.
Flotsam and Jetsam.
Langrishe, Go Down.
Scenes from a Receding Past.
Windy Arbours.
KEIZO HINO, *Isle of Dreams.*
KAZUSHI HOSAKA, *Plainsong.*
ALDOUS HUXLEY, *Antic Hay.*
Crome Yellow.
Point Counter Point.
Those Barren Leaves.
Time Must Have a Stop.
NAOYUKI II, *The Shadow of a Blue Cat.*
MIKHAIL IOSSEL AND JEFF PARKER, EDS.,
Amerika: Russian Writers View the
United States.
GERT JONKE, *The Distant Sound.*
Geometric Regional Novel.
Homage to Czerny.
The System of Vienna.

JACQUES JOUET, *Mountain R.*
Savage.
Upstaged.
CHARLES JULIET, *Conversations with*
Samuel Beckett and Bram van
Velde.
MIEKO KANAI, *The Word Book.*
YORAM KANIUK, *Life on Sandpaper.*
HUGH KENNER, *The Counterfeiters.*
Flaubert, Joyce and Beckett:
The Stoic Comedians.
Joyce's Voices.
DANILO KIŠ, *Garden, Ashes.*
A Tomb for Boris Davidovich.
ANITA KONKKA, *A Fool's Paradise.*
GEORGE KONRÁD, *The City Builder.*
TADEUSZ KONWICKI, *A Minor Apocalypse.*
The Polish Complex.
MENIS KOUMANDAREAS, *Koula.*
ELAINE KRAF, *The Princess of 72nd Street.*
JIM KRUSOE, *Iceland.*
EWA KURYLUK, *Century 21.*
EMILIO LASCANO TEGUI, *On Elegance*
While Sleeping.
ERIC LAURRENT, *Do Not Touch.*
HERVÉ LE TELLIER, *The Sextine Chapel.*
A Thousand Pearls (for a Thousand
Pennies)
VIOLETTE LEDUC, *La Bâtarde.*
EDOUARD LEVÉ, *Suicide.*
SUZANNE JILL LEVINE, *The Subversive*
Scribe: Translating Latin
American Fiction.
DEBORAH LEVY, *Billy and Girl.*
Pillow Talk in Europe and Other
Places.
JOSÉ LEZAMA LIMA, *Paradiso.*
ROSA LIKSOM, *Dark Paradise.*
OSMAN LINS, *Avalovara.*
The Queen of the Prisons of Greece.
ALF MAC LOCHLAINN,
The Corpus in the Library.
Out of Focus.
RON LOEWINSOHN, *Magnetic Field(s).*
MINA LOY, *Stories and Essays of Mina Loy.*
BRIAN LYNCH, *The Winner of Sorrow.*
D. KEITH MANO, *Take Five.*
MICHELINE AHARONIAN MARCOM,
The Mirror in the Well.
BEN MARCUS,
The Age of Wire and String.
WALLACE MARKFIELD,
Teitlebaum's Window.
To an Early Grave.
DAVID MARKSON, *Reader's Block.*
Springer's Progress.
Wittgenstein's Mistress.
CAROLE MASO, *AVA.*
LADISLAV MATEJKA AND KRYSTYNA
POMORSKA, EDS.,
Readings in Russian Poetics:
Formalist and Structuralist Views.
HARRY MATHEWS,
The Case of the Persevering Maltese:
Collected Essays.
Cigarettes.
The Conversions.
The Human Country: New and
Collected Stories.
The Journalist.

FOR A FULL LIST OF PUBLICATIONS, VISIT:
www.dalkeyarchive.com

PETROS ABATZOGLOU, *What Does Mrs. Freeman Want?*
MICHAL AJVAZ, *The Golden Age.*
The Other City.
PIERRE ALBERT-BIROT, *Grabinoulor.*
YUZ ALESHKOVSKY, *Kangaroo.*
FELIPE ALFAU, *Chromos.*
Locos.
IVAN ÂNGELO, *The Celebration.*
The Tower of Glass.
DAVID ANTIN, *Talking.*
ANTÓNIO LOBO ANTUNES, *Knowledge of Hell.*
ALAIN ARIAS-MISSON, *Theatre of Incest.*
IFTIKHAR ARIF AND WAQAS KHWAJA, EDS., *Modern Poetry of Pakistan.*
JOHN ASHBERY AND JAMES SCHUYLER, *A Nest of Ninnies.*
GABRIELA AVIGUR-ROTEM, *Heatwave and Crazy Birds.*
HEIMRAD BÄCKER, *transcript.*
DJUNA BARNES, *Ladies Almanack.*
Ryder.
JOHN BARTH, *LETTERS.*
Sabbatical.
DONALD BARTHELME, *The King.*
Paradise.
SVETISLAV BASARA, *Chinese Letter.*
RENÉ BELLETTO, *Dying.*
MARK BINELLI, *Sacco and Vanzetti Must Die!*
ANDREI BITOV, *Pushkin House.*
ANDREJ BLATNIK, *You Do Understand.*
LOUIS PAUL BOON, *Chapel Road.*
My Little War.
Summer in Termuren.
ROGER BOYLAN, *Killoyle.*
IGNÁCIO DE LOYOLA BRANDÃO, *Anonymous Celebrity.*
The Good-Bye Angel.
Teeth under the Sun.
Zero.
BONNIE BREMSER, *Troia: Mexican Memoirs.*
CHRISTINE BROOKE-ROSE, *Amalgamemnon.*
BRIGID BROPHY, *In Transit.*
MEREDITH BROSNAN, *Mr. Dynamite.*
GERALD L. BRUNS, *Modern Poetry and the Idea of Language.*
EVGENY BUNIMOVICH AND J. KATES, EDS., *Contemporary Russian Poetry: An Anthology.*
GABRIELLE BURTON, *Heartbreak Hotel.*
MICHEL BUTOR, *Degrees.*
Mobile.
Portrait of the Artist as a Young Ape.
G. CABRERA INFANTE, *Infante's Inferno.*
Three Trapped Tigers.
JULIETA CAMPOS, *The Fear of Losing Eurydice.*
ANNE CARSON, *Eros the Bittersweet.*
ORLY CASTEL-BLOOM, *Dolly City.*
CAMILO JOSÉ CELA, *Christ versus Arizona.*
The Family of Pascual Duarte.
The Hive.
LOUIS-FERDINAND CÉLINE, *Castle to Castle.*
Conversations with Professor Y.
London Bridge.
Normance.

North.
Rigadoon.
HUGO CHARTERIS, *The Tide Is Right.*
JEROME CHARYN, *The Tar Baby.*
ERIC CHEVILLARD, *Demolishing Nisard.*
MARC CHOLODENKO, *Mordechai Schamz.*
JOSHUA COHEN, *Witz.*
EMILY HOLMES COLEMAN, *The Shutter of Snow.*
ROBERT COOVER, *A Night at the Movies.*
STANLEY CRAWFORD, *Log of the S.S. The Mrs Unguentine.*
Some Instructions to My Wife.
ROBERT CREELEY, *Collected Prose.*
RENÉ CREVEL, *Putting My Foot in It.*
RALPH CUSACK, *Cadenza.*
SUSAN DAITCH, *L.C.*
Storytown.
NICHOLAS DELBANCO, *The Count of Concord.*
Sherbrookes.
NIGEL DENNIS, *Cards of Identity.*
PETER DIMOCK, *A Short Rhetoric for Leaving the Family.*
ARIEL DORFMAN, *Konfidenz.*
COLEMAN DOWELL, *The Houses of Children.*
Island People.
Too Much Flesh and Jabez.
ARKADII DRAGOMOSHCHENKO, *Dust.*
RIKKI DUCORNET, *The Complete Butcher's Tales.*
The Fountains of Neptune.
The Jade Cabinet.
The One Marvelous Thing.
Phosphor in Dreamland.
The Stain.
The Word "Desire."
WILLIAM EASTLAKE, *The Bamboo Bed.*
Castle Keep.
Lyric of the Circle Heart.
JEAN ECHENOZ, *Chopin's Move.*
STANLEY ELKIN, *A Bad Man.*
Boswell: A Modern Comedy.
Criers and Kibitzers, Kibitzers and Criers.
The Dick Gibson Show.
The Franchiser.
George Mills.
The Living End.
The MacGuffin.
The Magic Kingdom.
Mrs. Ted Bliss.
The Rabbi of Lud.
Van Gogh's Room at Arles.
ANNIE ERNAUX, *Cleaned Out.*
LAUREN FAIRBANKS, *Muzzle Thyself.*
Sister Carrie.
LESLIE A. FIEDLER, *Love and Death in the American Novel.*
JUAN FILLOY, *Op Oloop.*
GUSTAVE FLAUBERT, *Bouvard and Pécuchet.*
KASS FLEISHER, *Talking out of School.*
FORD MADOX FORD, *The March of Literature.*
JON FOSSE, *Aliss at the Fire.*
Melancholy.
MAX FRISCH, *I'm Not Stiller.*
Man in the Holocene.

FOR A FULL LIST OF PUBLICATIONS, VISIT:
www.dalkeyarchive.com

A leading figure in the Russian Formalist movement of the 1910s and 1920s, VIKTOR SHKLOVSKY (1893–1984) had a profound effect on twentieth-century Russian literature and on literary criticism throughout the world. Many of his books have been translated into English and are available from Dalkey Archive Press.

SHUSHAN AVAGYAN is the translator of Shushanik Kurghinian's *I Want to Live* and Viktor Shklovsky's *Energy of Delusion: A Book on Plot*. She is co-translator, with Ana Lucic, of several essays by Arkadii Dragomoshchenko included in *DUST*.